INTERNATIONAL GRAPHIC DESIGN, ART & ILLUSTRATION

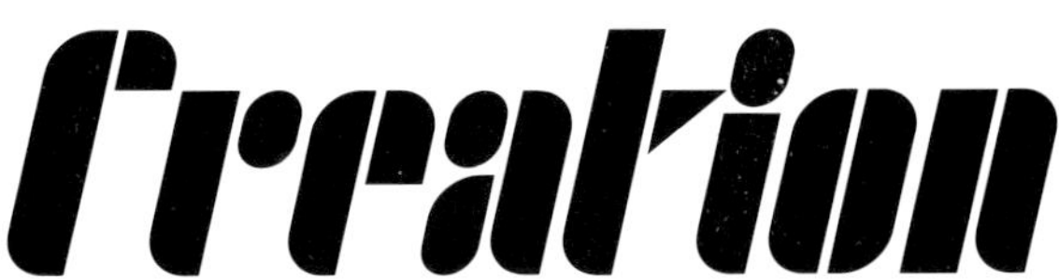

Editor: YUSAKU KAMEKURA

Publisher: RECRUIT CO., LTD.
Production: RECRUIT CREATIVE CENTER

Printing: TOPPAN PRINTING CO., LTD.
Distributors: RIKUYO-SHA PUBLISHING, INC.
ZOKEISHA (USA) INC.

編集長 ——— 亀倉雄策

編集アシスタント ——— 菊池雅美

アートディレクター ——— 亀倉雄策

デザイナー ——— 水上 寛
アシスタントデザイナー ——— 加藤正巳
廣田由紀子
プリンティングディレクター ——— 小嶋茂子
英訳 ——— ロバート・ミンツァー

発行 ——— 1989年6月1日
定価 ——— 3,200円(本体3,107円)
発行所 ——— 株式会社リクルート
〒104 東京都中央区銀座8-4-17
TEL.03-575-7074(編集室)
発行人 ——— 位田尚隆
制作 ——— リクルートクリエイティブセンター
印刷 ——— 凸版印刷株式会社
発売 ——— 株式会社六耀社
〒160 東京都新宿区新宿2-19-12 静岡銀行ビル
TEL.03-354-4020 FAX.03-352-3106

世界のグラフィックデザイン，アート＆イラストレーション

クリエイション

編集――亀倉雄策

発行――株式会社リクルート
制作――リクルートクリエイティブセンター

印刷――凸版印刷株式会社
発売――株式会社六耀社

Editor —— Yusaku Kamekura

Editorial assistant —— Masami Kikuchi

Art director —— Yusaku Kamekura

Designer —— Yutaka Mizukami
Assistant designers —— Masami Kato
Yukiko Hirota
Printing director —— Shigeko Kojima
Translator —— Robert A. Mintzer

CREATION No.1 1989
Publisher —— Recruit Co., Ltd.
8-4-17 Ginza, Chuo-ku, Tokyo 104, Japan
Production —— Recruit Creative Center
Printing —— Toppan Printing Co., Ltd.
Distributors —— Rikuyo-sha Publishing, Inc.
Shizuoka Bank Bldg., 2-19-12 Shinjuku, Shinjuku-ku, Tokyo 160, Japan
TEL. 03-354-4020 FAX. 03-352-3106
Zokeisha (USA) Inc.
51 East 42nd Street New York N.Y. 10017 USA
TEL. 212-986-3120 FAX. 212-986-3122

CONTENTS——目次

Cover: IKKO TANAKA
表紙:田中一光

PREFACE はじめに

Yusaku Kamekura 亀倉雄策

I had always assumed that I would spend my remaining active years as I have all along—proudly, as a graphic designer. It never crossed my mind that someday I would become editor of a magazine about design.

From around the spring of 1988, though, I began growing impatient with myself, filled with an urgency to *do* something on behalf of the design field. But just what that "something" might be, I could not pinpoint. So I continued to ponder the issue until, finally, an answer occurred to me: I should start a new design magazine and serve as its editor. I was not unaware, let me assure you, how hasty and infantile this conclusion was.

The puerile nature of my decision notwithstanding, I learned all too quickly that my idea was easier conceived than carried out. To begin with, the magazine had no promise of turning a profit. This was all the more true if I insisted on adhering strictly to my ideals. And yet I knew that unless I kept to my ideals, there could be no meaning in my producing a magazine in the first place.

Then I began to think again. Are there not already a number of superlative design magazines around the world with long and distinguished histories? "Graphis" of Switzerland, for example. Or "HQ" of Germany. Or, until several years ago, Japan's own "Graphic Design." The last work was edited by noted design critic Masaru Katzumie. Though it was highly respected by designers worldwide, the magazine was continually plagued by financial difficulties. Miraculously it endured for 100 issues, even overcoming the sudden and tragic death of its editor.

On the other hand I remembered the case of "Portfolio," a magazine produced way back in 1950 under the editorship of George S. Rosenthal and Alexey Brodovitch. Brodovitch's cover and layout work are striking even today. Still, the goddess of good fortune failed to smile even on this work of genius, and "Portfolio" was forced to discontinue publication after only two issues.

"Graphis" was inaugurated under the brilliant editorial leadership of Walter Herdeg, a long-time friend who had originally started out as a graphic designer. The magazine appeared shortly after WWII, and to those of us in Japan in the depths of post-war destitution, it was more beautiful than we could imagine. Through this work Herdeg's discerning views came to contribute significantly to the advancement of the design profession around the world.

When I met Herdeg at his office in 1984, however, he spoke of his decision to retire and of his search for someone to take over his duties at "Graphis." Naturally, I was saddened to hear this news. Yet today "Graphis" continues to be published under the able direction of B. Martin Pedersen, a dynamic young editor. Furthermore, under its new leadership the magazine has undergone outstanding transformations of remarkable scale.

"HQ," though a relatively new publication, in my opinion merits widespread attention because it manifests so distinctly the design philosophy of its astute editor, Rolf Müller. Müller is an ardent admirer of Masaru Katzumie, and their editorial stances have much in common. "HQ" is particularly attractive as a result of its bold experiments in eliciting visual effects from the printed page.

With excellent magazines like "Graphis" and "HQ" already in circulation, the question inevitably arises as to what on earth I can dare seek to accomplish that these outstanding works do not. The answer is both simple and complex. All I aim to do is to start my

私の一生は、グラフィックデザイナーとして誇りを持って終わりたいと思っていた。それが、例えデザイン誌といっても編集者になろうとは夢にも考えてみなかった。

1988年5月にAGI(世界グラフィック連盟)の東京大会が開催された。功成り名を遂げた巨匠たち、最先端で精力的に仕事をしているスターたちが、世界の国々から集まってきた。デザイン仲間だけに通じあう友情の融けあった交流も、短い会議と共に終わり、心温まる想いを胸に、それぞれの国へ帰っていった。後に言い知れぬ寂寥を残して……。

私は、その寂寥感の根底にあるものを自問し続けた。それが、デザイン界のために何かをしなければという焦躁感の疼きだということが次第にわかってきた。一体何をすべきか。キラリと光るものが脳裏をかすめ、それは何とデザイン誌を私自身が編集し、創刊することだった。あまりにも短絡的な、あまりにも幼児的な発想に自分ながらあきれ果てた。

あきれ果てたといっても、いざ実現出来るかといえば、これ程の困難な事業はないということが次第にわかってきた。先ず経営的に全く不可能なのである。理想を貫けば貫く程、物理的に経営は不可能になる。しかし理想を貫かなければ、私が編集する意義がない。

しかし、すでに世界には優れたデザイン誌が長い歴史をもって毅然と存在しているではないか。スイスの「GRAPHIS」、ドイツの「HQ」、日本でも数年前まで刊行されていた「グラフィックデザイン」。この本はデザイン評論家の勝見勝の編集だった。彼の良心的な編集は世界のデザイナーから尊敬されながらも、常に経営難に悩まされ続けた。彼の突然の死という悲劇を越えて100号まで出版されたのは驚くべきことである。

私が今、思い出すのは1950年にジョージ・ロゼンダールとアレクセイ・ブロードヴィッチの編集によって発刊された「PORTFOLIO」である。ブロードヴィッチの表紙と抜群のレイアウトは、今も魅力的である。この天才の理想的な本も経営の女神は微笑んではくれなかった。私の手元にあるのは1号と2号、遂に3号を見ることは出来なかった。私の昔からの友人で、偉大な編集者ワルター・ヘルデークも実はグラフィックデザイナーから編集者になった人である。終戦後いち速く、彼の手で「GRAPHIS」が創刊された。当時疲弊していた私達から見れば夢の様な美しい本だった。ヘルデークの高い見識眼は、編集を通して世界のデザイン界に偉大な貢献をした。

そのヘルデークに1984年、彼のオフィスで会った時、すでに彼は引退の決意をし、後継者を探していると言っていた。私はそれを悲しんだが、しかし現在マーチン・ペイデルセンという若い生き生きとした編集者が後を継いでいる。そして「GRAPHIS」は全く新しい感覚で、目を見はるばかりの見事な変貌をとげた。ドイツの「HQ」は発刊の歴史こそ浅いが、編集のロルフ・ミューラーのデザインに対する哲学がよく表現されていて、注目に価すると思う。ミューラーは勝見勝を尊敬していて、その編集精神は勝見と通じるものがある。しかも本の誌面効果に大胆な試みがなされていて魅力的である。

own design magazine... a magazine that reflects my personal views on the essence and philosophy of design... a magazine embodying design aesthetics in line with my artistic sensibilities... a magazine arranged by my own hand to spotlight what I see to be the unique characteristics of various designers.

The content of "my" magazine reflects my design philosophy closely. I am not interested, for example, in introducing "current topics" in the design field. In this respect, I will not curry favor with the drift of the times: outstanding designs are outstanding whether they are new or old. Nor do they have to be from a designer of great renown. My only criteria are exceptional talent and artistic ability.

I am curious, of course, to know what impressions you, the reader, have of this inaugural issue. Naturally I must be concerned too—perhaps most—with the financial fortunes of this magazine. As you can imagine, many obstacles stood in the way before I succeeded in bringing my dream to fruition. Several times I thought of giving up in despair. Then at last I found a company that understood my stubborn adherence to my ideals, a company that agreed to publish a magazine that had no financial viability. That company is Recruit.

As is widely known, the Recruit Company is presently at the center of a political scandal of undeniably serious dimensions. I would particularly like to take this opportunity therefore to thank the members of the Board of Directors of Recruit for believing in me and agreeing, in the midst of their current troubles, to publish this magazine as a potential contribution to global progress in design. When the time is opportune, I hope to write more on my views of the events surrounding the unfortunate Recruit affair.

Although I had early decided upon "CREATION" as the ideal title for "my" magazine, I subsequently discovered that the name was already registered and therefore not usable. To complicate matters, the registrant was a German company, which made the situation appear all the more hopeless. About the only thing I could do was to curse Japan's outdated laws that prevented me from using the title of my choosing.

Ultimately, I decided that my last hope was to try negotiating with the German company. Through special intermediators I conveyed to the firm the purpose of my forthcoming publication. I also submitted my already completed logo design for the "CREATION" title, along with a list of my credentials.

More than a month passed when finally I received a truly wonderful reply. The firm granted me permission to use the "CREATION" title in perpetuity, citing the "high cultural value" of the magazine in planning. I could not have been happier. I was also deeply moved by the noble judiciousness of such a firm to support a cultural pursuit of this kind. I wish to use this opportunity to express my heartfelt appreciation to this exceptionally fine firm: Elegance, Rolf Offergelt GmbH.

And so it is, through the kind understanding of my financial backers and personal supporters, that the magazine "CREATION" has been brought into this world. I feel most fortunate that my dream has been realized. Now all that remains is for me to pursue my editorial ideals as I have long hoped to.

この様なデザイン誌の状況の中で、一体お前に何が出来るかと問われるに違いない。これに答えることは易しいようで、実に難しい。唯ひとつ、私のデザイン誌をつくりたいということだけである。私の考えるデザインの本質と哲学。私の感性によるデザインの芸術性。芸術家の個性の輝きをとらえ、誌面の上に、私自身の手によって構成する。その構成が私のデザイン論だということが出来よう。私はこの本では決してニュースを扱わない。だから時流に媚びない。古くても新しくてもいいものはいい。デザインの本道でも、脇道でも、路地でもいい。有名も無名もない。優れた才能と芸術家としての力量を重視するだけである。

さて皆さん。創刊第1号を手に取られて、どんな印象を持たれたであろうか。そして当然、一番懸念されたのは経営のことではなかろうか。もちろん、この本が実現するまでに色々な曲折はあった。時として絶望もした。ところが頑固に初心を貫こうとする私のひたむきさに理解を示し、経済的に成り立たないこの本を出版してくれる企業があった。リクルートである。リクルートは現在、政治とマスコミの間にスキャンダルとしてゆれ動いている。この激動の中で、世界のデザイン界に貢献出来るならと、私を信じて出版を決定して下さった役員会議に心から感謝したい。この間の事情については折りを見てふれたいと思うが今はその時期でない。

本誌の「CREATION」というタイトルは、私が編集を決意した時点で、すでに登録済みで使用不可能だった。しかも厄介なことにドイツの企業が登録していた。すっかり絶望して仕方なくデザインを連想する名称を探したが全部登録済みだった。我国の時代遅れの悪法を恨んだ。最後の望みはドイツ企業に交渉するしかない。そこで専門家を通じてドイツの会社に、すでに出来上がっている「CREATION」のロゴタイプと私の経歴を提出して、出版目的を訴えた。

それから1ヶ月も過ぎた頃、ドイツから素晴らしい通知が来た。「我社は文化的に高い出版に対しては、我社の存続する限り、タイトルの使用を許可するものである」。うれしいではないか。さすがにドイツの企業は文化に対して高い見識を持っていると、改めて感動した。その会社名をここに記して、私の心からなる感謝の気持ちを伝えたい。

Elegance, Rolf Offergelt GmbH

エレガンス社の深い理解で、このデザイン誌「CREATION」が誕生した。幸運な船出と言えよう。後は理想の追求を持続するのみである。

IKKO TANAKA 田中一光

Mamoru Yonekura 米倉 守

Yusaku Kamekura, widely recognized as Japan's leading figure in graphic design today, has said that Japanese designers broadly divide into three camps: Tadanori Yokoo on the right, Kohei Sugiura on the left and Ikko Tanaka in the middle. This notion is quite on target. Yokoo and Sugiura stand at opposite poles, one swayed by emotion, the other by reason. Ikko Tanaka represents the orthodox midstream. His works are completely devoid of anything that smacks of fantasy, deception or unreality. Their greatest appeal lies in their purity of expression, supported by the mechanical process known as printing.

Tanaka has completely mastered the "ABC's" of the printing art. In coloring, for example, he brings out the pure brilliance of printing ink. He also achieves a simple beauty through juxtaposition of black and white in a manner possible only through printing. He further knows how to capture the interesting effects unique to printing through combination of letters and pictures or photographs. These traits he then utilizes to maximum effect in advertising.

The designer is an artist eternally caught between the demands of the client and the tastes of the general public. Ikko Tanaka, however, is a designer who, through the medium of advertising, has continually pursued what might be called a "morality of form or color" in his quest to open up a new genre of social art. This is a task of extremely great importance today, one which has far greater substance than the cheap paintings sold off by so-called "pure artists."

The elegant aesthetics of Japanese tradition were refined almost entirely through the hands of the common populace. In all areas from dyeing, weaving, architecture, furniture, lacquerware and ceramics to cooking and theater arts, elegant design, meticulous technical skill and supreme practicality all evolved in the process of everyday life. It is this affinity for everyday practicality which, I believe, serves as the starting point for Ikko Tanaka's design inspiration.

In the fall of 1988, Tanaka held highly successful one-man shows in New York, Los Angeles and Paris. Overseas, his works are always greeted with an element of great surprise. This is because they represent a fascinating blend of art and design. Moreover, they are created in a style that is clearly "Japanese" yet which also embraces elements that are ultimately of Western origin, resulting in a unique "hybrid" of aesthetics.

"Sometimes I wonder if I truly have a style all my own," Tanaka has said of himself. "Maybe I haven't been severe enough in asserting myself." Where Tanaka's secret strength lies, however, is in his ability to place himself at the fulcrum and respond flexibly to everything around him. This capacity also gives Tanaka's works a unique individuality by virtue of their lack of rigid form, an underlying tenacity blended with a willingness to change.

This character may perhaps invite misunderstanding abroad, where Tanaka might sometimes be viewed as a man who throws himself into a new endeavor with great fury but who is also quick to lose interest. Yet Tanaka is in fact quite different. The power of his design capability lies in his broad receptiveness for the sake of harmony and equilibrium.

Furthermore, his open receptiveness and magnanimity, I believe, are like national treasures. They should be highly admired, and passed down to future generations.

田中一光は昨秋(1988年9月)、ニューヨーク、ロサンゼルスに続いてパリのフランス広告美術館で個展を開催、成功をおさめた。日本のグラフィック・デザイナーをリードする亀倉雄策は、この国のデザイン人脈を「右側に横尾忠則、左側に杉浦康平、そして中央に田中一光という図式がある」と指摘した。情と理の2人を両極にすえて、正統に田中一光をすえた図式は的を得ている。

田中の仕事に空想的な嘘っぽいリアリティーのない作品は皆無だ。その魅力は、印刷というメカニックな過程を経た清潔な表現にある。色彩にしても印刷インクの純粋な輝き、印刷でなければ出ない白と黒の対比の簡素な美しさ、あるいは文字と絵や写真との印刷プロセスによる独自の合成の面白さ、といったいわば印刷美学のいろはを完璧につかみ、それが宣伝の効率と結びついているところにある。デザイナーは注文者と大衆との間に板ばさみになった美術家だが、宣伝、訴えを通しながら形、色彩のモラルとでもいいたいものを追求して、新しい社会芸術のジャンルを切り開いてきたのが田中である。これは安易な売り絵を描いている「純粋画家」よりもはるかに抵抗のある、今日的な偉大な仕事であるはずだ。

日本の伝統であるみやびやかな美意識は、ほとんど大衆の手で火花を散らせて磨かれてきた。それが日本の文化の質になっているところは、権力者の所有物を大衆にも見せるという西欧近世のオペラなどの浸透の仕方とはちがっている。染、織、建築、家具、漆器、陶器から料理、芸能までの優美な意匠と精巧な技術、質の高い合理性、それらが平凡な日常生活のなかでたえず創意、工夫を重ねて生きてきた。田中一光のデザインはここのところを自らのかんどころにしていると思う。

欧米での展覧会で、田中の仕事が驚きの目で迎えられたのも、アートとデザインの境界を超えた、しかも田中にとって血肉化しているこの日本的様式に、これまでこの国が吸収してきた西欧的なものがプラスされて、独特の混種ができていたからである。

「私は、『私のかたち』を持っていないのではないかと考えることがある。もちろん狭義な『かたち』を言うのだが、長い間のデザイナーとしての習慣がそうさせたのか、あるいは、自己を主張する厳しさが欠けていたせいかもしれない。ともかく、頑固でなかった自分が残念だが、しかし、それがデザイナーにとって決定的な不名誉なことだとは、少しも思ったことがない」。

一見難解な田中の言葉だが、田中作品の「強さ」の秘密がここにある。その才能は、自己を主軸としてあらゆるものに柔軟に適応するというバランスの良さを持つ。が、それは硬ばった形などは持たぬという独自性に貫かれており、田中の根底には粘り強く、しかも変化的で機敏な自己が確としてあるということである。外国から見れば、熱しやすくさめやすい、などと誤解されかねないが、これはもっとちがった本質である。調和と均衡のための幅広い受容力が田中一光のデザインの根底をなす力である。

田中の目下の関心事は、世界に向って日本からいかなる文化を発信することができるか、ということだ。

その受容力と視野の広い寛容さこそ、新世紀の日本の貴重な宝石であろうと思うのである。

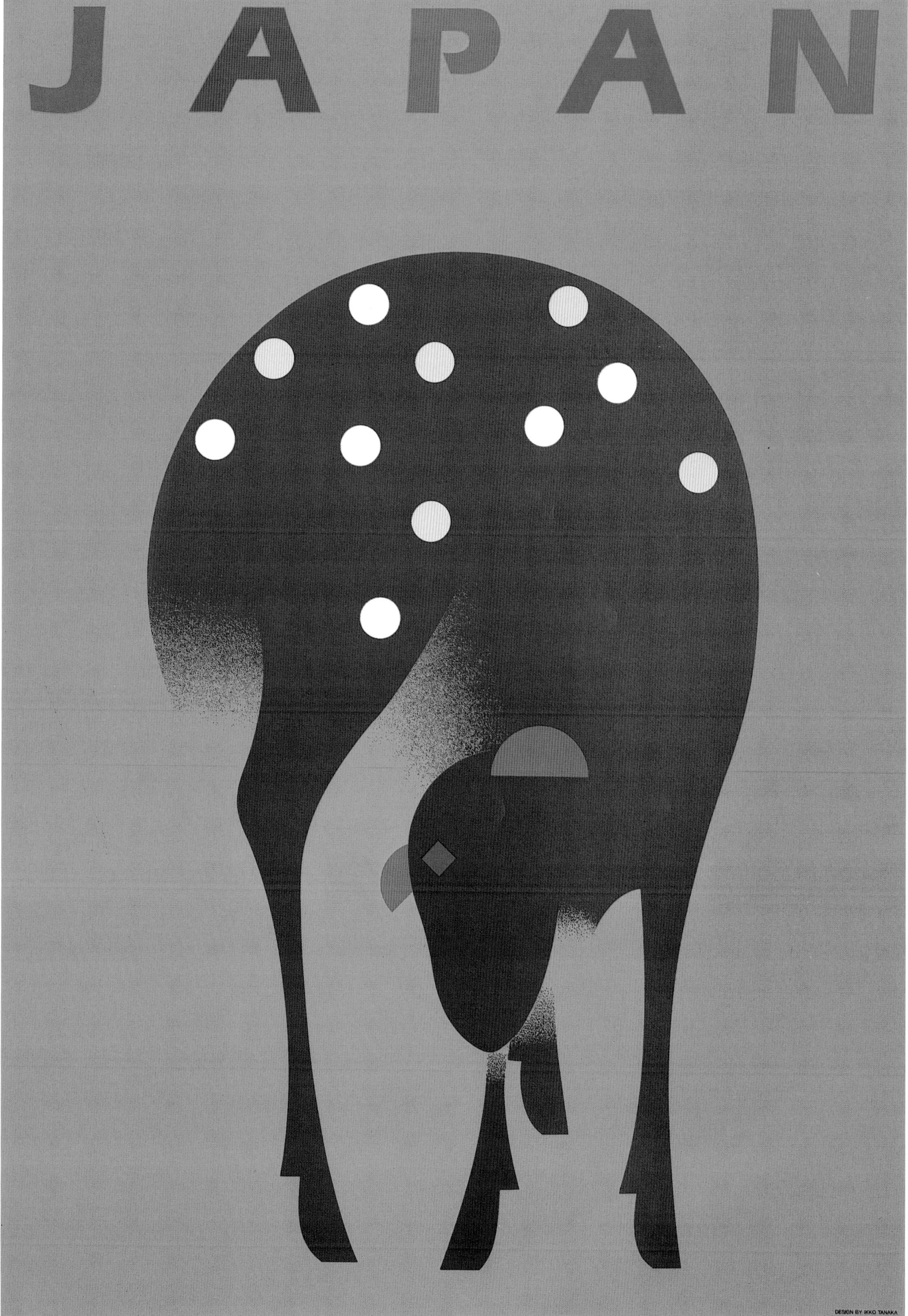

1 Image poster イメージ・ポスター 1987

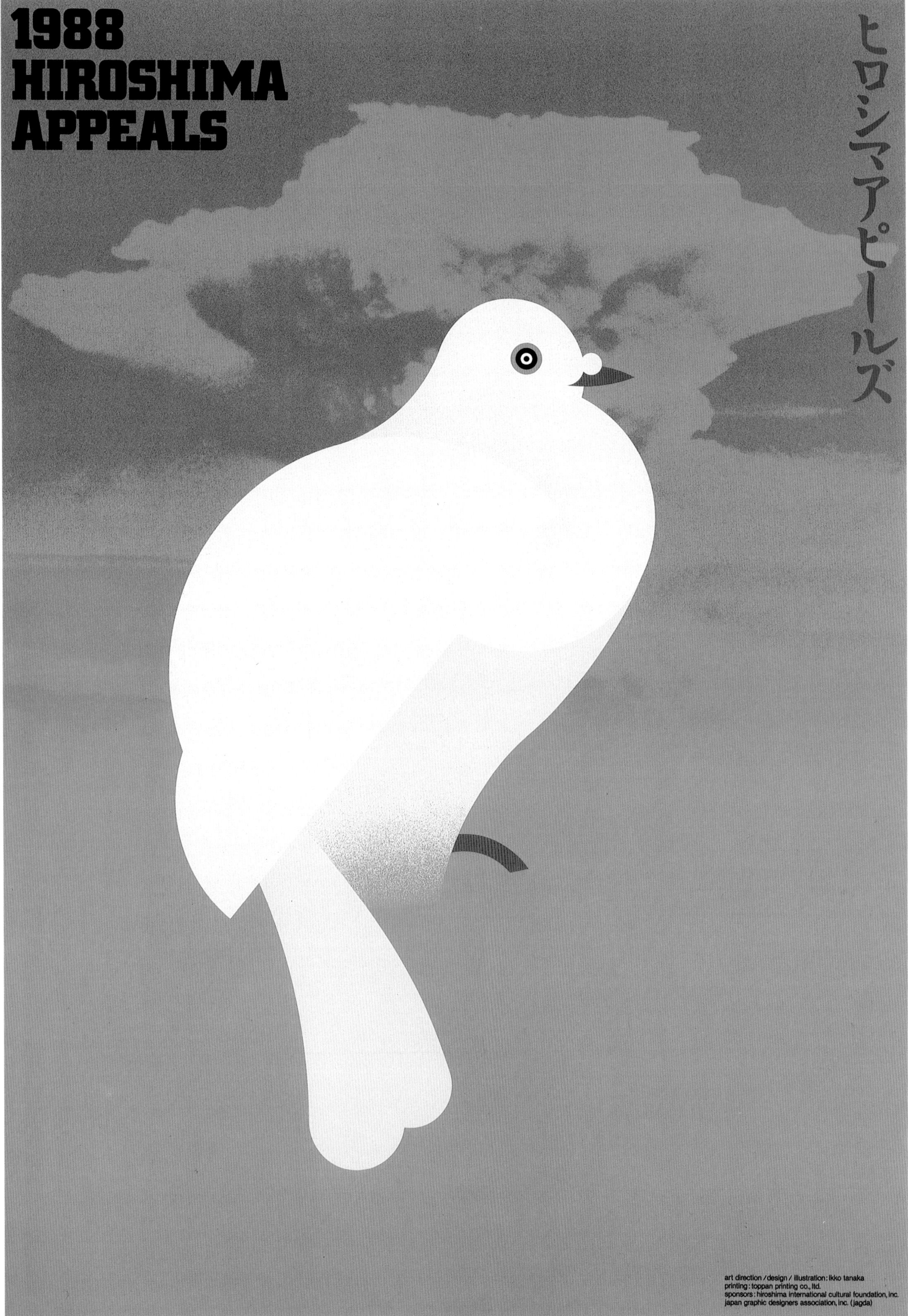

2 Peace poster 平和ポスター 1988

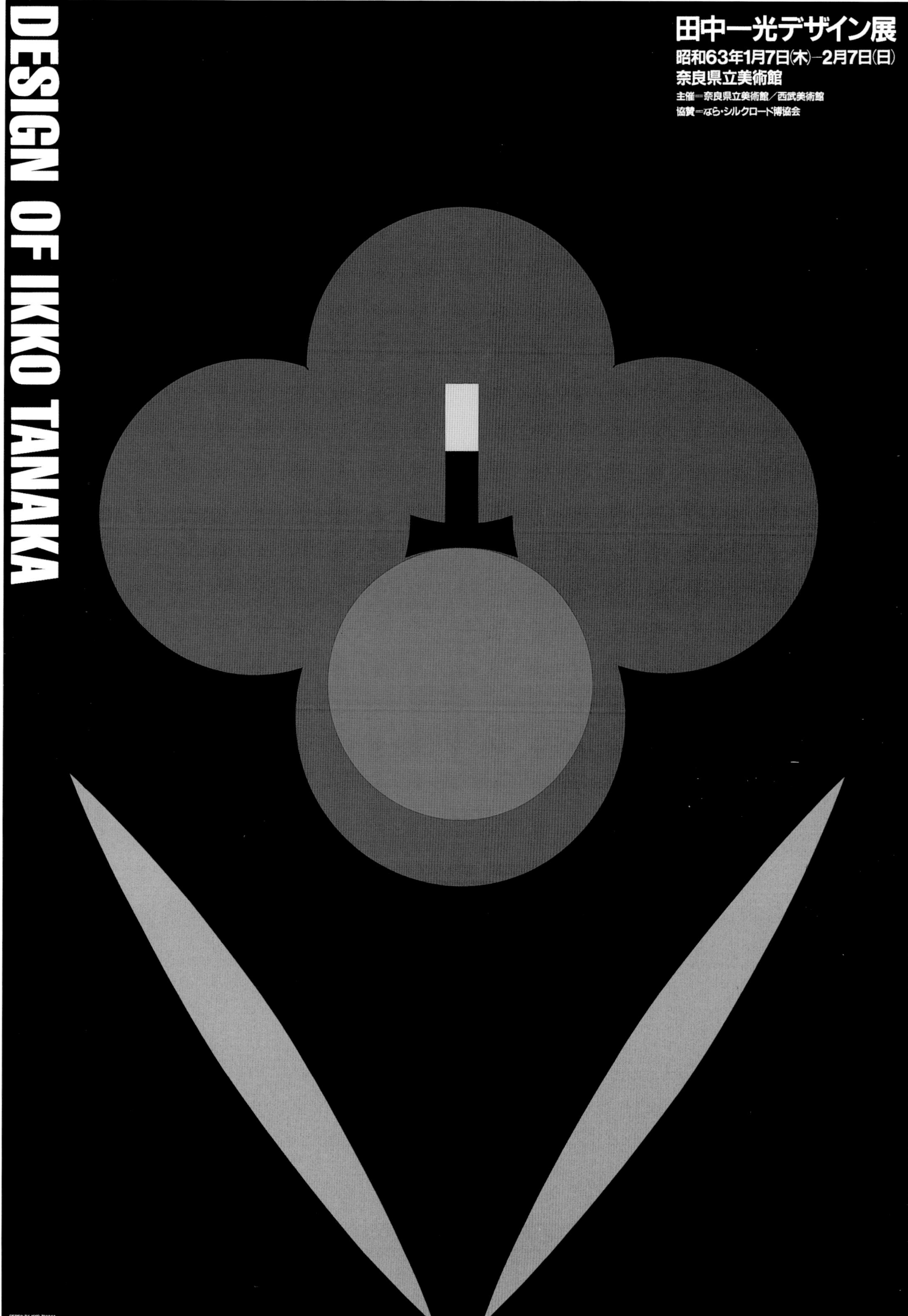

3 Exhibition poster 個展ポスター 1987

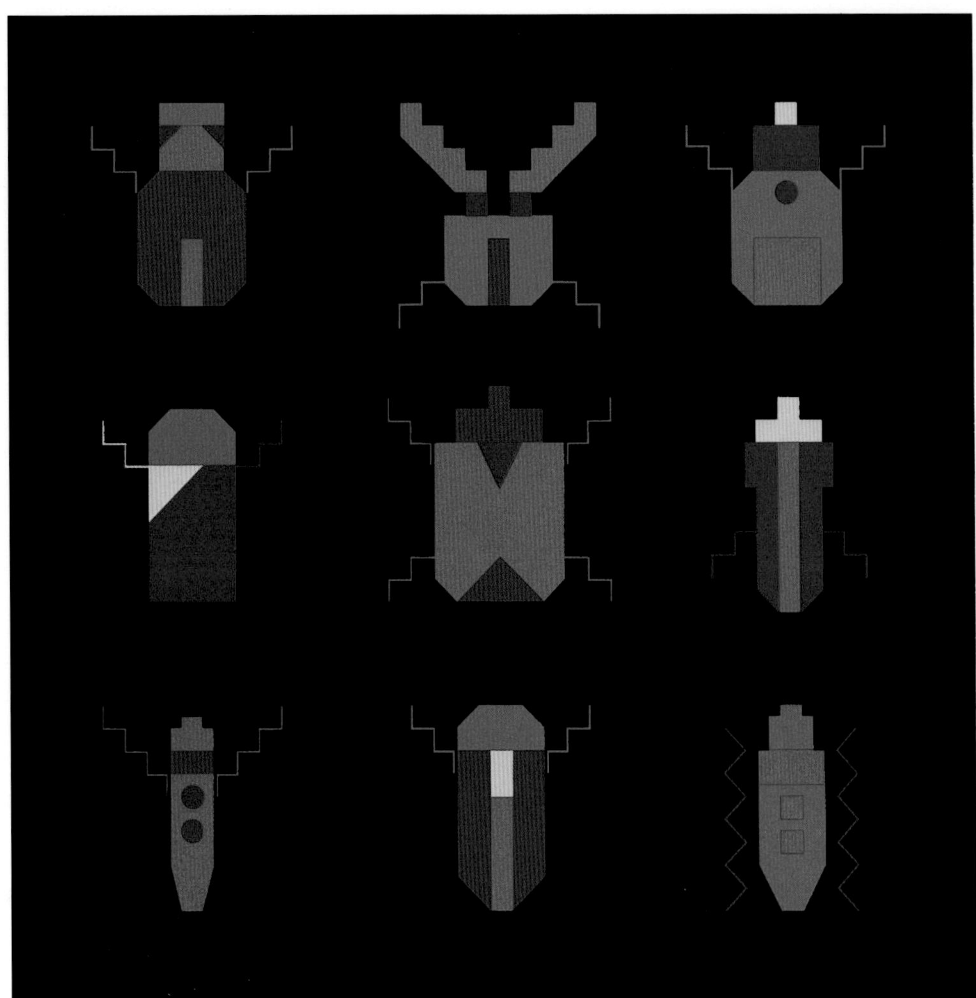

4 Illustration for calendar カレンダーのイラストレーション 1985

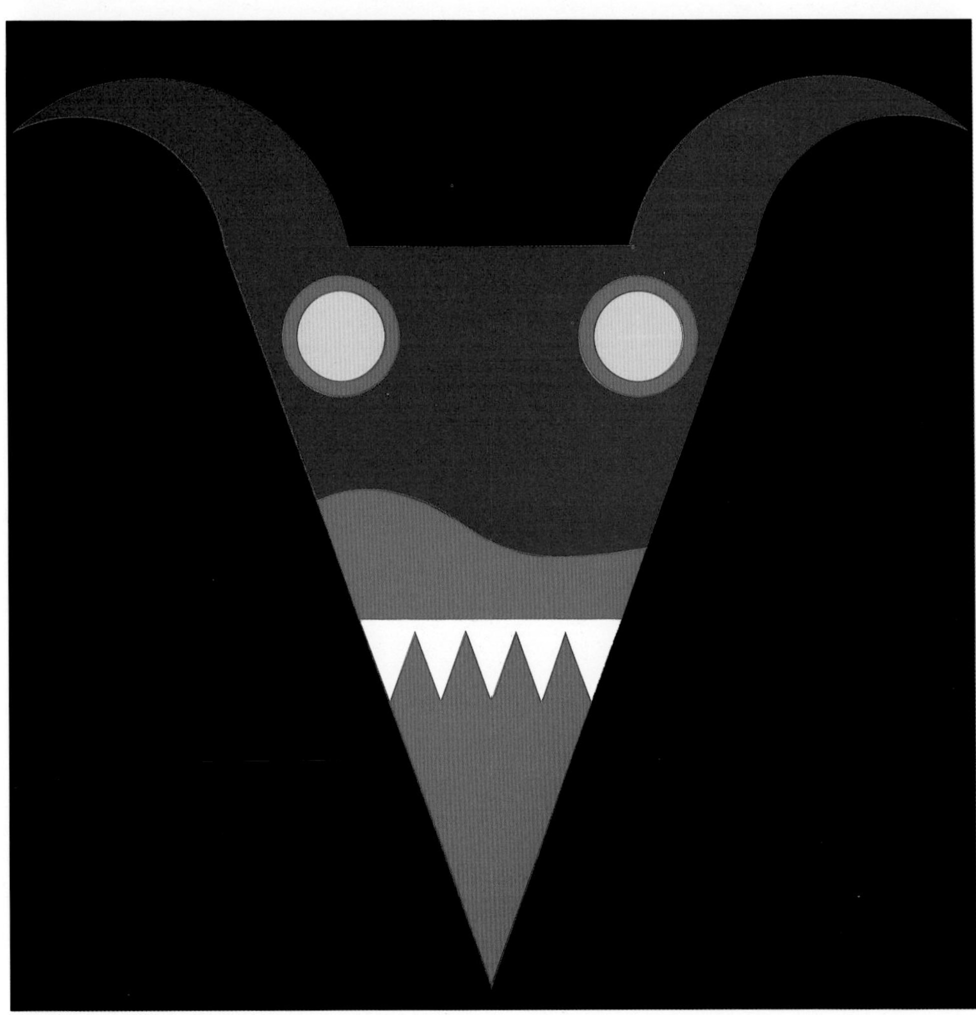

5 Illustration for concert poster 音楽会ポスターのイラストレーション 1973

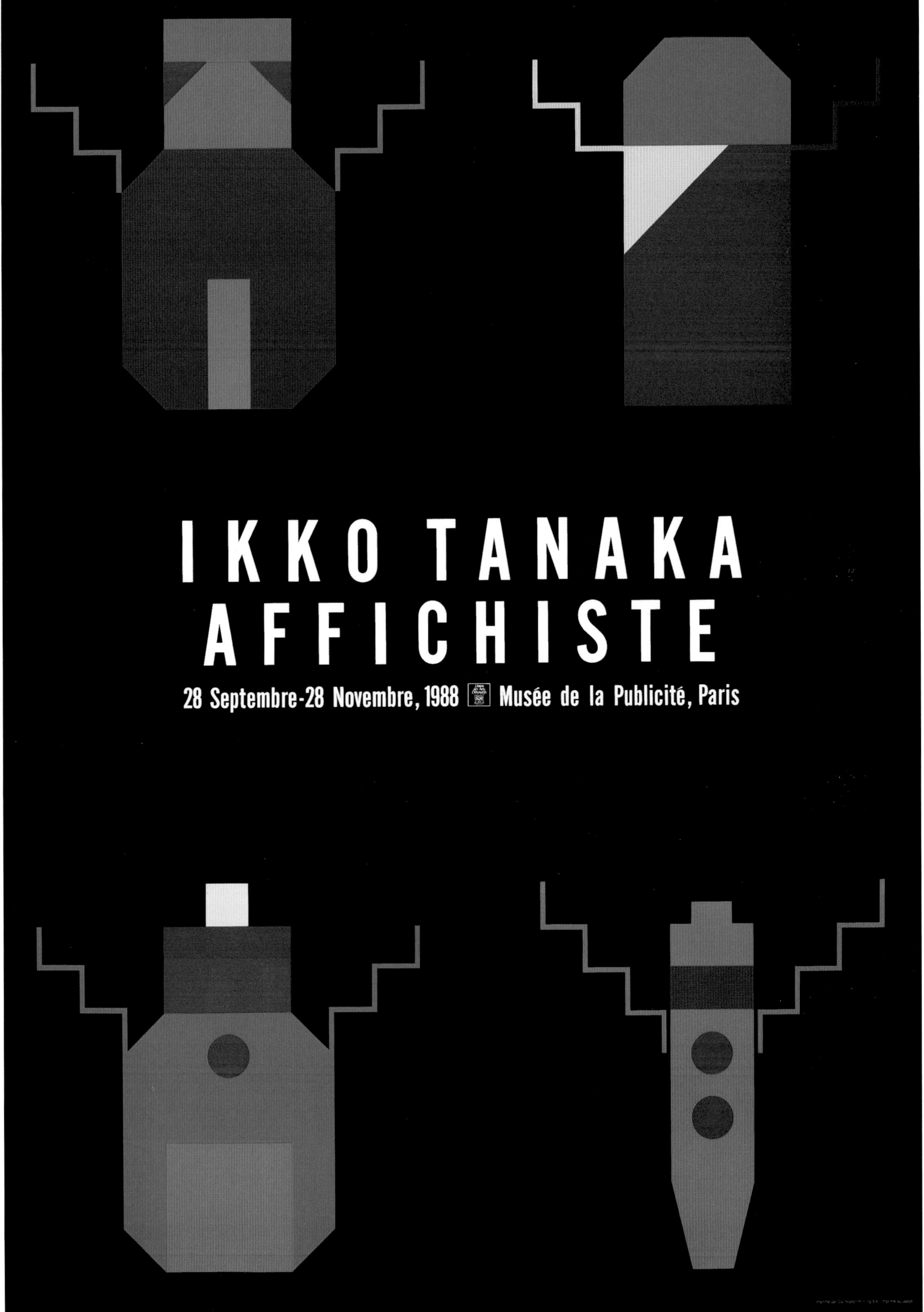

6 Exhibition poster 個展ポスター 1988

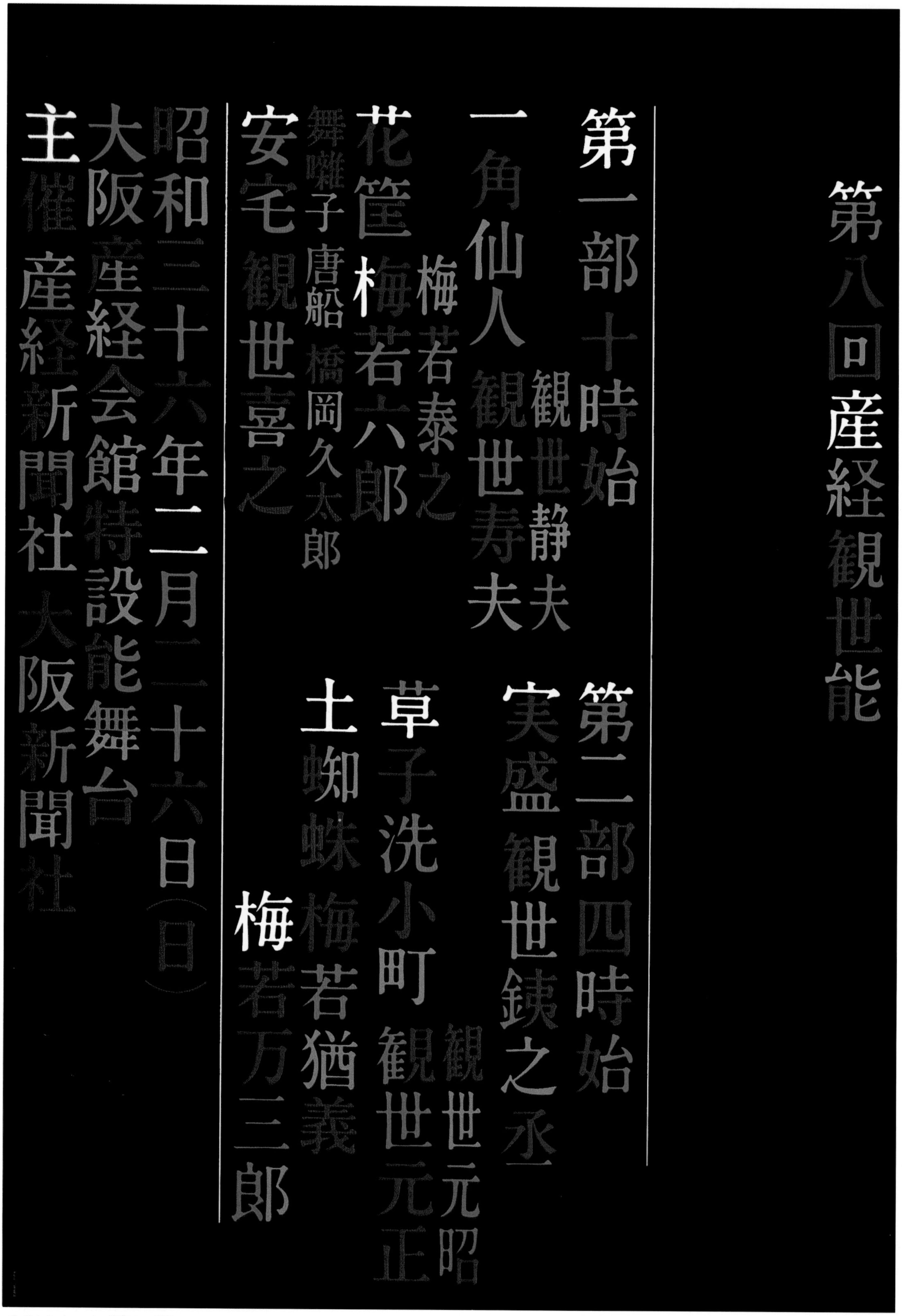

第八回産経観世能

第一部十時始

観世静夫
一角仙人 観世寿夫

梅若泰之
花筐 梅若六郎

舞囃子 唐船 橋岡久太郎

安宅 観世喜之

第二部四時始

実盛 観世銕之丞

観世元昭
草子洗小町 観世元正

土蜘蛛 梅若猶義
梅若万三郎

昭和三十六年二月二十六日(日)
大阪産経会館特設能舞台
主催 産経新聞社 大阪新聞社

7 Noh theater poster 能ポスター 1961

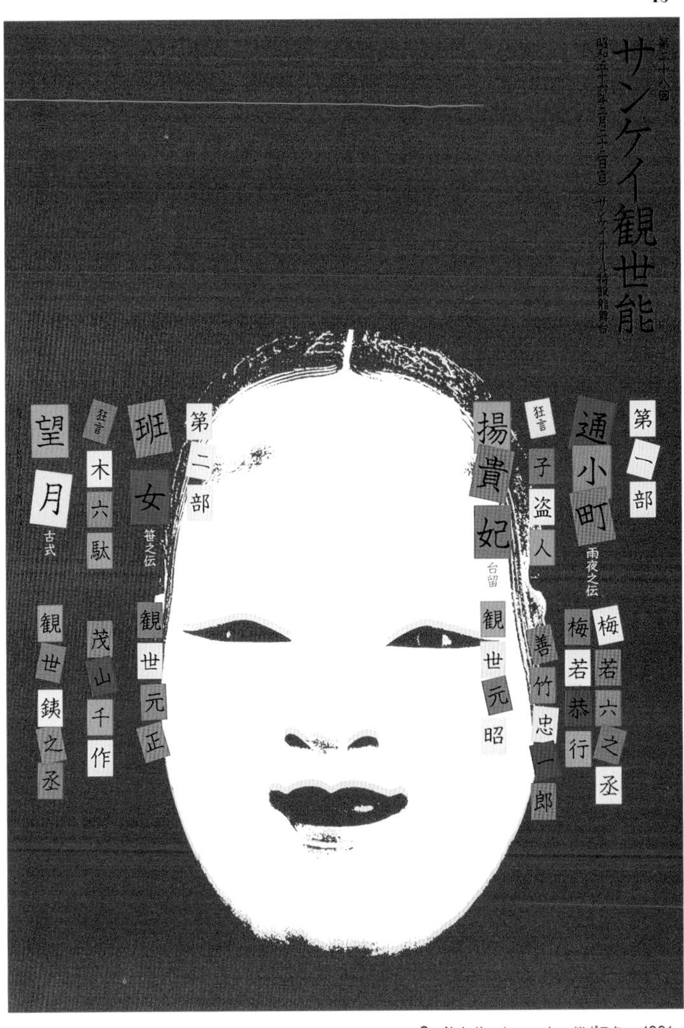

8 Noh theater poster 能ポスター 1981

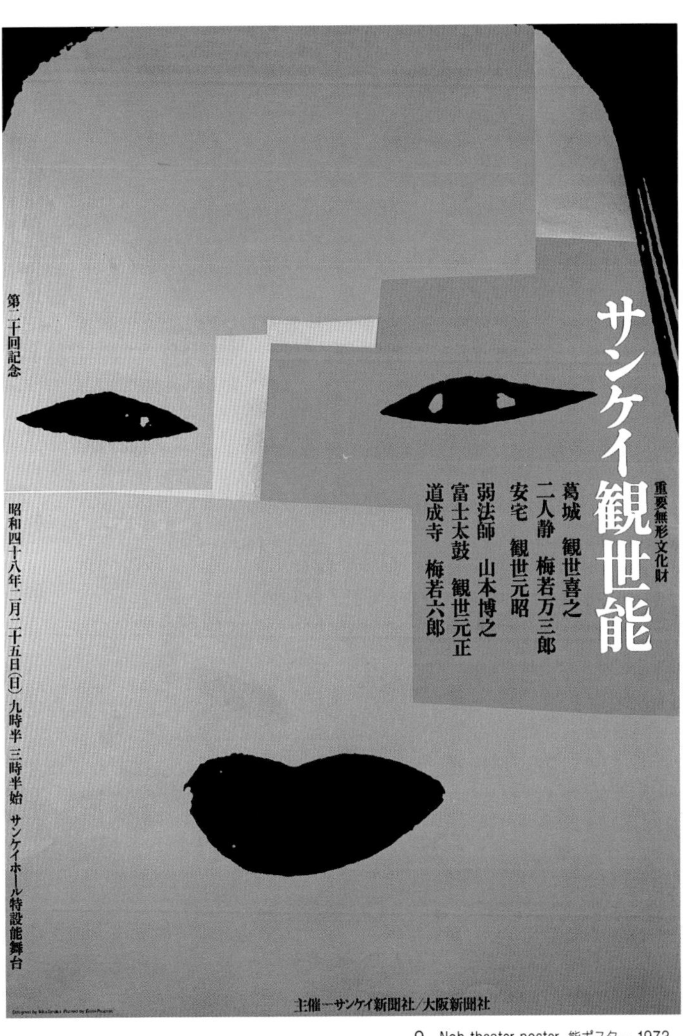

9 Noh theater poster 能ポスター 1973

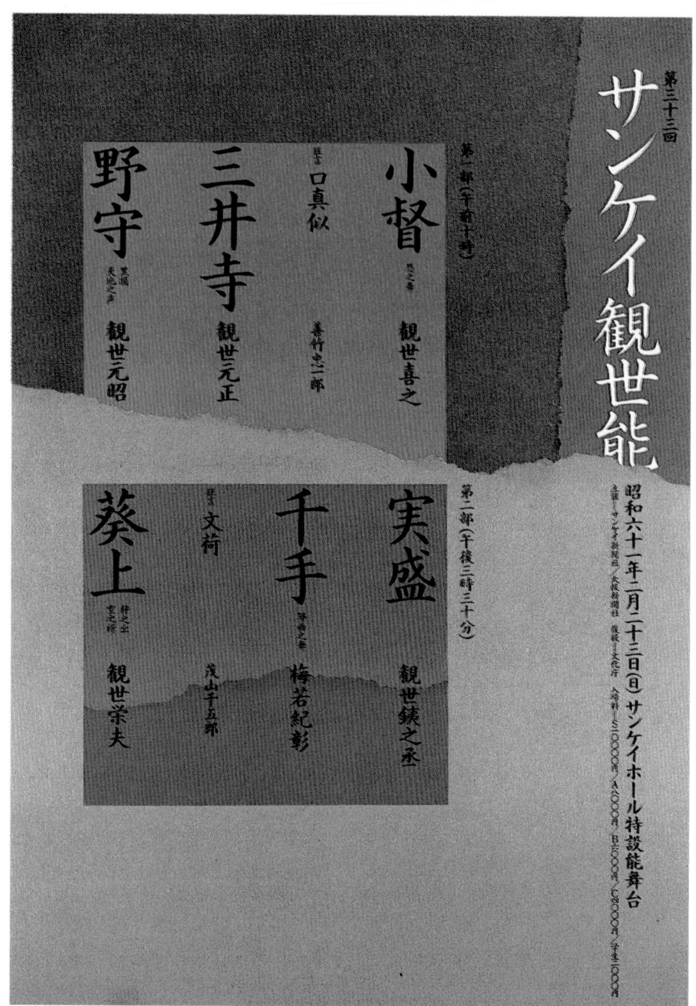

10 Noh theater poster 能ポスター 1986

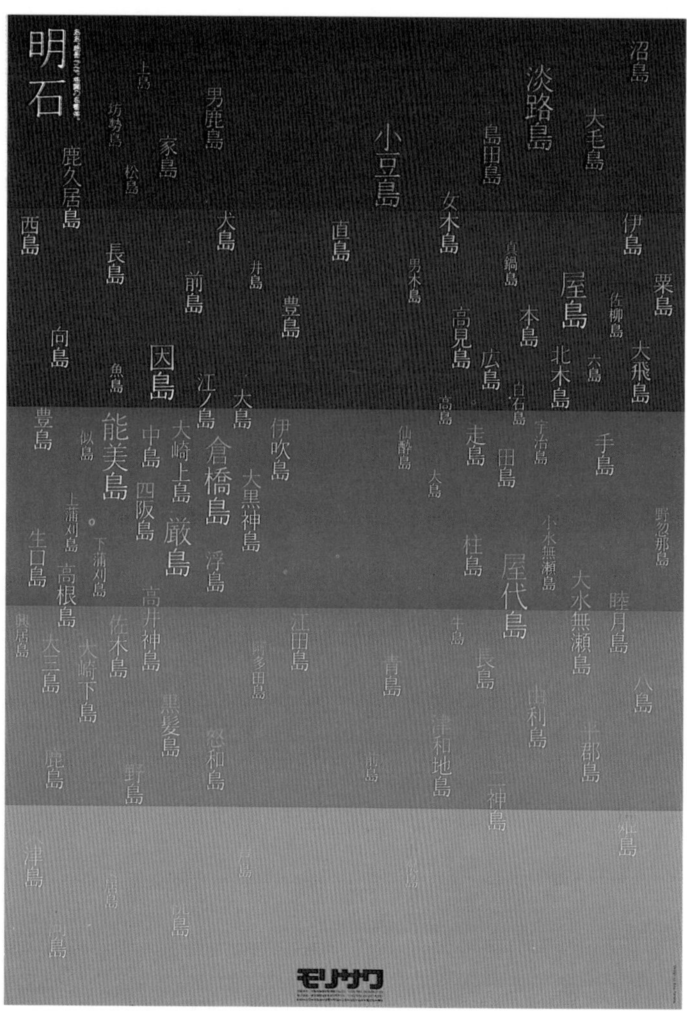

11 Poster for new typeface 写植新書体のポスター 1984

百の「花」は誇りたかく、百の「華」を競う。

第十四回いけばな日本百傑展

出品作家
阿川恵石　新井日新　有川悦子　飯村素翠　池田昌弘
市川光松　稲井理善　猪熊系惠　上田千代　上野理彰　宇田川理登
内田一油　海野彰人　榎本鶴遊　江見岬樹　役正風軒　太田光
大橋泉秀園　大野理瀞　岡婦美　岡田広山　尾中千草　小原夏樹
柿谷理閑　粕谷明弘　粕谷明光　香取柳知　金子理栄　蒲田素石
神尾芳翠　川浪冷祥　川原田湖秀　神崎華今
木下瀟雲　工藤和彦　熊井理総　熊沢仙華　小泉道生
小島喜艸　小島美陽　後藤喜舟　小林一阿彌
小室尚翠　佐藤秀抱　沢井剛　渋井玲虹　七五三月璋
七五三月窓　白澤春草　新藤華盛　末野尚霞　杉崎宜宗
須田芳枝　関江松風　千羽理芳　平光波　高橋松登
高橋梛翠　立原清香　立原広明　田津原楳陽
田辺宗風　谷野春光　角田一忠　東香舟　新呑傾月
野呂華宗　花井一柳　早川研一　林映里　原田淑水
原田春光　原野理筆　日向洸二　堀川晶仙　細田一弘　増野雪舟
松谷真月　松友義明　松野理鶴　宮上崇顕　宮下一風　宮田方圓居
望月義耀　森一森　森笙抱　山口草樂　山根由美　山本一水
山本斎月　横地宗象円　吉村隆　渡辺汀華
運営委員　池田理英
池坊専永　小原豊雲　下田天映　勅使河原宏　早川尚洞　吉村華泉

いけばな日本
百傑

11月6日(金)—11日(水)　西武池袋店12階　西武美術館　主催—東京新聞/西武美術館　後援—文化庁　入場料—800円

12 Ikebana exhibition poster いけばな展ポスター 1981

第10回いけばな日本百傑展　百の「花」は誇りたかく、百の「華」を競う。

安達潮花　新井日新　有川悦子　飯村素翠　池田昌弘　池坊専永　市川光松　今泉映草　猪熊系惠　上野理彰　植村春水　宇田川理登　内田一油　海野彰人　榎本理福
江見岬樹　役正風軒　大橋泉秀園　大野理瀞　大貫文夫　岡田広山　尾中千草　小原夏樹　粕谷明弘　粕谷明光　香取柳知　蒲田素石　神尾芳翠　川上香華　川崎草心
川浪冷祥　川原田湖秀　神崎華今　木下瀟雲　工藤和彦　久保映泉　熊井理総　熊沢仙華　小島喜艸　小島美陽　後藤喜舟　五島泰雲　小林一阿彌　小室尚翠　米野理愛
佐藤秀抱　渋井玲虹　島村芳雲　七五三月窓　白沢春草　新藤華盛　末野尚霞　須賀柏葉　鈴木理藻　杉崎宜宗　関江松風　千羽理芳　平光波　宝井理湖　竹内杏哉　立原清香
立原広明　田津原楳陽　角田一忠　勅使河原霞　長島桂仙　中村幾次郎　花井一柳　早川研一　林映里　原田淑水　原田春光　原野理筆　原悠光　日向洸一　藤原幽竹　堀川晶仙
細田一弘　増野雪舟　松谷真月　宮上崇顕　宮下一風　宮田方圓居　望月義耀　森一森　森笙抱　守谷紅沙　山崎尚釆　山本一水　山本斎月　横地宗象円　吉岡晋月　渡辺汀華
運営委員　池田理英　小原豊雲　金子霞璋　下田天映　勅使河原蒼風　早川尚洞　吉村華泉

いけばな日本
百傑

9月30日(金)—10月5日(水)　入場料—700円　西武美術館
主催—東京新聞・西武美術館　後援—文化庁　西武百貨店池袋店12階

13 Ikebana exhibition poster いけばな展ポスター 1977

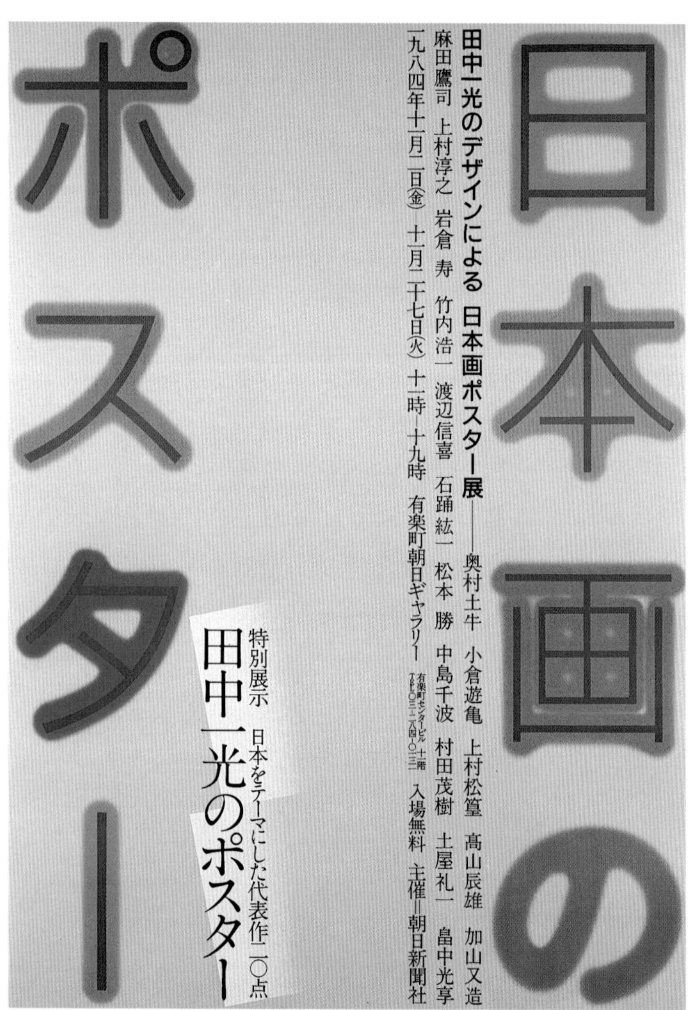

14 Exhibition poster 展覧会ポスター 1984

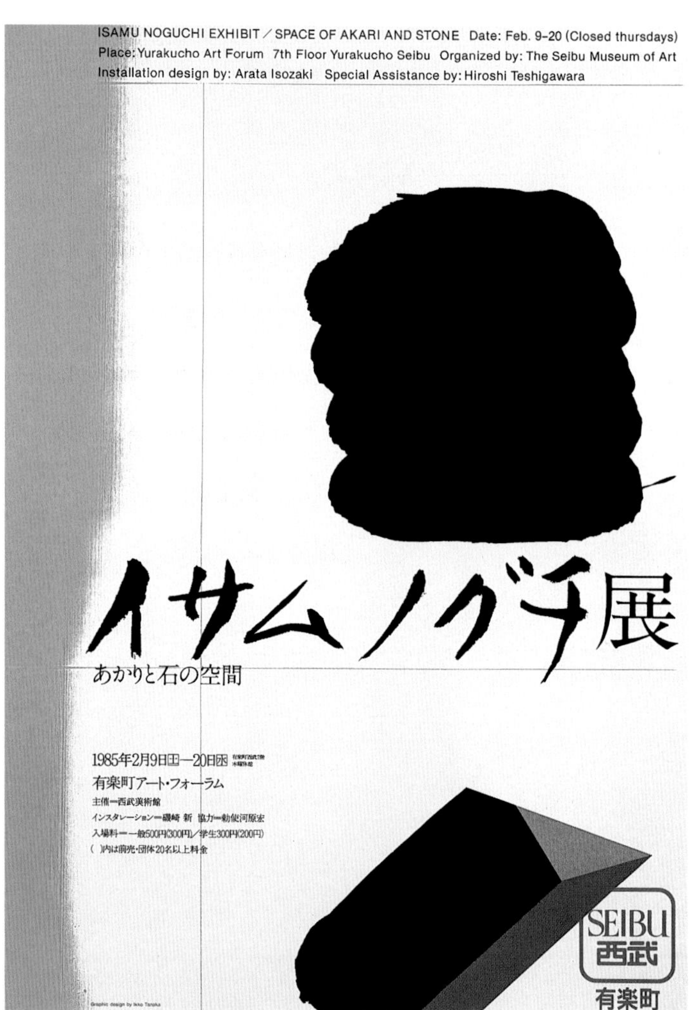

15 Exhibition poster 展覧会ポスター 1985

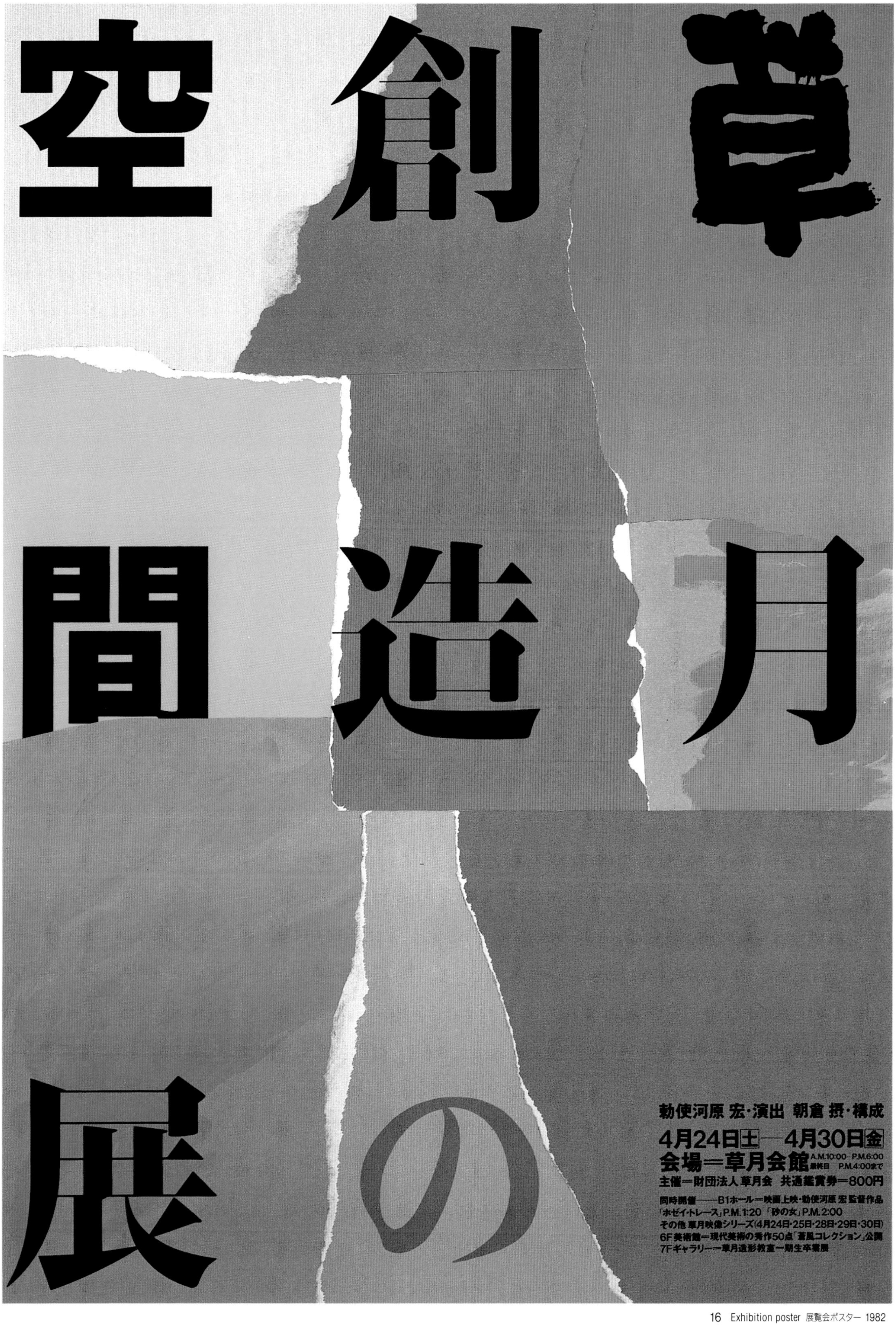

草月
創造
空間
の展

勅使河原 宏・演出 朝倉 摂・構成

4月24日(土)—4月30日(金)

会場＝草月会館 A.M.10:00–P.M.6:00 最終日 P.M.4:00まで

主催＝財団法人 草月会 共通鑑賞券＝800円

同時開催——B1ホール＝映画上映・勅使河原 宏 監督作品
「ホゼイ・トレース」P.M.1:20 「砂の女」P.M.2:00
その他 草月映像シリーズ(4月24日・25日・28日・29日・30日)
6F美術館＝現代美術の秀作50点「蒼風コレクション」公開
7Fギャラリー＝草月造形教室一期生卒業展

16 Exhibition poster 展覧会ポスター 1982

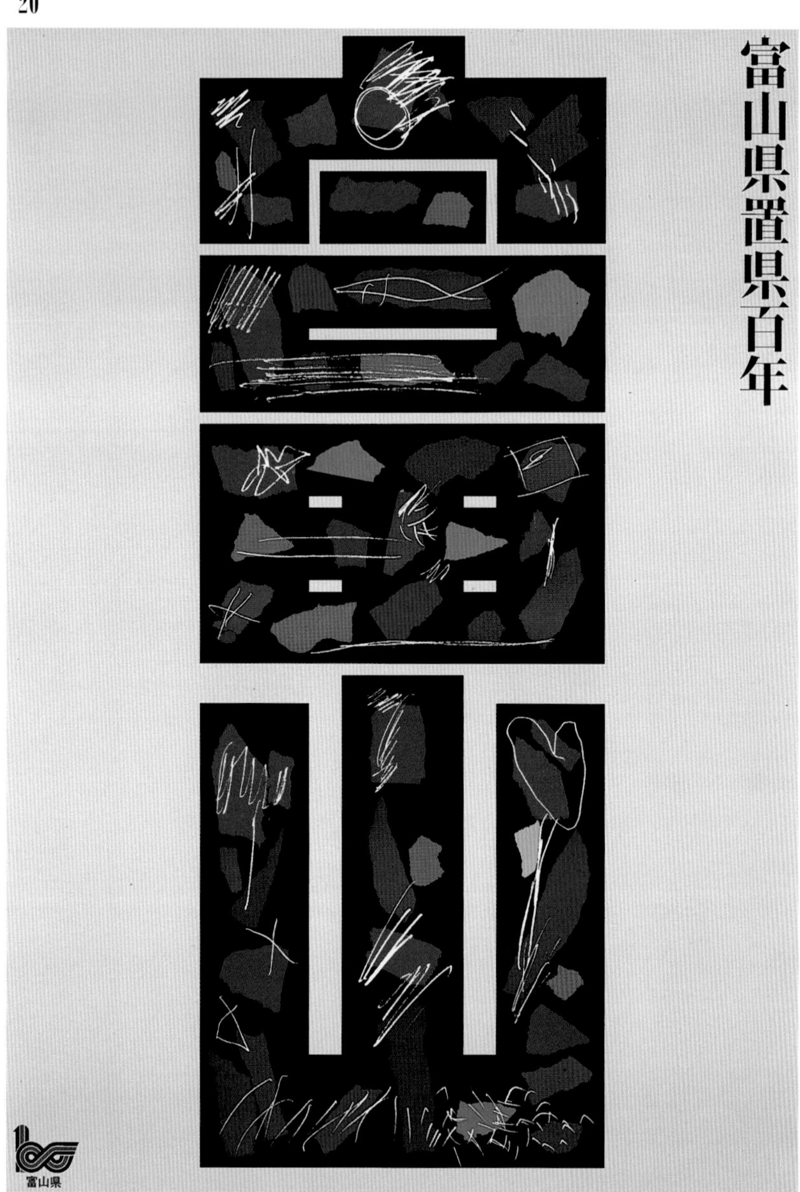

17 Poster for prefectural centennial 置県100年ポスター 1983

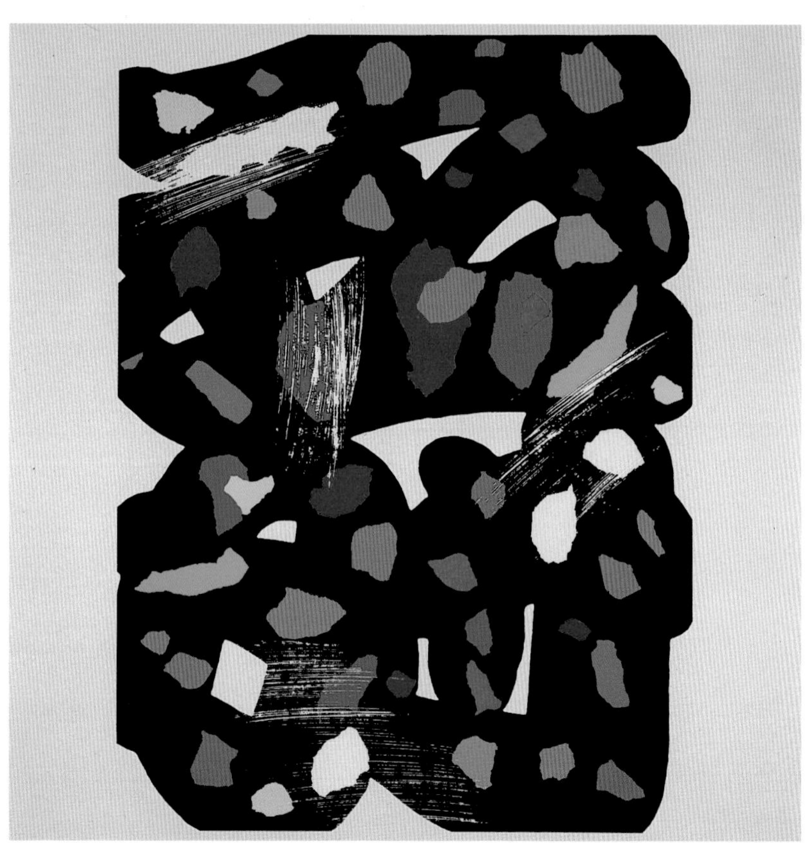

18 Illustration for exhibition poster 個展ポスターのイラストレーション 1979

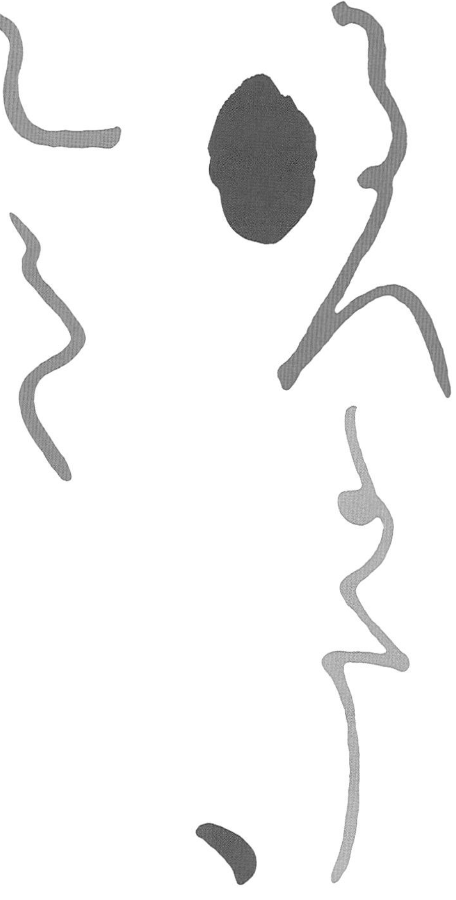

20b Calligraphy print カリグラフィ・プリント 1983

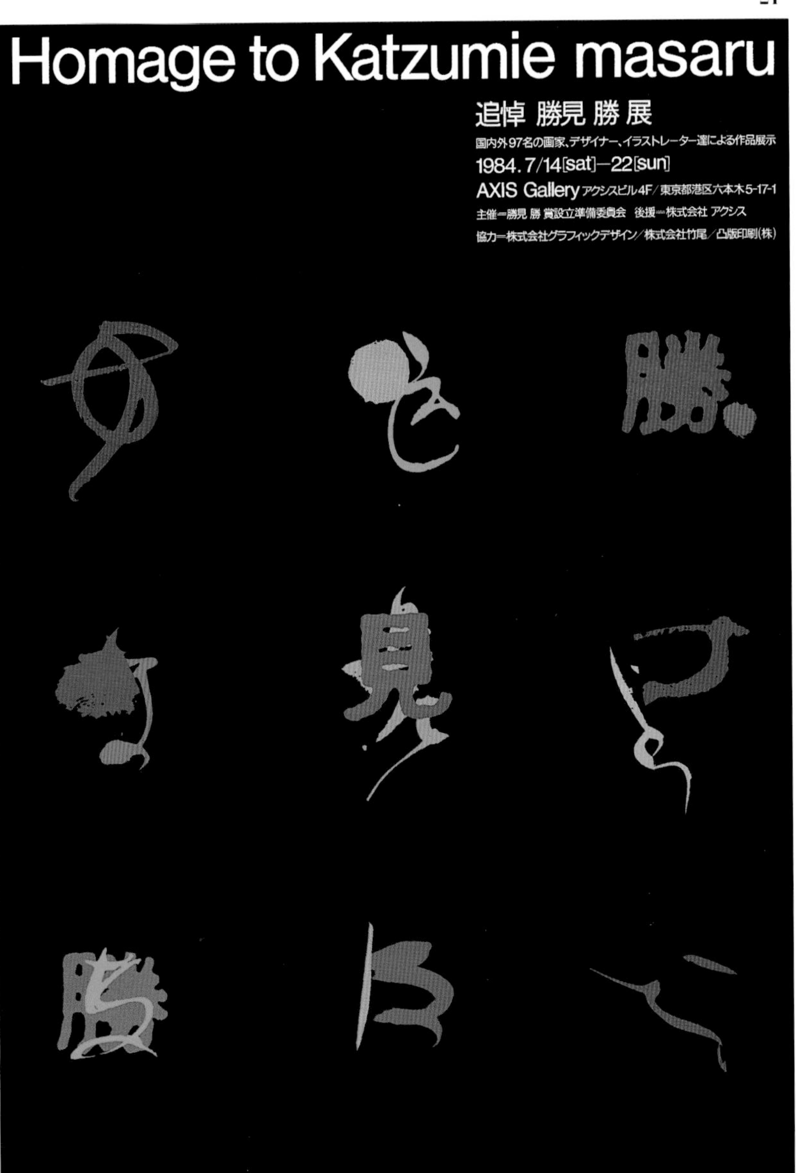

19 Exhibition poster 展覧会ポスター 1984

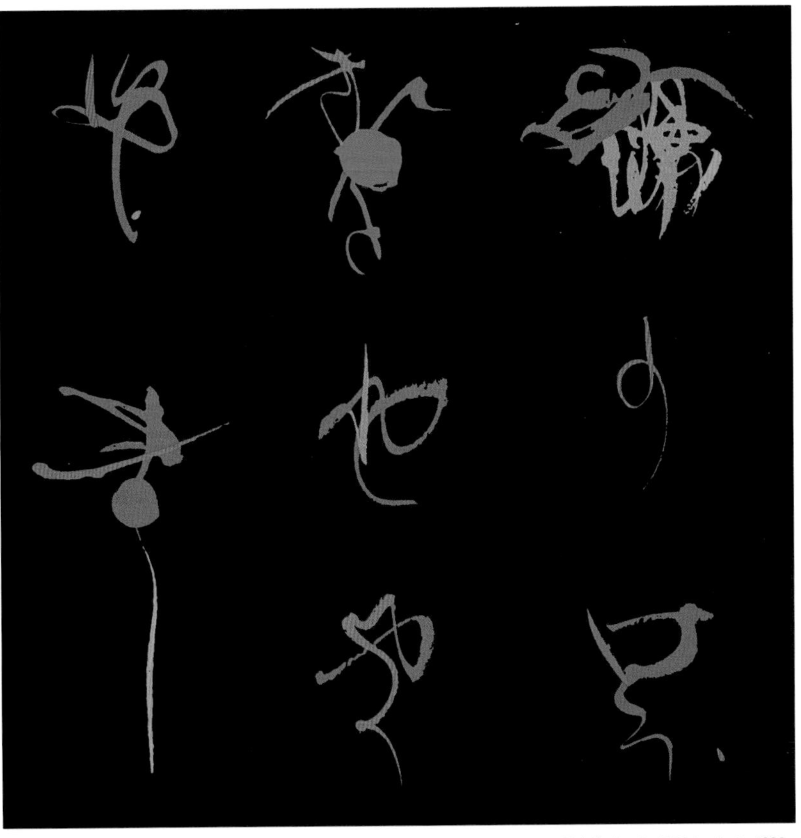

20a Illustration for exhibition poster 展覧会ポスターのイラストレーション 1982

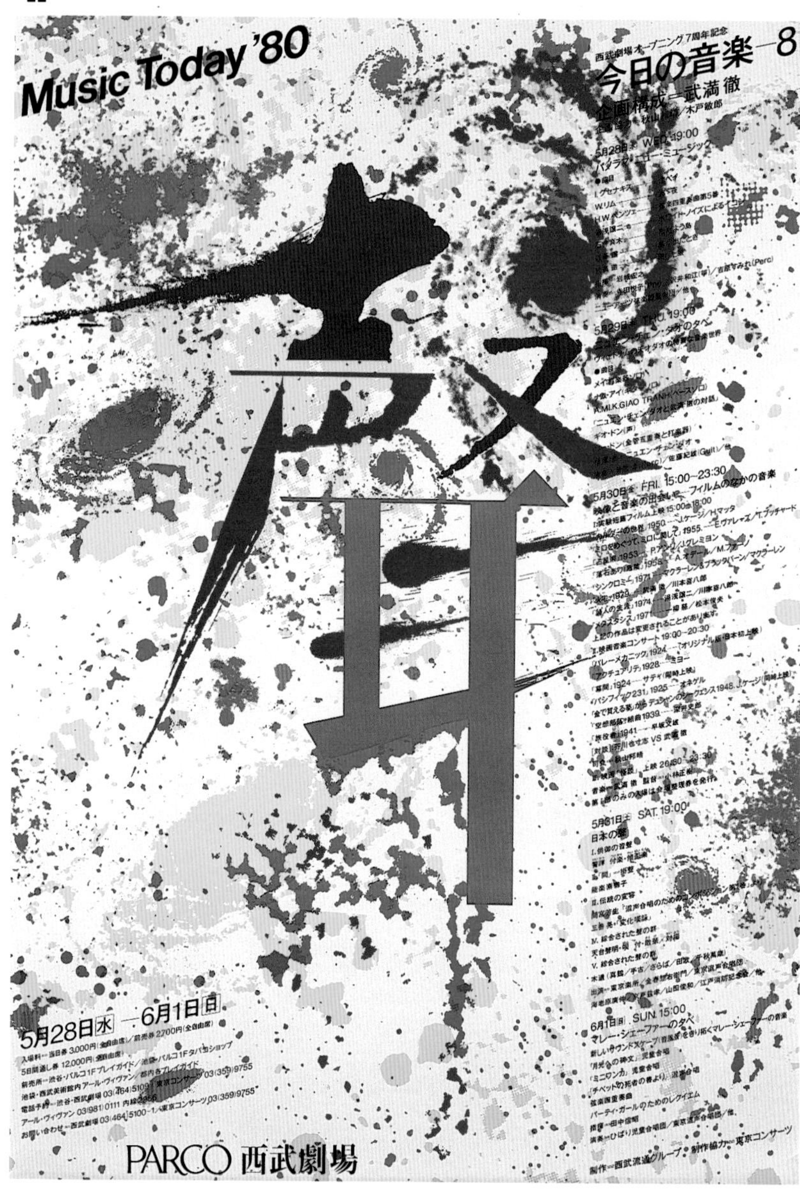

21 Concert poster 音楽会ポスター 1980

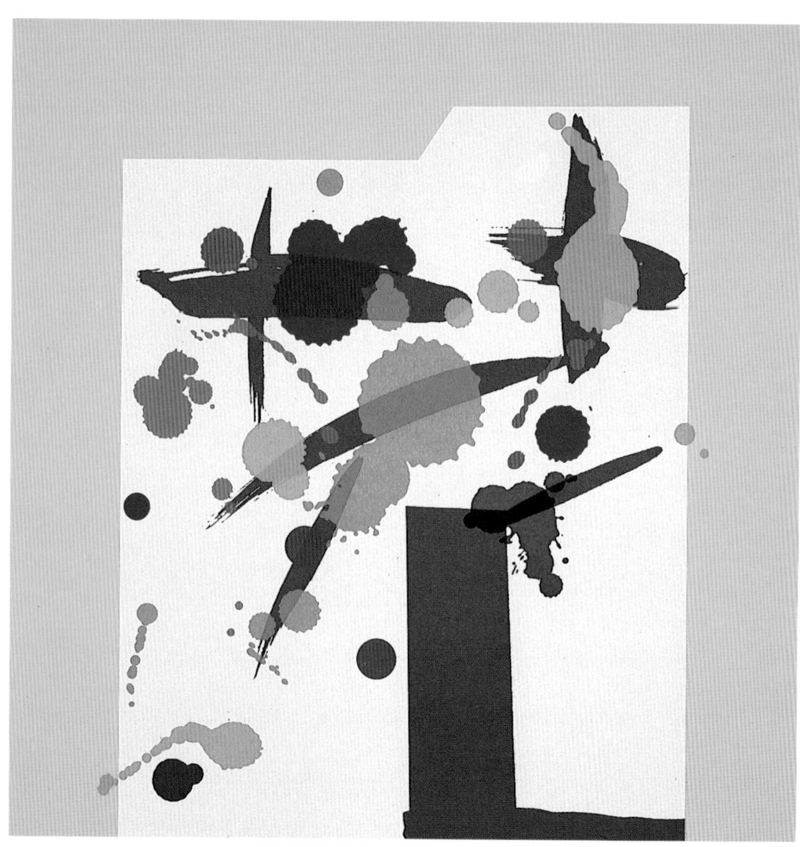

22 Calligraphy print カリグラフィ・プリント 1979

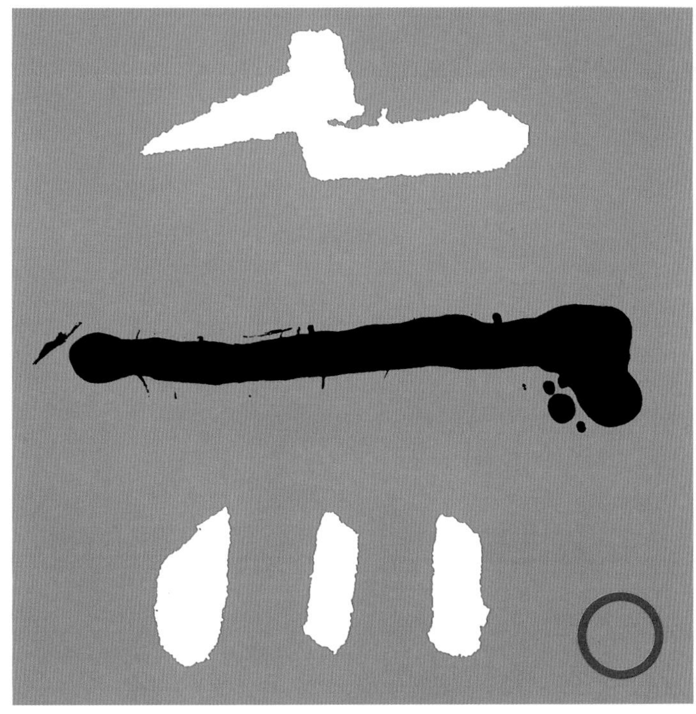

23 Calligraphy print カリグラフィ・プリント 1979

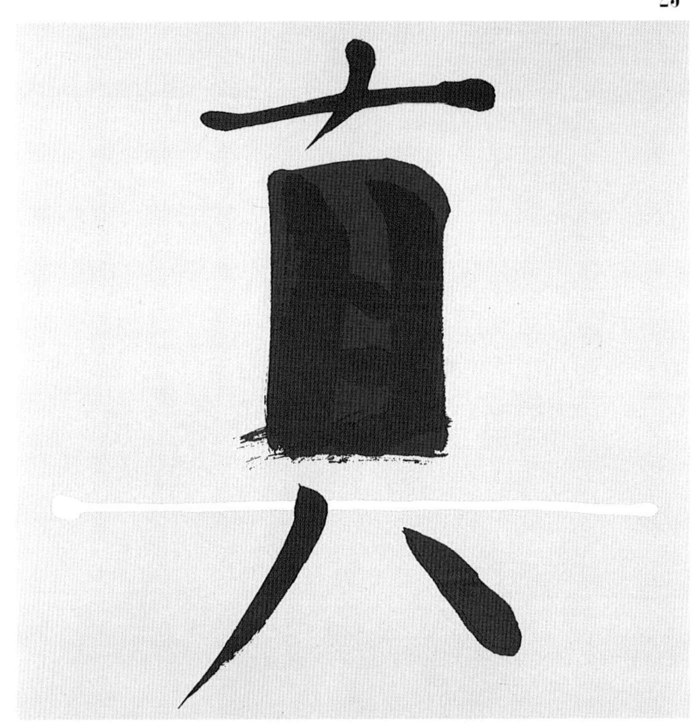

26 Calligraphy print カリグラフィ・プリント 1980

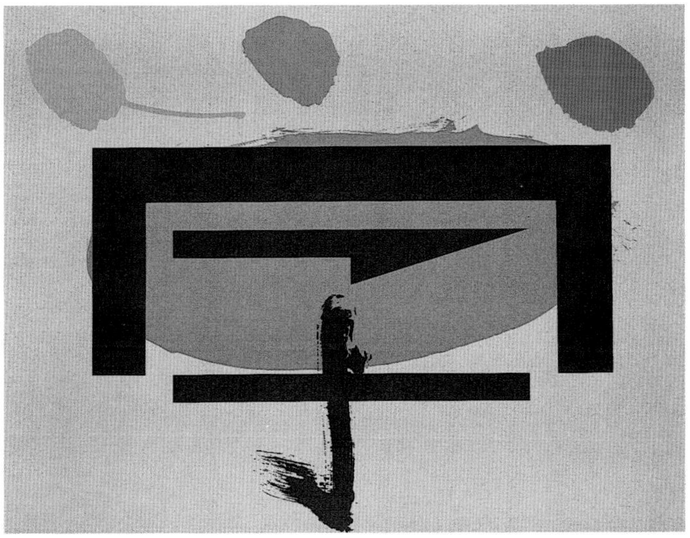

24 Illustration for calendar カレンダーのイラストレーション 1988

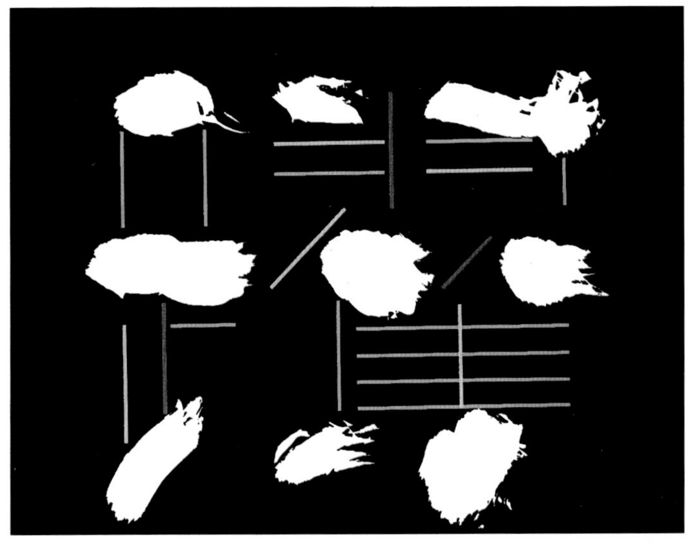

27 Illustration for calendar カレンダーのイラストレーション 1988

25 Calligraphy print カリグラフィ・プリント 1983

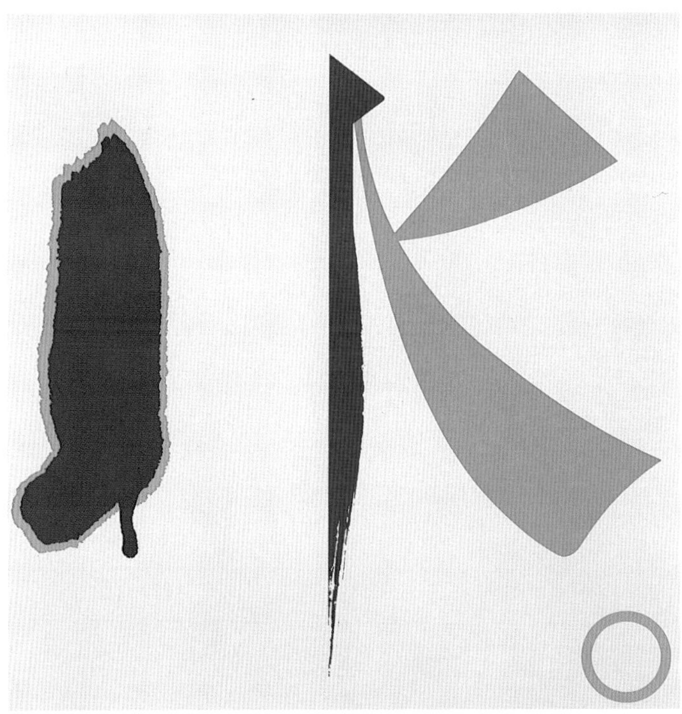

28 Calligraphy print カリグラフィ・プリント 1979

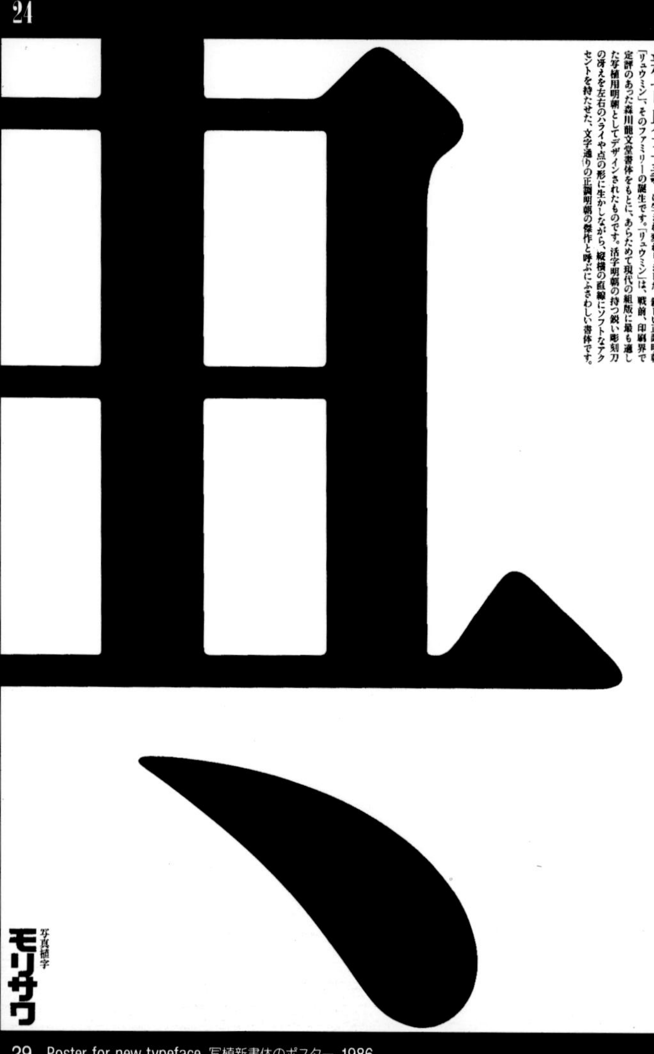

29 Poster for new typeface 写植新書体のポスター 1986

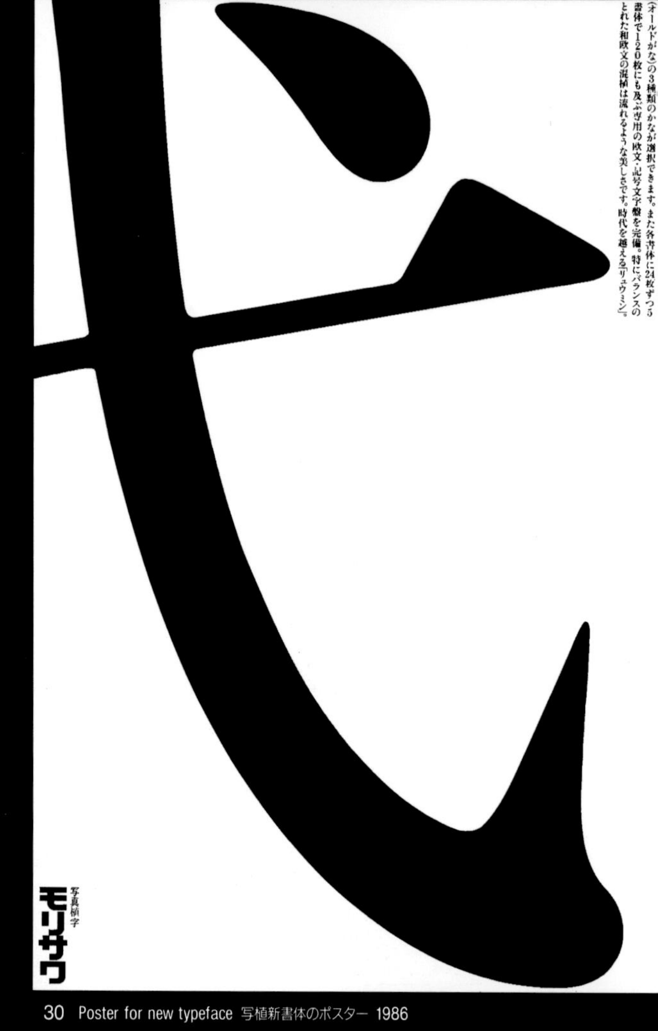

30 Poster for new typeface 写植新書体のポスター 1986

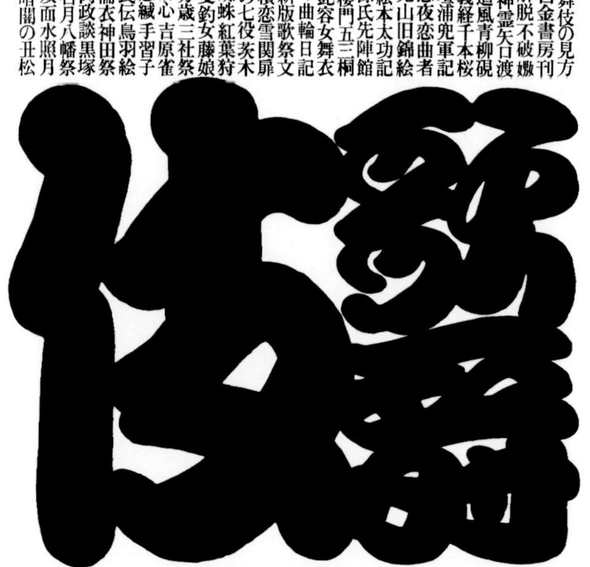

31 Poster for book on Kabuki 歌舞伎の本ポスター 1974

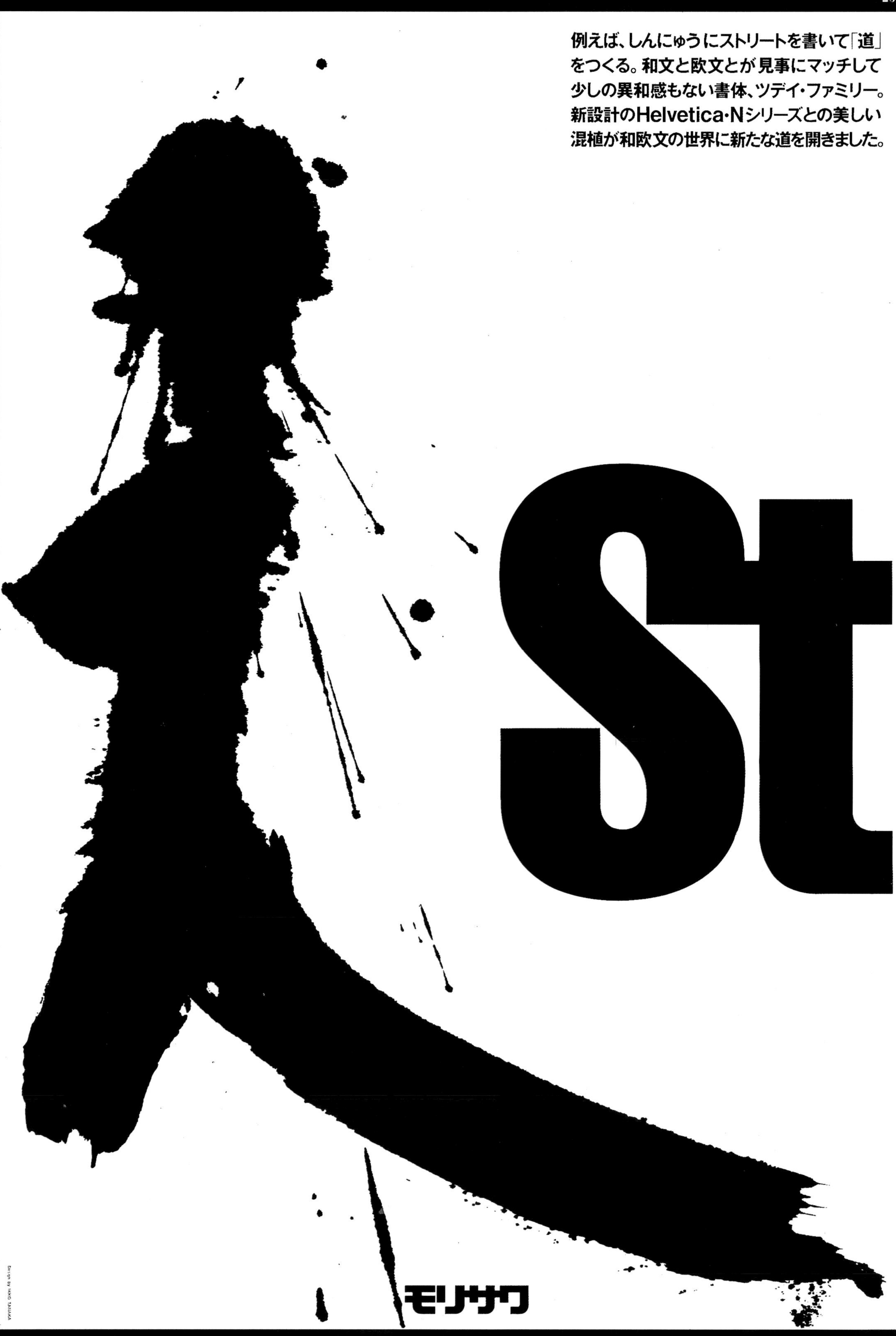

32 Poster for new typeface 写植新書体のポスター 1988

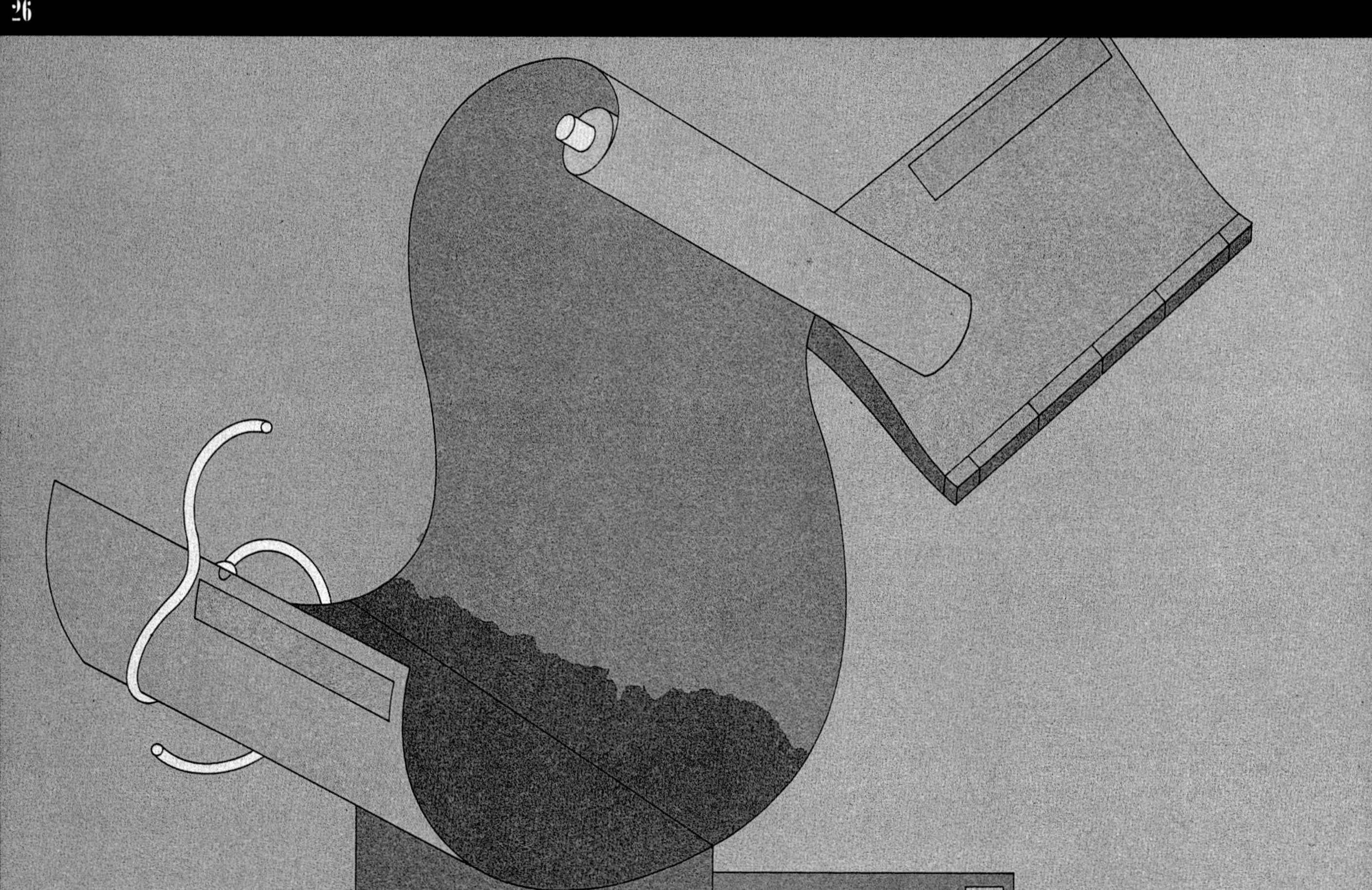

33-36 Illustrations for desk diary デスクダイアリーのイラストレーション 1982

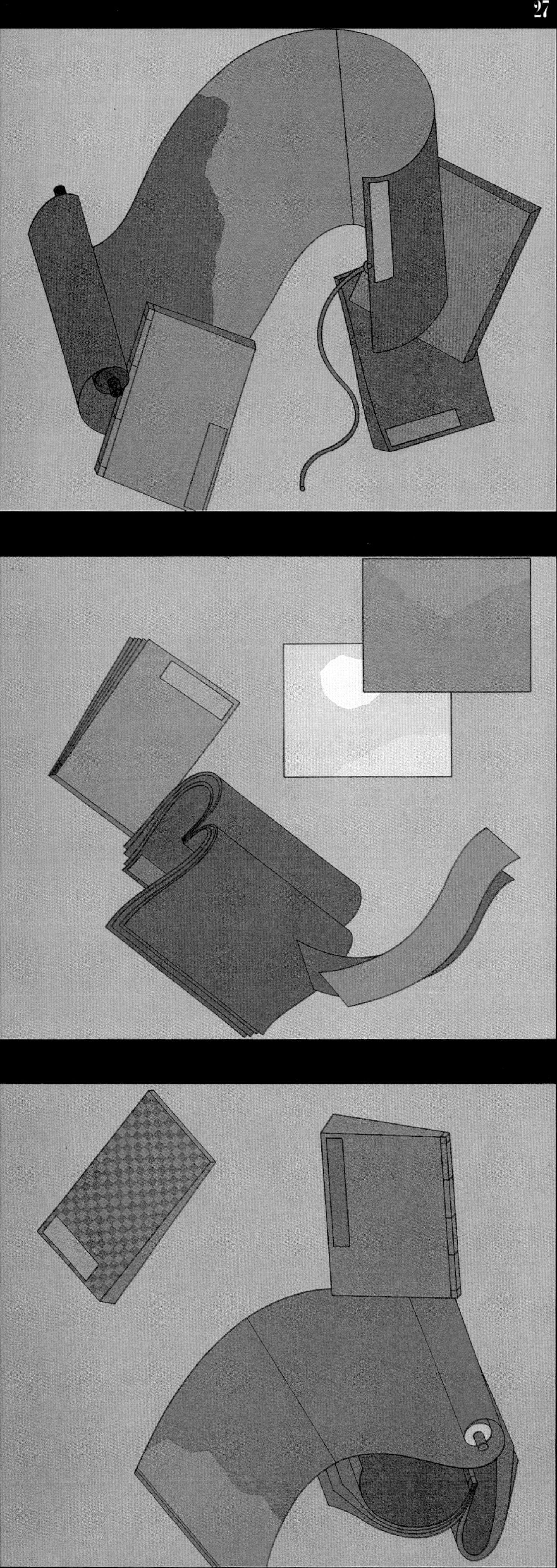

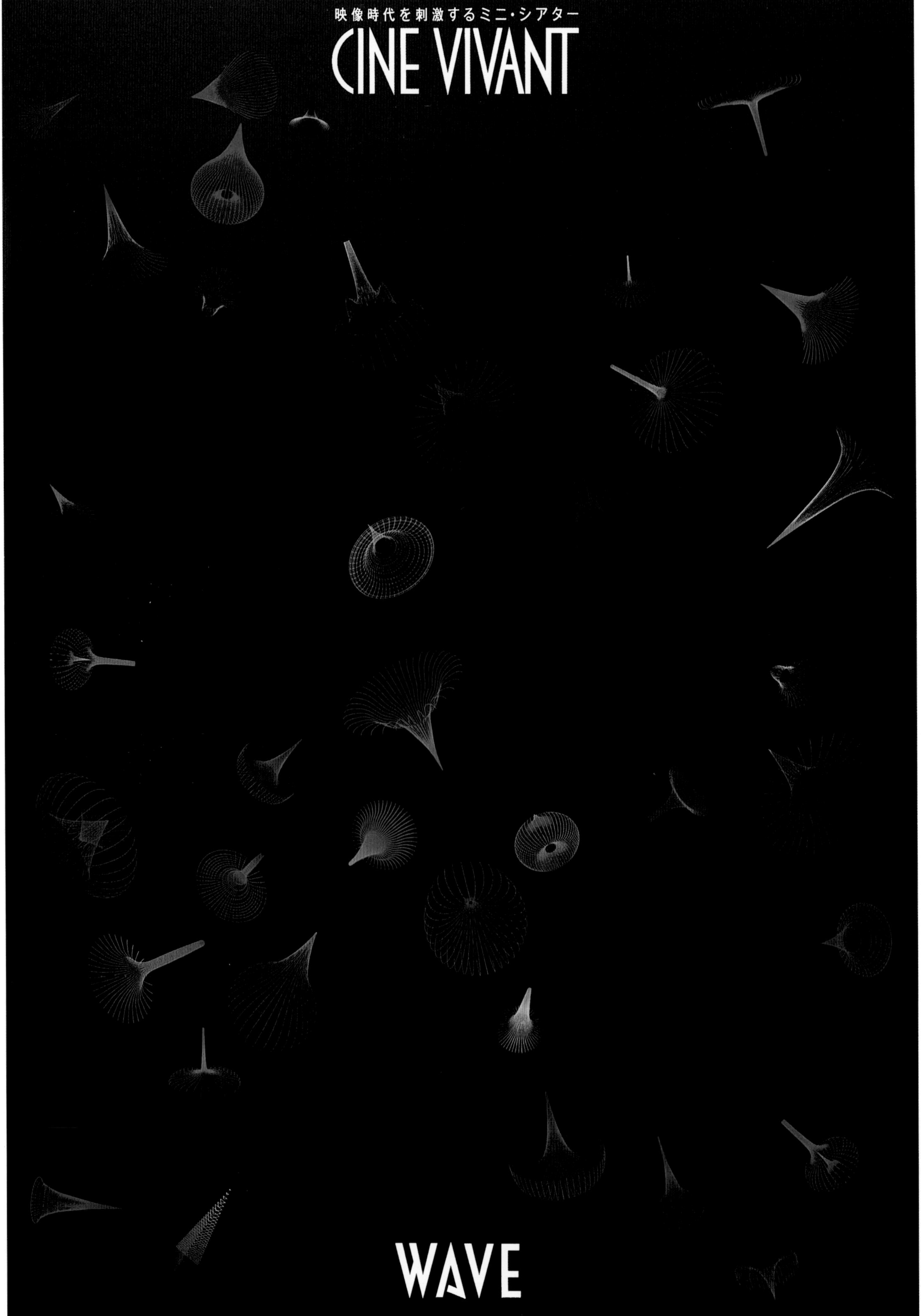

37 Movie theater poster 映画館オープンポスター 1984

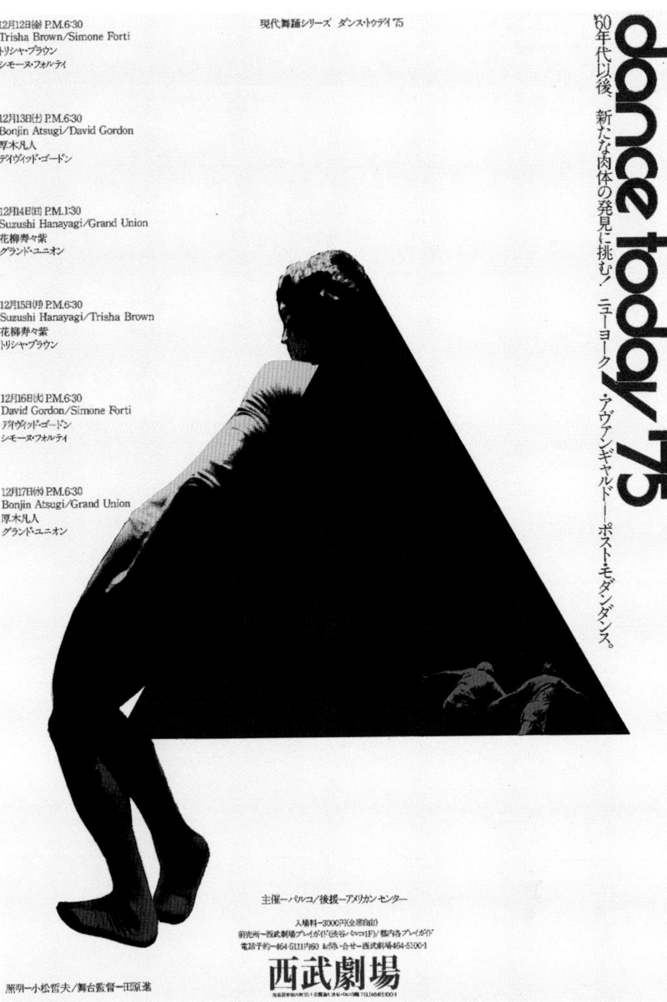

38 Poster for dance performance ダンスポスター 1975

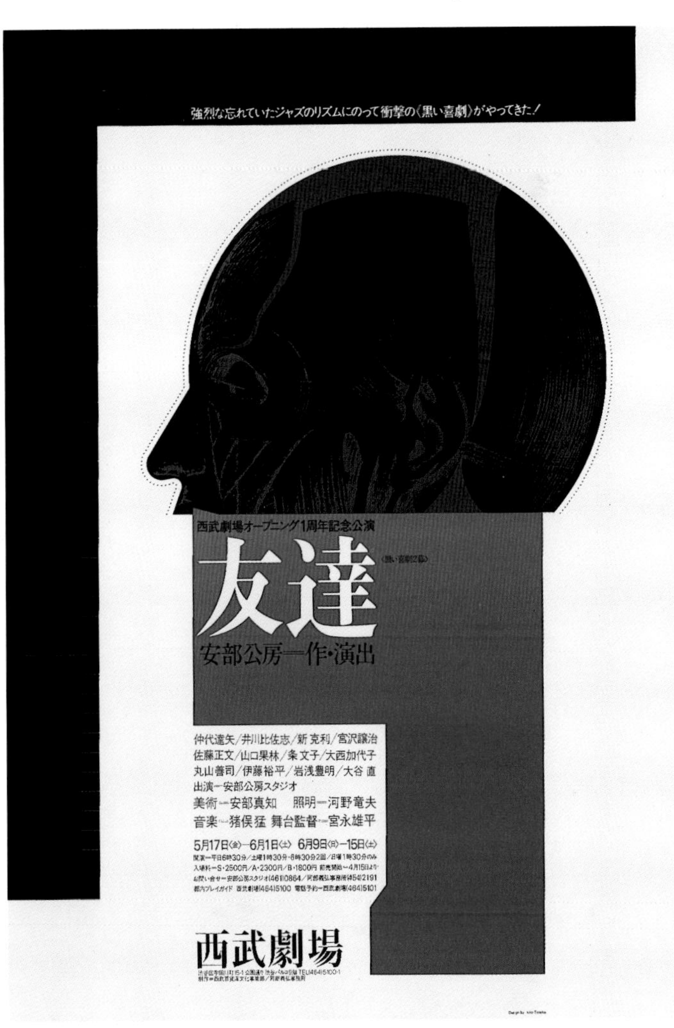

39 Poster for stageplay 演劇ポスター 1974

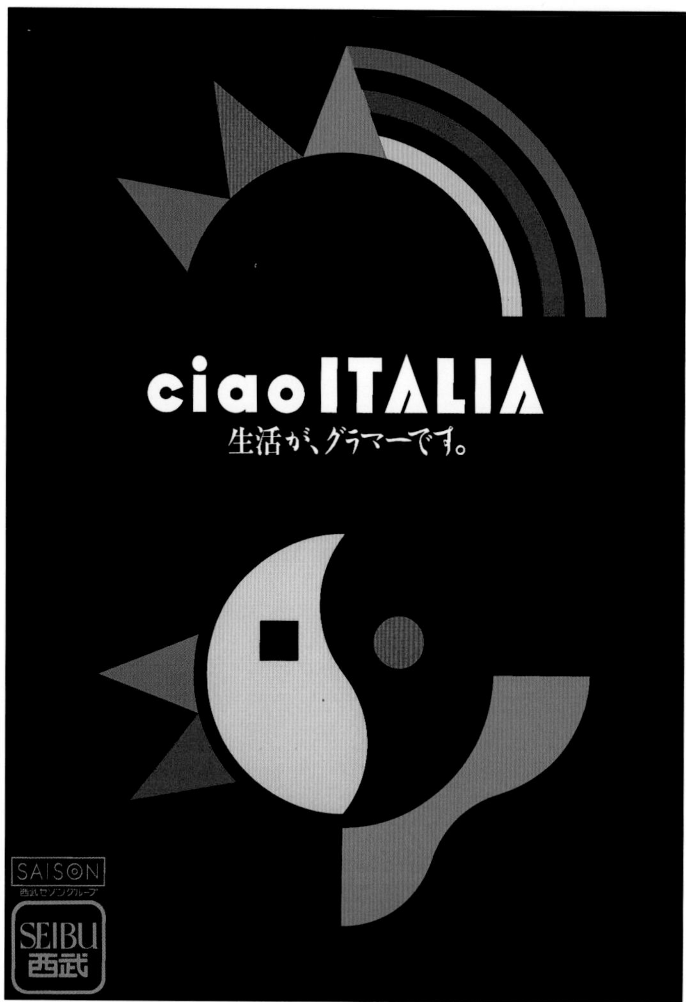

40 Poster for Italian Fair イタリア・フェアポスター 1986

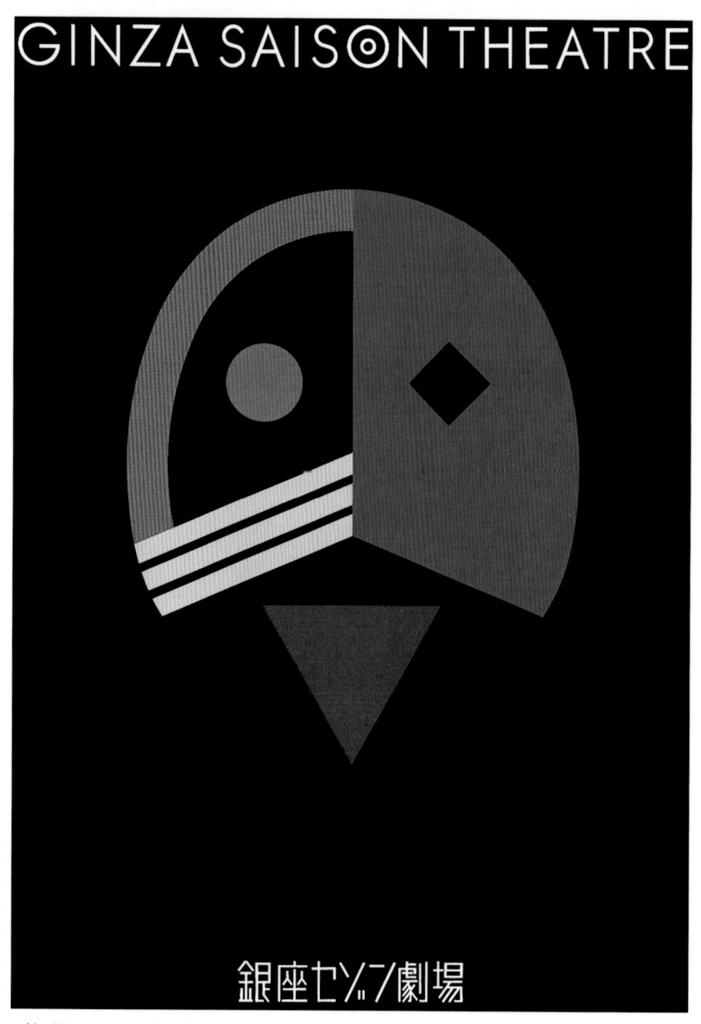

41 Theater poster 劇場ポスター 1986

ハート●インドの手

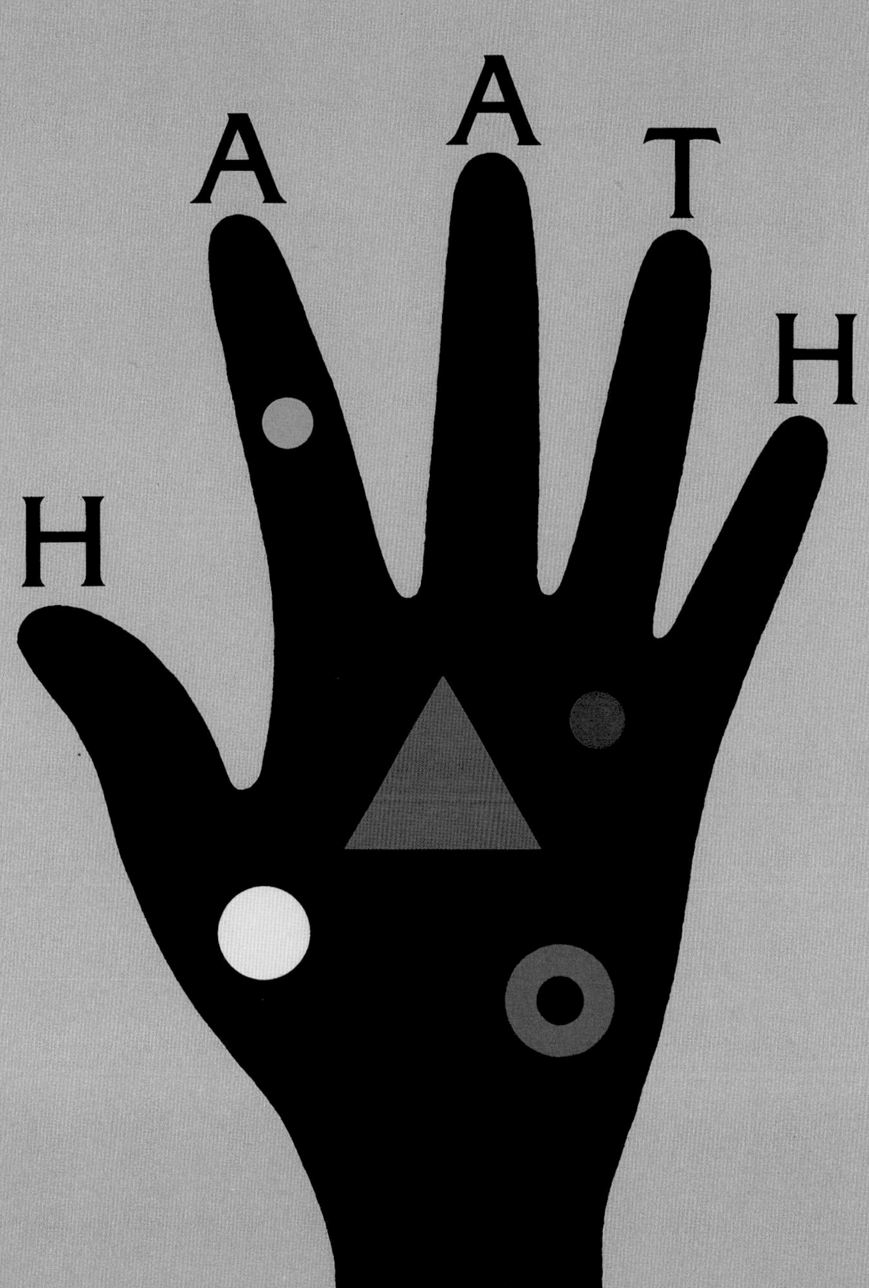

5月2日〔金〕―28日〔水〕
各階特別会場
●5月2日〔金〕―13日〔火〕
HAATH ハート展――
インド手織と三宅一生
有楽町アート・フォーラム
●5月16日〔金〕―27日〔火〕
HAATH――――
インドクラフトマーケット
有楽町アート・フォーラム

西武セゾングループ

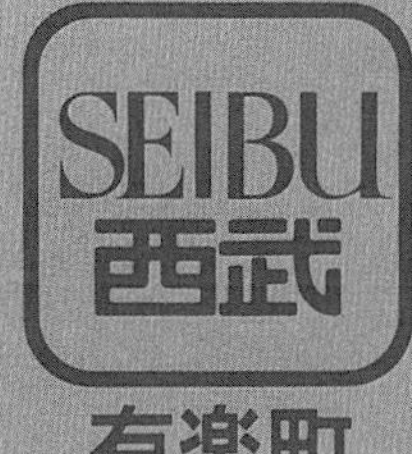

有楽町

Design by Ikko Tanaka

42 Poster for Indian Fair インド・フェアポスター 1986

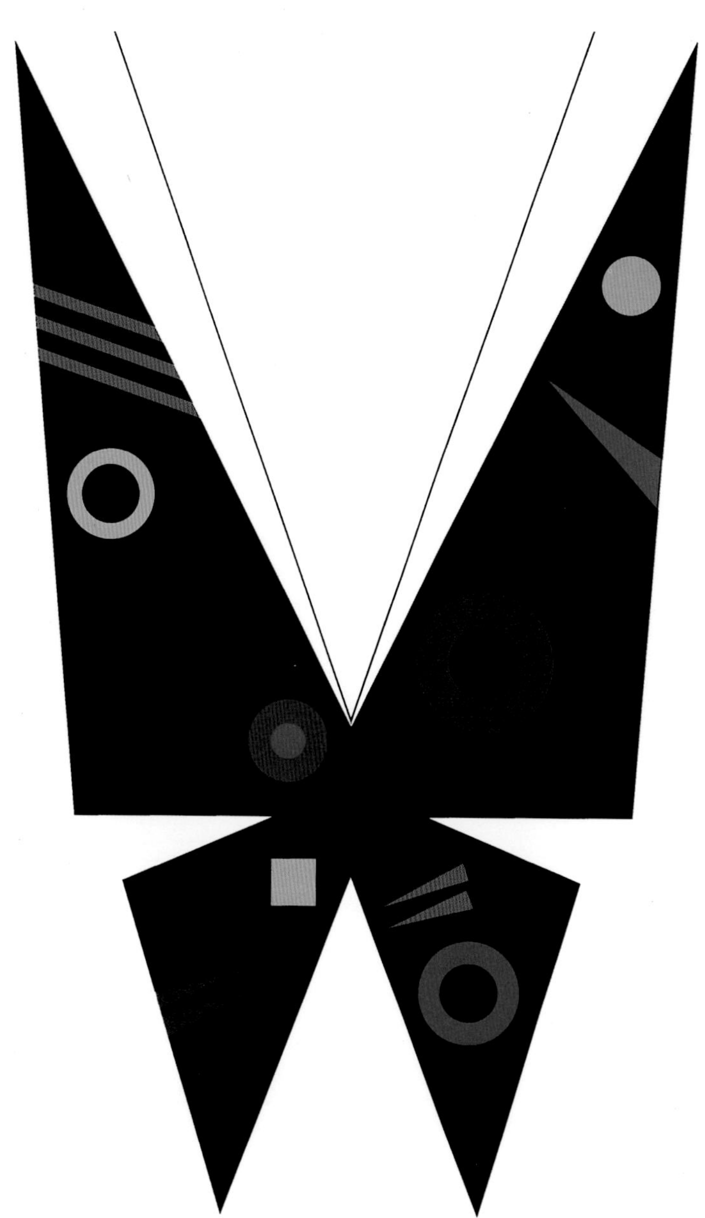

43 Symbol mark シンボル・マーク 1978

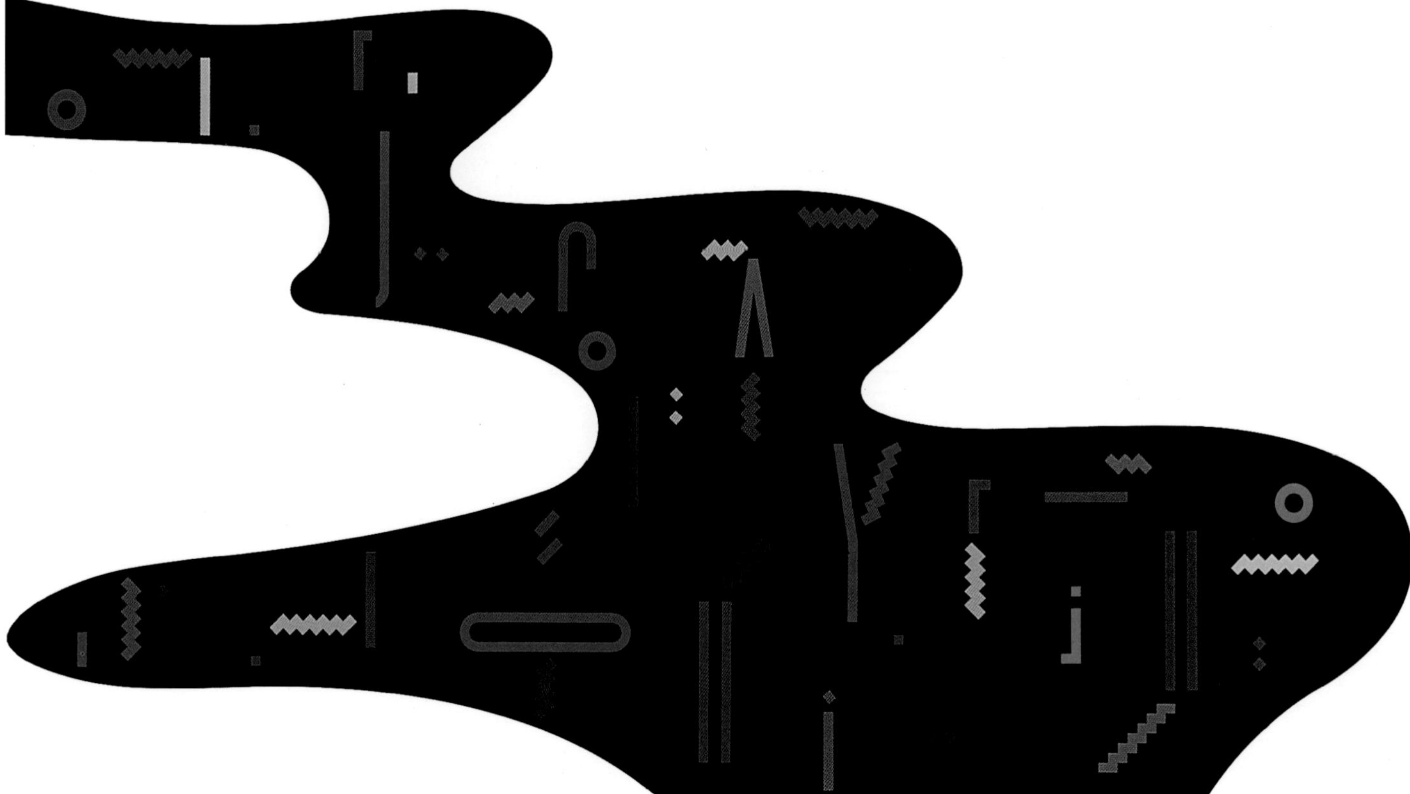

44 Illustration for concert poster 音楽会ポスターのイラストレーション 1985

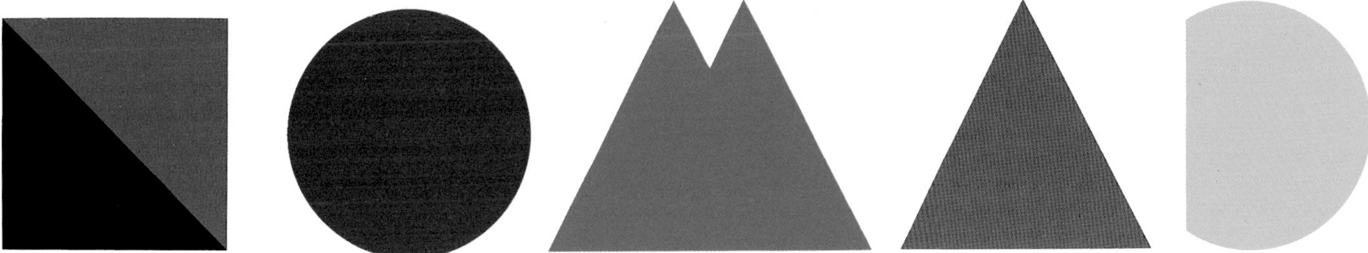

NOUVELLE
ORGANISATION
MAÏMÉ AND
DENISE

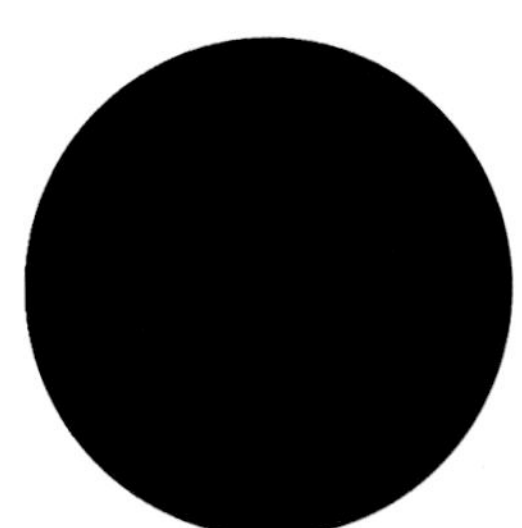

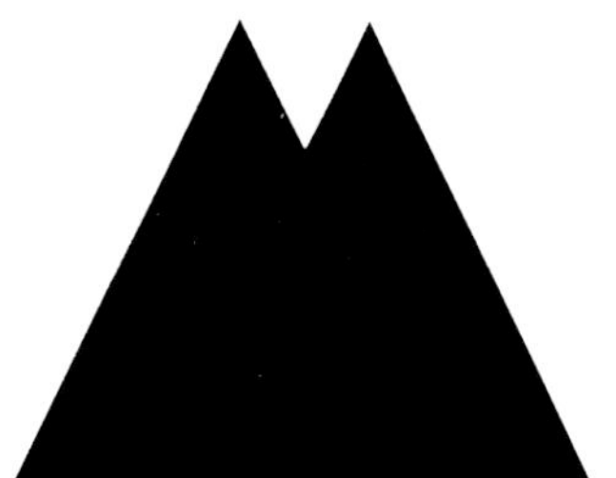

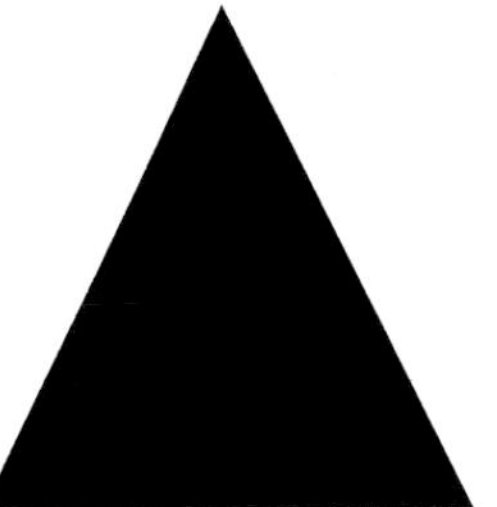

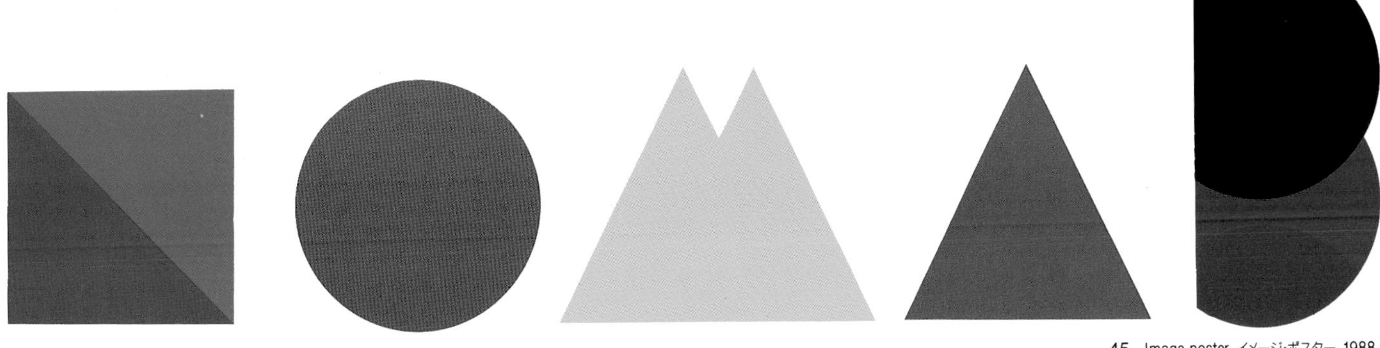

45 Image poster イメージ・ポスター 1988

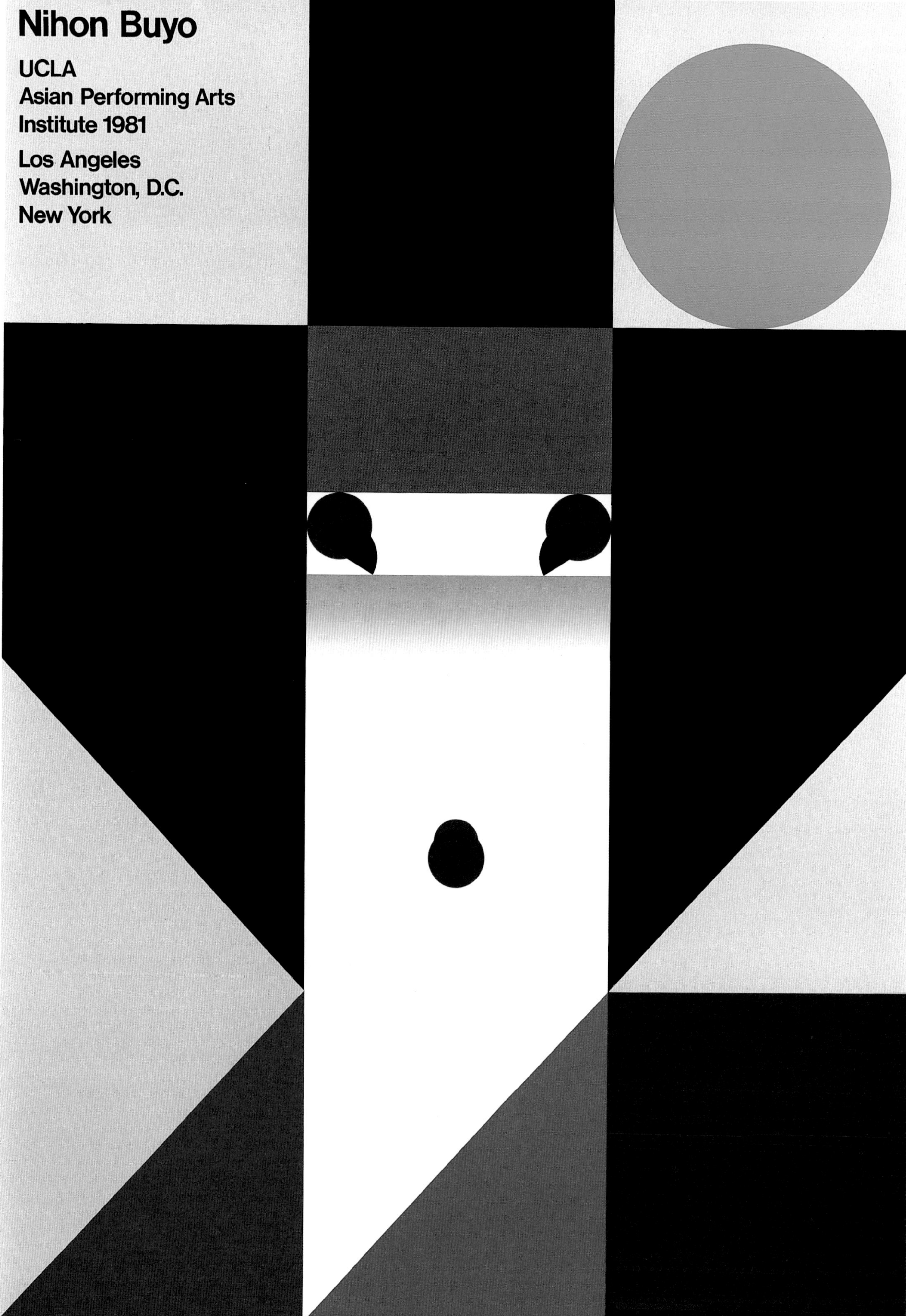

46 Poster for Japanese dance performance 日本舞踊ポスター 1981

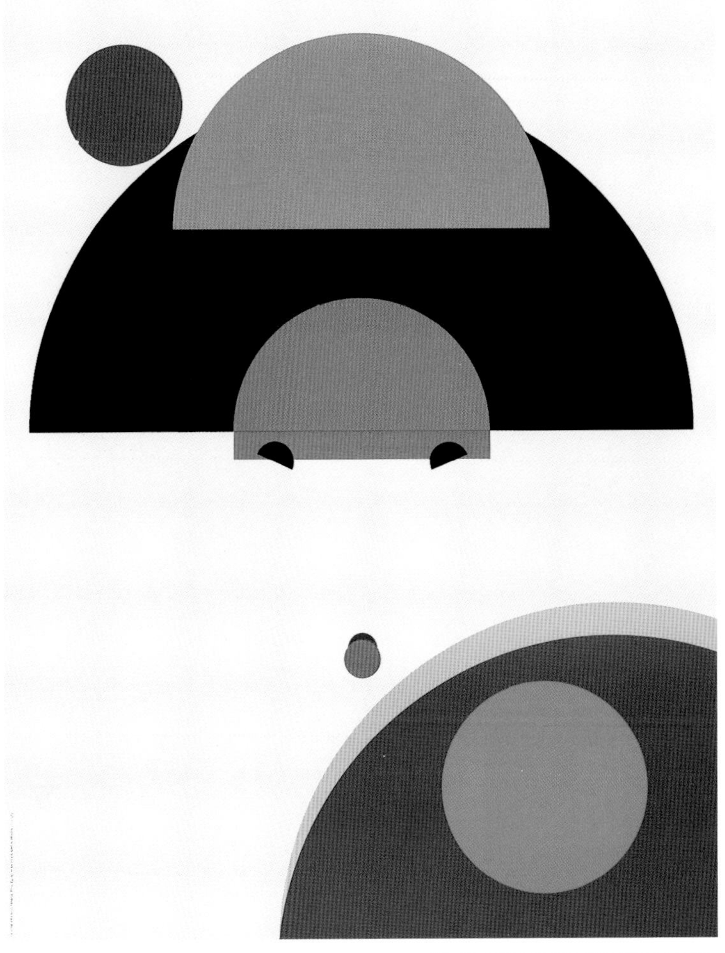

47 Magazine cover design 雑誌表紙 1984

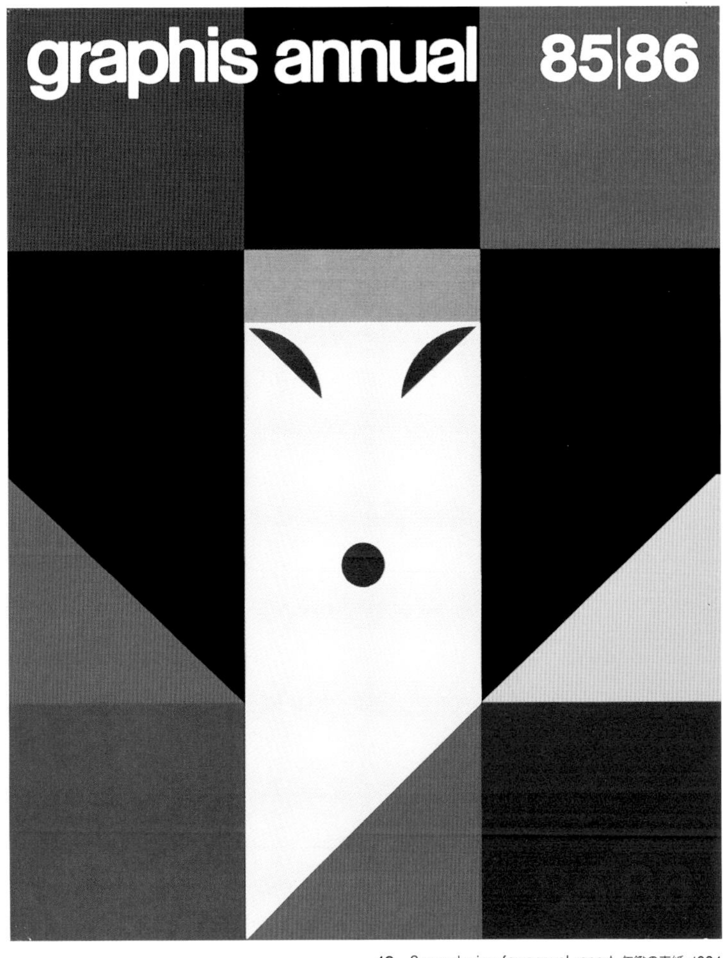

48 Cover design for annual report 年鑑の表紙 1984

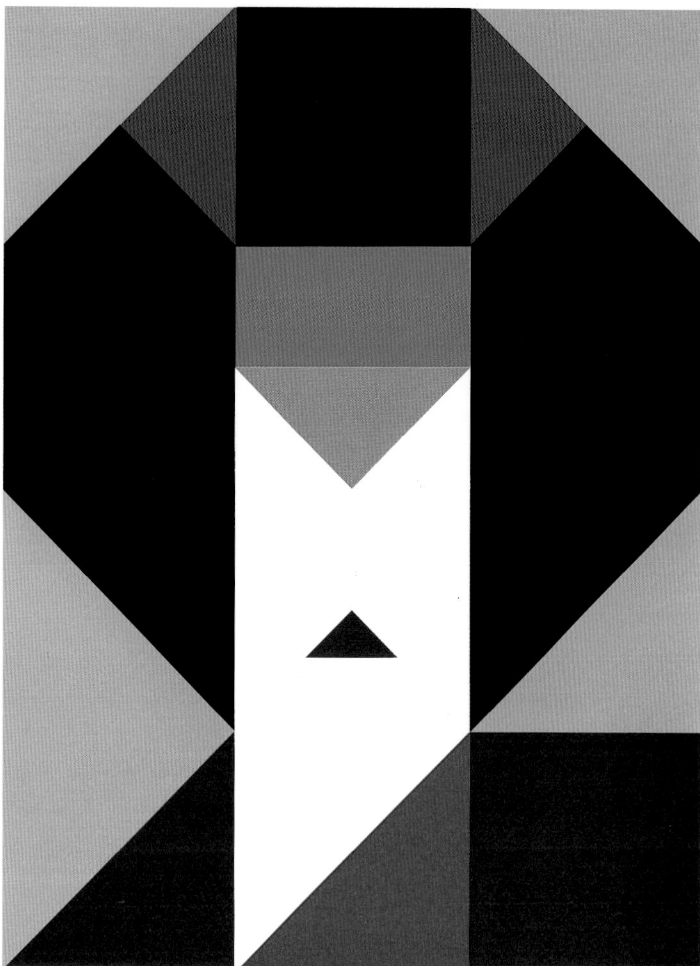

49 Illustration for special event poster イベントポスターのイラストレーション 1985

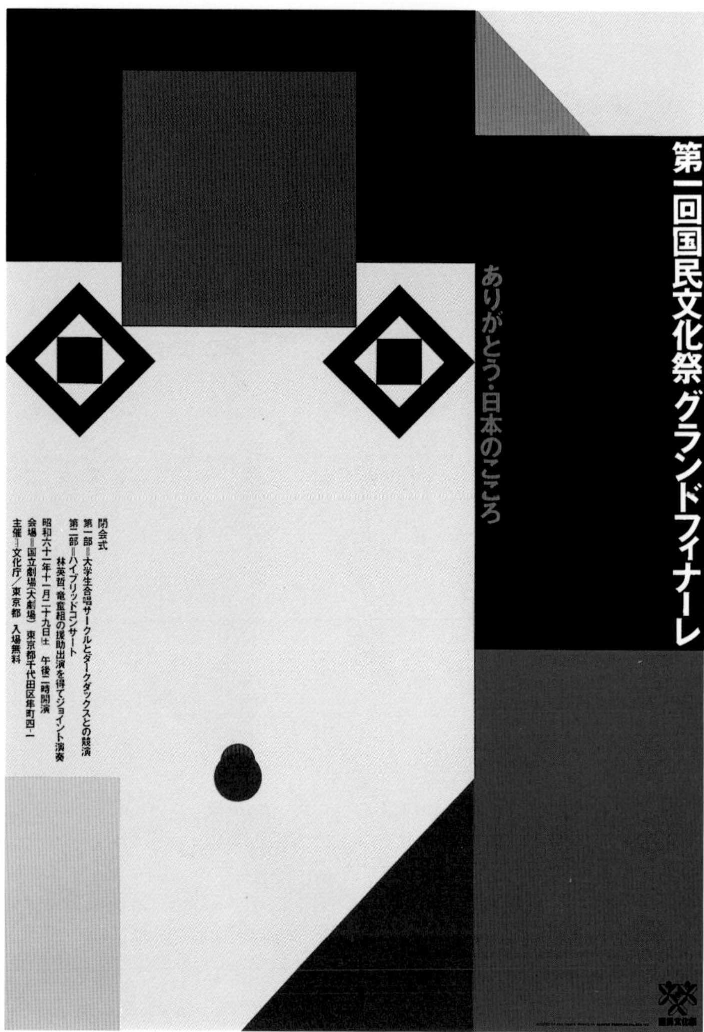

50 Poster for National Cultural Festival 国民文化祭ポスター 1986

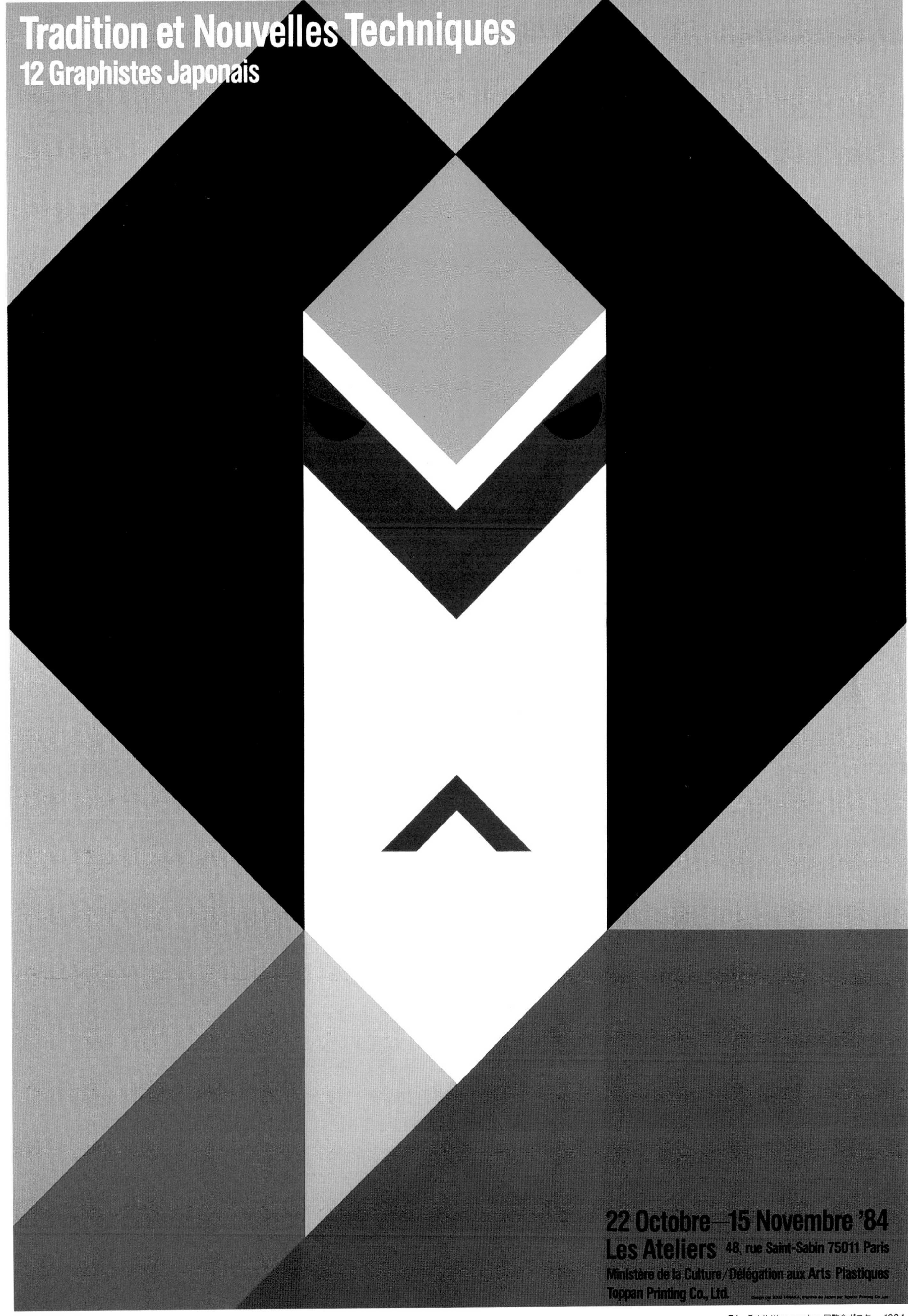

51 Exhibition poster 展覧会ポスター 1984

BRUNO BRUNI ブルーノ・ブルーニ Painter

Shunsuke Kijima 木島俊介

Bruno Bruni frequently refers to himself as a "fantastical realist." In ancient art history fantasy and realism were contradicting terms. But to those of us familiar with surrealistic art, the world of "fantastical realism" is by no means inconceivable. On the contrary, in today's modern age of intertwining values "true" reality is perhaps attainable only through sublation with its inherently conflicting phenomenon, fantasy. The term "fantastical" as used here refers to that which is imagined, and as we who are involved in art all know, imagination is the wellspring of creation.

From his earliest years of artistic activity, Bruni already experienced a search for reality amid two antimonious forces. On one hand he was born into an era of Italian classicism with its insistence on clear forms. On the other he was educated under German romanticism with its insatiable admiration of the mysterious and unknowable. As we may recall, early this century the Italian painter Giorgio de Chirico, a strong proponent of Nietzsche, created a strange world blending fantasy and reality. Formerly we were able to explain this world only using the ambiguous adjective "metaphysical." In our contemporary context, however, we now know that this obscure and visionary realm has adequate realism. Bruno Bruni, by virtue of his Latin and German backgrounds, similarly creates an artistic world that sublates fantasy with reality.

It is significant to note that Bruni learned stone lithography in Hamburg under Paul Wunderlich. Unlike recent print techniques where zinc or aluminum plates are substituted, in traditional lithography using limestone artistic advantage is made of the property of water absorbed into the fine grain of the stone to repel oil-based paint. This characteristic enables the subtle nuances of the natural stone to come through in endless variety and ambiguity, producing on paper areas of diaphanous shadow and soft light, as well as superb colors of mysterious shading. Onto this ambiguous "cloud" of color Bruni creates a contrasting line-drawing of great beauty and detail, suggesting a finely drawn sketch. Yet the form created by these lines is not classical but rather manneristic. It tends to convolutions, exaggerations, abbreviations, along with a propensity toward length and fineness. These extremely self-willed and artificial lines do not, however, recoil from a fetishistic tenacity with real objects—and this is where the world of sublation comes into play.

As an example, fine lines forming the contour of a nude female are sufficient to arouse a sense of eroticism. Yet the long, thin body has only a shadowy color that precludes a sensation of life, thereby causing the woman to retreat from the viewer like an apparition. Though she may stretch and remove her undergarments over her head, throwing her arms upright and setting her bosoms erect in an erotic pose, her facial expression remains concealed under a shapeless veil of cloth.

Flowers, leather gloves, birds, hats, bedsheets, shoes, raincoats. Though these at one moment seem to be spirited away into the fetishistic realm of inanimate object worship, in another they immediately come back to life: the glove as a living fish, the hat as a woman's private parts. Bruni seems to be telling us that the true meaning of life can be known only through melancholy, in the chasm between eroticism and iniquity.

ブルーノ・ブルーニは自分を称して「ファンタスティック・リアリスト」だと言っている。古い美術史のなかでは、幻想的であることと現実的であることは相容れない性格だが、超現実主義の美術を知っているわれわれには、決して不可解な世界ではないだろう。そればかりか、現代という価値観の錯綜している時代にあってはもはや、背反する事象のあいだに止揚されるファンタスティックな価値によってしか真のリアリティーは得られないのかもしれない。この場合ファンタスティックとは「想像された」という意味であって、想像することが創造することの源泉であることはアートに関与するわれわれには周知の事実である。

ブルーニは、その初期の経歴からしてすでに、二律背反するもののなかにリアリティーを模索するような環境を体験してきている。彼は形態に明快さを求めるイタリアの古典的風土のなかに生まれながら、神秘と不可知とを憧憬してやまないドイツの浪漫主義的風土のなかで教育を受けているのである。ニーチェの哲学に傾倒したイタリアの画家デ・キリコが、今世紀の初頭に、幻想と現実とが交錯する不思議な世界を現出させたことはわれわれの記憶に新しい。かってわれわれはその世界を〔形而上的〕という曖昧な言葉でしか説明できなかったのだが、その空漠とした白日夢の空間は、現代という時のなかでは、充足とたとえていいほどのリアリティーを持つものとなったことを知っている。ブルーノもまた、ラテン人とゲルマン人の意識の拮抗するさなかで、幻想と現実とが止揚する作品世界を創出させて来ているのである。

ブルーノが、ハンブルグにおいてパウル・ウンダーリッヒから石版画（ストーン・リトグラフ）を学んだことには大きな意味がある。周知のごとく、最近この版画法に代用されている亜鉛版やアルミ版とは異なり、石灰石を版に用いる伝統的なリトグラフ版画は、細かな石のきめのなかにすいこまれている水が油性の絵具をはじく性格を利用した版画法である。自然石の肌の微妙で曖昧で変化にとんだ組成が、紙の面に、おぼろげな闇とやわらかな光を、また神秘な陰翳をかもす精妙な色彩を転写させるのだ。ブルーノは、雲のごとくたちこめているこの曖昧な色域に、デッサンの正確さをうかがわせるに充分な美しい線描を対照させるのである。その線のつくるフォルムが古典的だというのではない。フォルムはむしろマニエリスモ的で、よじれと誇張と省略、そしてまた長さと細さにたいする嗜好とを見せている。だがその極めて恣意的な、アーティフィシャルな線も、現実の事物にたいするフェティシュなまでの執着を止めはしないのである。ここに止揚の世界が生まれる。たとえば女の裸身にそって細く流れている線は、充分にエロティスムを生みだす。だが、細く長くのびるその体には、化肉をこばむ影のような色がただようばかりで、女は幻のごとくこちらから遠ざかる。時に彼女は、身をのばし、乳房を隆起させ、腋をひらいて、頭上から下着をはずすエロティスムを見せるが、彼女の生きた表情は不定形な薄衣のしたに隠されたままで見ることができはしない。

花、皮手袋、鳥、帽子、シーツ、靴、レインコート、これらの物が、フェティシスムの、死物崇拝の彼岸へと拉致されてゆくかと思えば、その彼岸の雲のなかから、手袋は生きた魚となり、帽子は女の秘所となって蘇ってくる。エロティスムと死のはざま、その憂愁のもとにしか生の意味はないと、ブルーノは語っているかのようである。

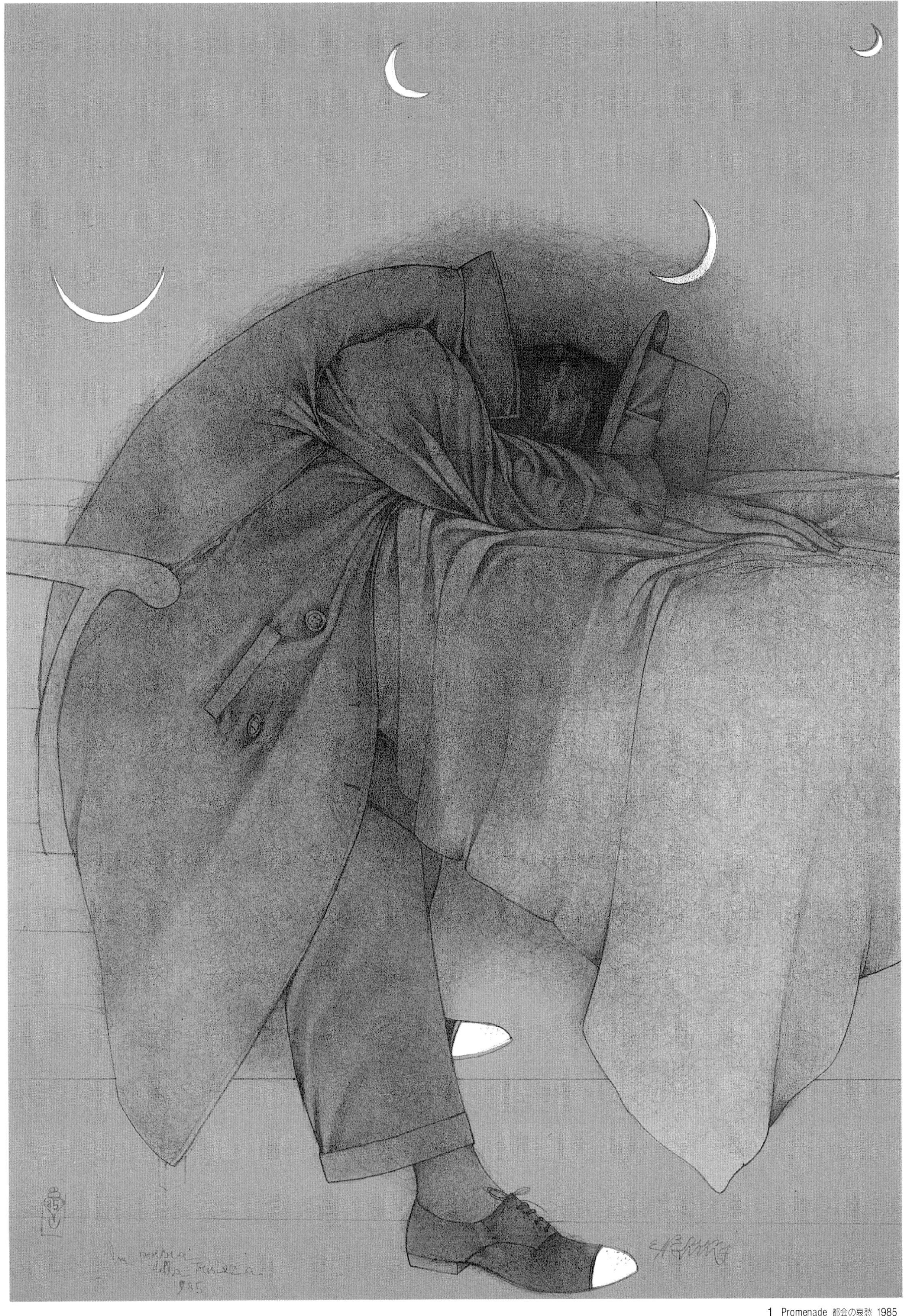

1 Promenade 都会の哀愁 1985

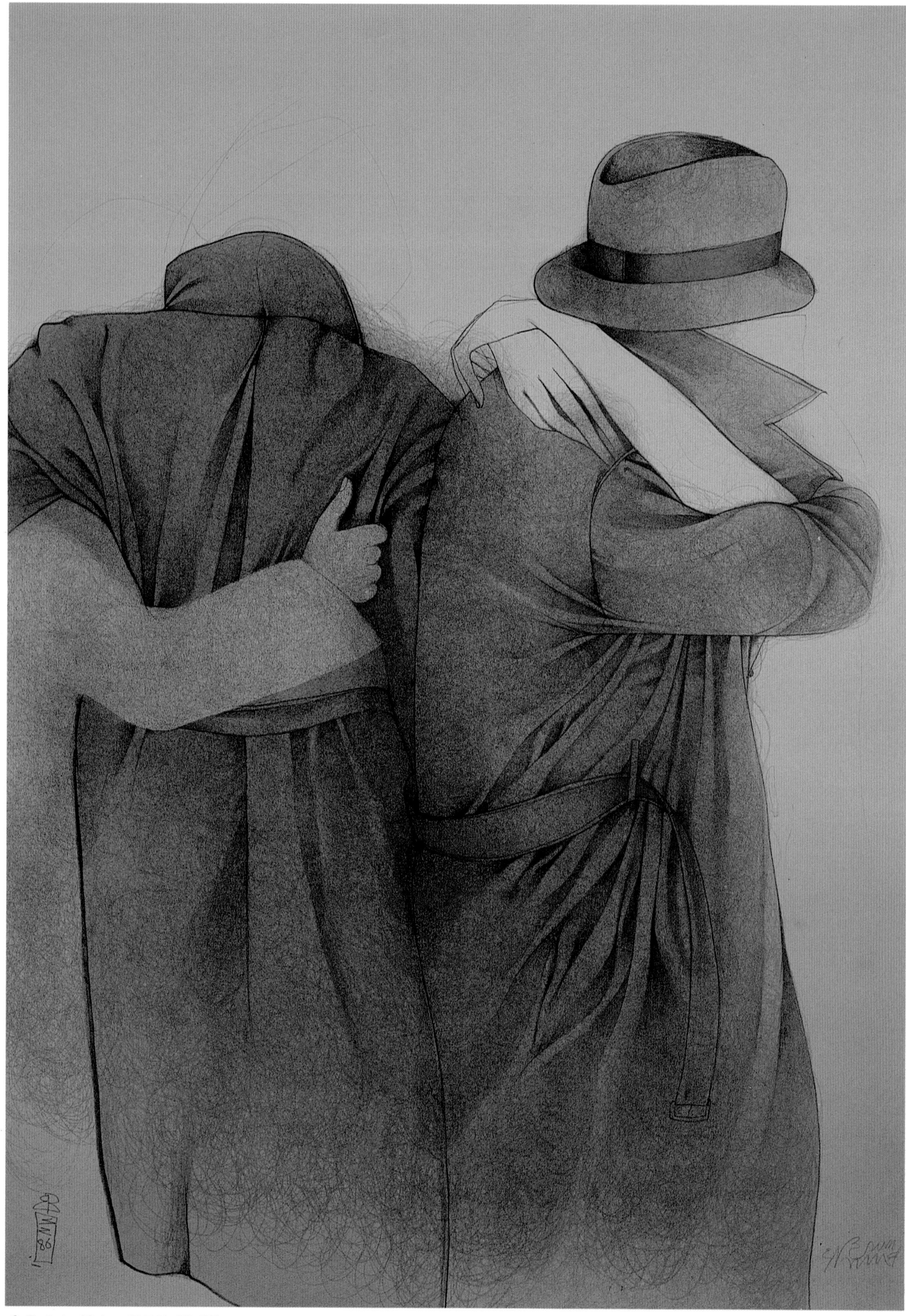

2 The Poetry of Sadness 都会のシリーズより 1986

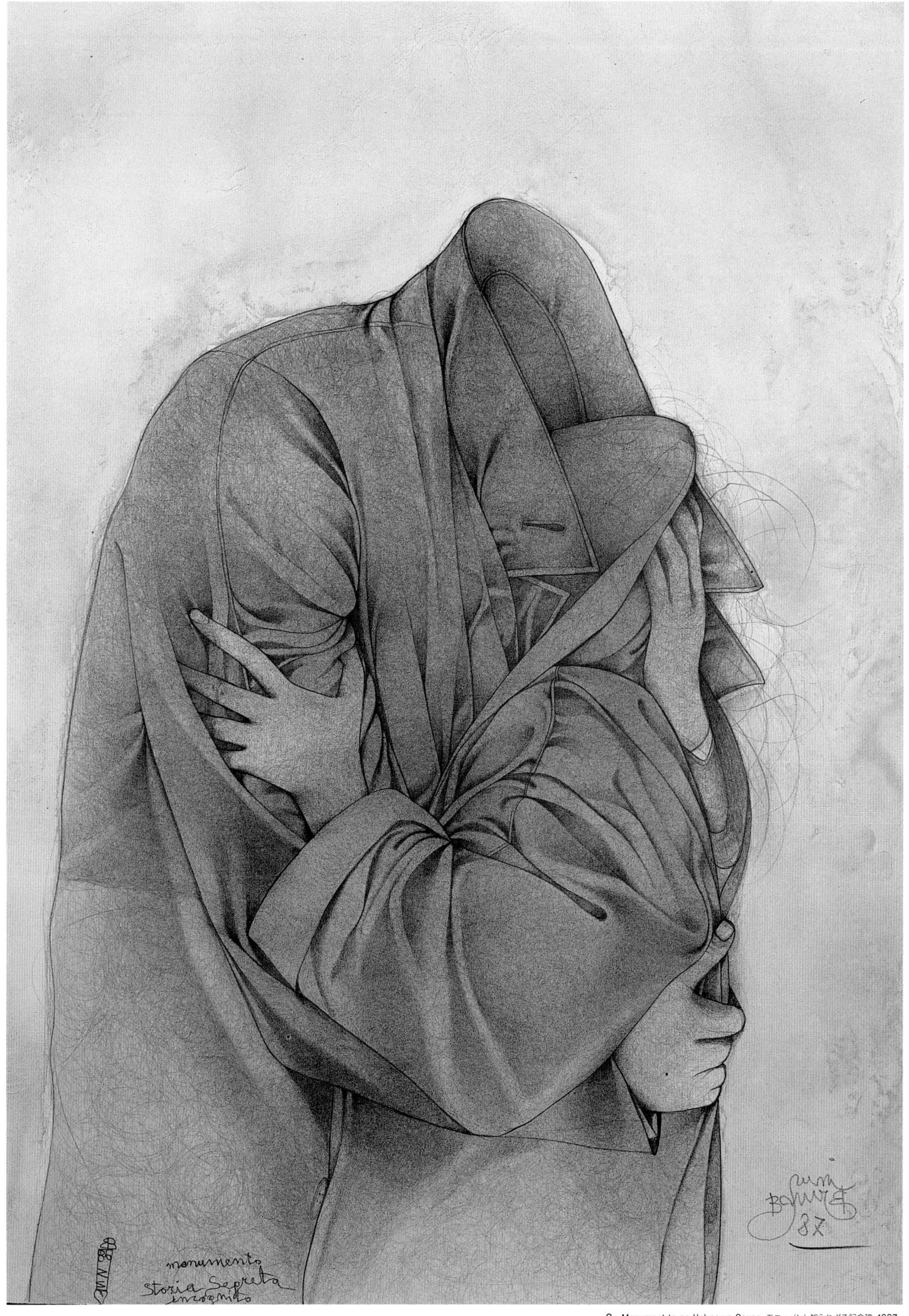

3 Monument to an Unknown Cause モニュメント知られざる記念碑 1987

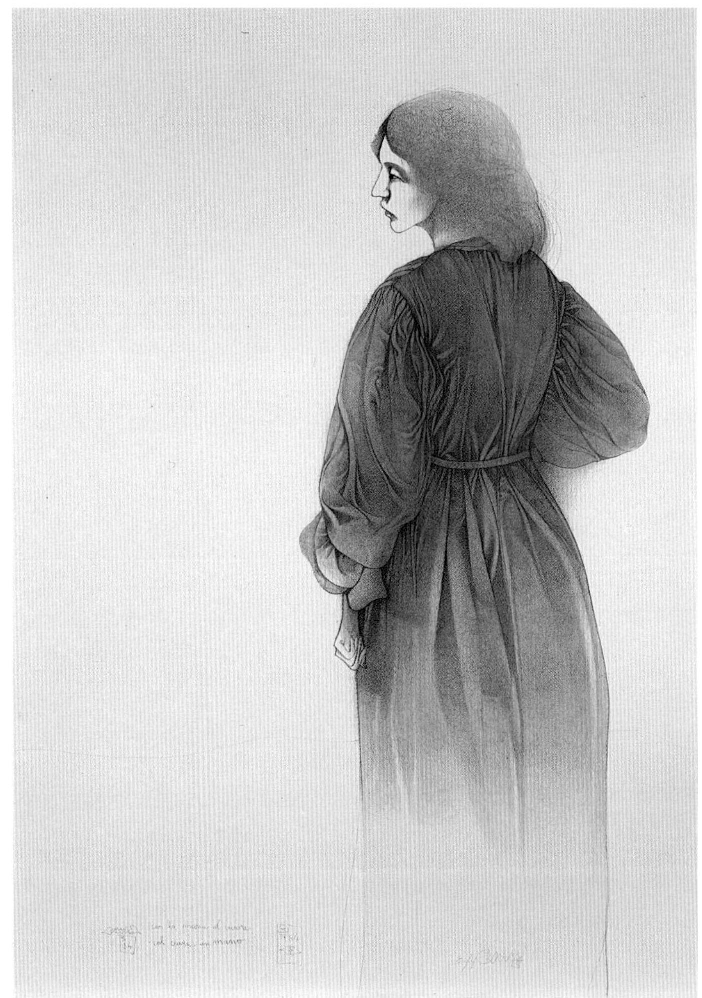

4 With Hand on Heart 胸に手をおく女性 1984

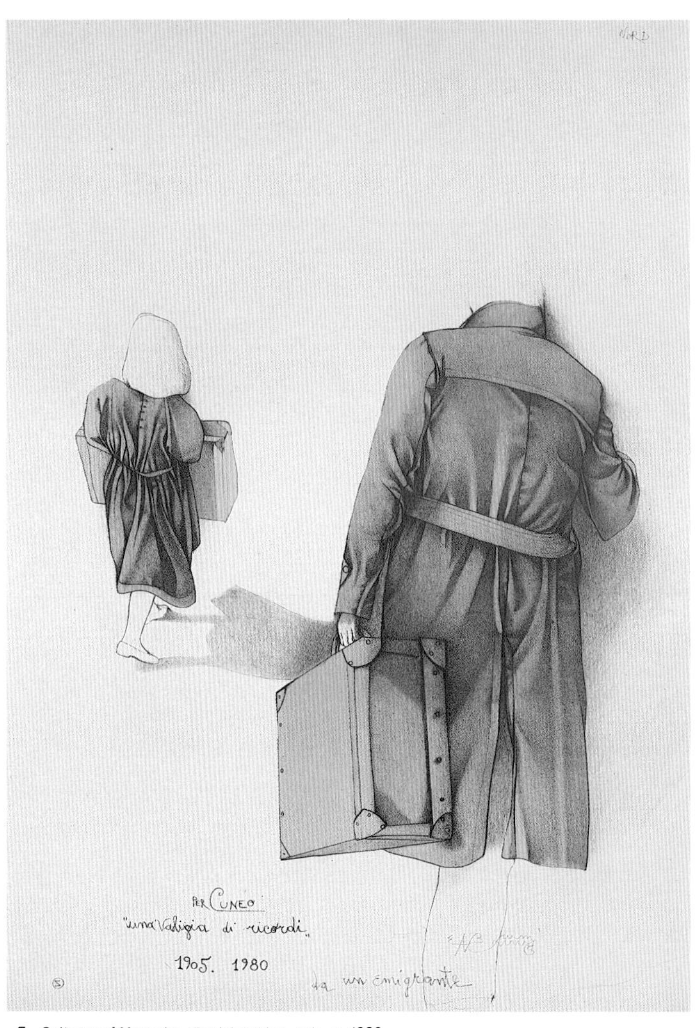

5 Suitcase of Memories 思い出をつめたスーツケース 1980

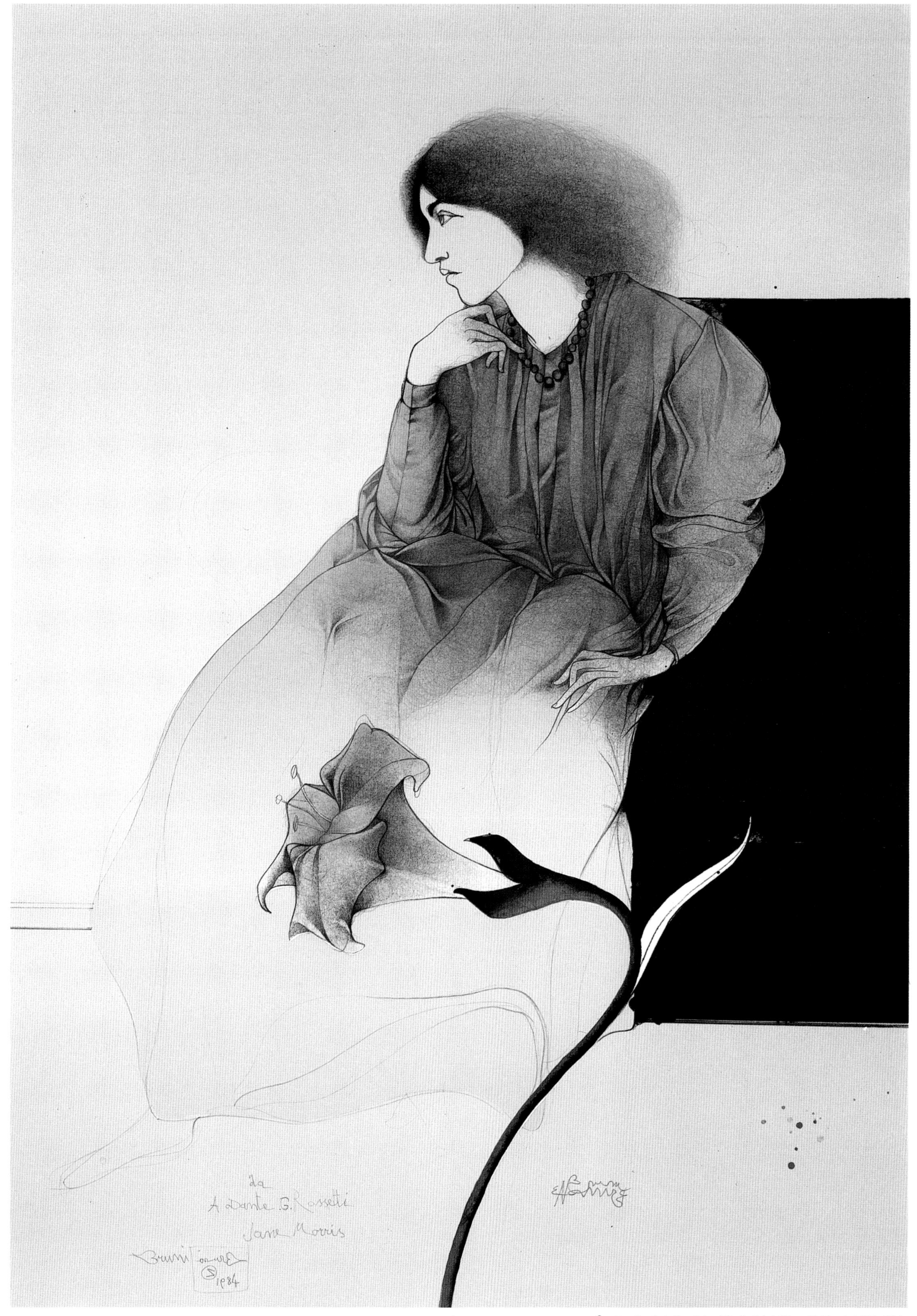

6 Jane Morris, in the style of Dante Gabriel Rossetti ジェーン・モリス 1984

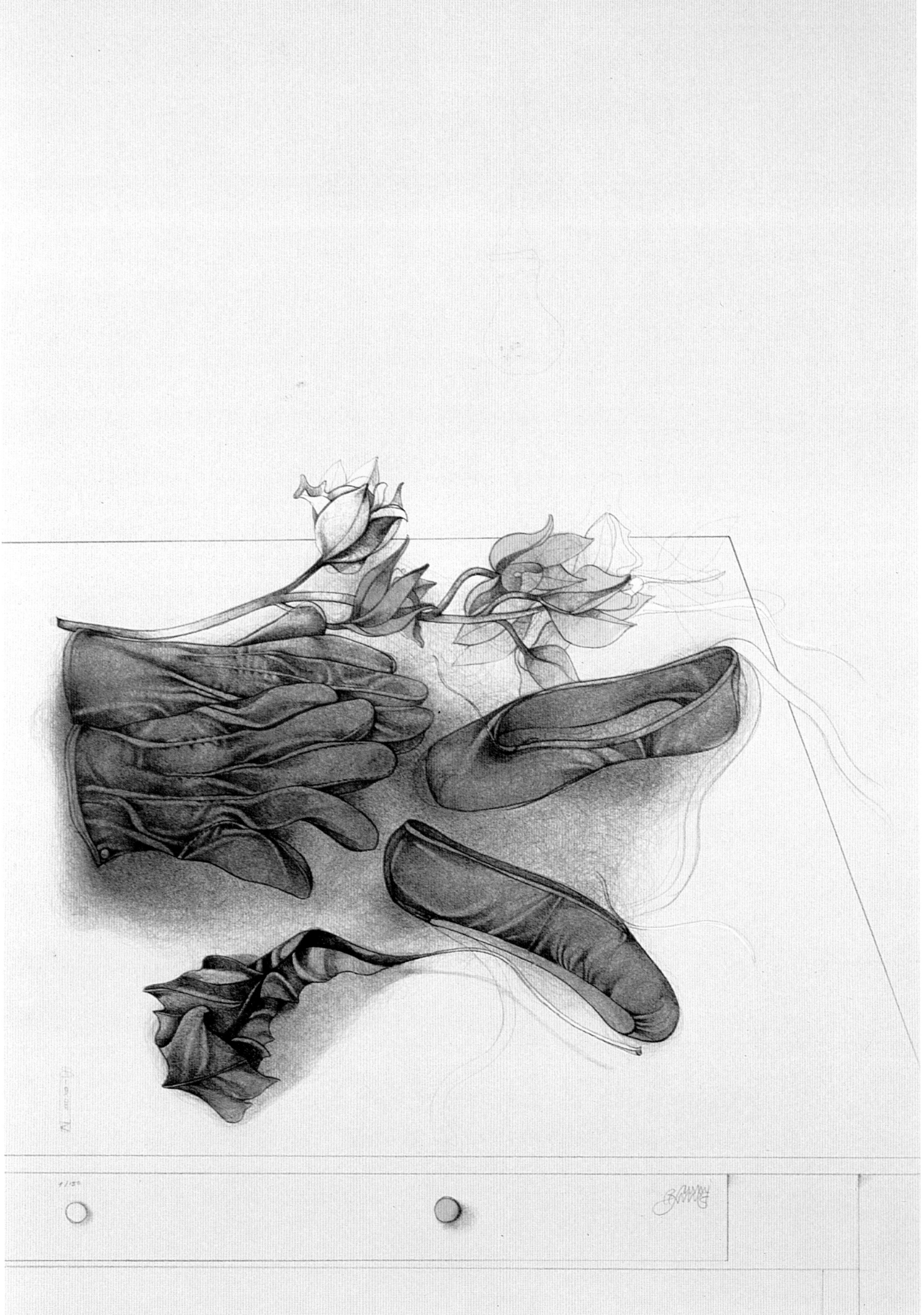

7 Still Life 静物 1988

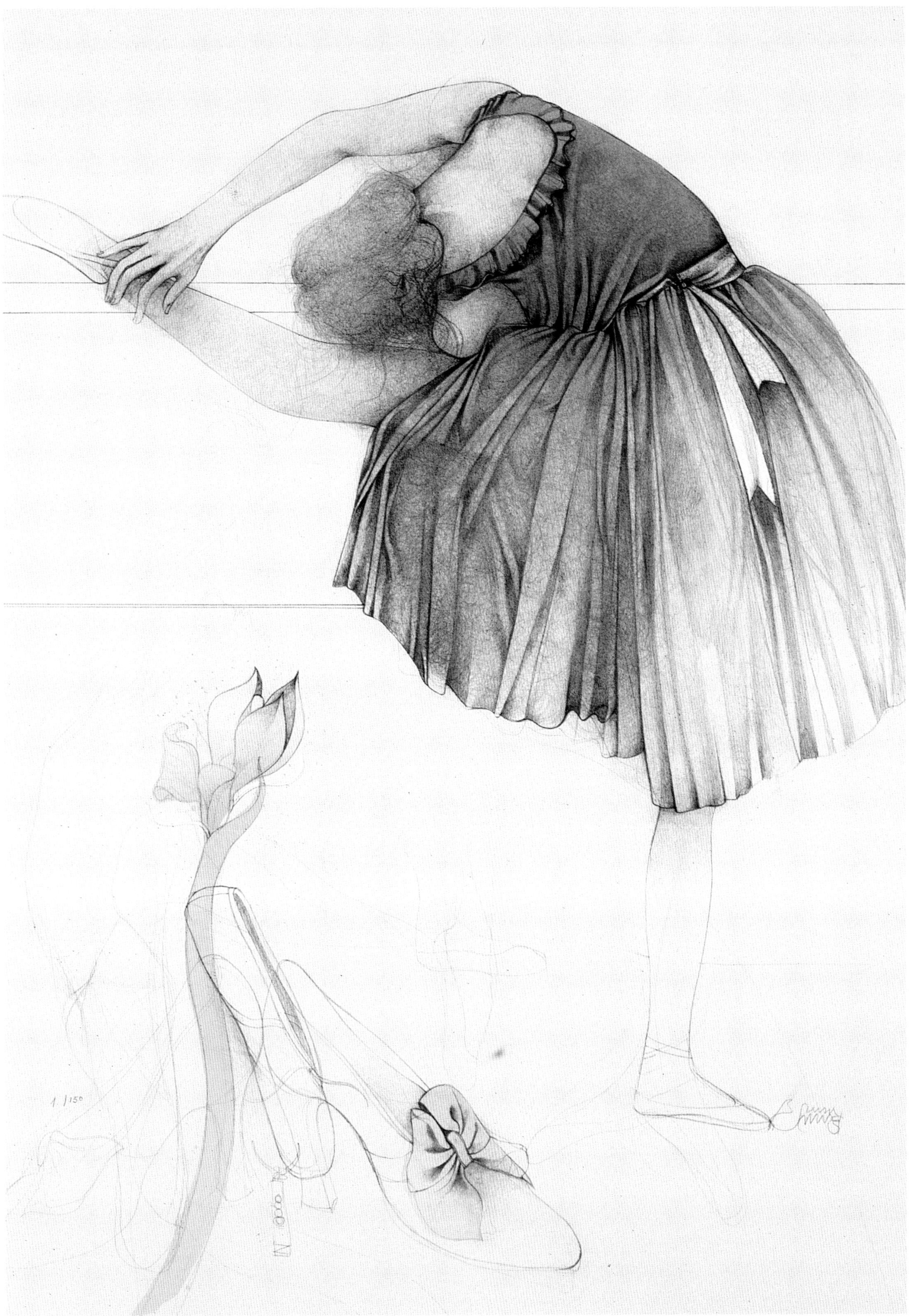

8 Ballerina バレリーナ 1988

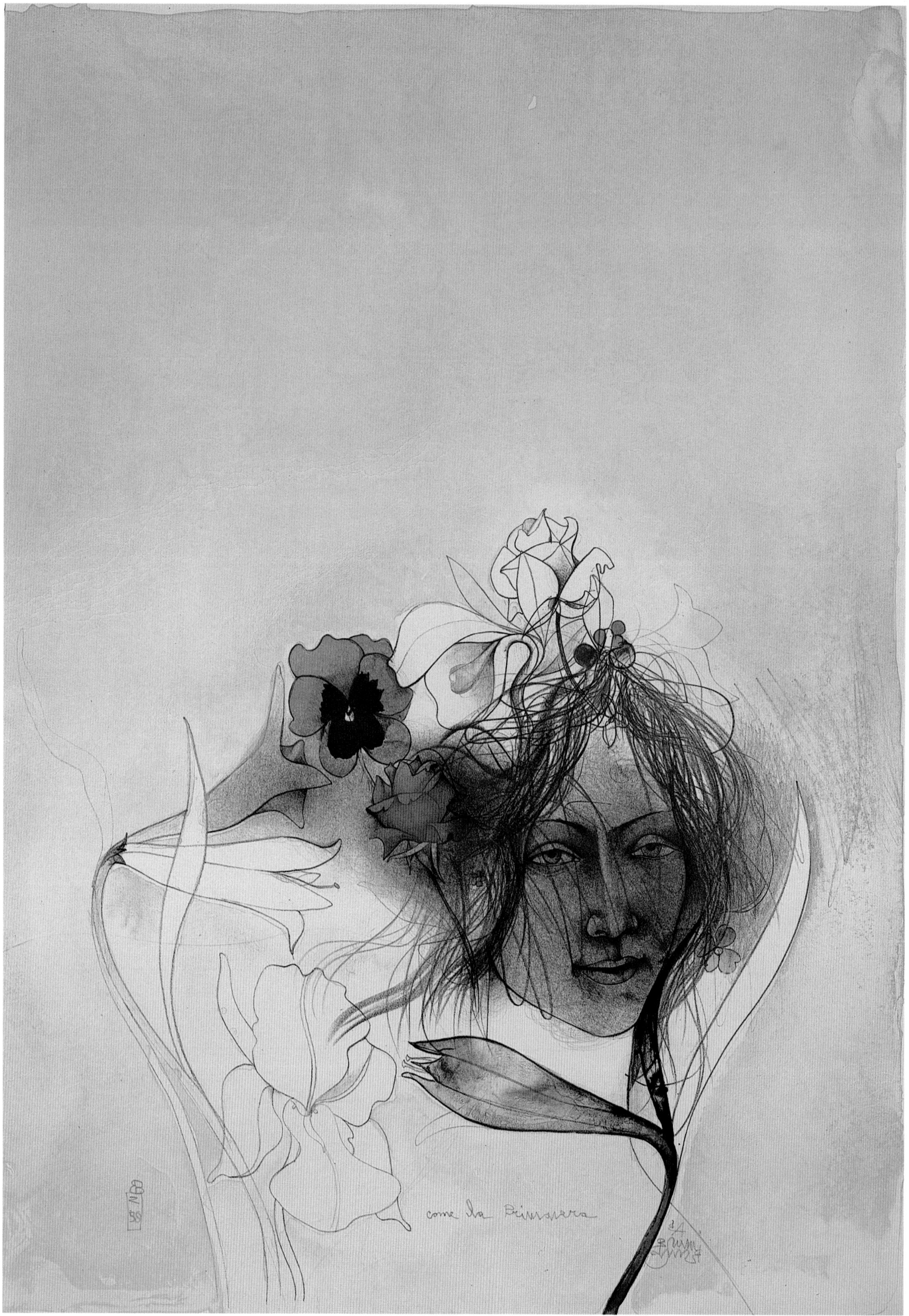

9 Like Spring 春のように 1985

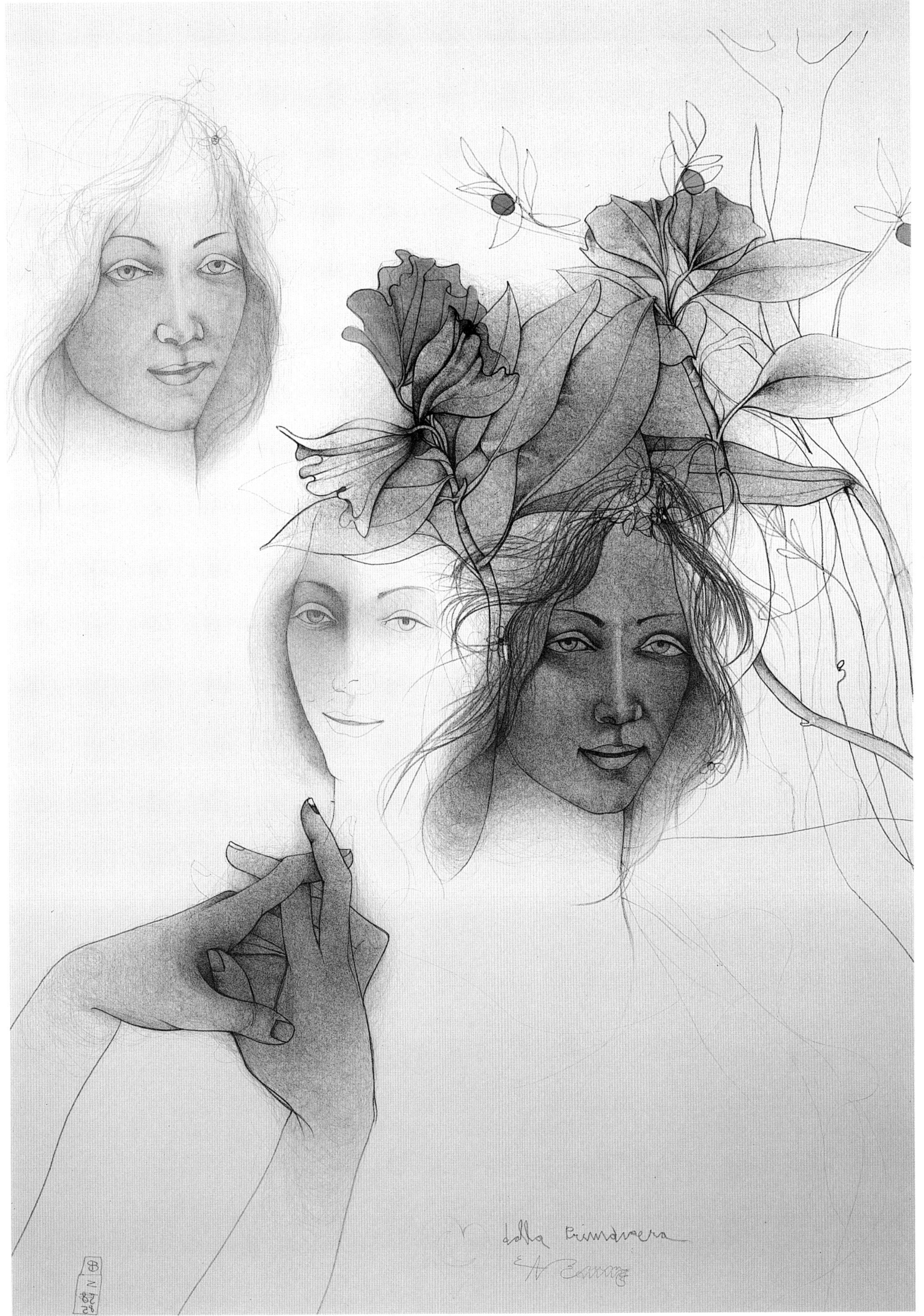

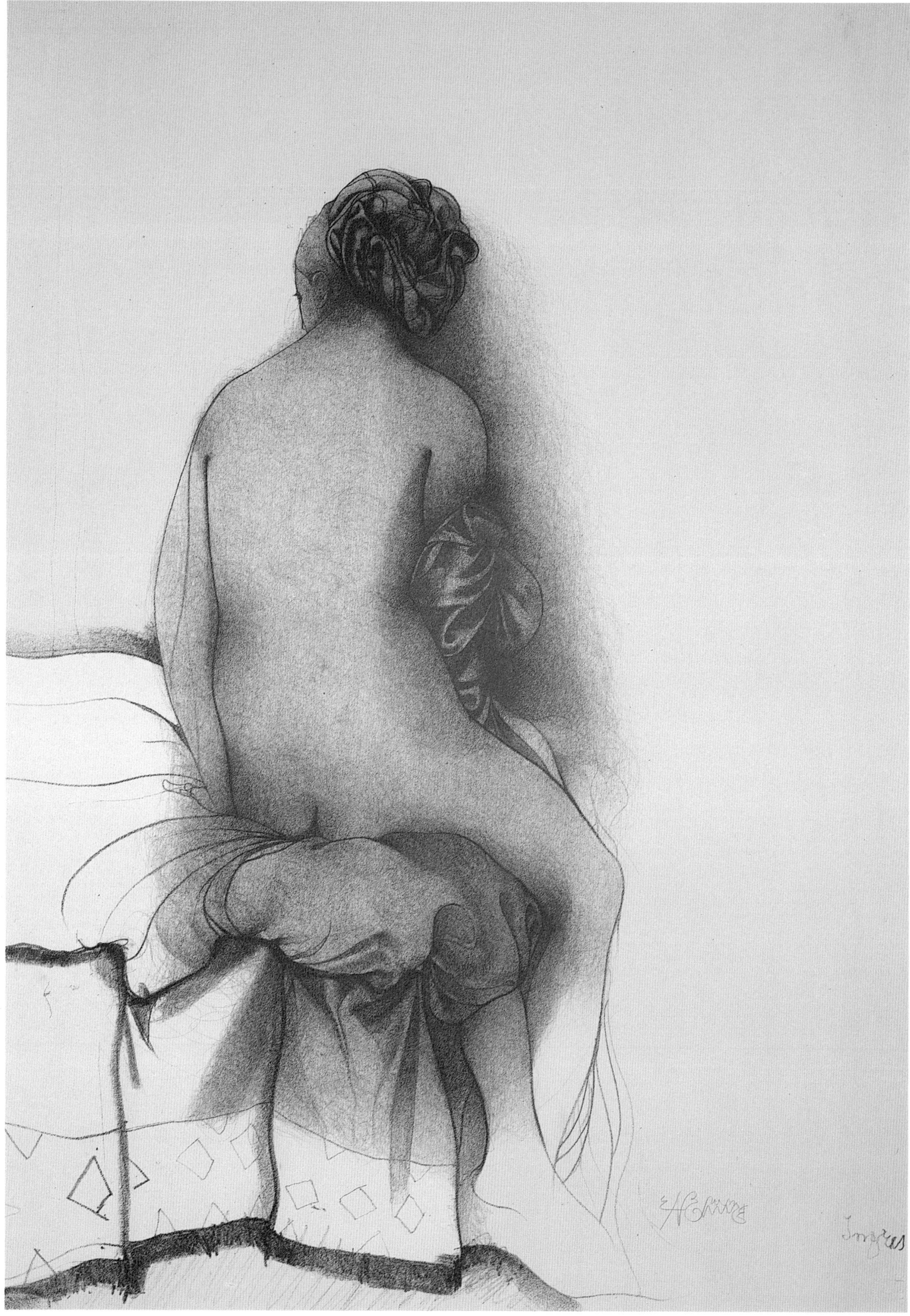

11 In the style of Ingres アングルのように 1980

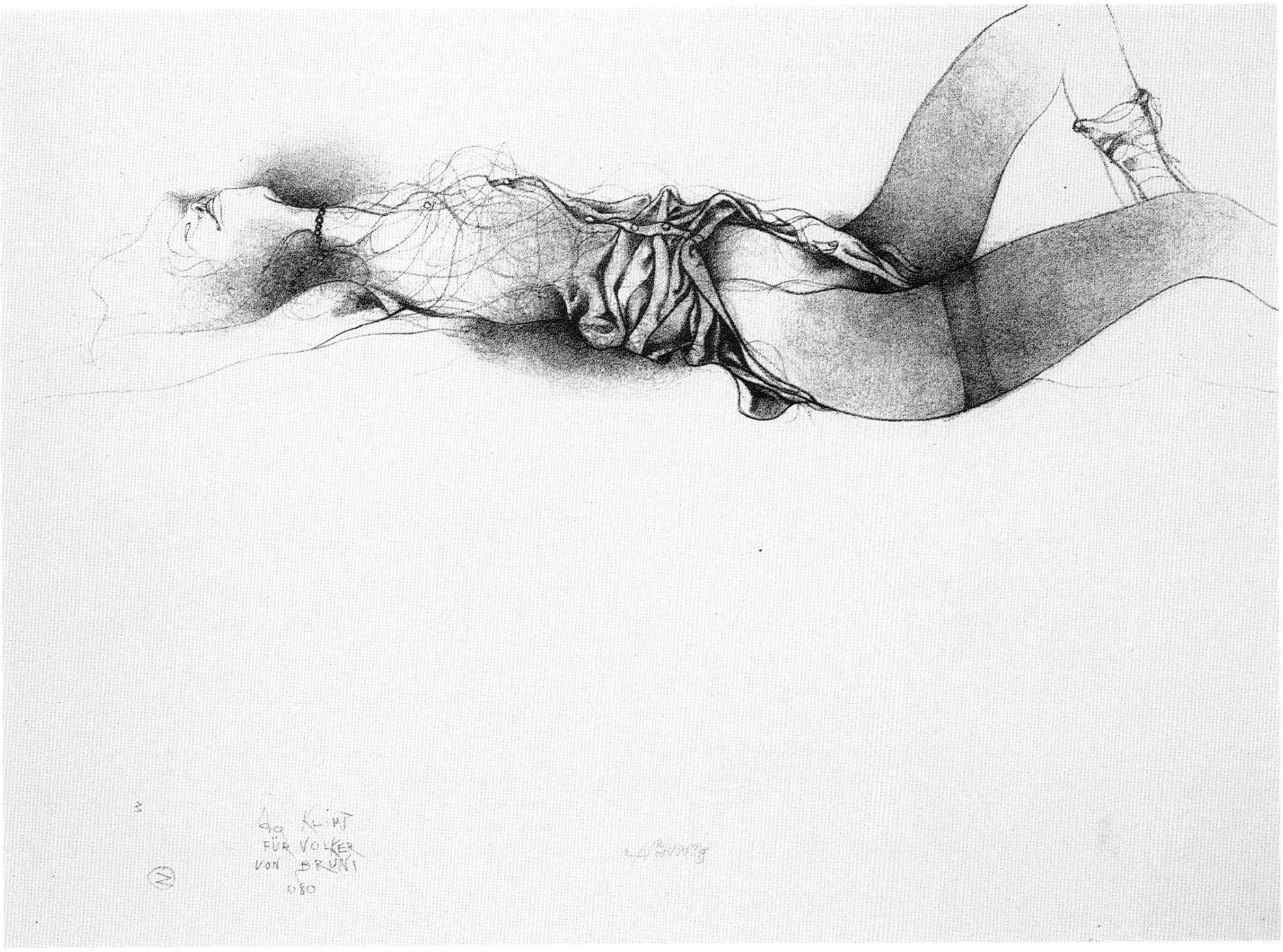

12 In the style of Klimt クリムトのように 1980

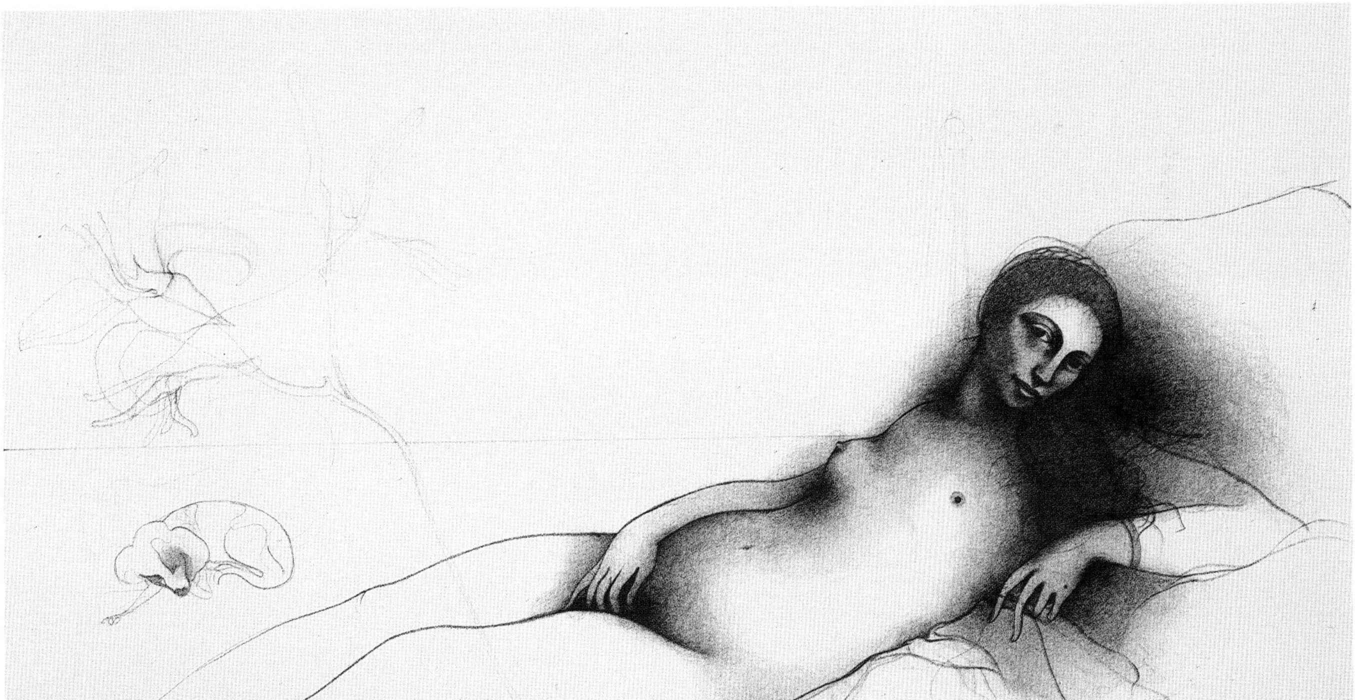

13 Venus of Urbino, by Tiziano テッチアーニのように 1980

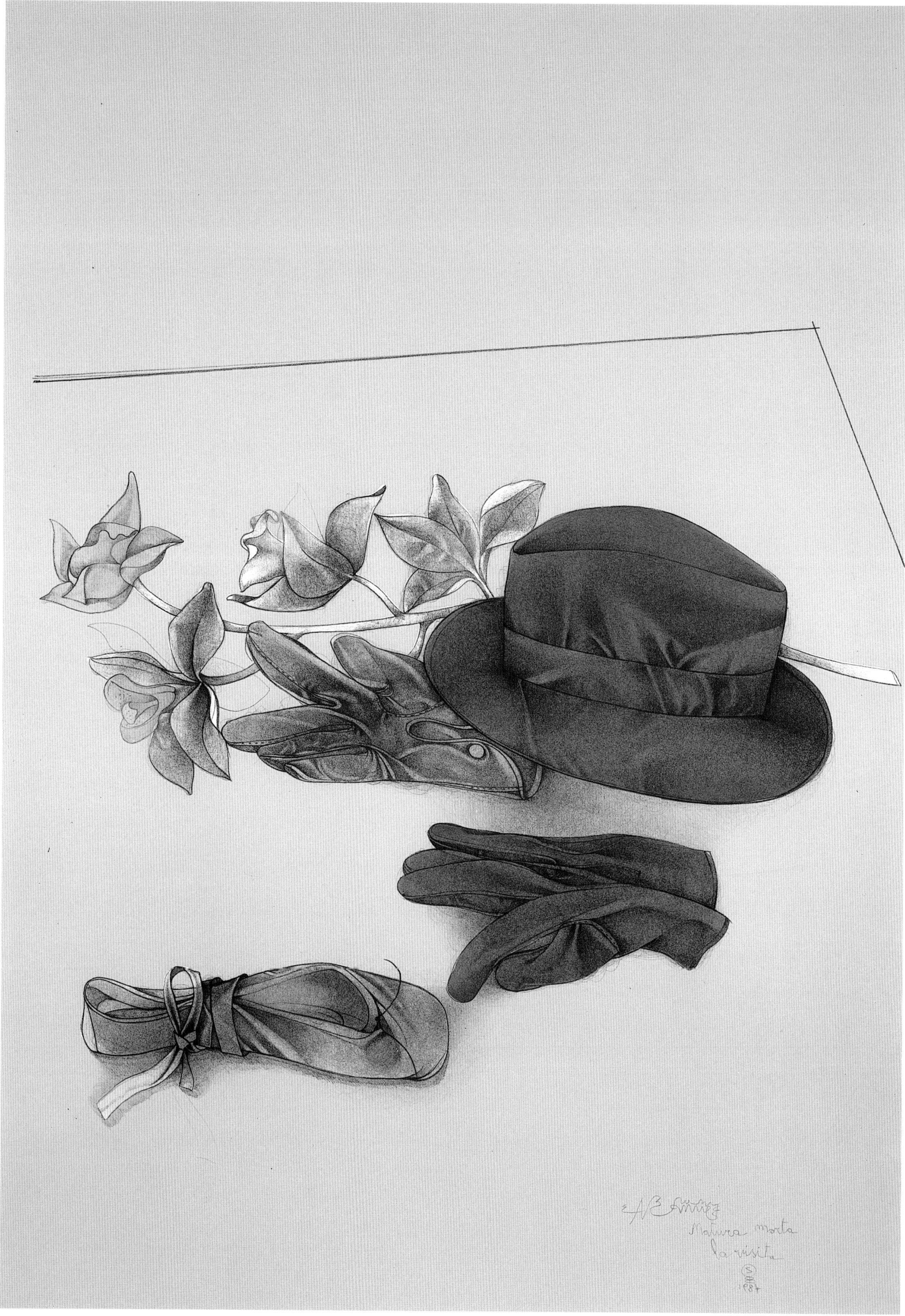

14 Still Life of Hat and Orchids 帽子と蘭のある風景 1984

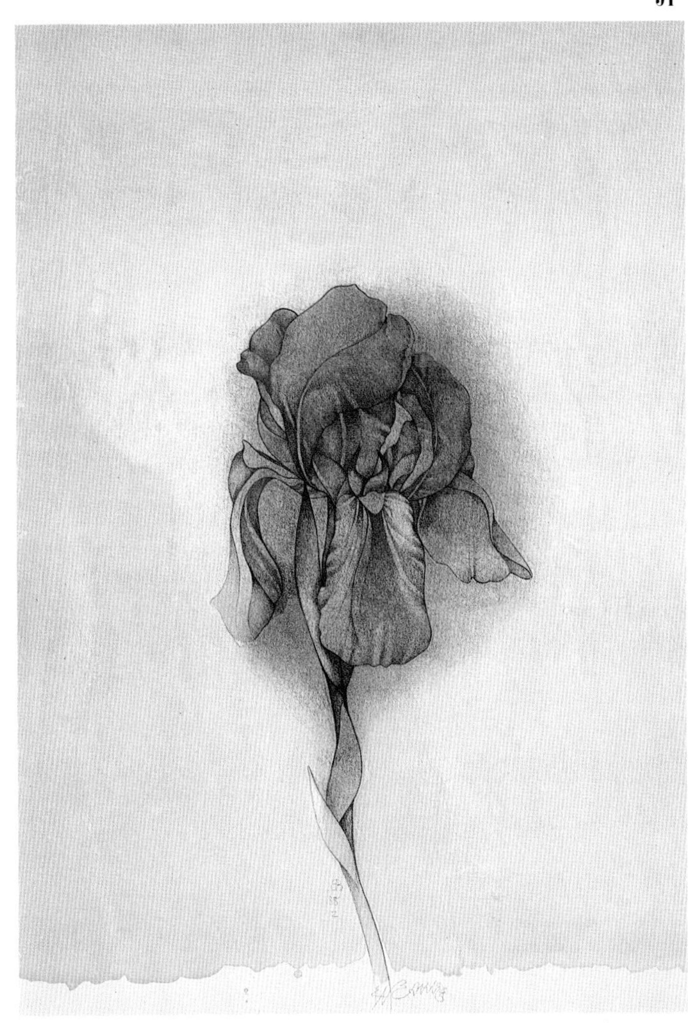

15 Iris Germanica ドイツのアイリス 1985

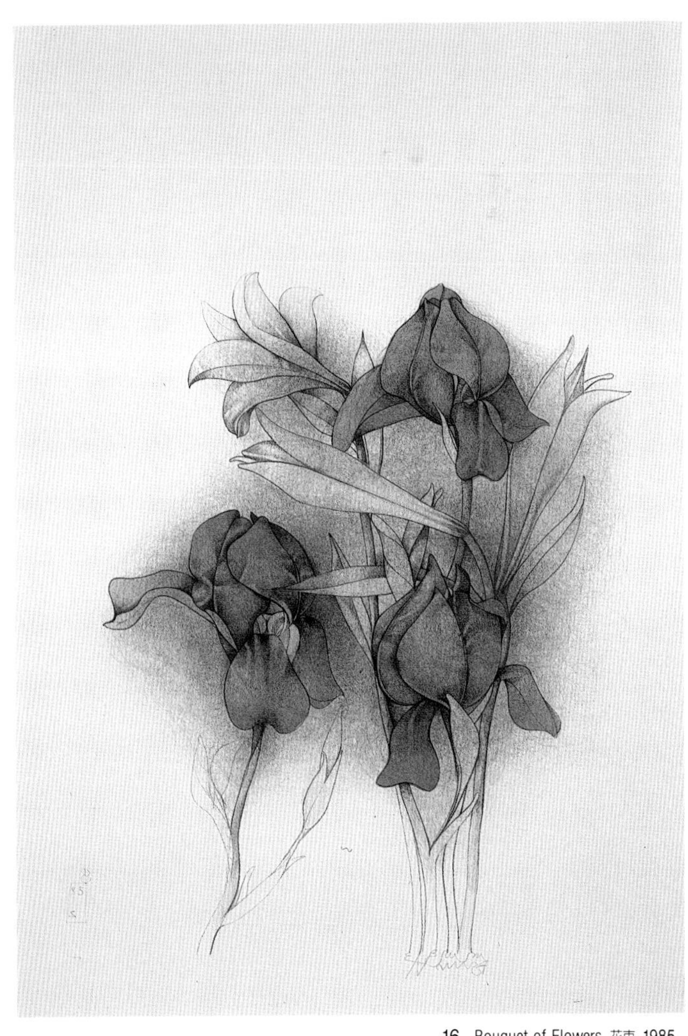

16 Bouquet of Flowers 花束 1985

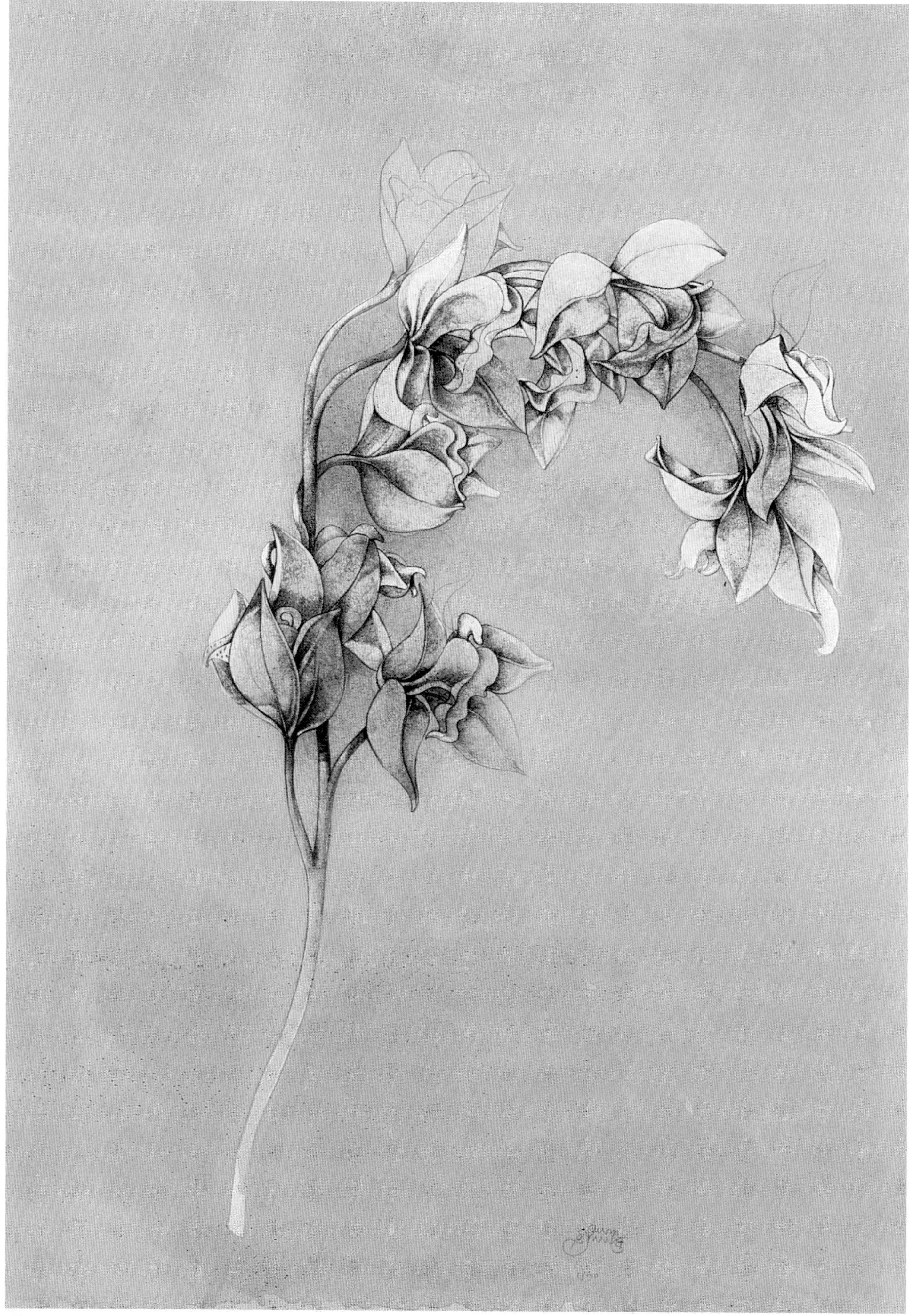

17 Orchid 花 1988

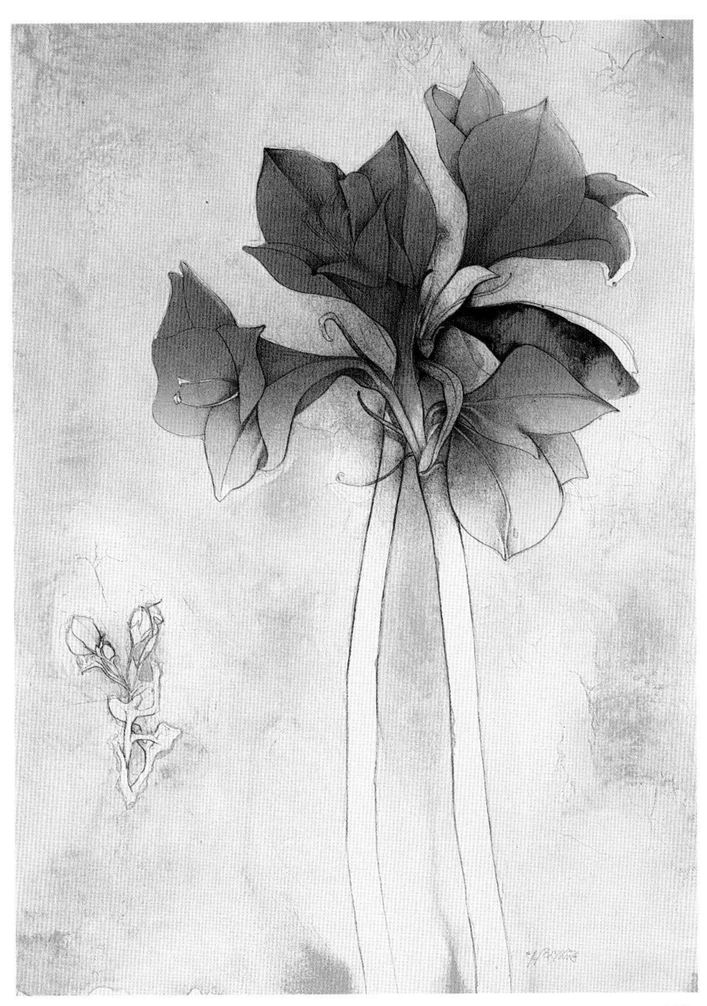

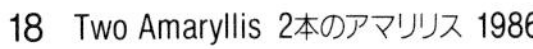
18 Two Amaryllis 2本のアマリリス 1986

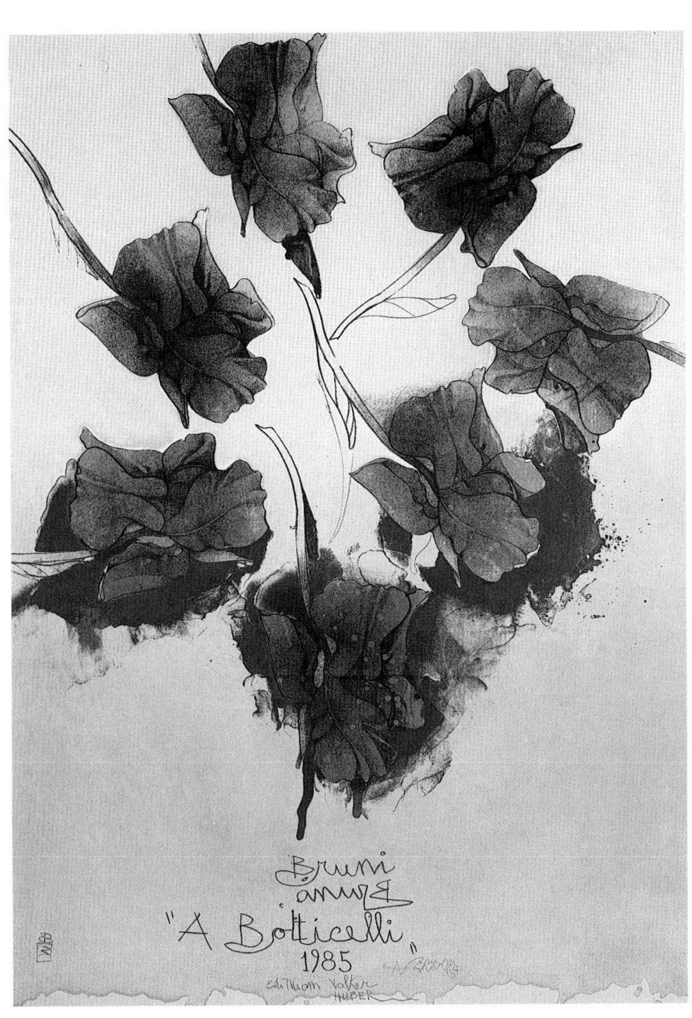

19 To Botticelli ボッティチェリ 1985

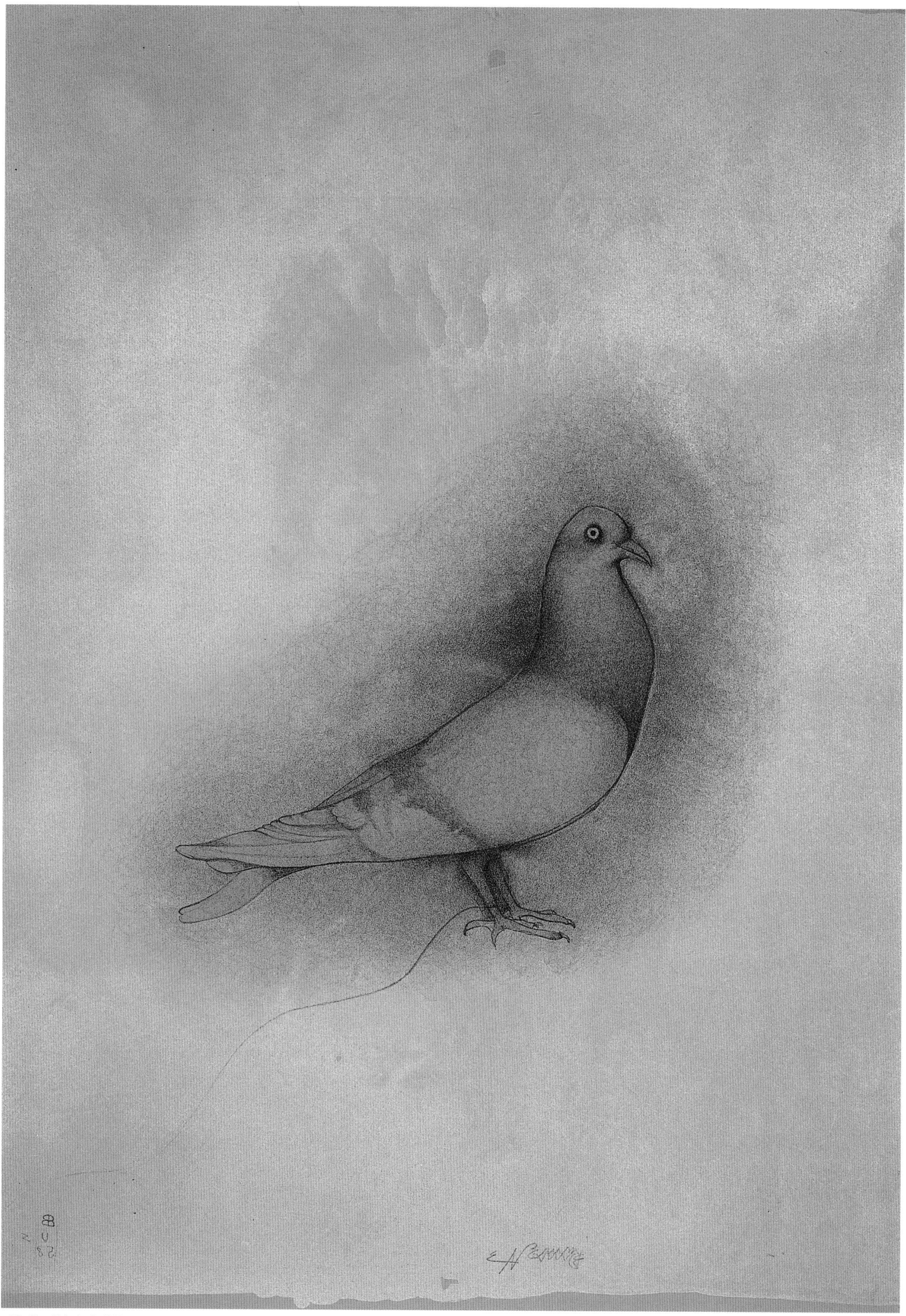

20 Blue Bird 青い鳥 1985

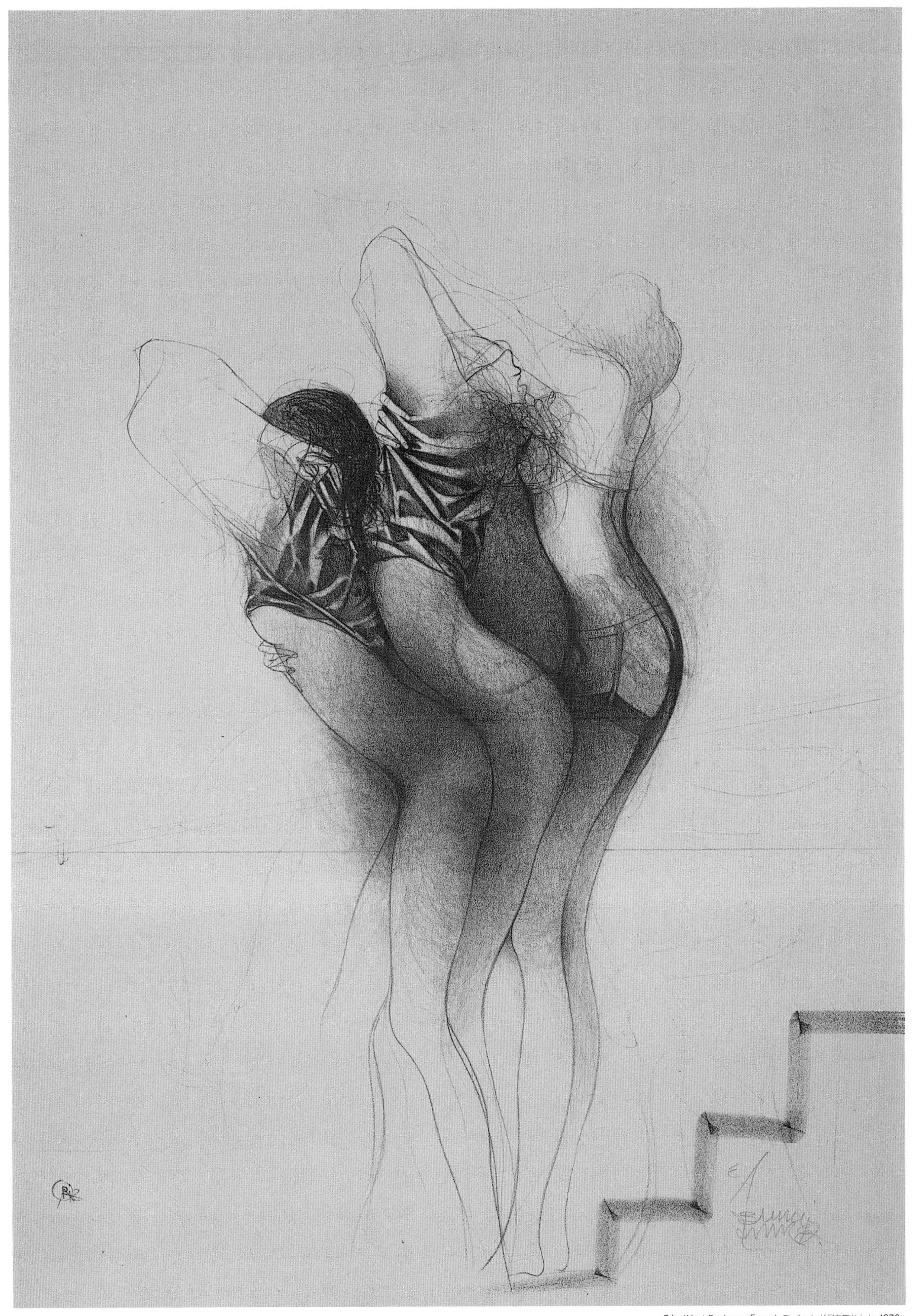

21 What Duchamp Forgot デュシャンが何を忘れたか 1976

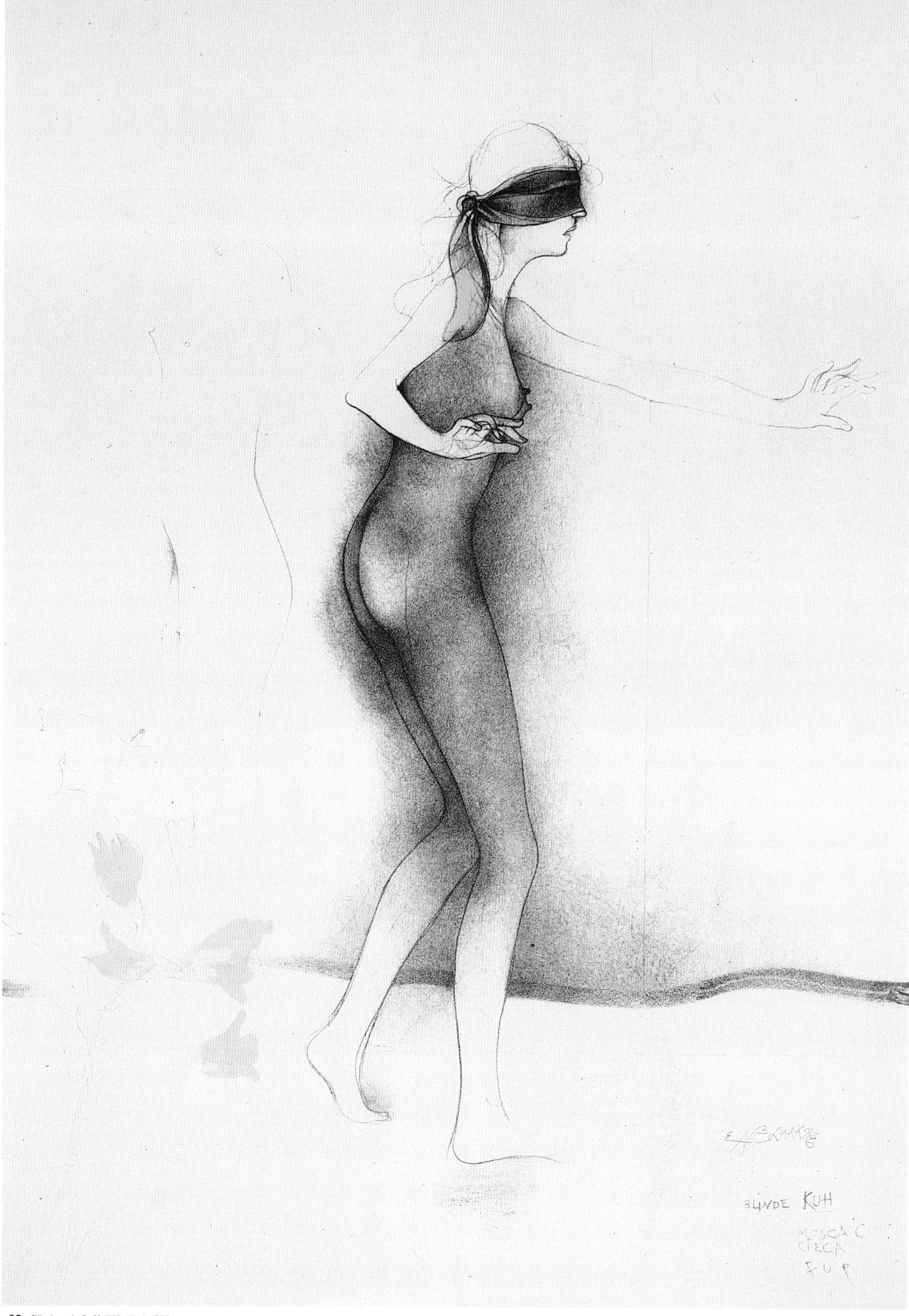

22 Blindman's Buff 目隠し遊び 1979

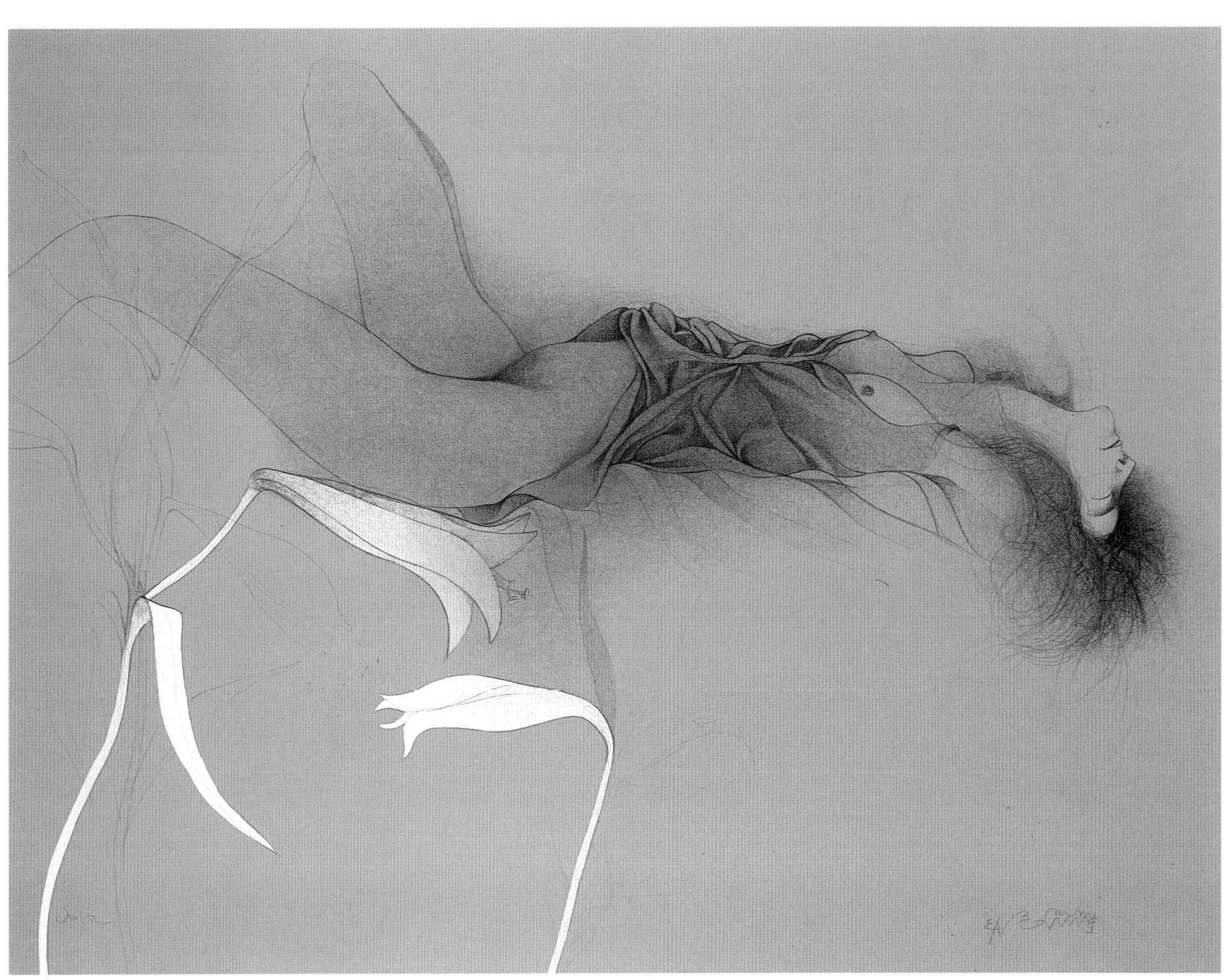

23 Solitude 孤独 1987

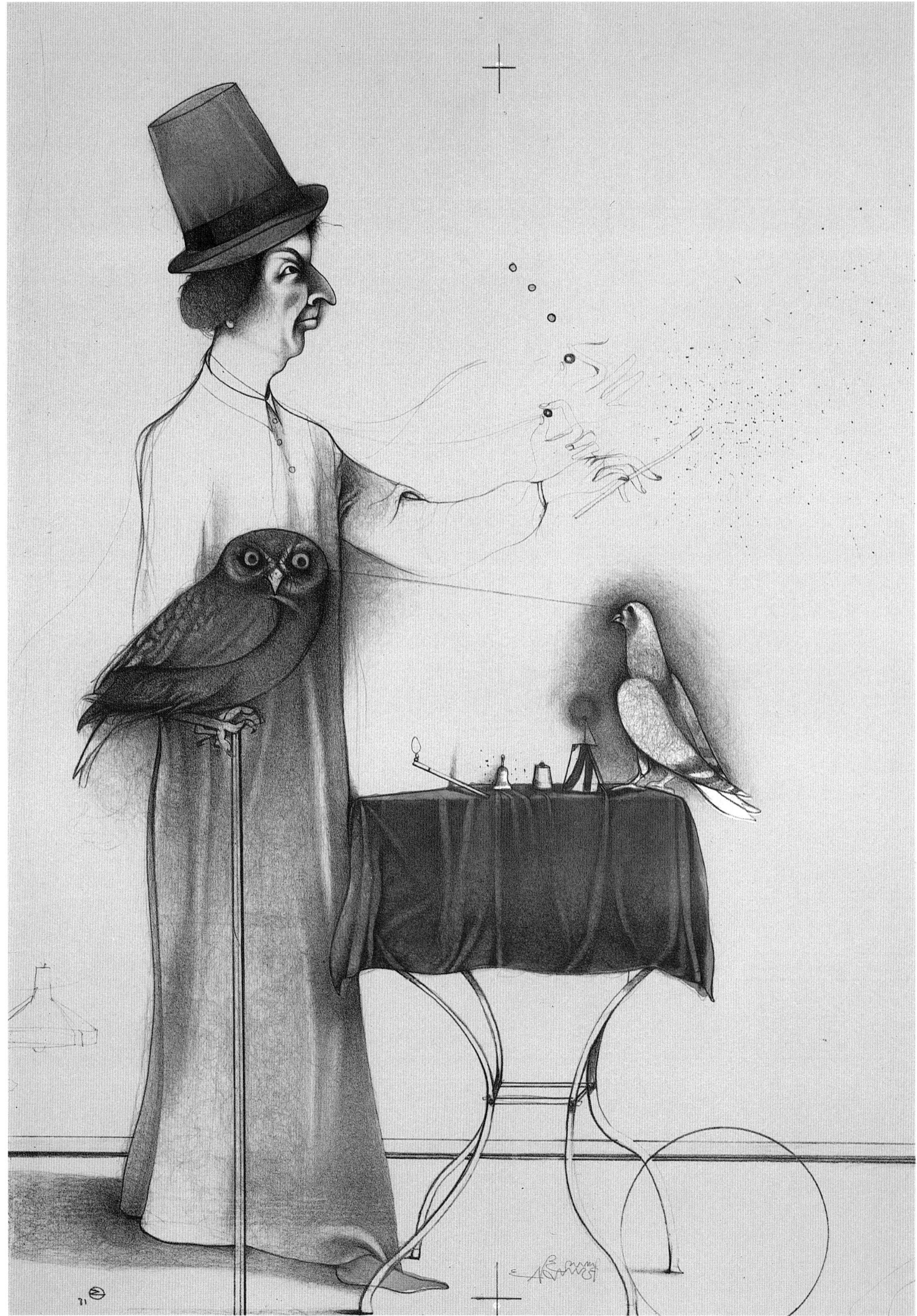

24 Magic Afternoon I 奇術 1981

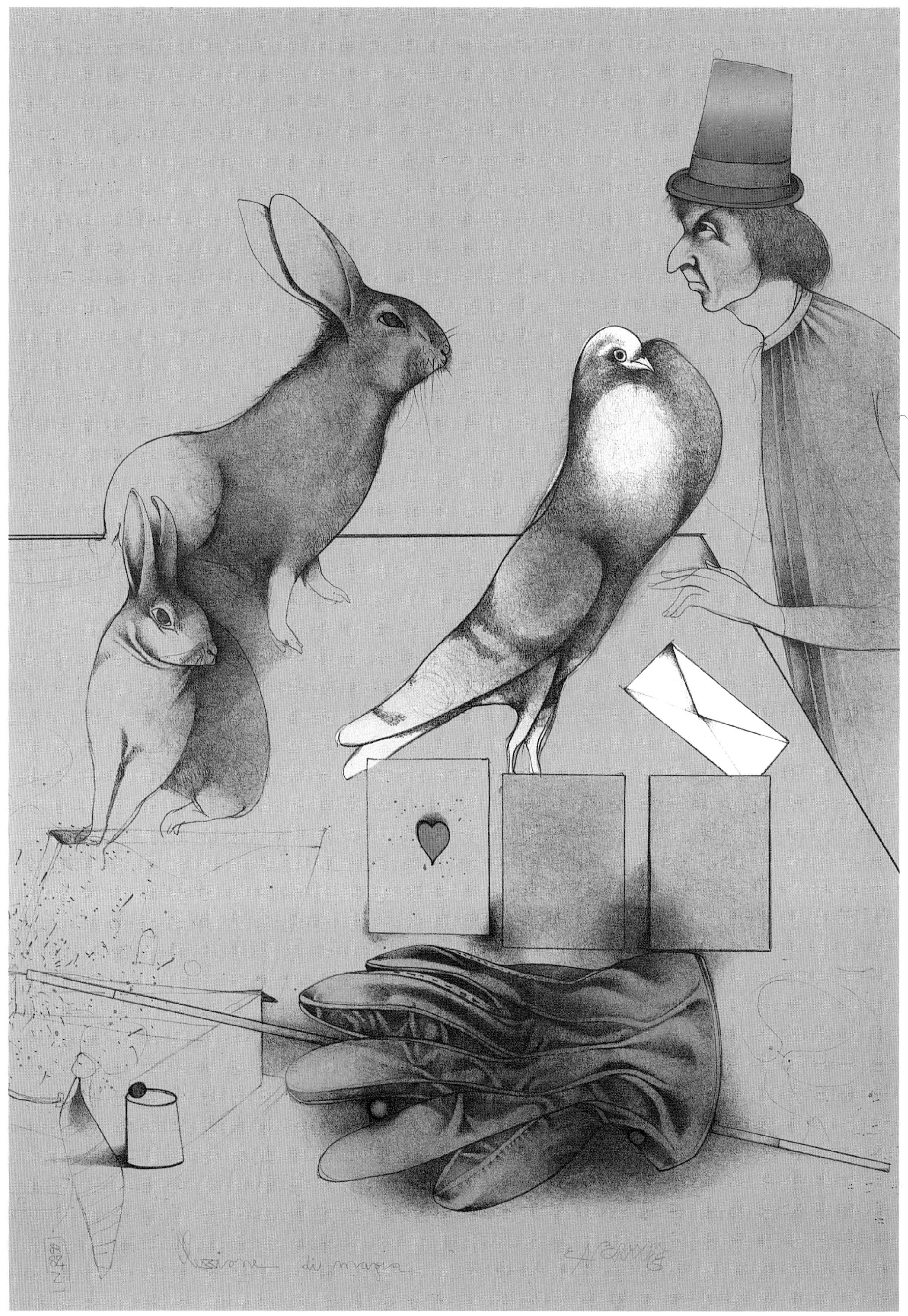

25 Magic Lesson 魔法のレッスン 1985

Grand Master Series 巨匠シリーズ—1

PAUL RAND ポール・ランド

Shigeo Fukuda 福田繁雄

Every designer must possess three highly demanding traits. Each is unquestionably desirable in any individual seeking to pursue a career in design, yet none are easily acquired.

First, a designer must have a flair for form. This is not an acquired skill but rather an innate sensitivity. Second, a designer must have insight, an inborn wisdom which transcends knowledge and enables prediction of the trends and social fabric of the future. Third, the designer must have a clear doctrine vis-à-vis design. This doctrine may be understood as an awareness that design constitutes culture.

Paul Rand is an American designer who is blessed with all three of these traits. He is also a man who has shaped and influenced the course of 20th century graphic design to a remarkable degree. His talent, wisdom and philosophy fuse to produce a designer of rare individuality, a designer who sets a shining example for graphic designers not only in America but around the world.

Paul Rand has scored his professional successes in the highly competitive vortex of New York, one of the most demanding arenas for design work. His creative activities and design philosophy are totally integrated and ideally balanced in everything he does, colored by a sense of humor emanating from his inner warmth. His achievements are as surprising as they are awe-inspiring.

Among the highlights of Paul Rand's many accomplishments are the following: cover design for "Direction" magazine (1938); book jacket for *Modern Art In Your Life*, published by the New York Museum of Modern Art (1949); "No Way Out" poster for 20th Century-Fox (1950); symbol marks for IBM and Westinghouse (1956); cover design for "AIGA 50 Books" (1972); "The Prepared Professional" poster for the World Design Conference in Aspen (1982); and the "3rd International Exhibition" poster for the New York ADC (1988).

A successful design, it has been said, has the power to stir emotions in any age, spanning all time frames. Retracing Paul Rand's long path of creative endeavor, we discover that his designs indeed transcend time in this way. Even today they shine bright above our heads like stars in the firmament. Each of his works, regardless of date of origin, shares the spry wit that characterizes his brand of design to perfection.

The supreme source of Paul Rand's achievement lies in his vast knowledge of his field and his rigorous design philosophy. Yet at the same time, one cannot overlook his brilliant accomplishments in design education. For many years he has devoted himself, with the same enthusiasm as to his creative activities, to teaching graphic arts to students at Cooper Union, Pratt Institute and Yale University.

Perhaps Paul Rand's foremost greatness, however, is found elsewhere than his talent, wisdom and convictions and the way they all entwine to form a distinctly individual style. Nor is his greatness the manner in which his style has enabled him to establish his own niche in the world of graphic design. His greatness rests rather in his never-abating enthusiasm, despite all his many achievements, to continue creating and pursuing new challenges in his field.

To me, Paul Rand is a grand master who has infused new culture into the graphic design of the 20th century. Through his individuality and unique philosophy, he has raised graphic design to the pinnacle of its development as we know it today.

デザイナーは3つの厳しい条件を持たなければならない。それは、この道に進む誰もが、望んでいるのだが、容易に身につけられる条件ではない。

その第1は、造形に対する才能である。技術ではなく、自分の造形を発見する感性である。第2は、新しい時代、明日の社会を読み取る知識以上の〈先見の明〉という知恵である。第3番目は、デザインに対する確固たる信念である。それは、デザインは文化であるという意志でもある。

このめぐまれた、すべての力をもって、今世紀、世界のグラフィックデザインに大きな影響と希望を与えてくれたデザイナーが、アメリカの生んだポール・ランドである。才能と知恵と信念が、1つになって類いまれなデザイナーの個性になって、その存在は、アメリカはもとより、世界のグラフィックデザイナーの光になっている。

ニューヨークという、巨大な先進デザインの厳しい渦の中を歩んできた、ポール・ランドの創造活動とデザイン哲学が、人間味あふれたユーモアの感性で、すべてに一貫して、バランスされていることは、驚きでもあり、素晴らしさでもある。

個性と意志のないデザインは、ビジネスだけのコマーシャル作業の壁に突きあたる。ポール・ランドのデザイン哲学は、心ならずも、人間性を離れて、ますます爛熟して行く現代デザインへの警告でもあり、大切な道標でもあると思う。ポール・ランドのぼう大なデザインの歩みを列記することは、不可能だし、不必要だと思うが……。

マガジンカバー〈DIRECTION〉1938、ニューヨーク近代美術館のブックジャケット〈MODERN ART IN YOUR LIFE〉1949、20世紀フォックス社の映画ポスター〈NO WAY OUT〉1950、シルボルマーク〈IBM〉〈WESTINGHOUSE〉1956、カバーデザイン〈AIGA, 50 BOOKS〉1972、アスペン国際デザイン会議のポスター〈THE PREPARED PROFESSIONAL〉1982、そして、最近作のニューヨークADCの公募ポスター〈3RD INTERNATIONAL EXHIBITION〉1988。

〝デザインは時を超えて、感動的である。〟ポール・ランドの創造の軌跡をたぐると、それらのデザインは、まさに時を超越して、輝く天空の星のように、頭上に輝いている。どの時代の作品も、ゆるぎない完璧なランドデザインといえる軽快なウィットによって、貫かれている。

それは、デザインに対する深い造詣と、ランドの確固たる信念と良心に他ならない。さらに、その素晴らしい創造活動と同じような情熱で携わってきた、クーパー・ユニオン、プラット・インスティテュート、そして、イエール大学のグラフィックコースの長期にわたるデザイン教育の成果も見のがせない輝かしい業績だと思う。

ポール・ランドの偉大さは、才能と知恵と信念が、1つの個性となって、世界のグラフィックデザイン界に、確固たる地位を築き、今日も、現役のクリエーターとして、かくしゃくとして、新しいグラフィックデザインに、孤高の挑戦をしていることである。

ポール・ランドは、今世紀のグラフィックデザインに文化を、そして、その心に個性と哲学を吹き込み、完成させた巨匠であると思う。

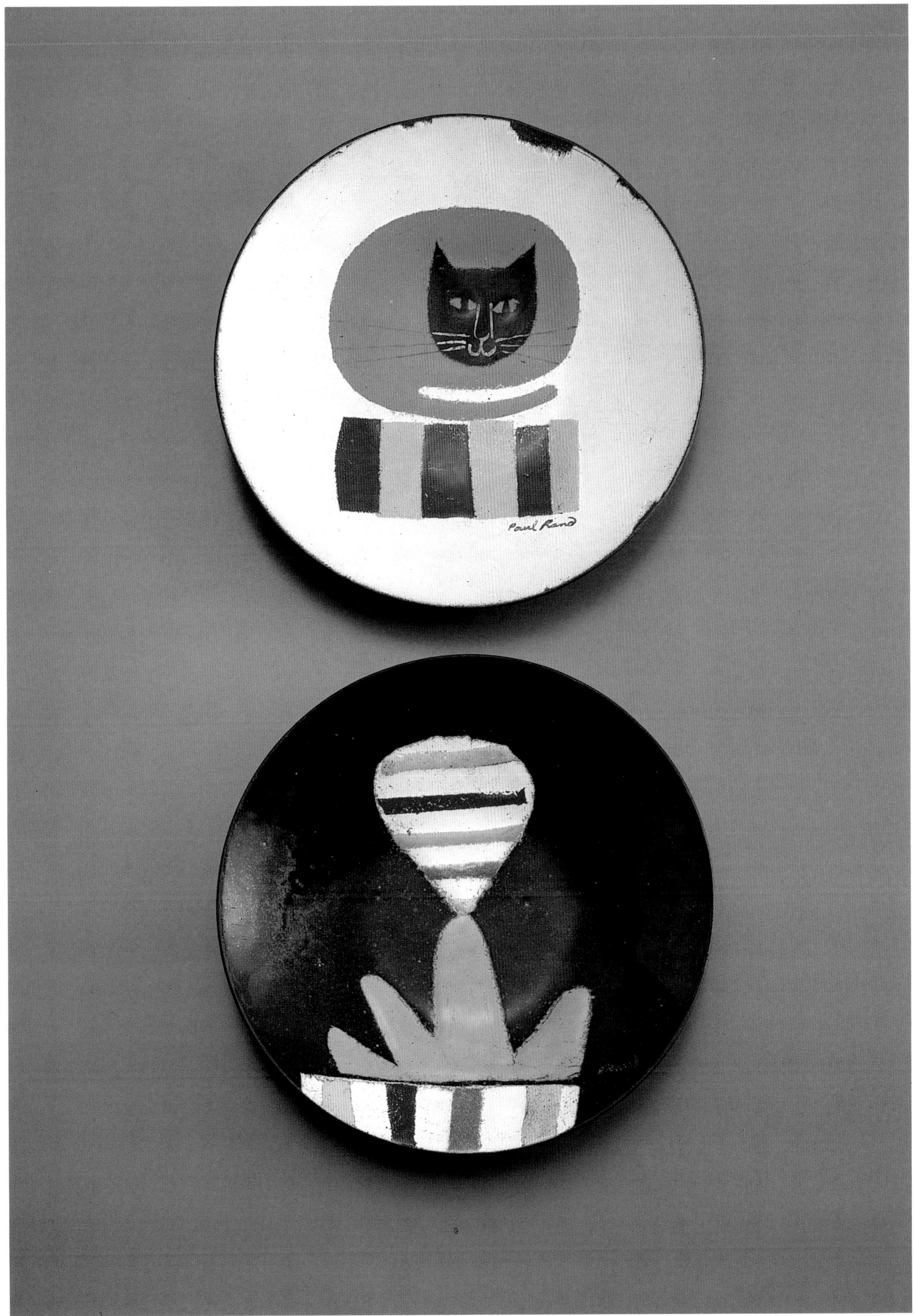

1　Designs for dishes 絵皿のデザイン 1956-1957　　Photo:Yasuhiro Ishimoto

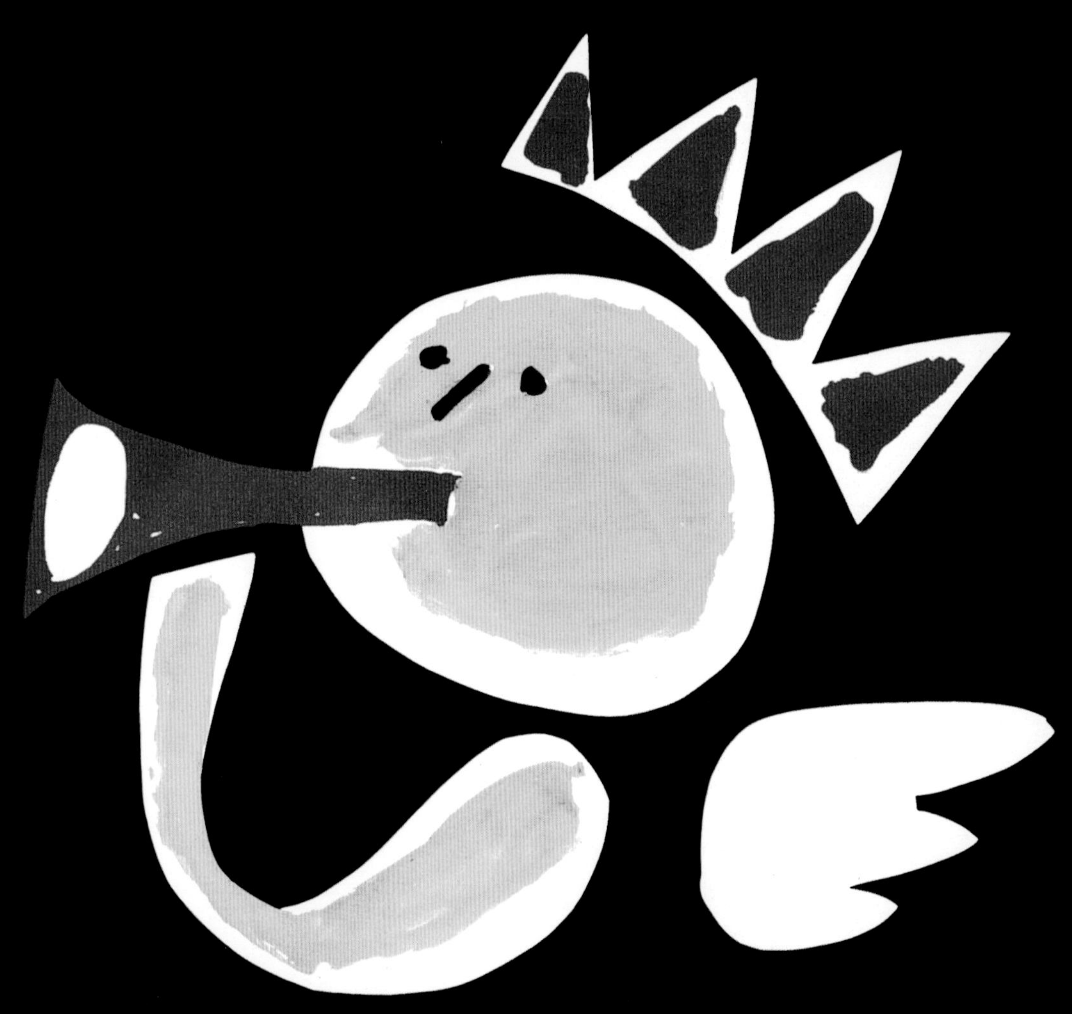

2 Interfaith Day poster インターフェイスデイ・ポスター 1954

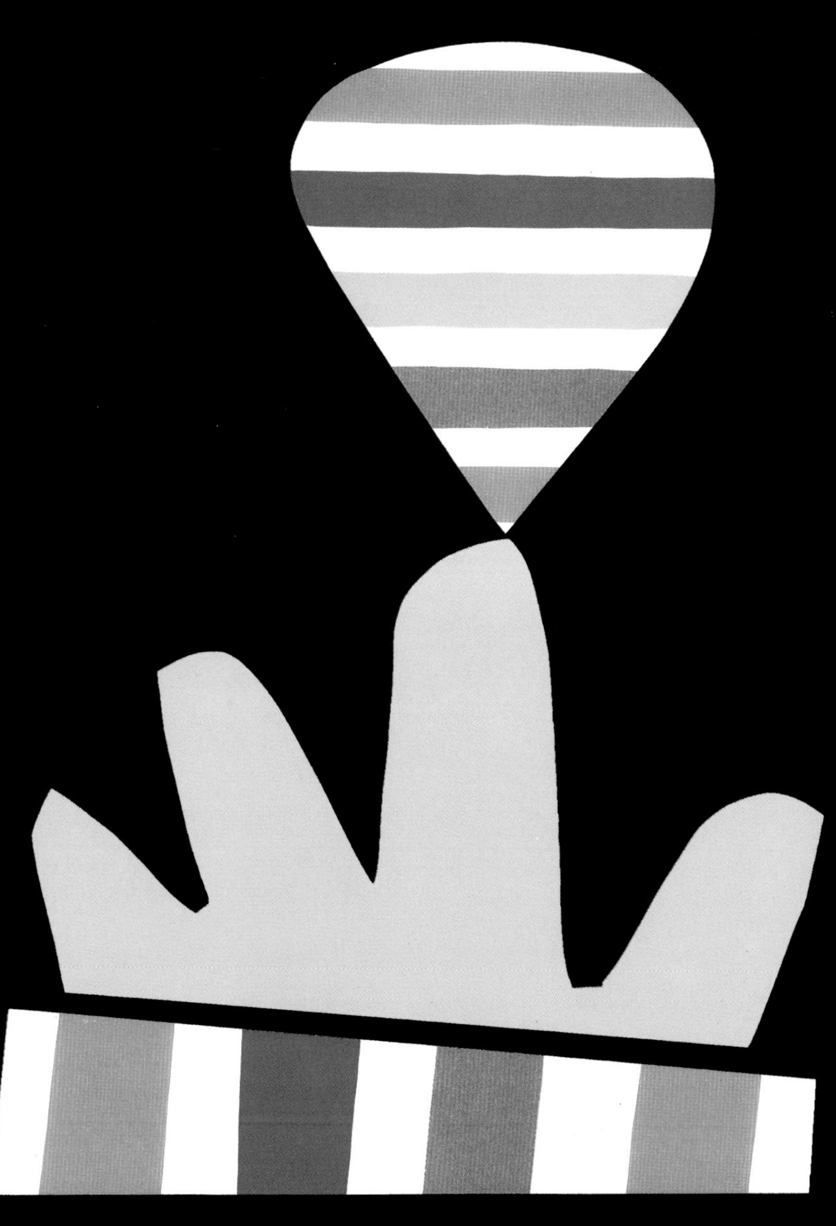

3 Book illustration 本の挿絵 1957

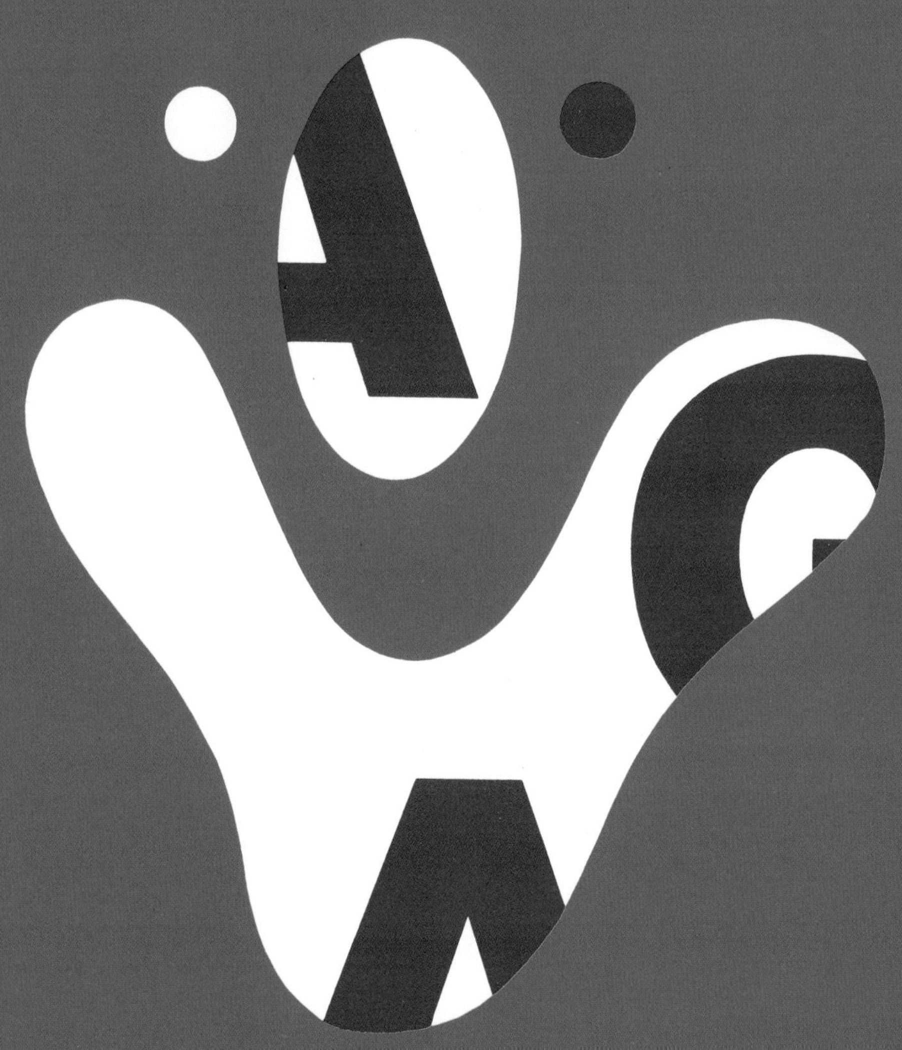

4 Cover design 表紙デザイン 1968

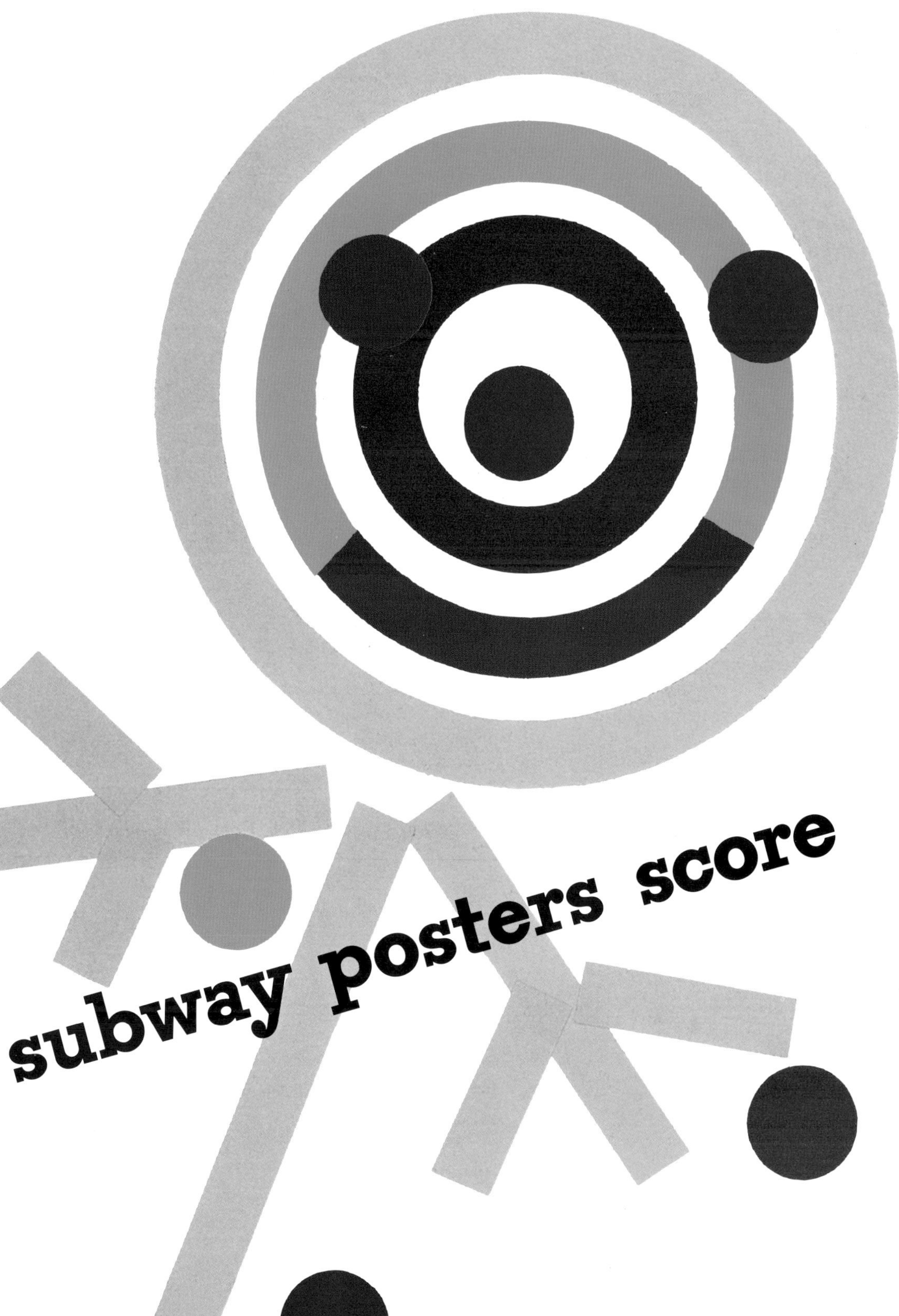

5 Poster for subway advertising company 地下鉄広告会社のポスター 1947

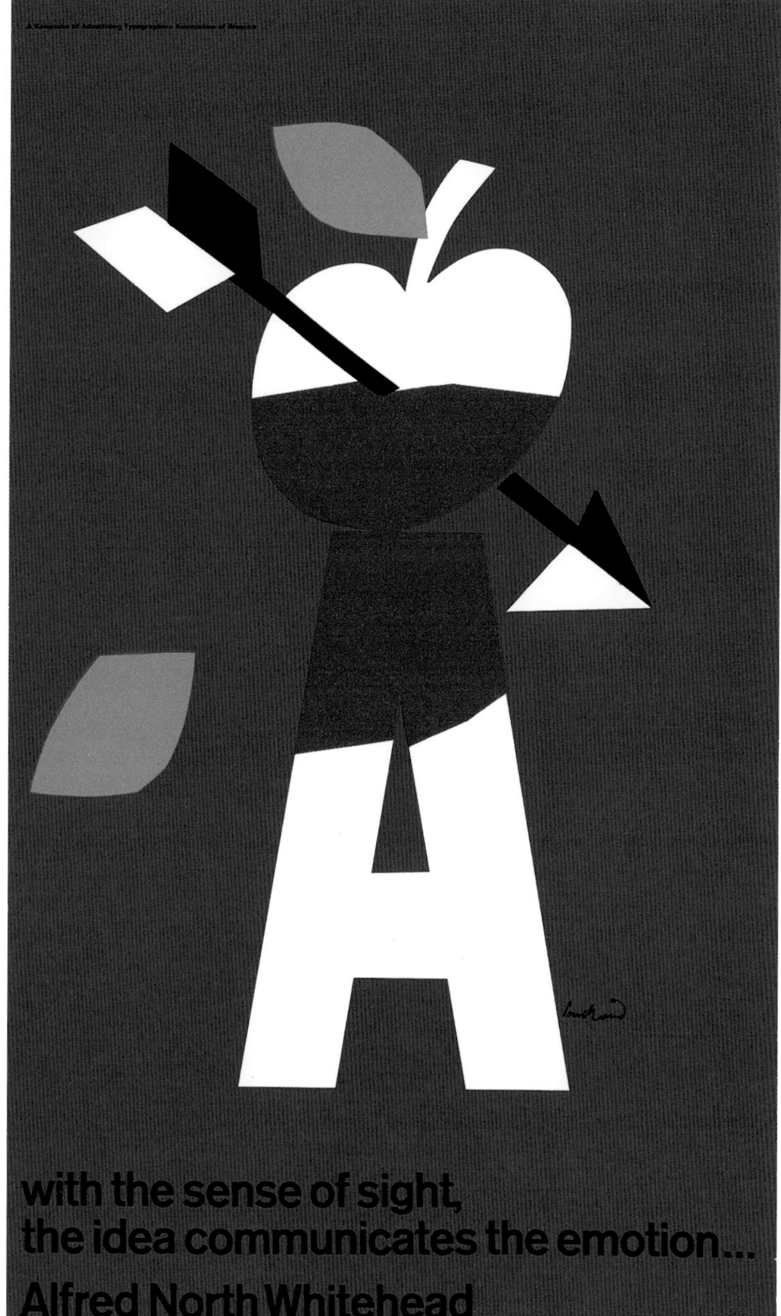

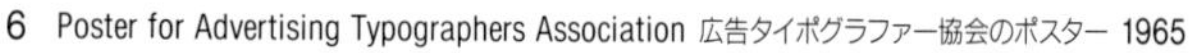
6 Poster for Advertising Typographers Association 広告タイポグラファー協会のポスター 1965

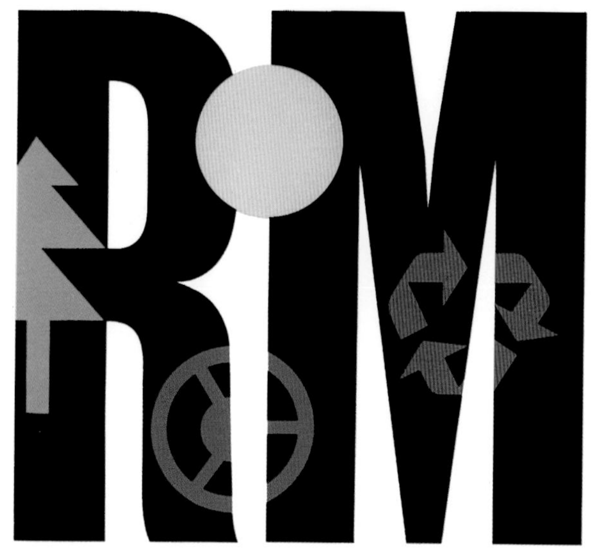

Resource Management:
Energy and
Materials Conservation
Ridesharing
Environment Protection
IBM

7 IBM poster IBMポスター 1980

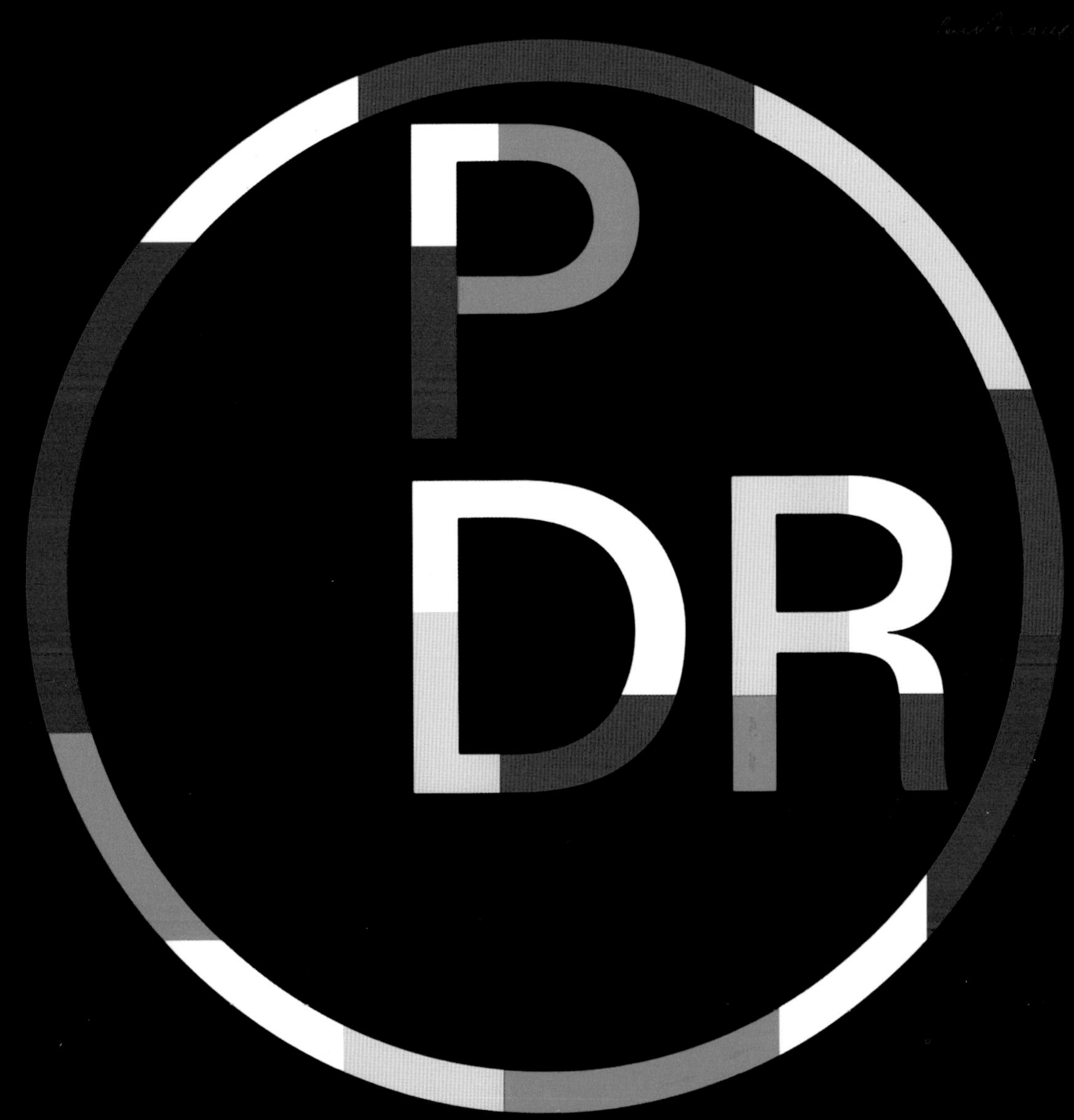

Computer Graphic Services:
Digital B&W Pre-Press
Custom Line Art & Typography
Process Color Separations

PDR Computer Impressions
303 Park Avenue South
New York, NY 10010
212 477 3300

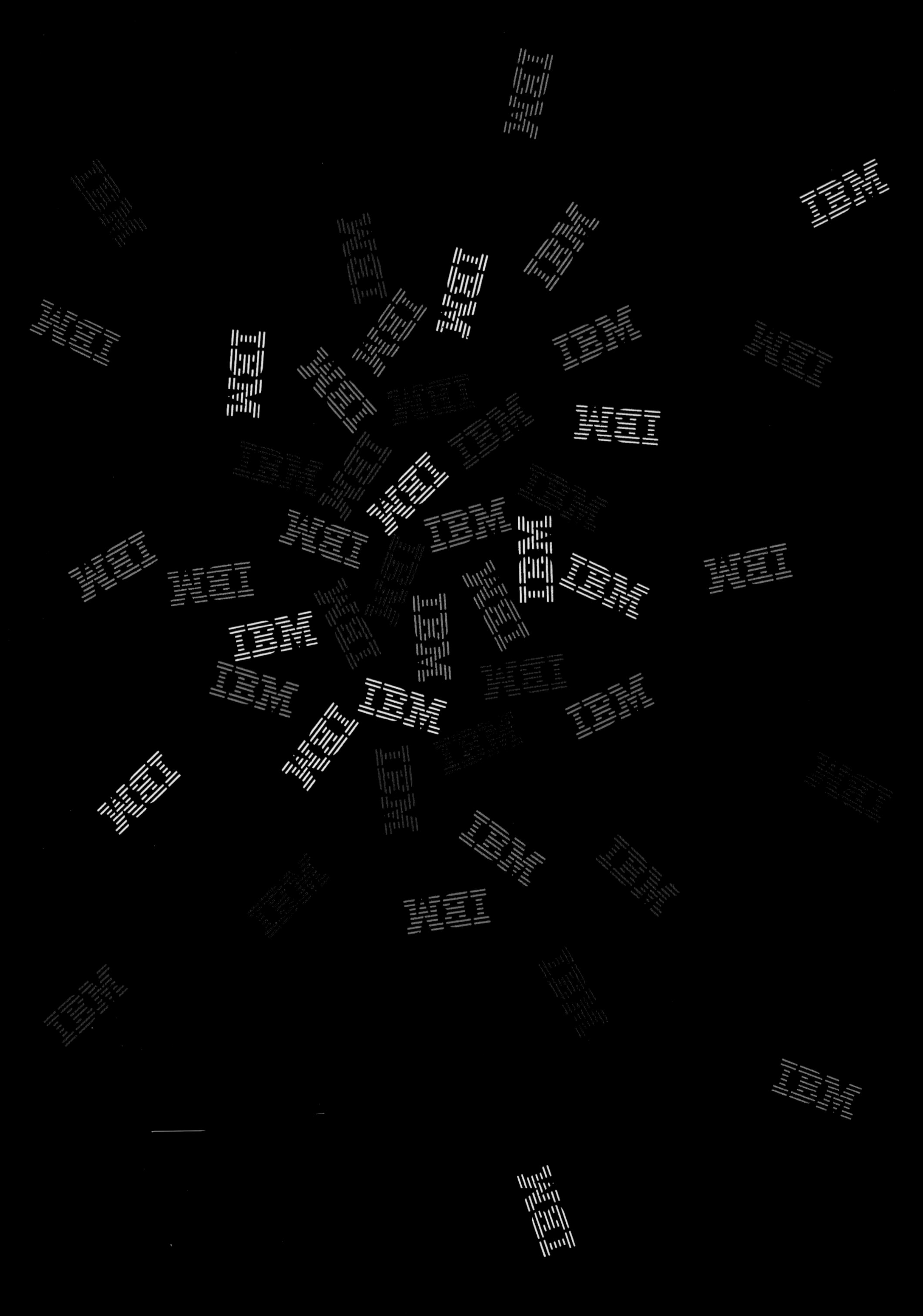

9 Cover design 表紙デザイン 1982

MIN
UTE
MAN

Minute Man National Historical Park
National Park Service
U.S. Department of the Interior

10 Poster for US Department of the Interior 米国内務省のポスター 1974

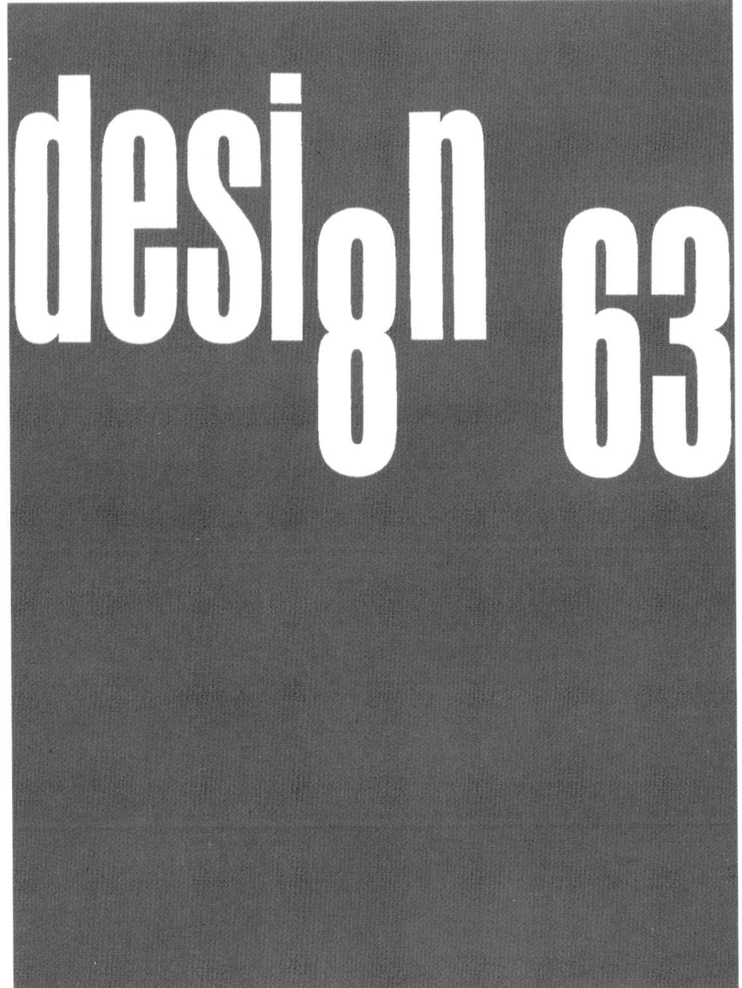

11 New York ADC poster ニューヨークADCポスター 1963

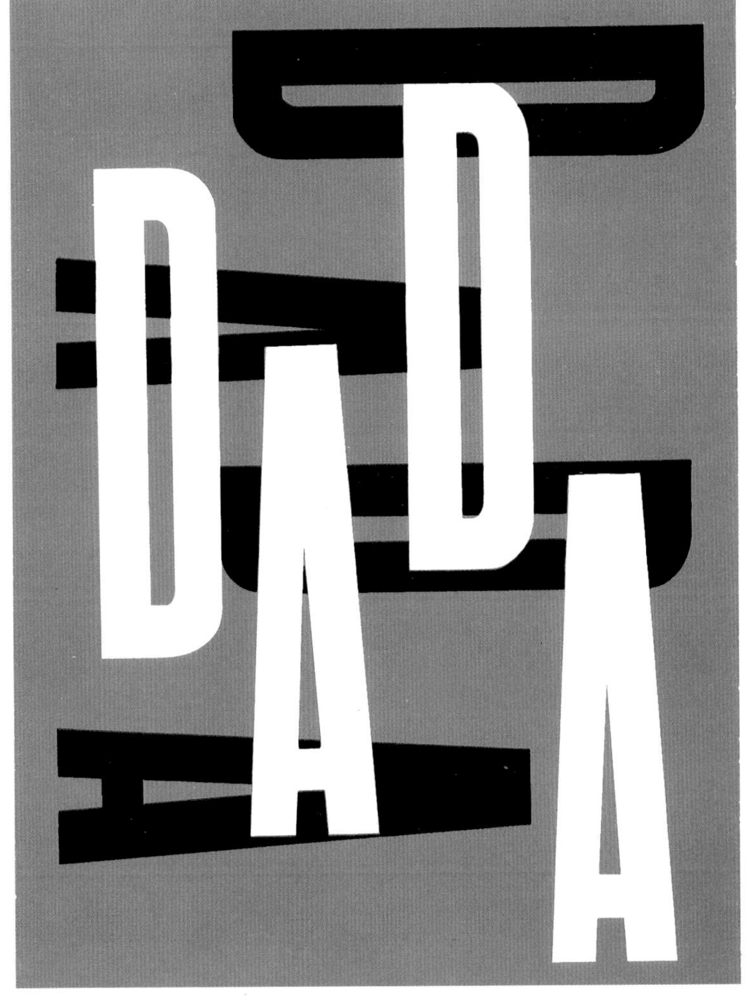

12 Book jacket design 本のカバー 1951

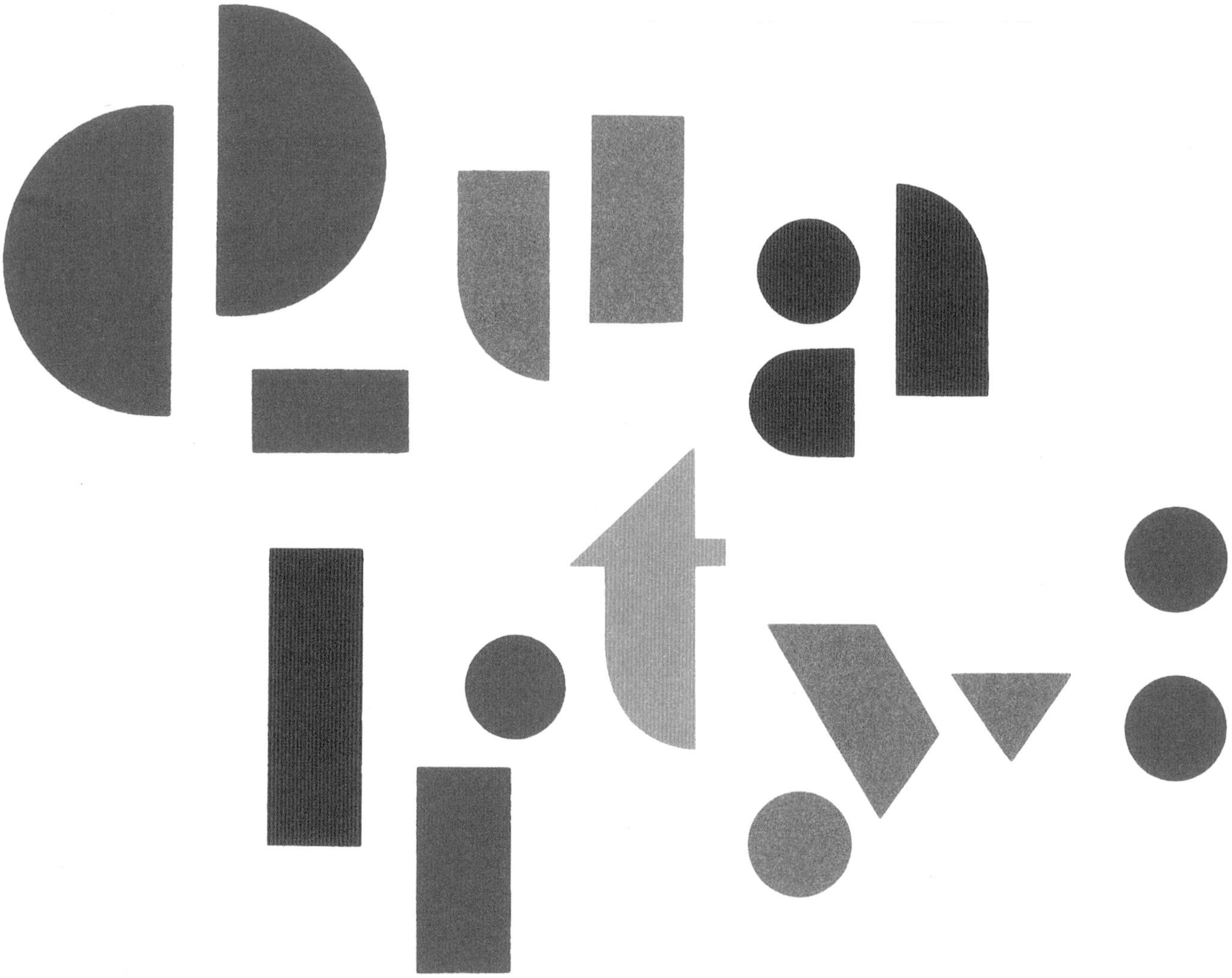

The concept of quality is difficult to define, for it is not merely seen, but somehow intuited in the presence of the work in which it is embodied.
Quality has little to do with popular notions of beauty, taste, or style; and nothing to do with status, respectability, or luxury. It is revealed, rather, in an atmosphere of receptivity, propriety, and restraint. Paul Rand

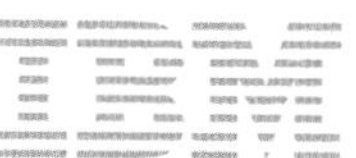

13 IBM promotion IBM PR用ちらし 1989

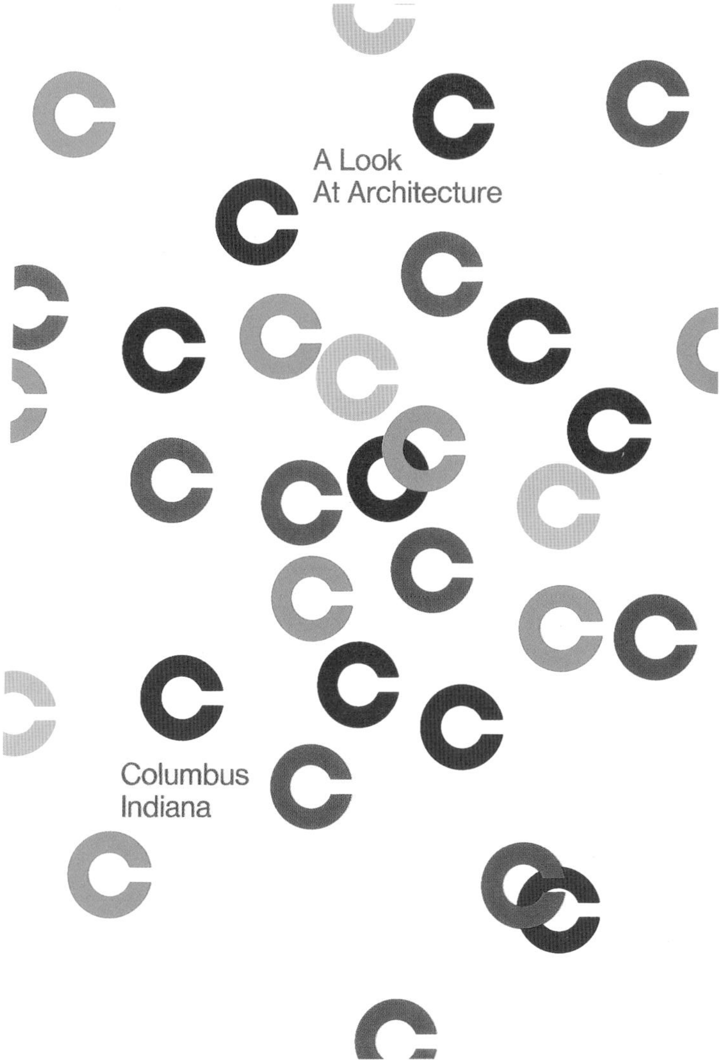

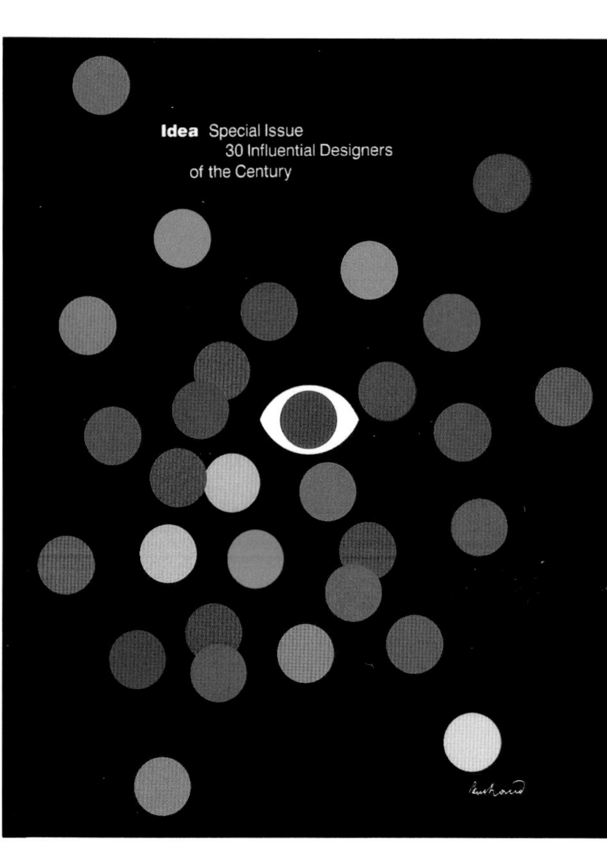

14 Magazine cover 雑誌の表紙 1984

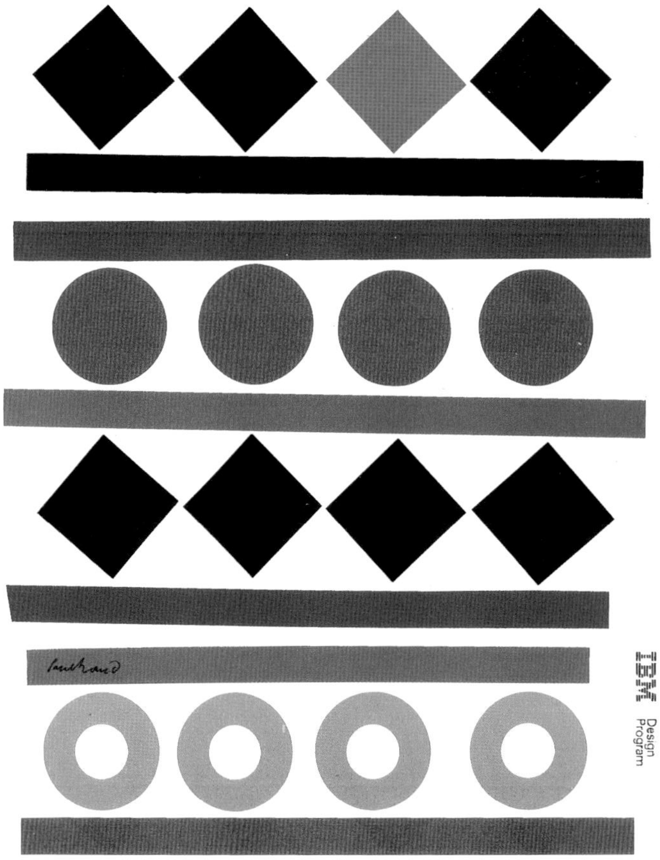

A Look
At Architecture

Columbus
Indiana

15 Book cover design 本の表紙 1974

IBM
Design
Program

16 Corporate folder design フォルダーのデザイン 1984

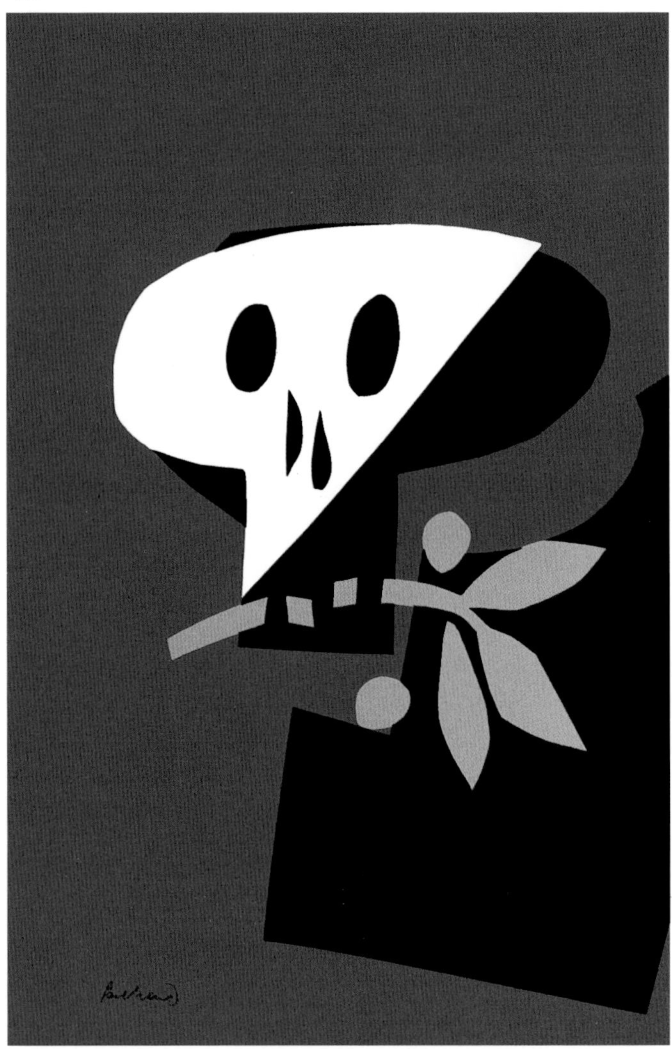

17 Poster against war 反戦ポスター 1968

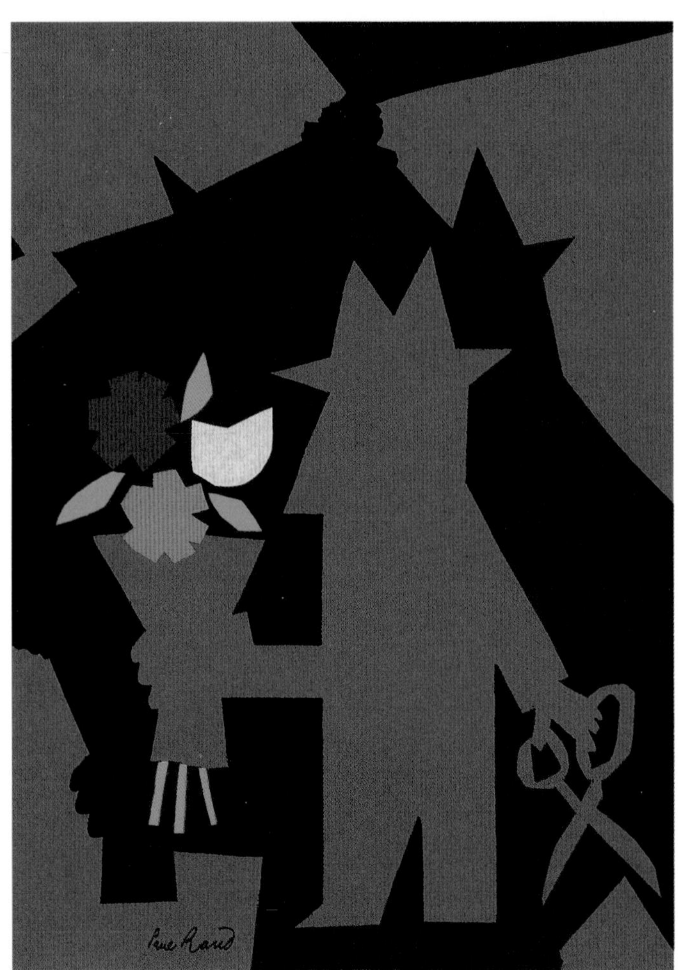

18 Magazine advertisement 雑誌広告 1960

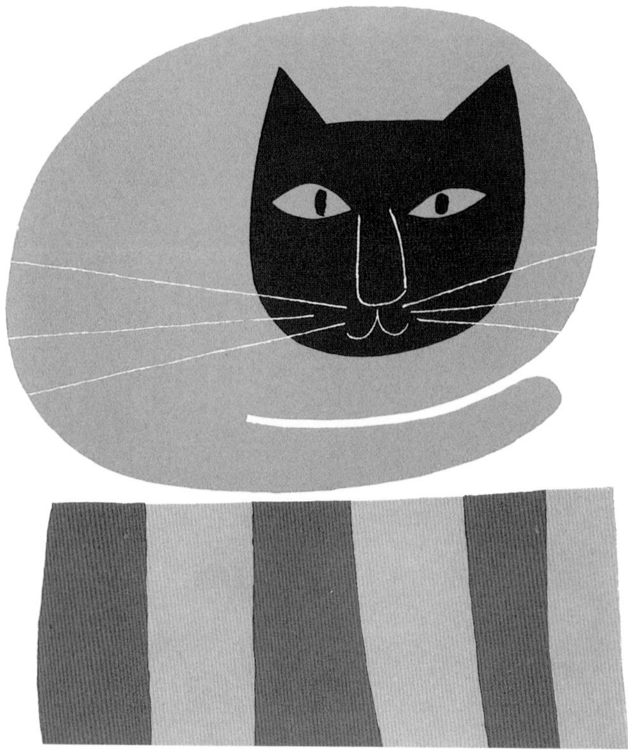

19 Book illustration 本の挿絵 1956

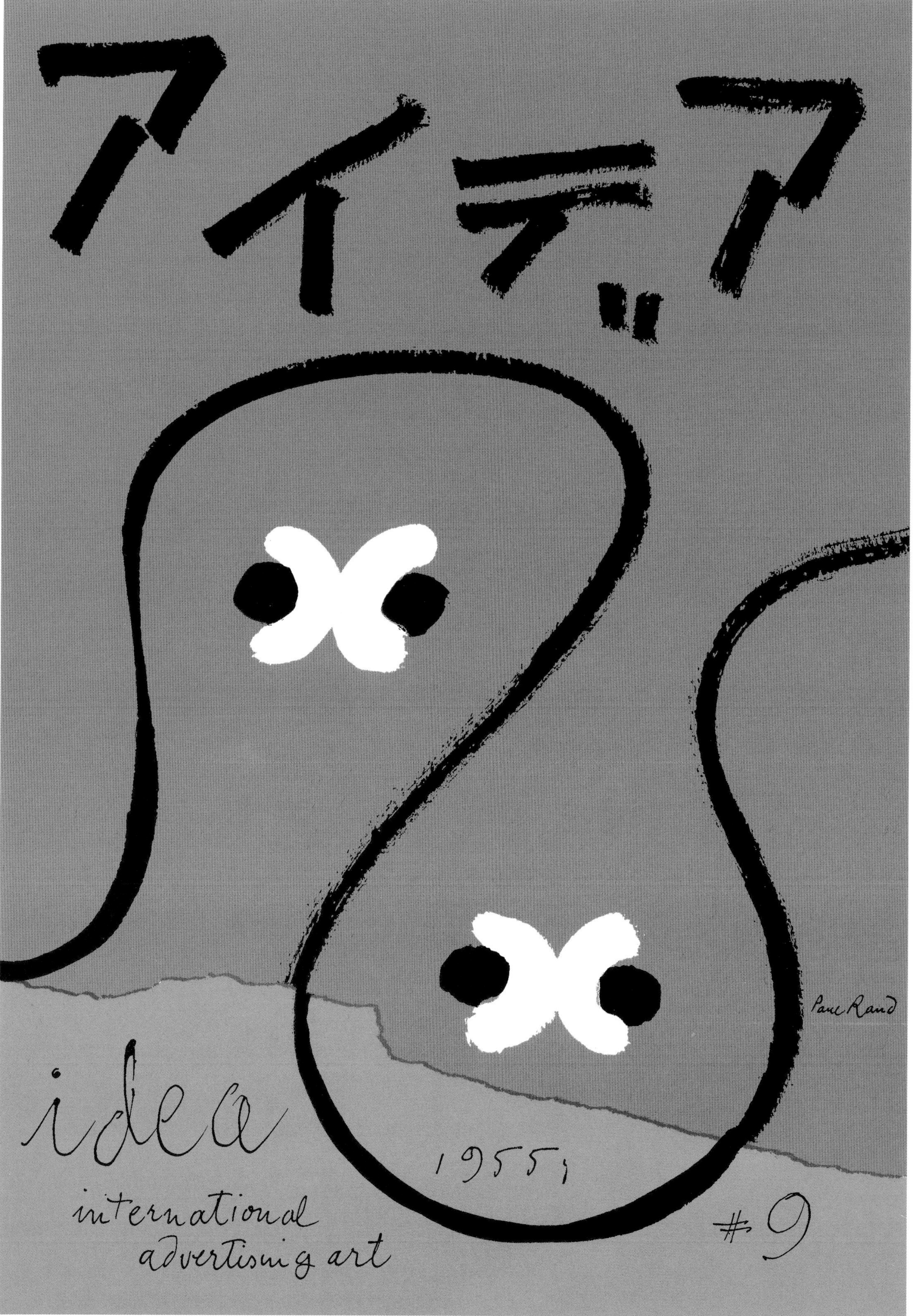

20 Magazine cover 雑誌の表紙 1955

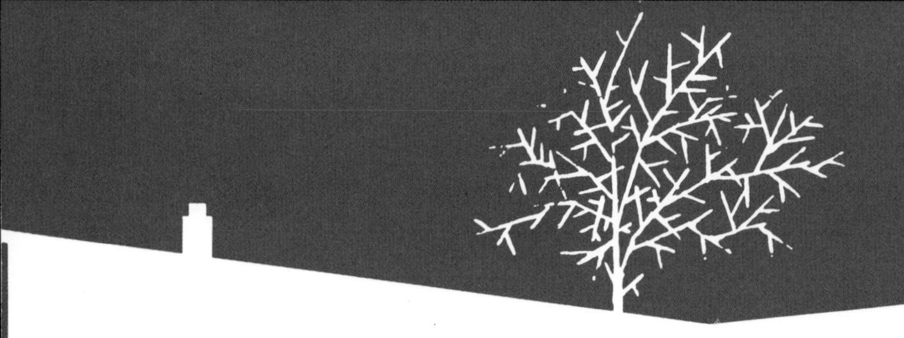

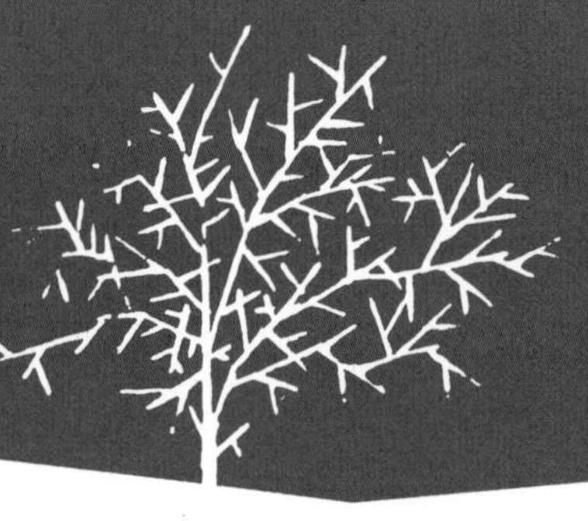

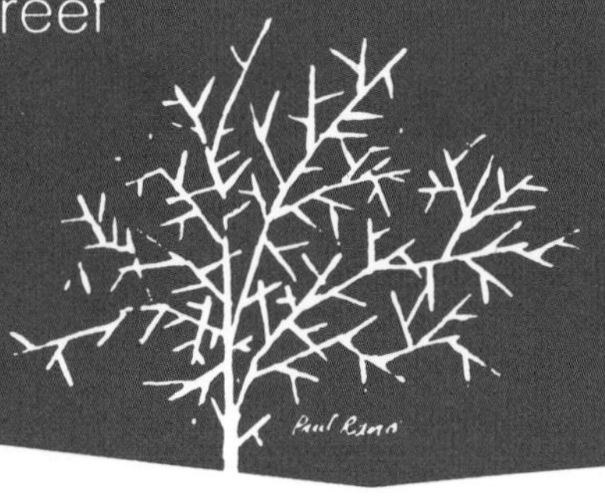

21 "The House in the Museum Garden" poster 美術館庭園の家ポスター 1949

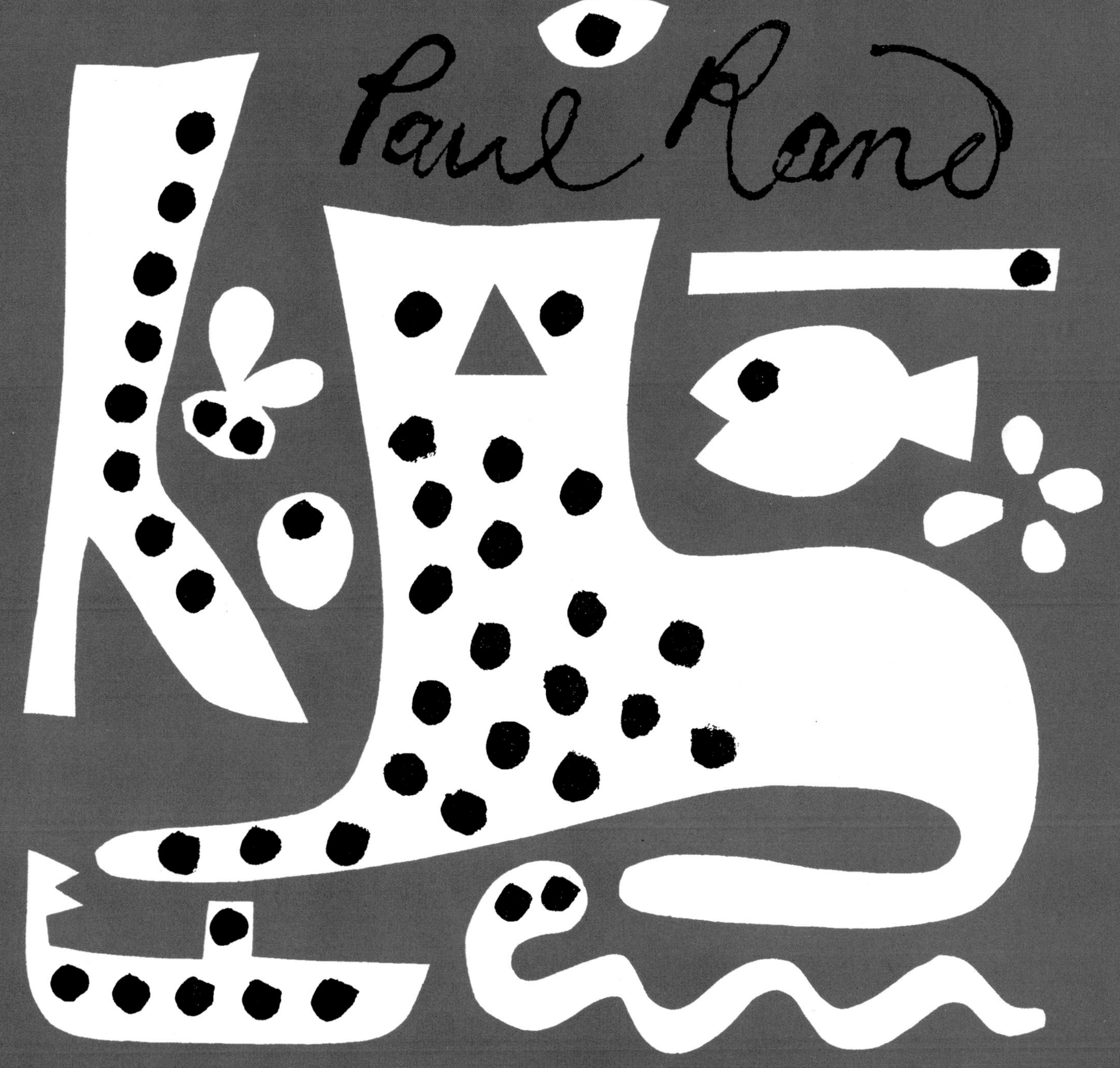

22 Book jacket design 本のカバー 1959

Westinghouse **1970 Annual Report**

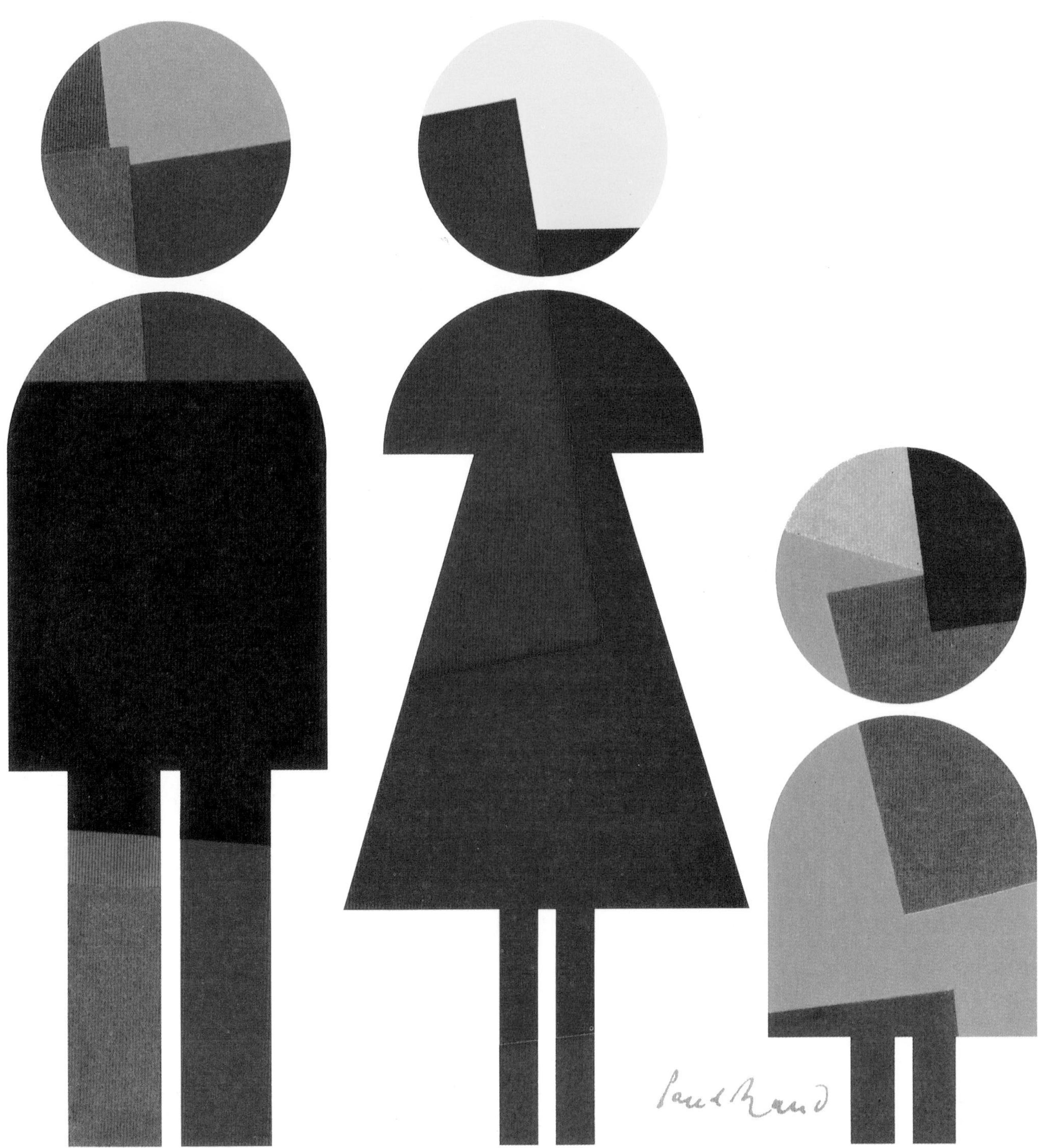

23 Annual report cover アニュアルレポートの表紙 1970

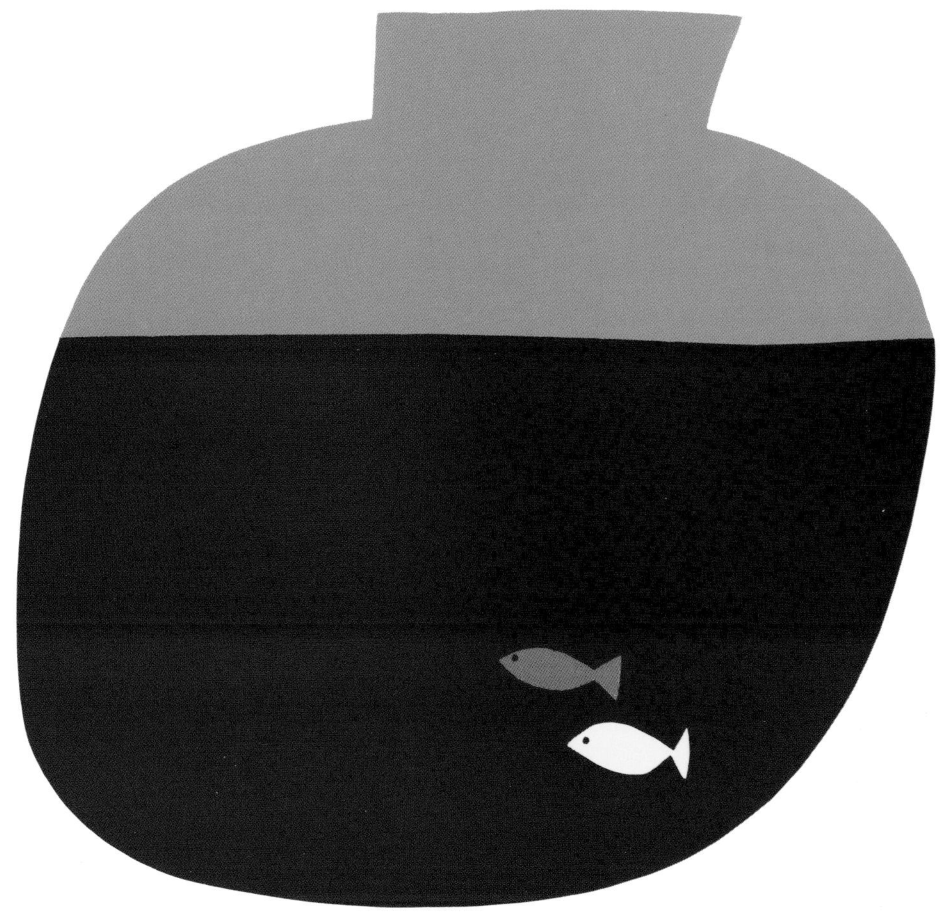

24 Magazine advertisement 雑誌広告 1962

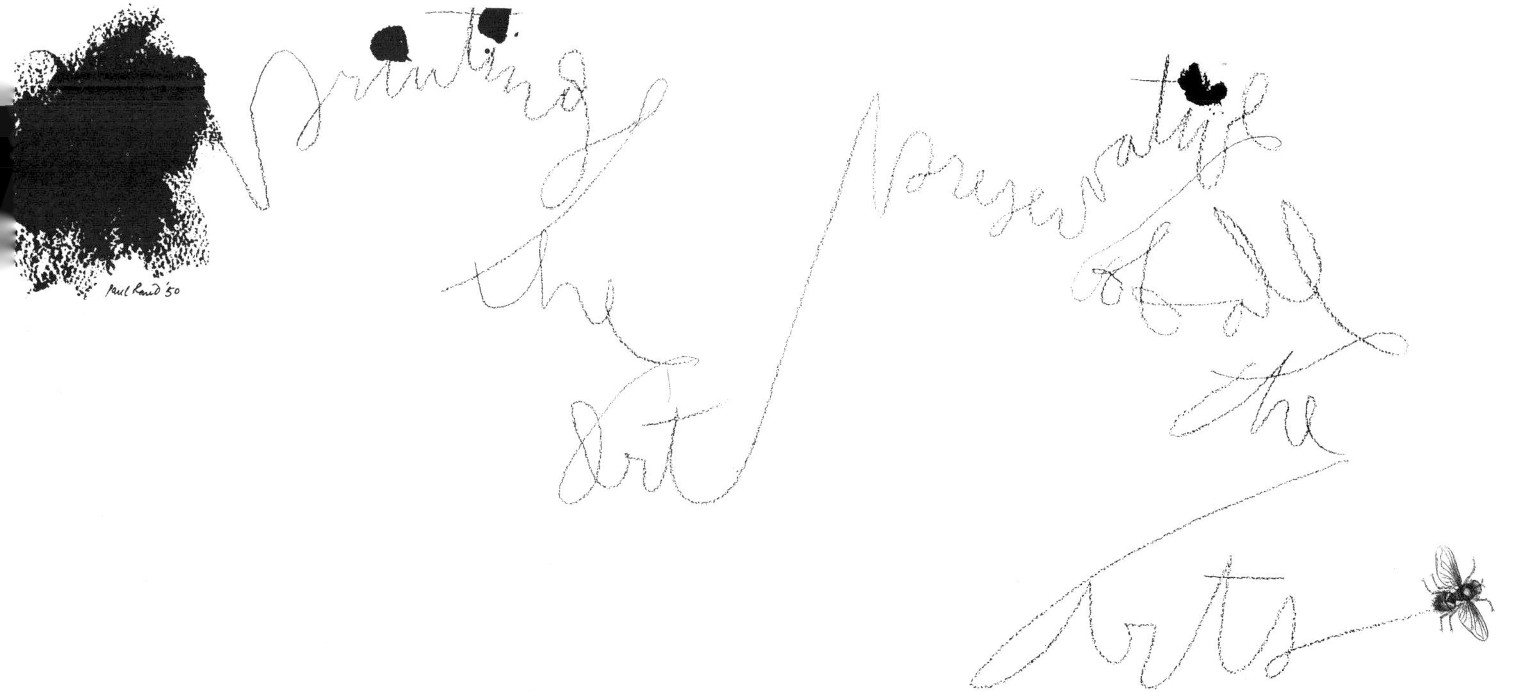

25 Editorial spread 本の見開きのイラストレーション 1950

yale

Yale University School of Art
Graduate Program

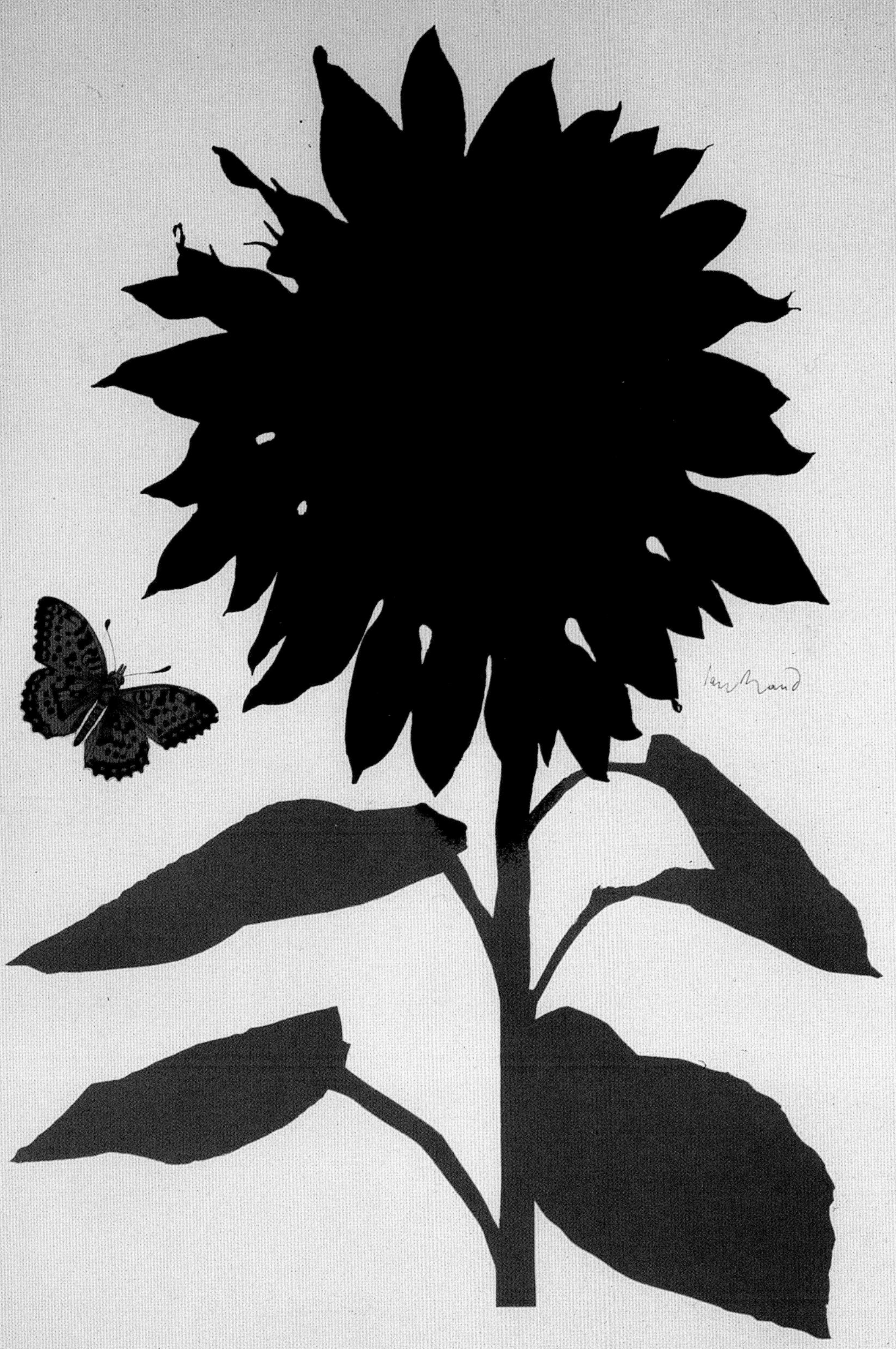

"What would life be if we had no courage to attempt anything?"

Vincent van Gogh

27 Poster for typographers タイポグラフ会社のポスター 1985

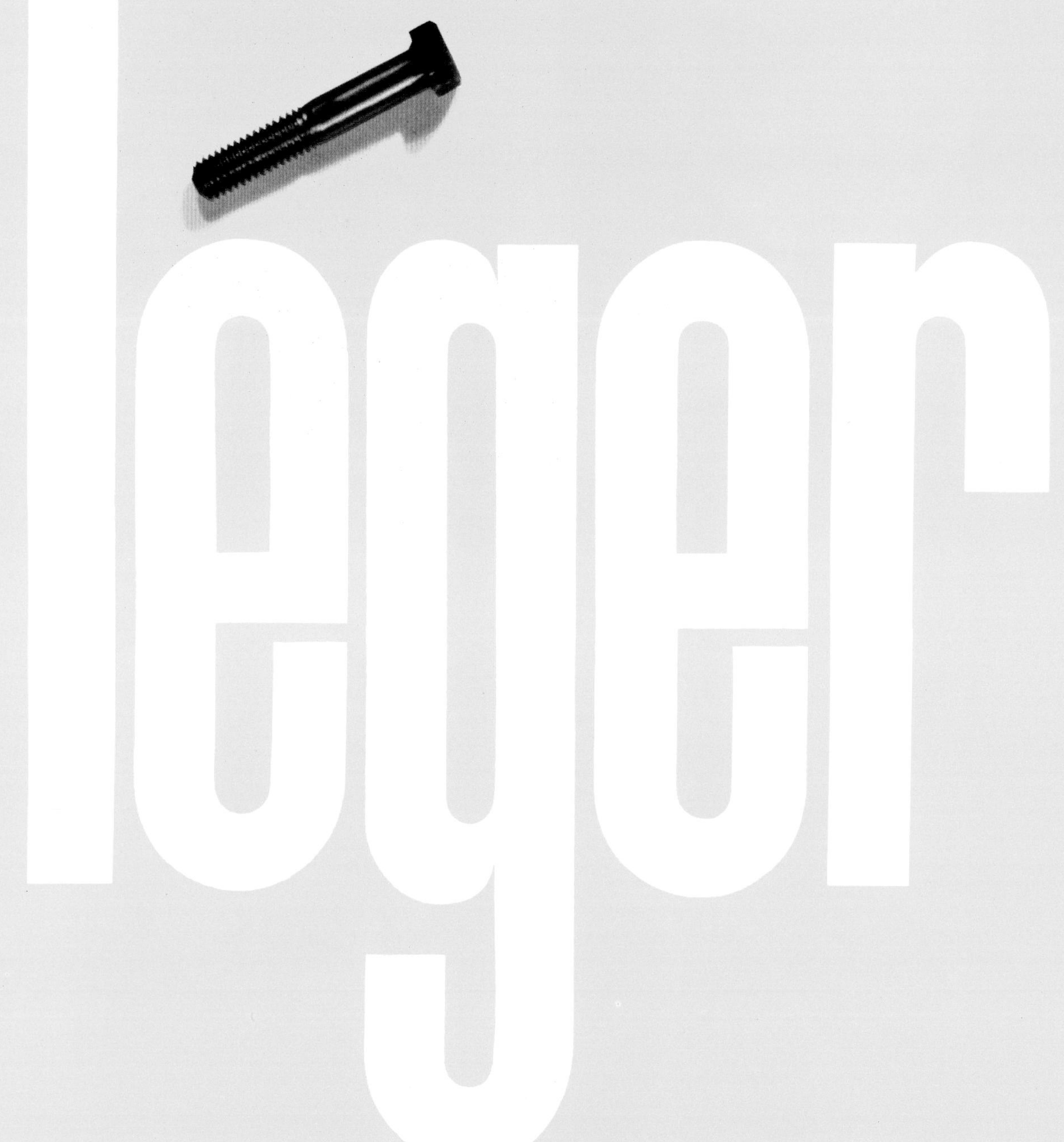
leger

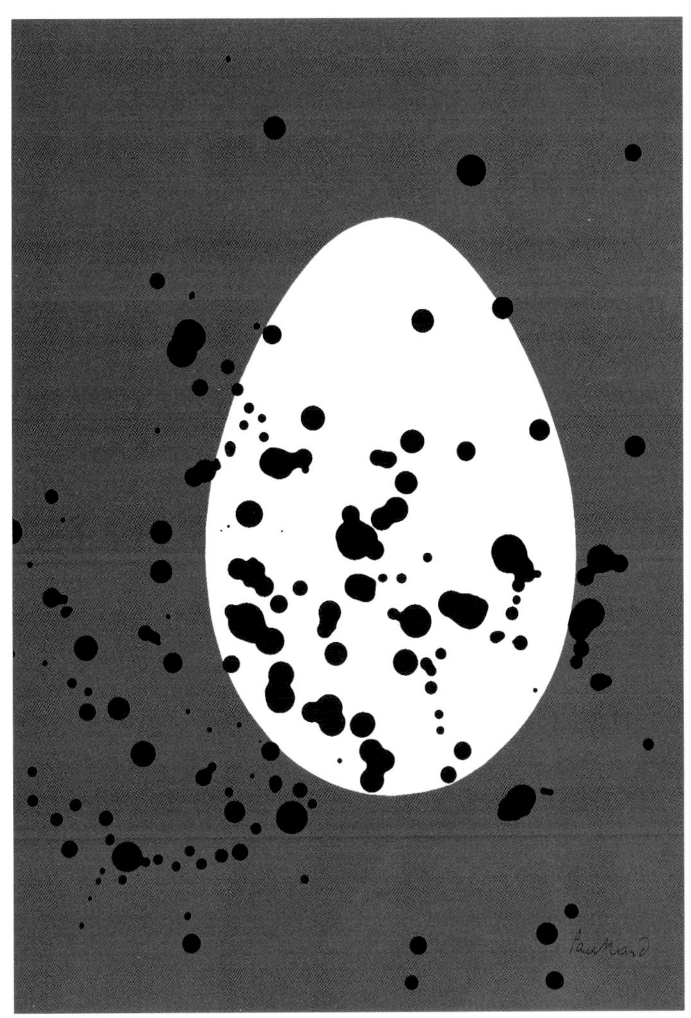

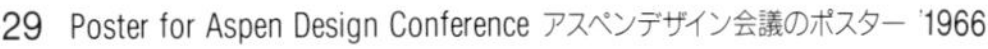
29 Poster for Aspen Design Conference アスペンデザイン会議のポスター 1966

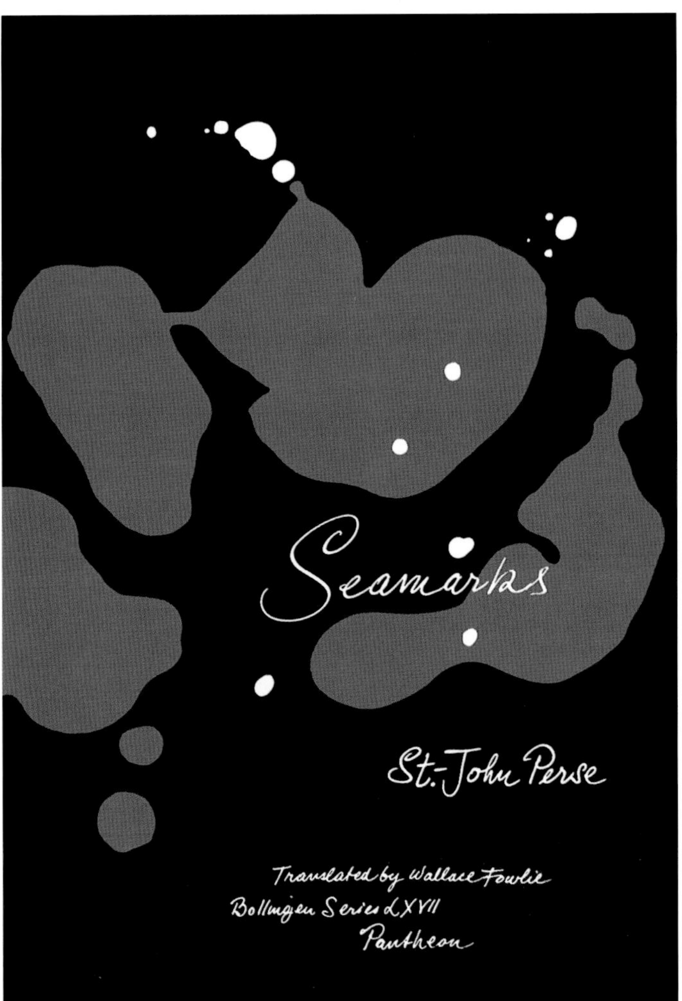

30 Book jacket design 本のカバー 1958

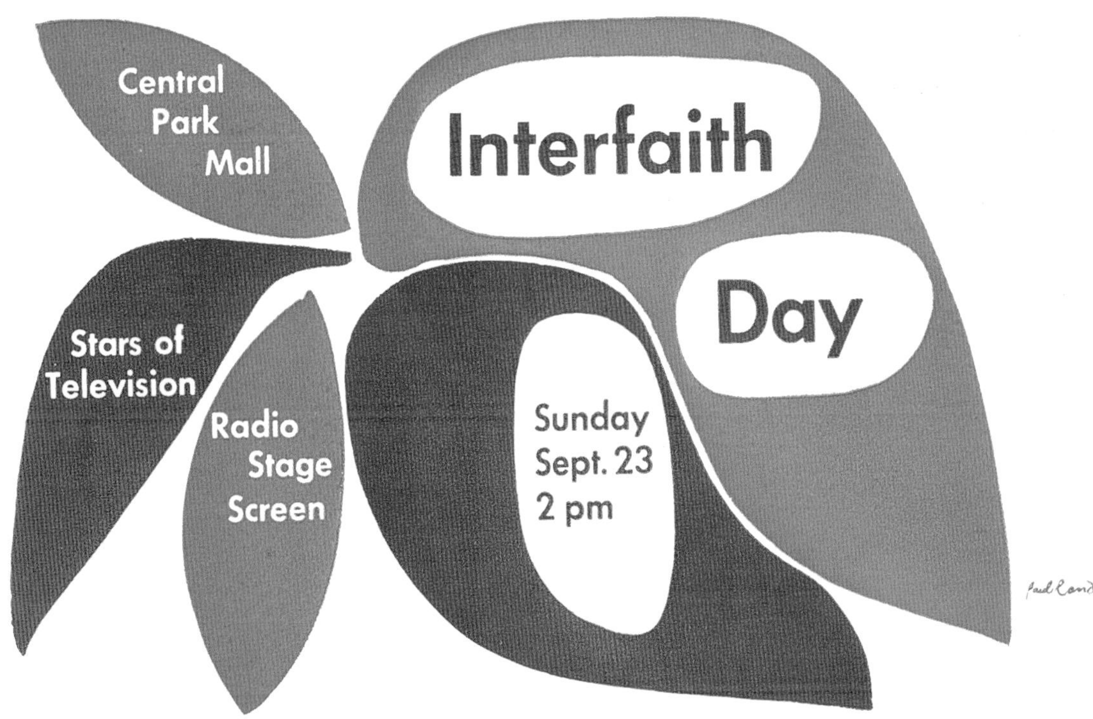

31 Interfaith Day card インターフェイスデイ・カード 1951

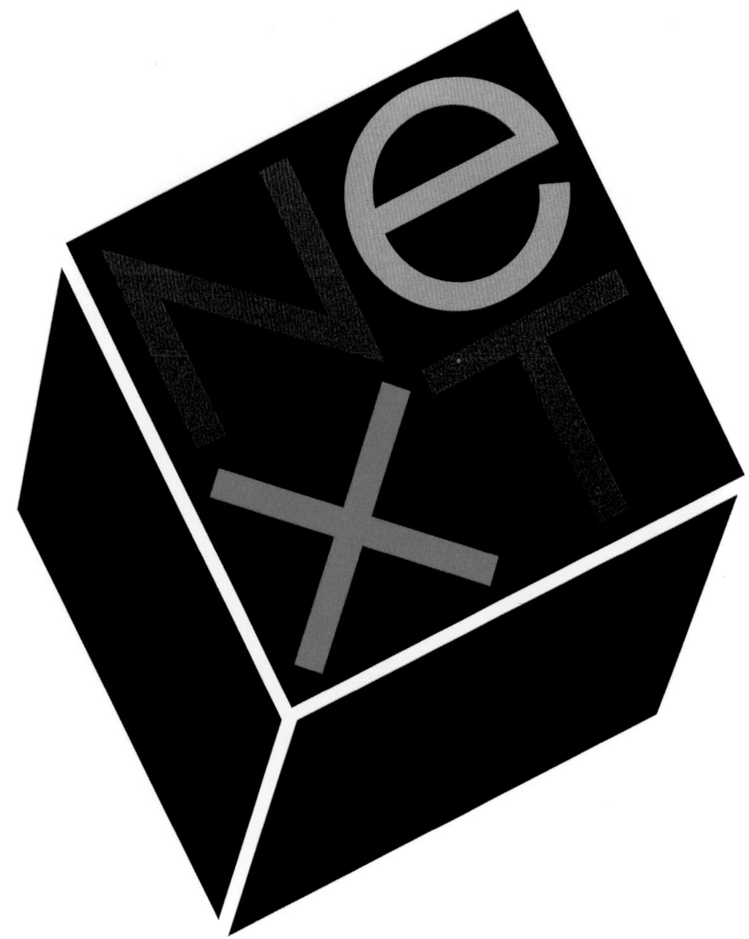

32 Trademark トレードマーク 1986

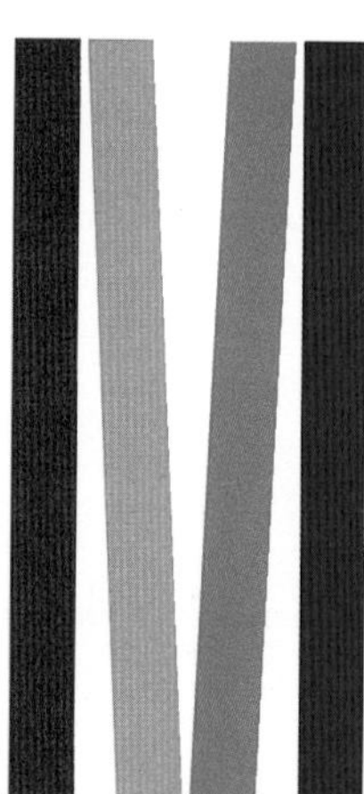

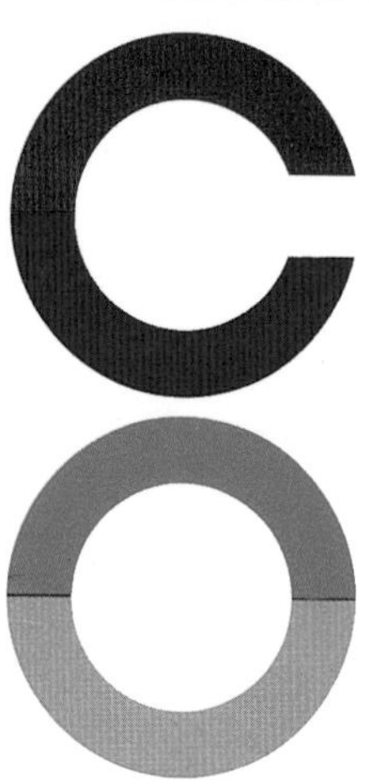

33 Logo ロゴマーク 1988

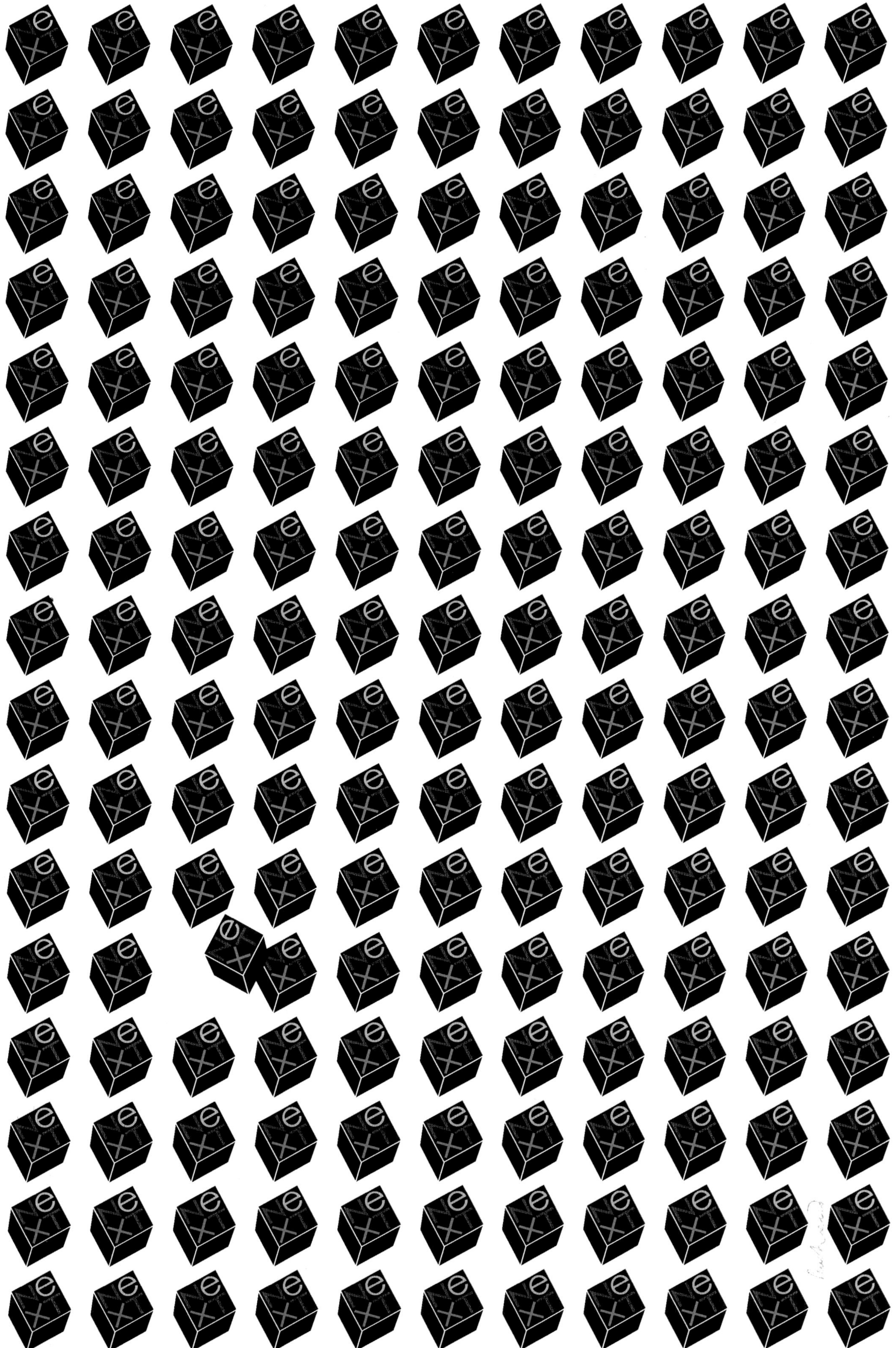

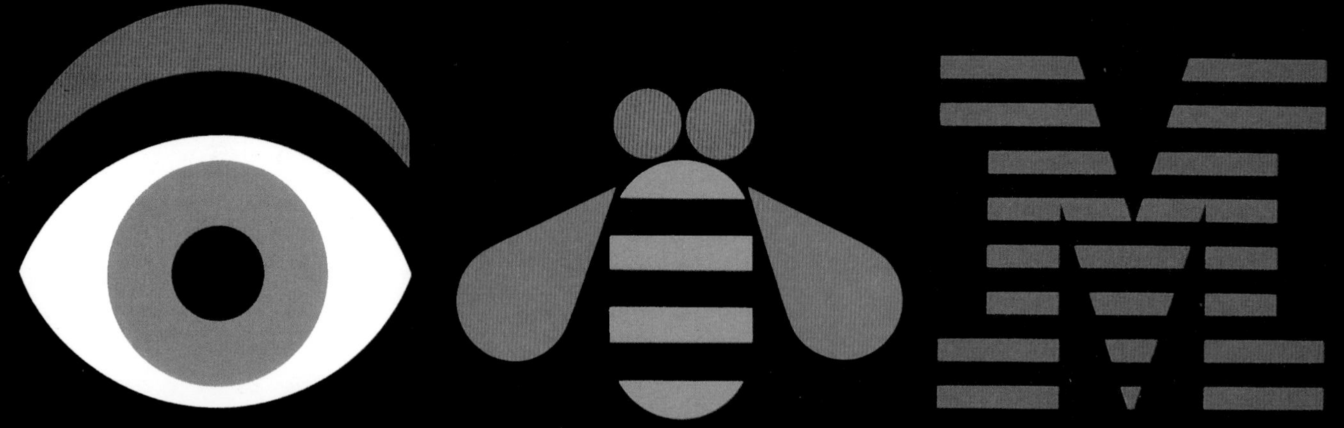

35 IBM poster IBMポスター 1981

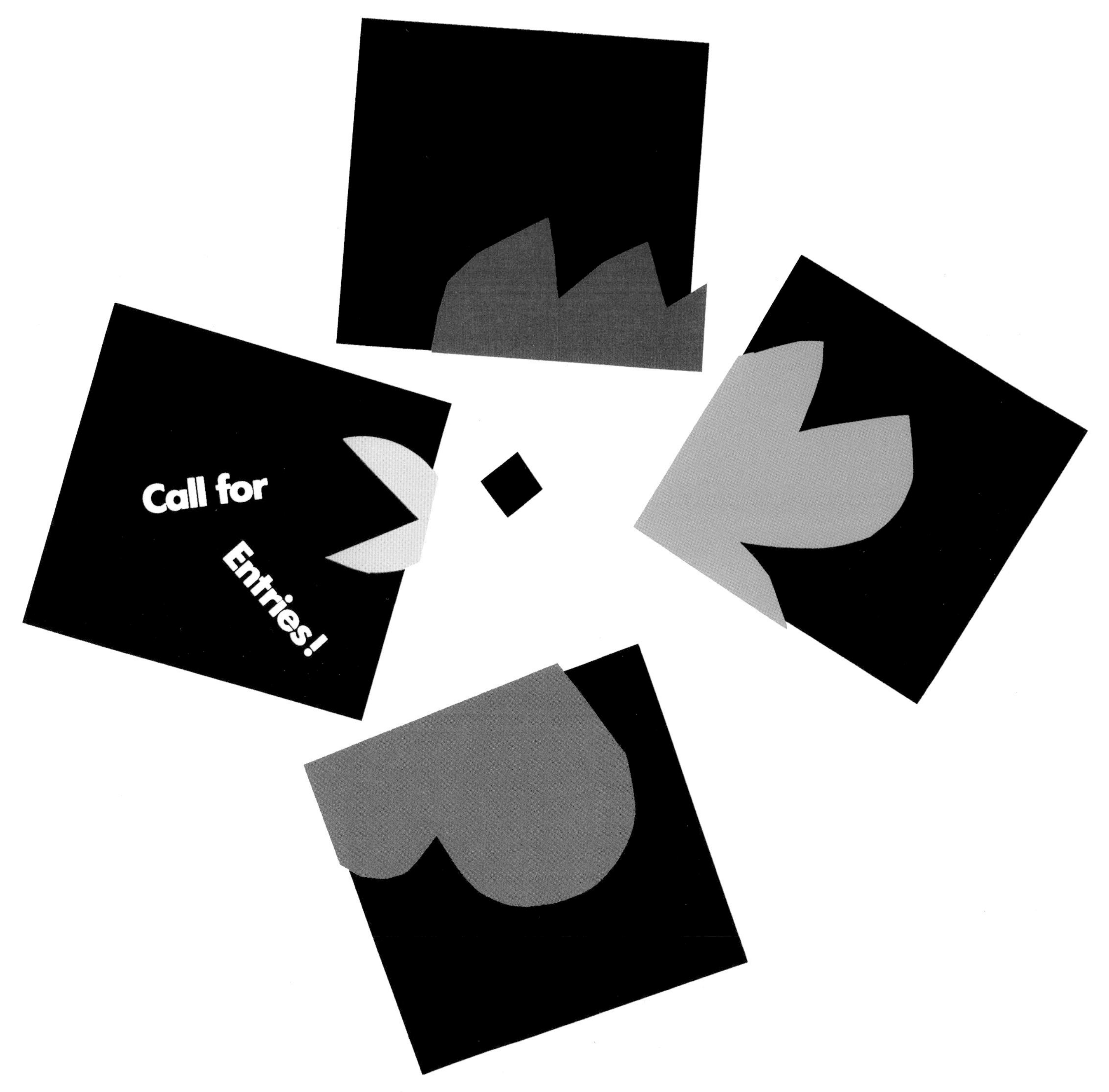

The Art Directors Club, Inc.
3rd International Exhibition
New York, N.Y. U.S.A.
Deadline: 16 December 1988

STASYS EIDRIGEVIČIUS スタシス・エイドリゲヴィチウス

Hiroshi Kojitani 麹谷 宏

The posters of Stasys Eidrigevičius are embued with a strange and mystical power: once seen, they are never forgotten. They evoke feelings of loneliness and melancholy. They are poetic and gentle. Yet they are frightening, as well.

Stylistically they betray their Polish origins almost instantly. Underlying all Polish works there seems to be a common mood—heavy and quiet, dark and introspective. Some would attribute this unique ambience to Poland's long and troubled history, or to its romantic despair and aspirations as seen in its literature. Others would say it is the product of a socialist society long isolated from external contacts.

It must be remembered, however, that Stasys is in fact not of Polish birth. He was born and raised in Lithuania, where he received his artistic training. Only later, as an adult, did he emigrate to Poland. How interesting that his works should be fully evocative of Polish poster art, nonetheless.

Stasys is an artist who has long piqued my interest. The first time I set eyes on one of his posters, I was so moved by the experience that a chill ran down my spine. Normally quite imperturbable, I found myself rocked with fear on viewing his imaginary world. It was almost as though something crazed within me were speaking in a murmur in the poster. Never before had I ever experienced anything so sensitive or so beautifully frightening in my life.

For many years, Stasys was involved in the production of children's coloring books. He scored great success in this field through his unique use of surrealistic ideas and expressions. In my view, these years of fanciful musing dramatically affected Stasys's work even after he became a poster artist. For unlike the sensual sweetness of Salvador Dali or Giorgio de Chirico, in Stasys's works we find people and animals who are expressionless, serious and restrained, each possessing an air of mysterious yet frightening allure.

In recent years Stasys's fame has gradually spread through frequent one-man shows in the United States, Switzerland and West Germany, and through numerous Grand Prizes he has garnered in Italy, France and elsewhere. At one of his most recent exhibitions in Tokyo, included were several of Stasys's original works that had been printed in Japan. The printing had been specially arranged by Ikko Tanaka.

During a visit to Poland last year Mr. Tanaka had gone to Stasys's studio and viewed his works in their original form. It was then for the first time that he recognized the poor quality of reproduction of Stasys's works as generally available, and so he arranged for the special printings in preparation for the Tokyo show. Because Stasys is open to using any medium that he feels can convey his artistic images—tempera, pastels, gouache, watercolor—he is said to have taken great pleasure in seeing his painstakingly selected shades and textures reproduced to such stunning effect.

When I went to view Stasys's works at the Tokyo showing, I was overwhelmed by the weight of his tableaux lined upon the walls. Stasys's posters are more than mere illustrations. They are posters incorporating paintings. This is what makes them so weighty. This is why they are so frightening.

I look forward to viewing his new works again at some time in the future. I long to feel once again the strangely frightening allure that only Stasys can evoke.

スタシス・エイドリゲヴィチウスの作品は、不思議な雰囲気で人をひきつけ、一目みたら忘れられない魅力を持っている。それは、寂しく、憂うつで、詩的で、やさしくて、そして怖い。その作風には、すぐにポーランドのポスターだと理解させるものがある。

確かに、ポスター王国ポーランドには、多数の個性と才能が存在しながら、その底部には、重く、静かで、暗く、内向的な、一種独特の共通した雰囲気がある。その理由を、あの有名なポーランド分割の長い苦難の歴史や、文学運動にみられたロマン主義的な絶望と希求の理念の影響だという人もいれば、また、長年の閉鎖的な社会主義社会が生み出した風土のせいとみる人もいる。

しかし、スタシスはポーランド人ではない。戦後の1947年にソビエトのリトアニア共和国に生れて、そこで芸術教育を受け、成人後にポーランドに移住してきたのである。(そして、母国人以外は彼の姓を発音できないので、外国では簡単にスタシスと呼ばれている)。にもかかわらず、スタシスの作品は、ポーランドのポスターそのものという雰囲気を持っているから面白い。

スタシスは、ぼくには、少々気になるアーチストなのである。はじめてスタシスのポスターの前に立った時、思わず身ぶるいが出たのだ。彼の描く幻想的な世界は、柄にもなくぼくを怖気だたせた。まるで、ぼく自身のなかにある何か狂おしいものが、その絵の中でぼくに向ってささやいたような気がしたのだ。このような繊細で美しい怖さといったものを感じたのは、はじめての体験だった。

スタシスは、若いころから長年、絵本の仕事に関わってきた。そして、「私は馬のいうことがわかる」と書いたりしているように、彼独特のシュールレアリスティックな発想と表現を駆使してその分野に挑み、成功した。この、超現実的で幻想的な世界に遊ぶ経験が、その後にポスター作家になってからも、ダリやキリコなどが見せる官能的な甘さといったようなものに走ることもなく、まじめで無表情な人たちや、抑制された動物たちというキャラクターを生み、不思議な魅力と怖さを見せる、スタシスの世界を築いたのだろうと思う。

スタシスは、近年、アメリカ、スイス、ドイツなど多くの国で個展を開き、また、イタリア、フランスなどのこれまた多くのコンテストで、グランプリを獲得している。最近の個展は、東京のgggギャラリーで開かれ、この時は、日本で印刷されたオリジナル作品も展示された。これは、昨年のポスター・ビエンナーレの審査でワルシャワに滞在中に、スタシスのアトリエを訪れた田中一光が、彼の原画を見て、印刷再現があまりにも違いすぎるのに同情し、特別に企画されて実現したものである。スタシスは、テンペラ、パステル、グワッシュ、水彩等と、イメージの表現のためには手法にこだわらない。だから、彼が大切にするその微妙な色彩とマチエールが、見事に再現されたこの日本での印刷には、とても喜んだという。

このスタシス展の会場に立って、ぼくは、タブローの並ぶ展覧会の重さを感じていたことを思い出す。スタシスのポスターは、単なるイラストレーションではなく、スタシスの絵画を使ったスタシスのポスターなのだ。だからしっかりと重く、だからやはり怖いのである。

またいつの日か、彼の新作の前に立って、あの不思議な怖気を感じてみたいものだ。

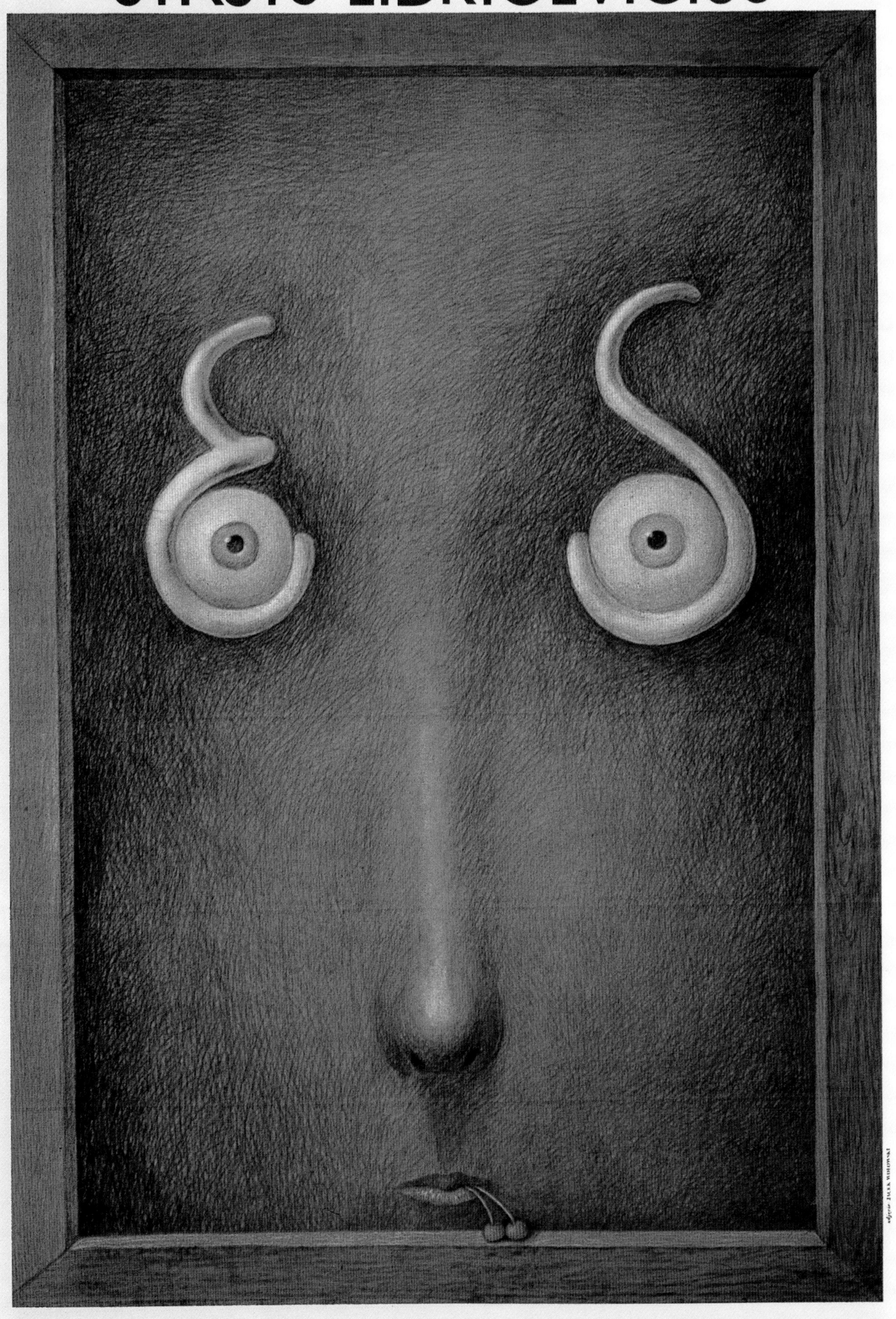

1 Exhibition poster 個展ポスター 1986

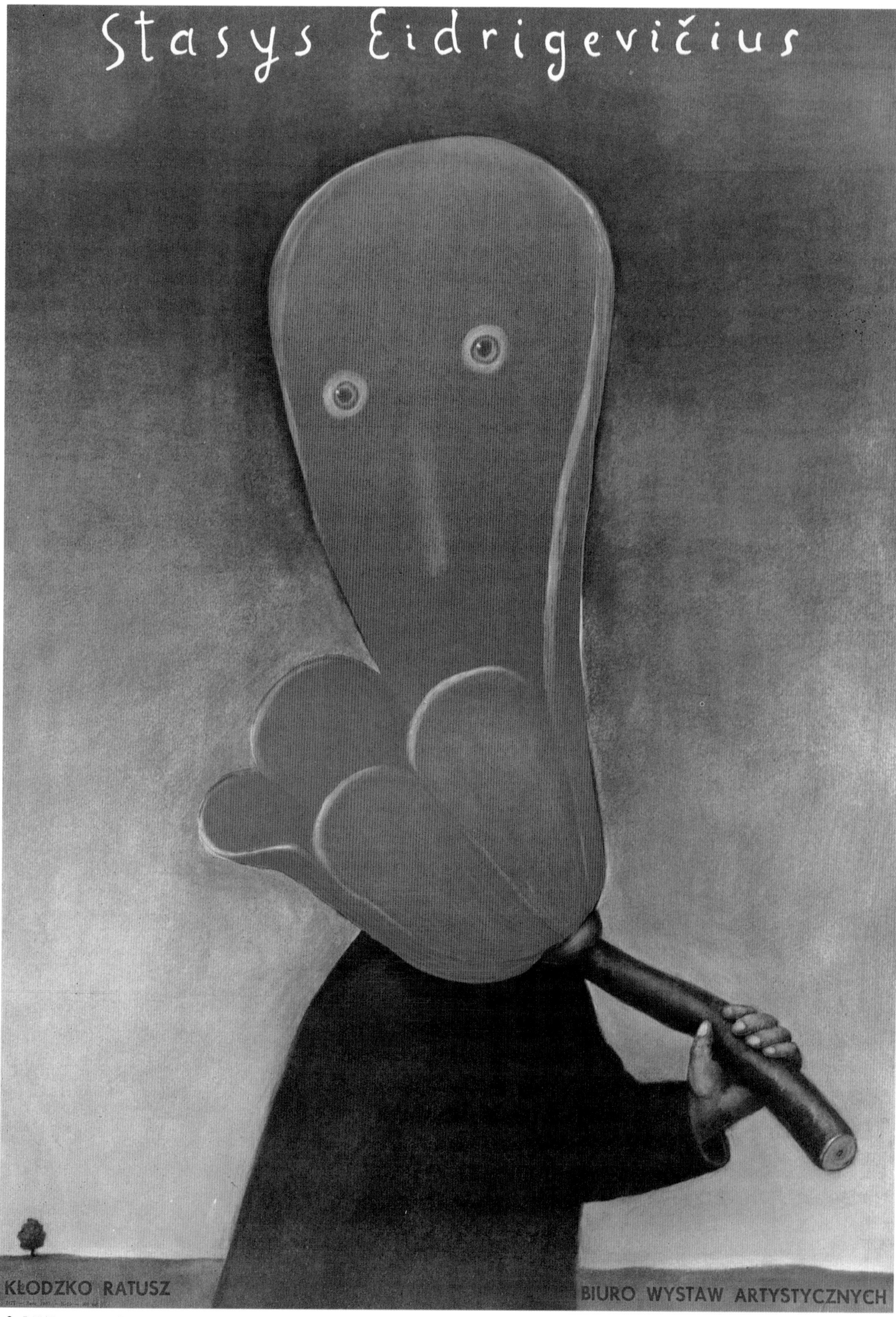

2 Exhibition poster 個展ポスター 1985

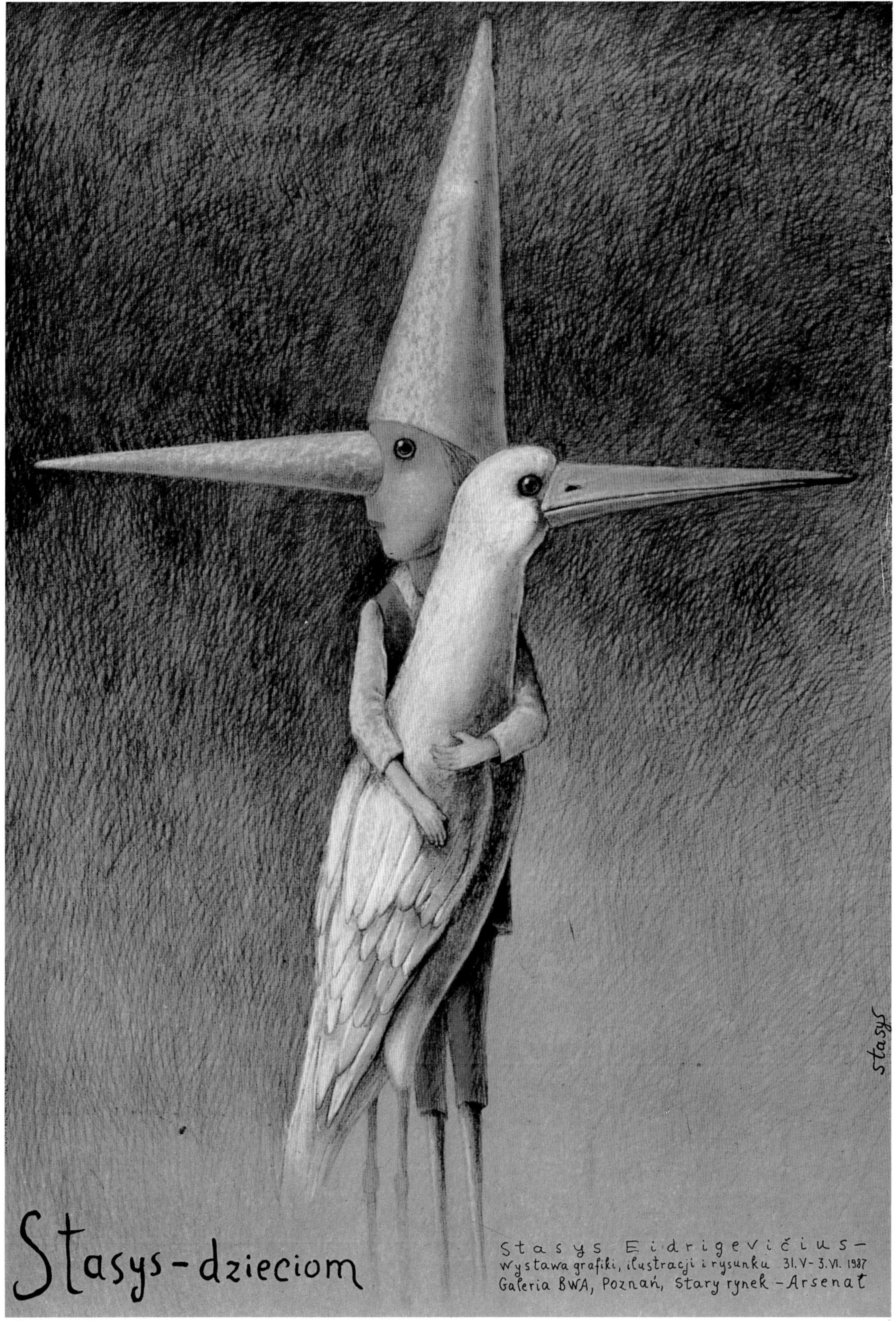

3 Poster for exhibition of illustration for children's books 絵本のイラスト展ポスター 1987

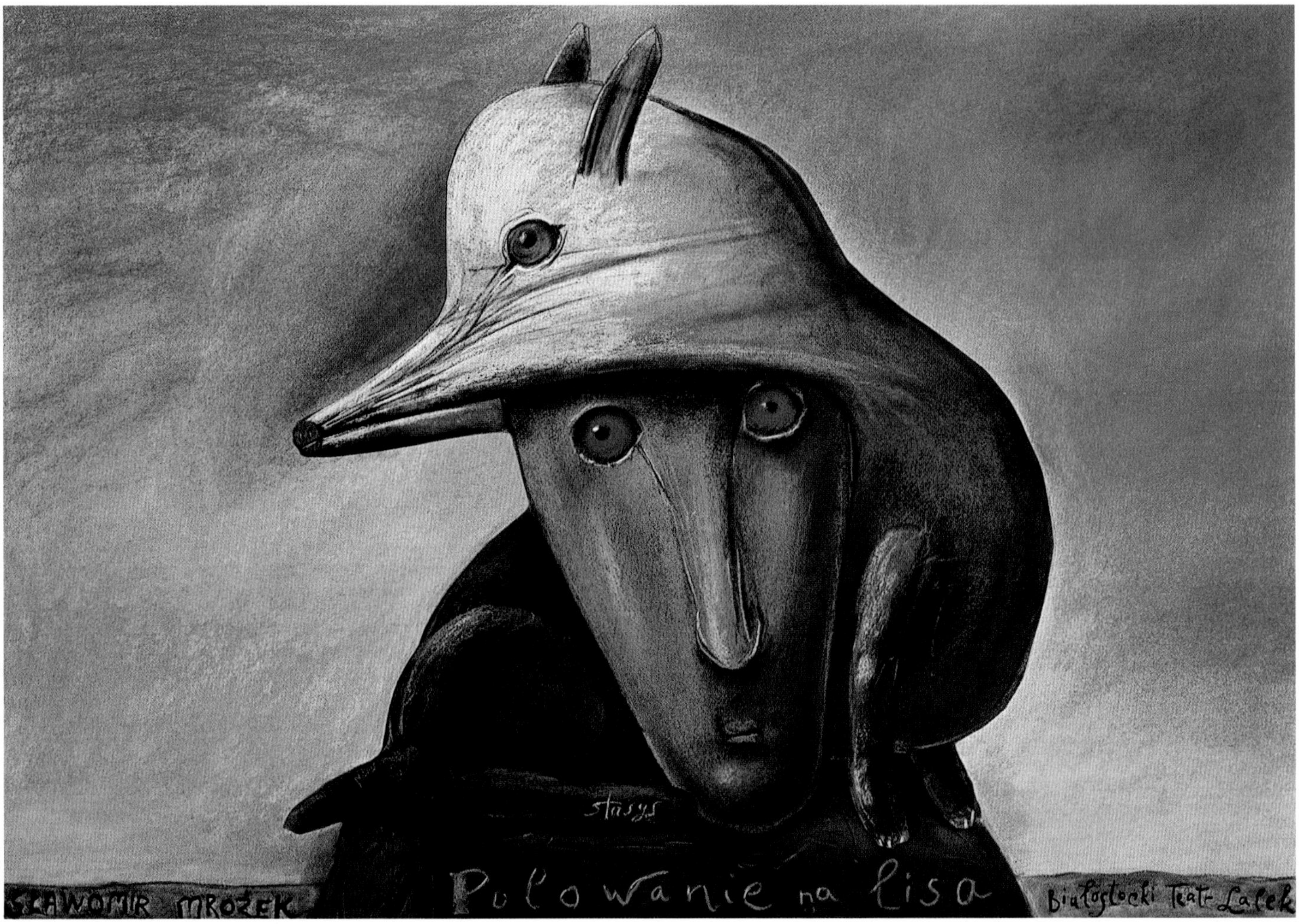

4 Poster for puppet show 人形劇ポスター 1988

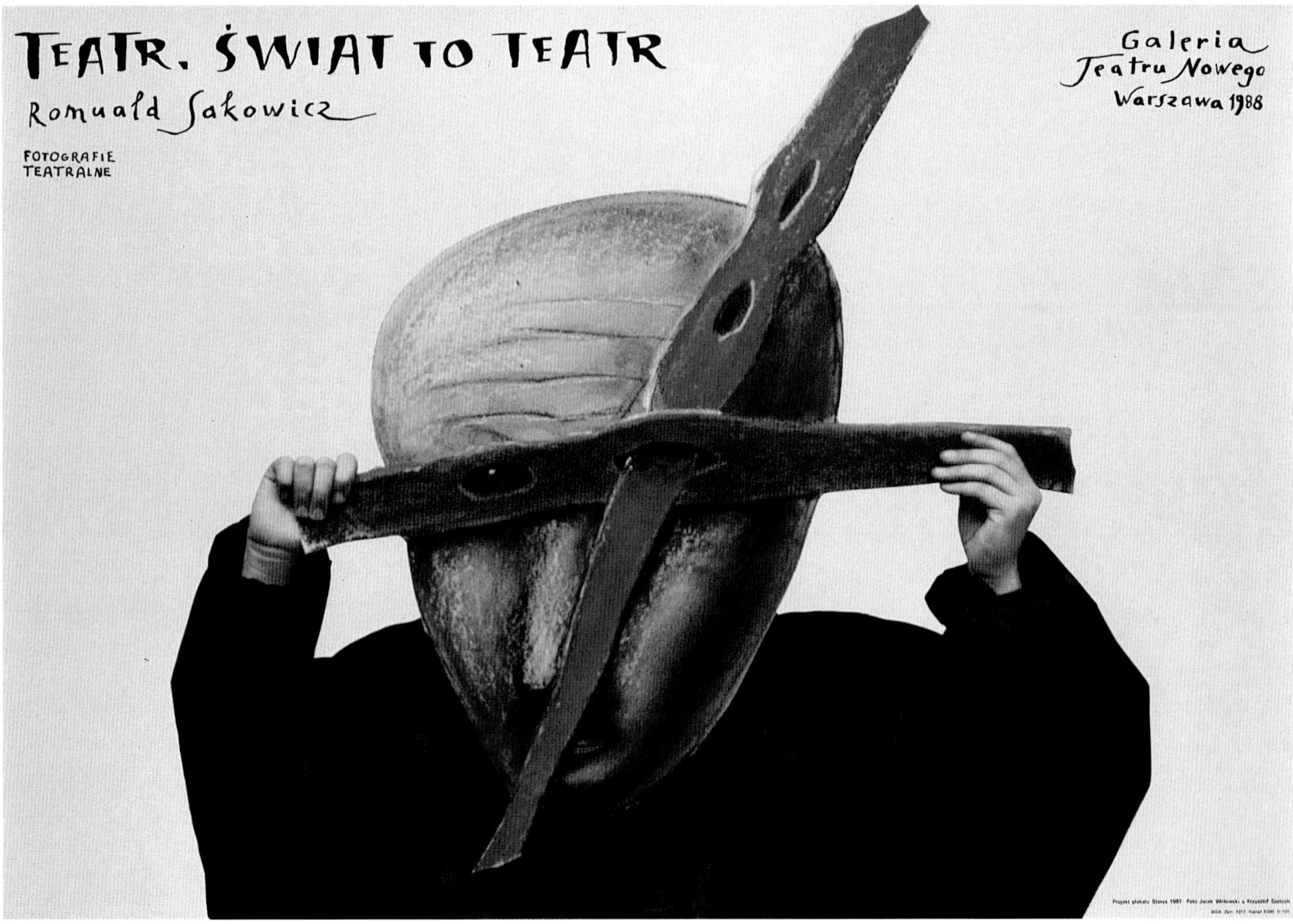

5 Poster for photo exhibition 写真展ポスター 1988

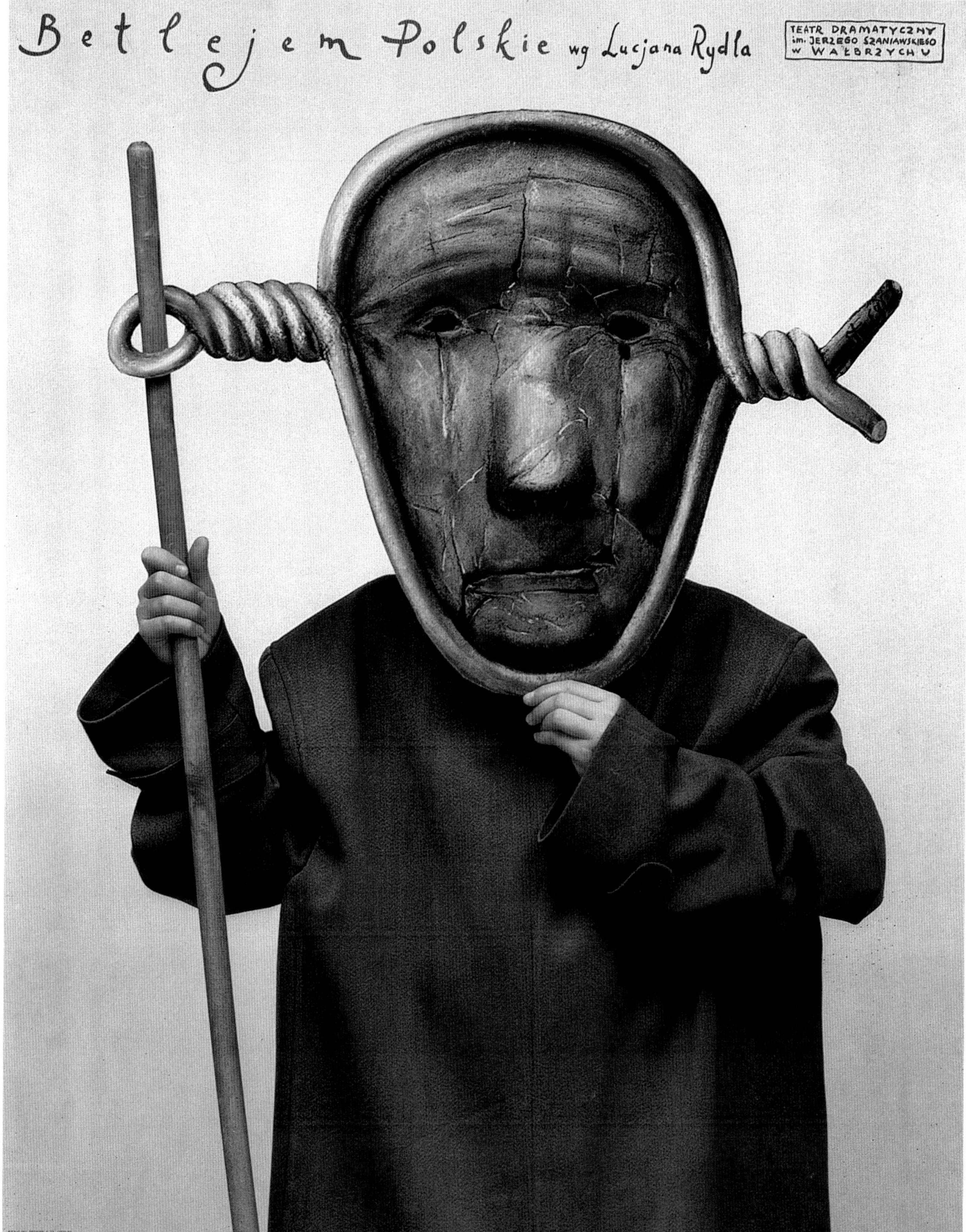

6 Poster for stageplay 演劇ポスター 1988

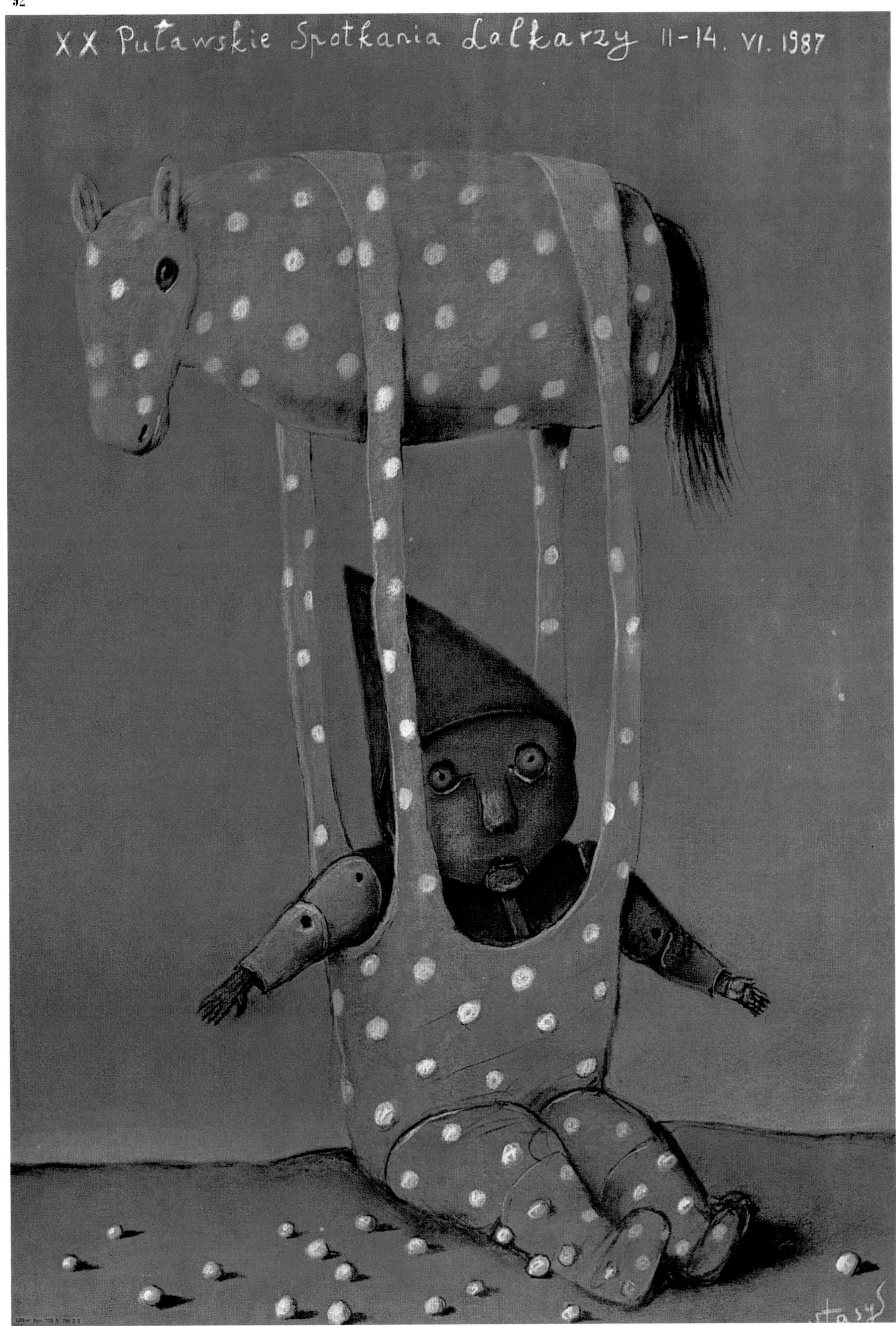

7 Poster for puppet show festival 人形劇フェスティバルポスター 1987

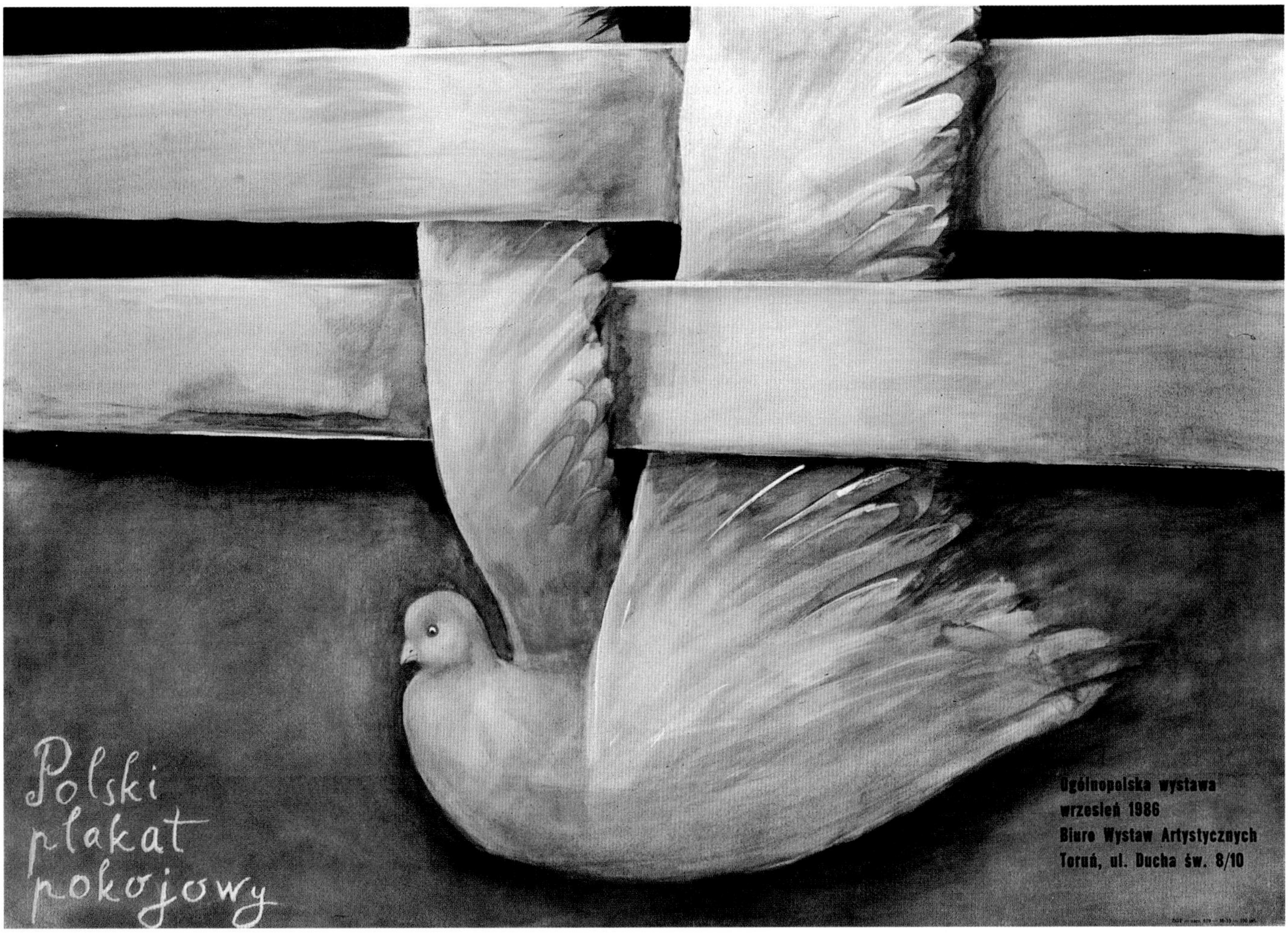

8 Peace poster 平和ポスター 1986

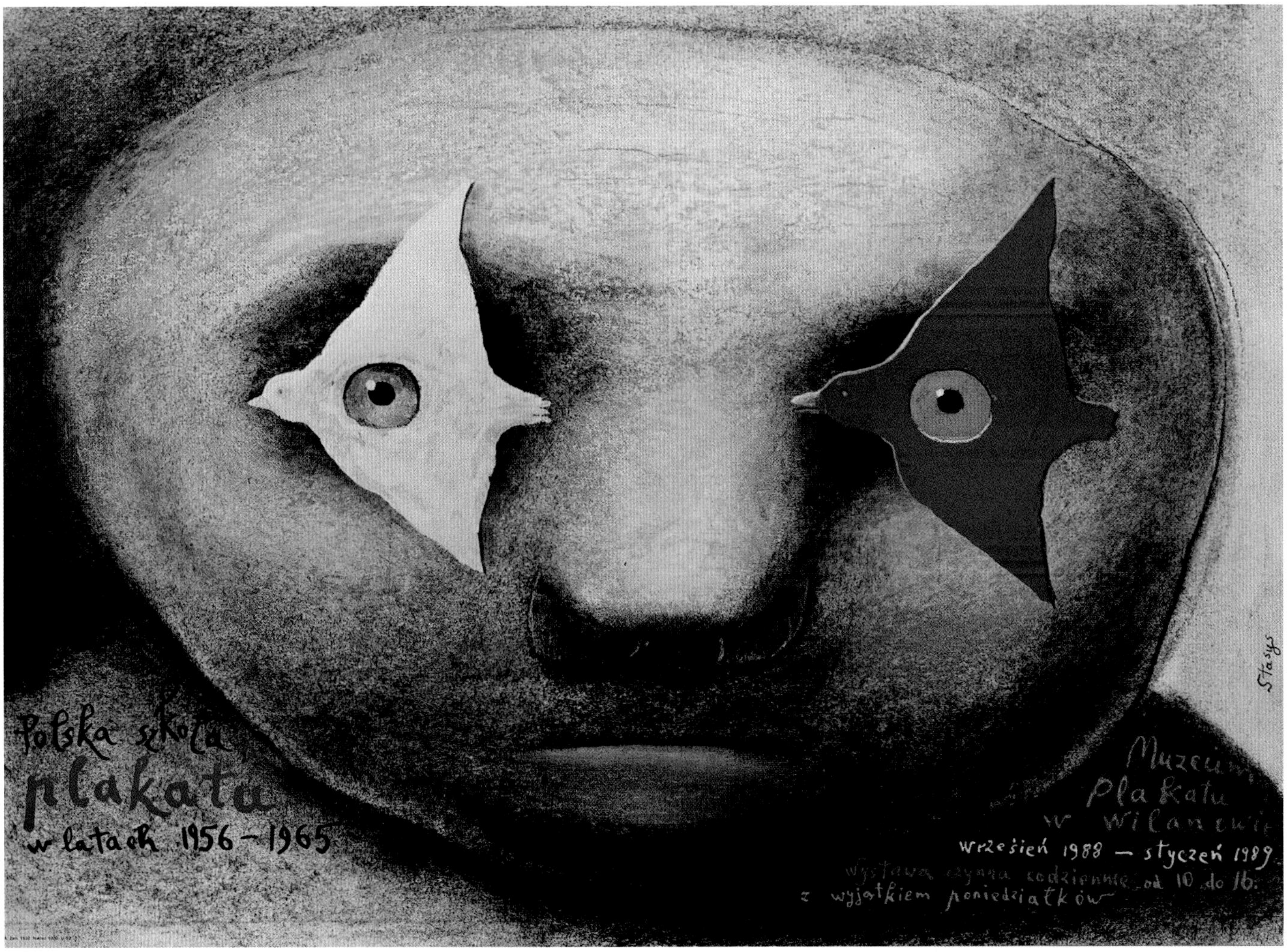

9 Poster for poster exhibition ポスター展のポスター 1988

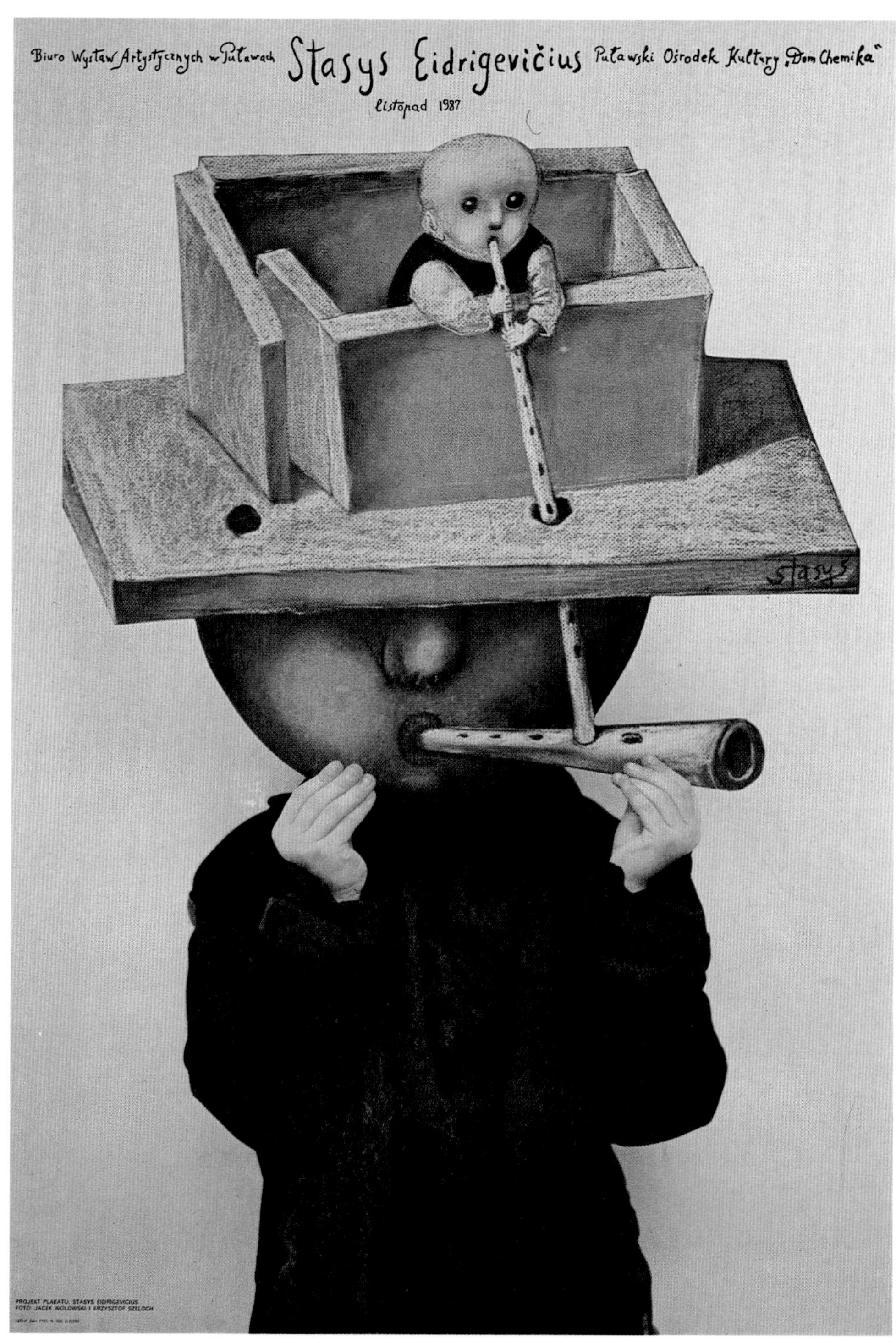

10 Exhibition poster 個展ポスター 1987

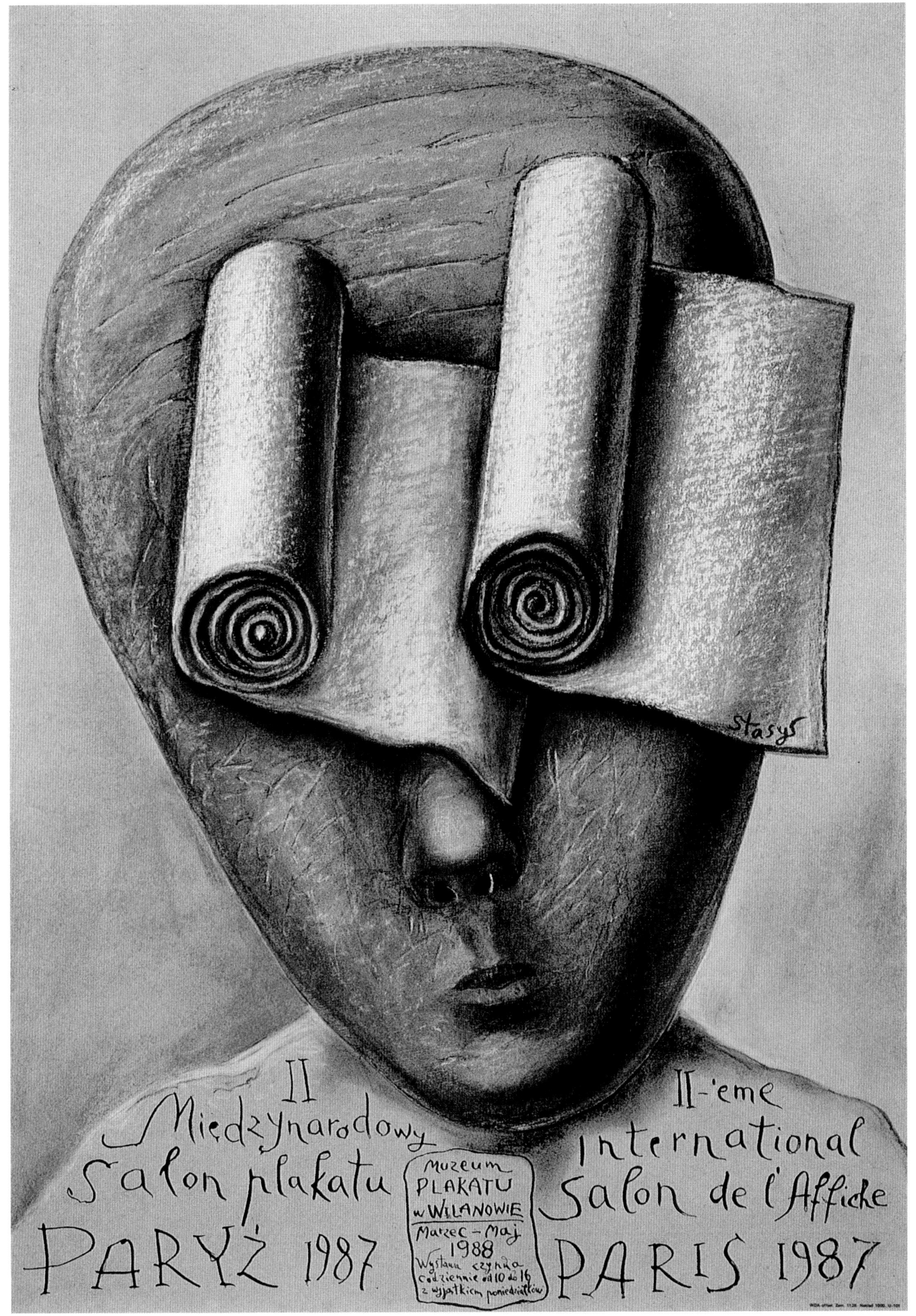

11 Poster for International Poster Salon in Paris パリ国際ポスターサロンポスター 1988

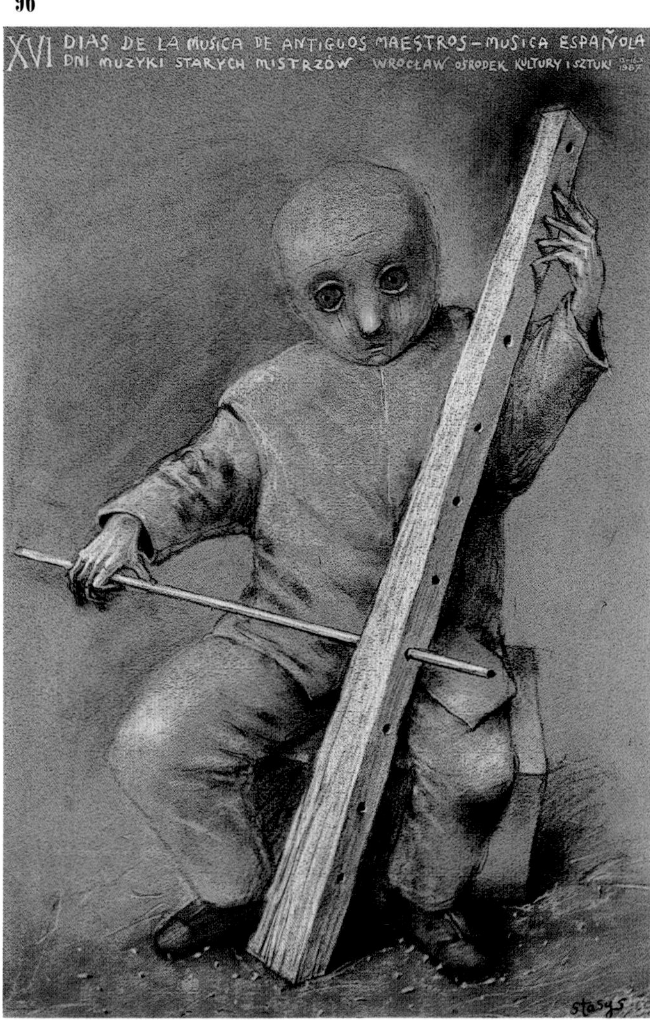

12 Concert poster 音楽会ポスター 1987

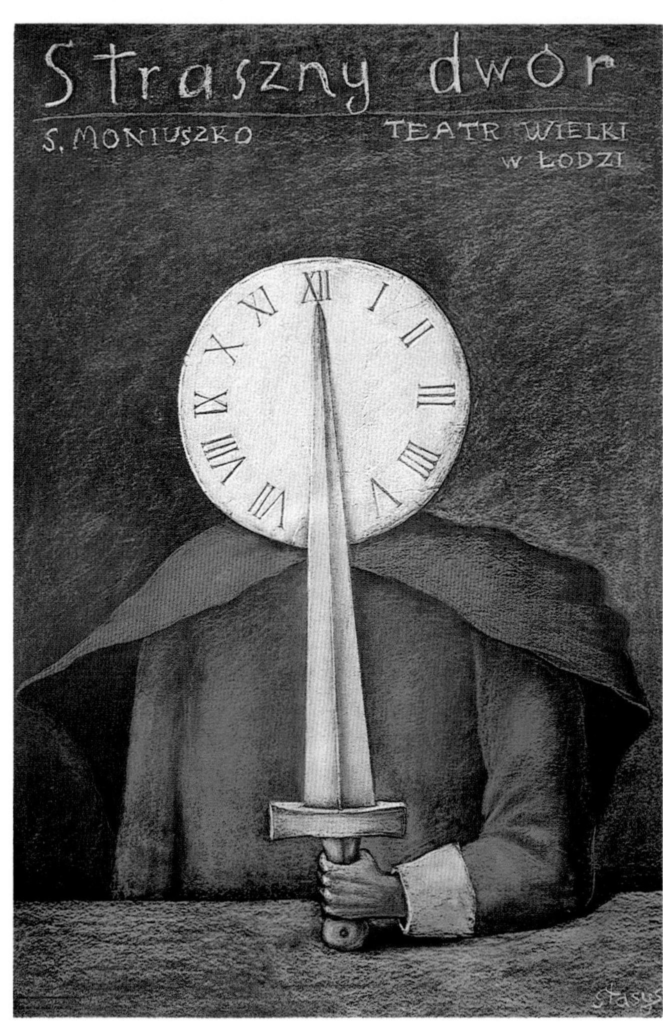

13 Poster for opera オペラポスター 1985

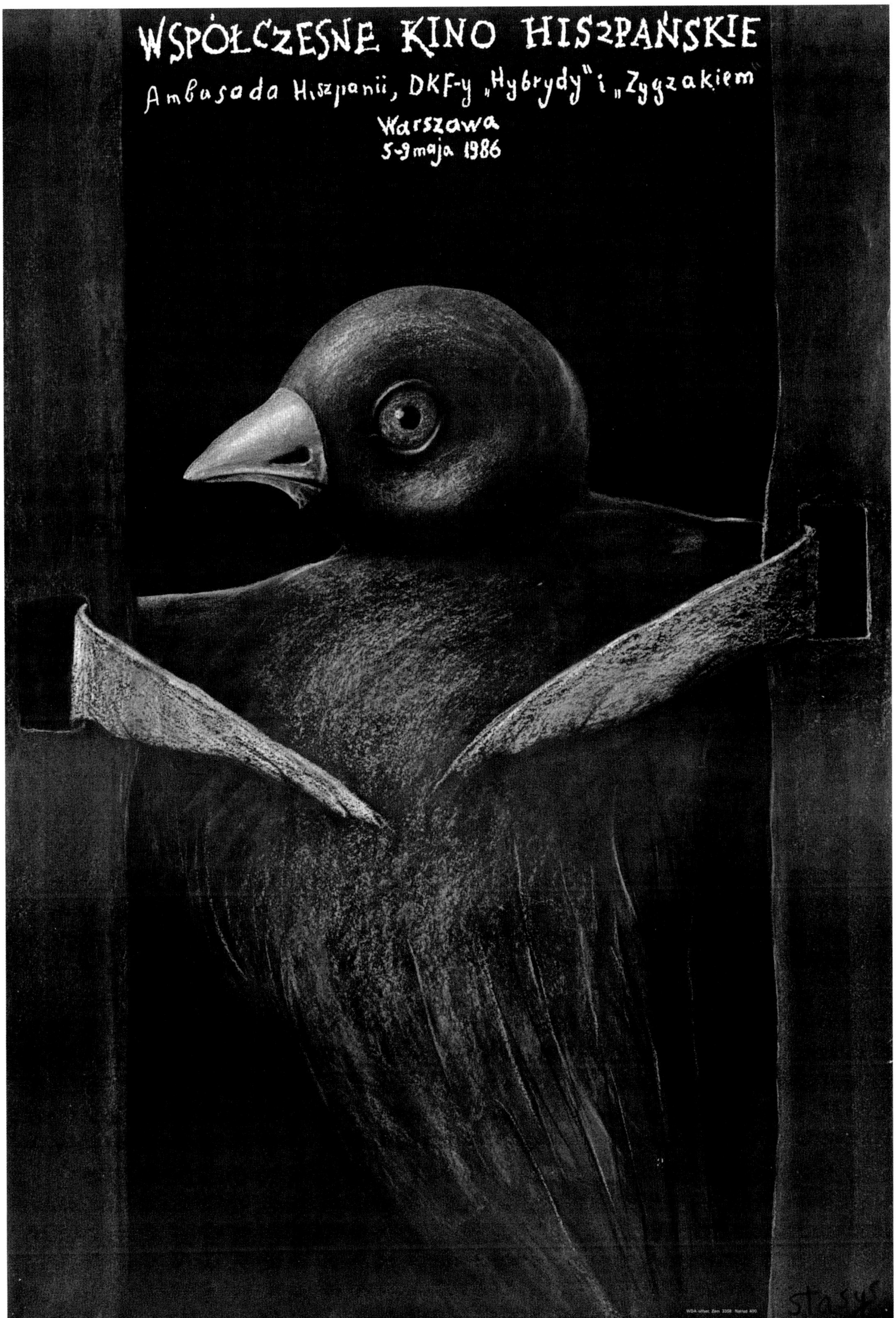

14 Poster for Spanish Movie Week スペイン映画週間ポスター 1986

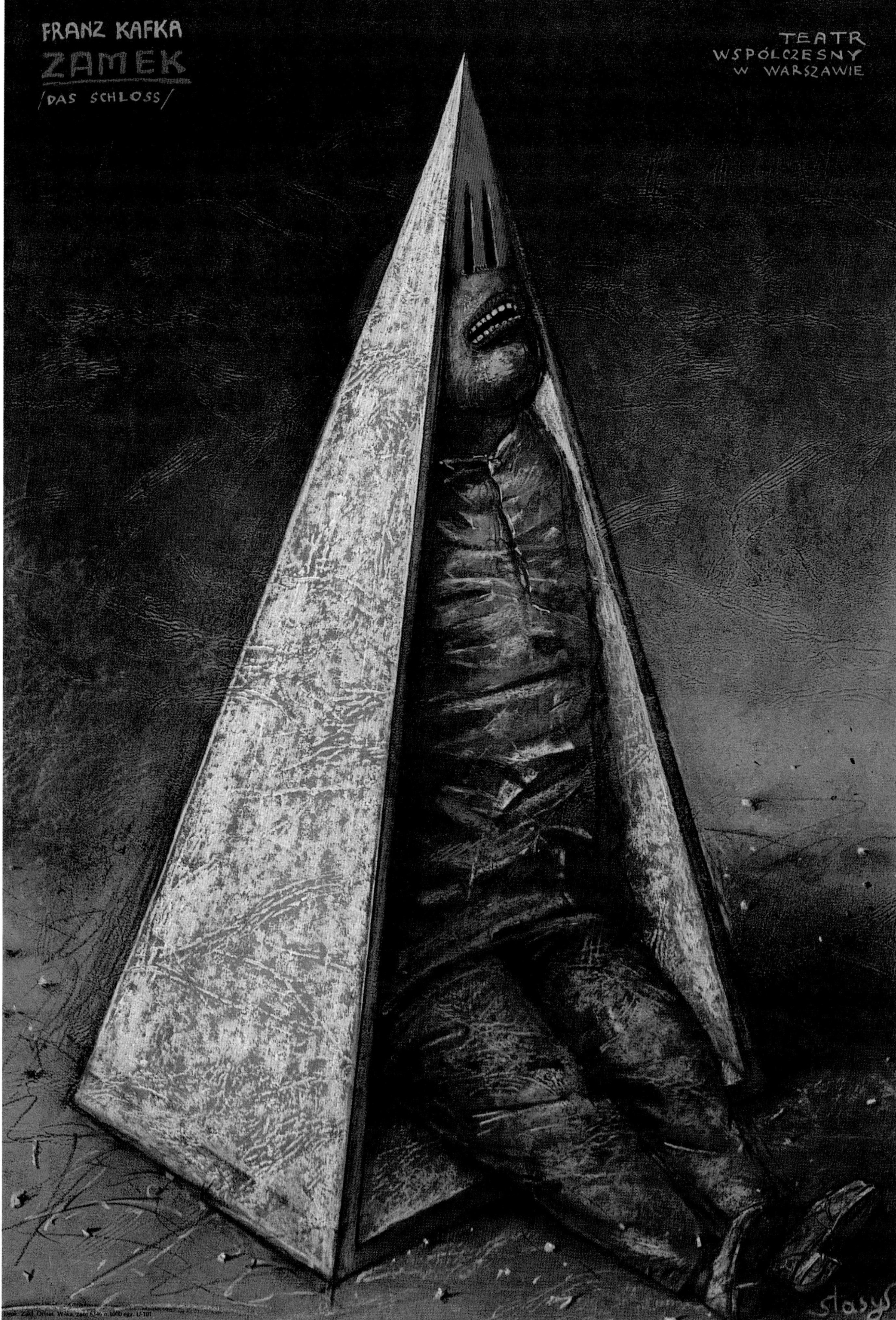

15 Poster for stageplay 演劇ポスター 1988

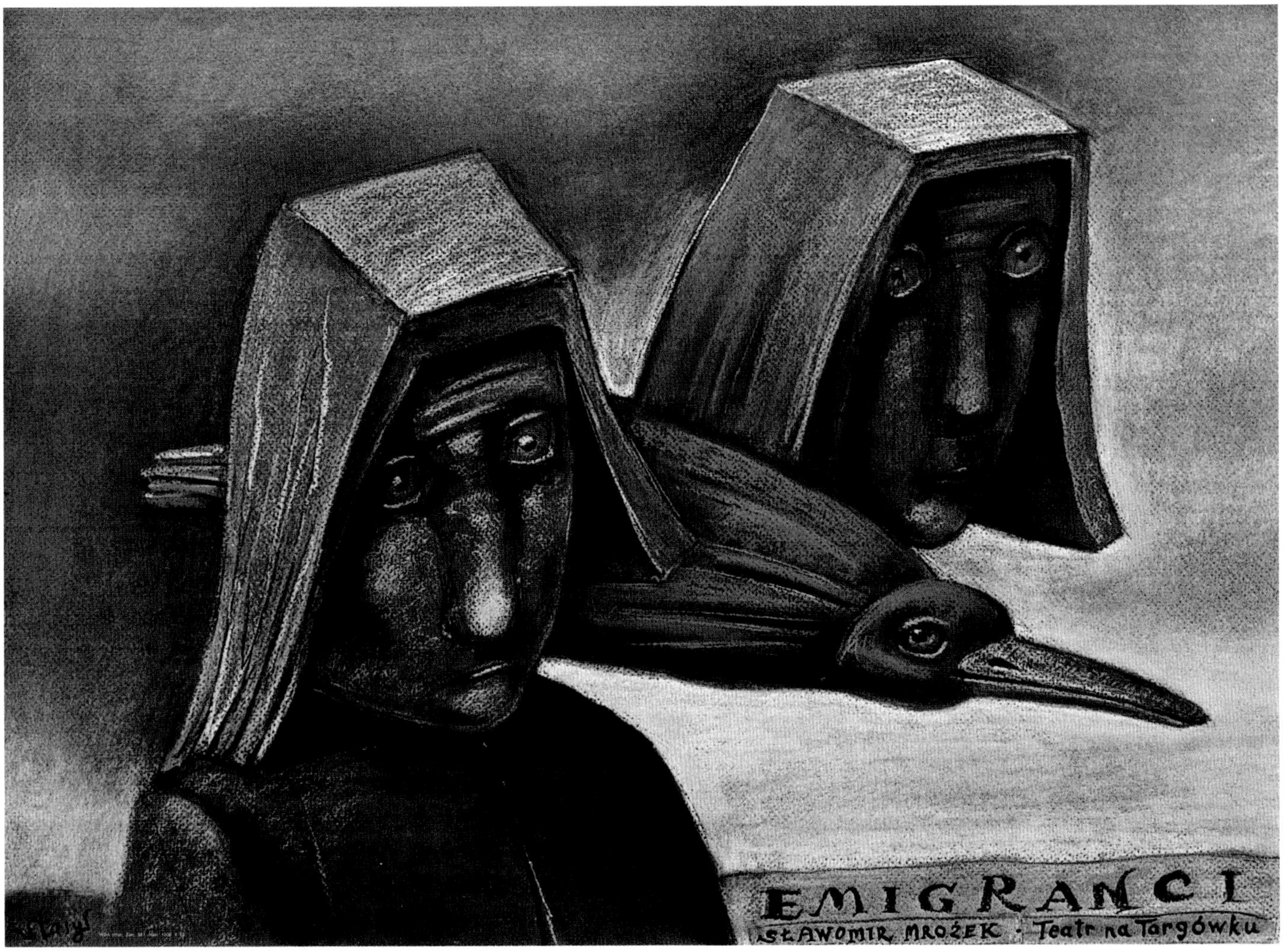

16 Poster for stageplay 演劇ポスター 1987

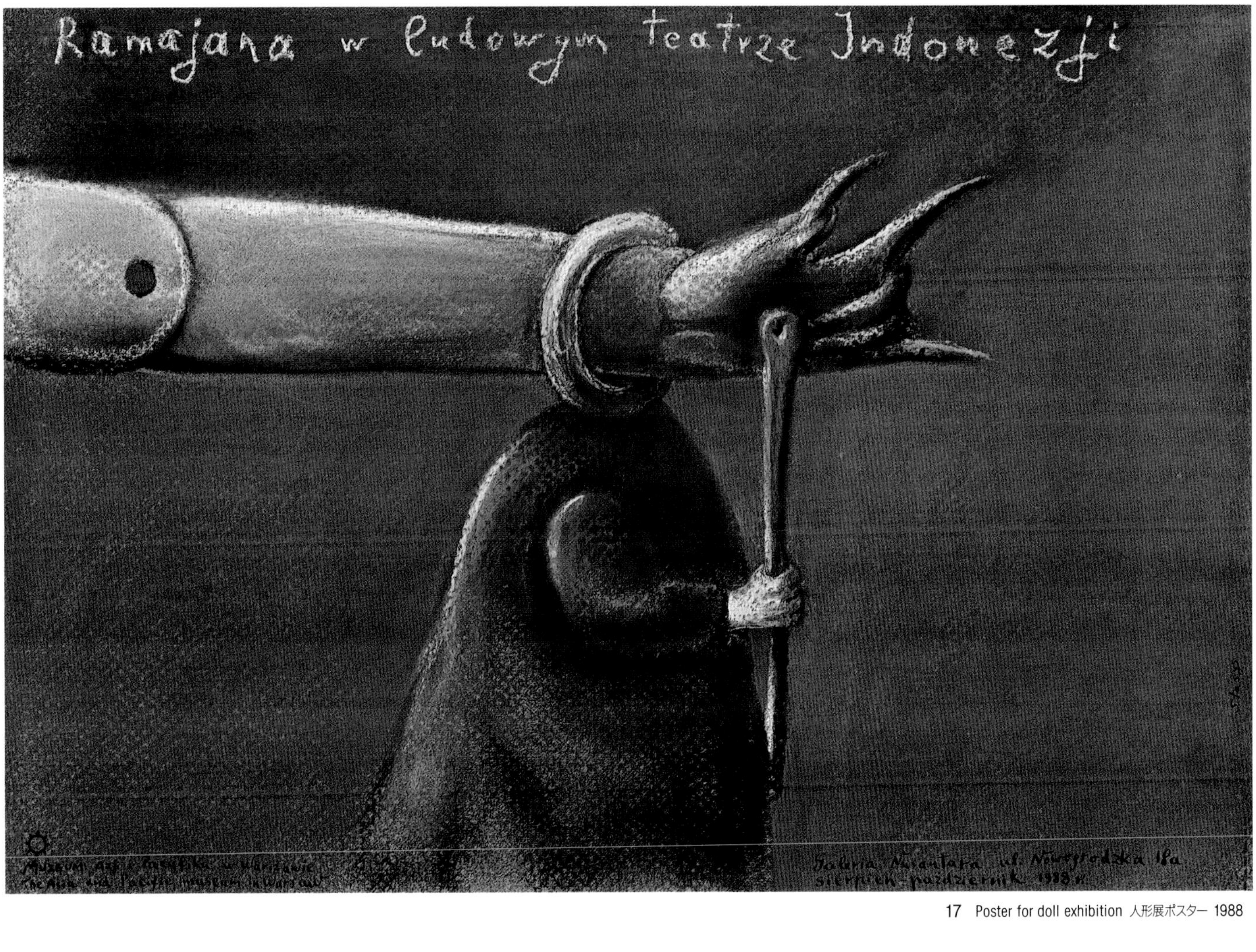

17 Poster for doll exhibition 人形展ポスター 1988

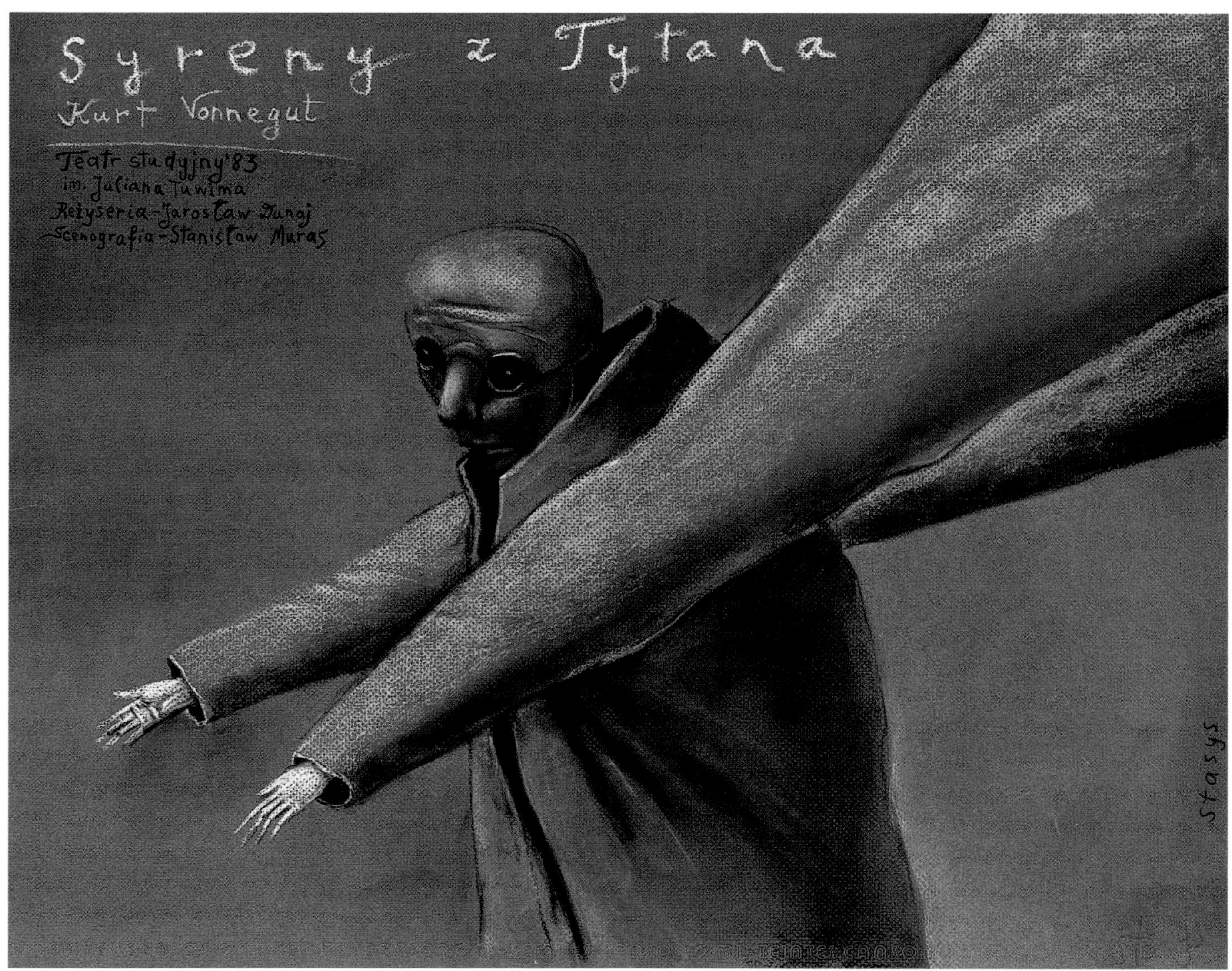

18 Poster for stageplay 演劇ポスター 1986

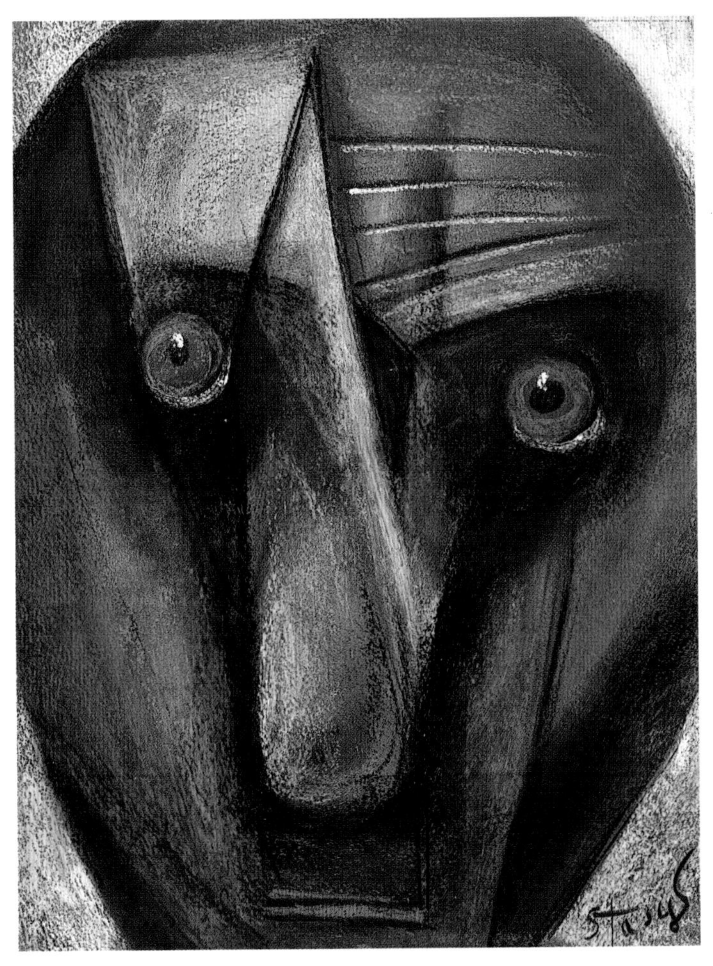

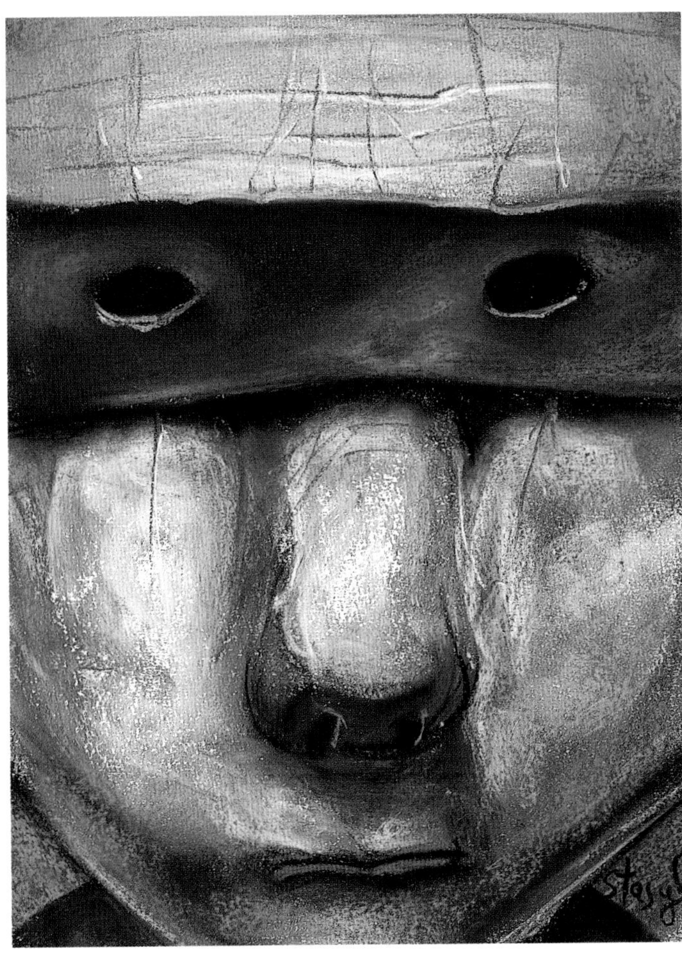

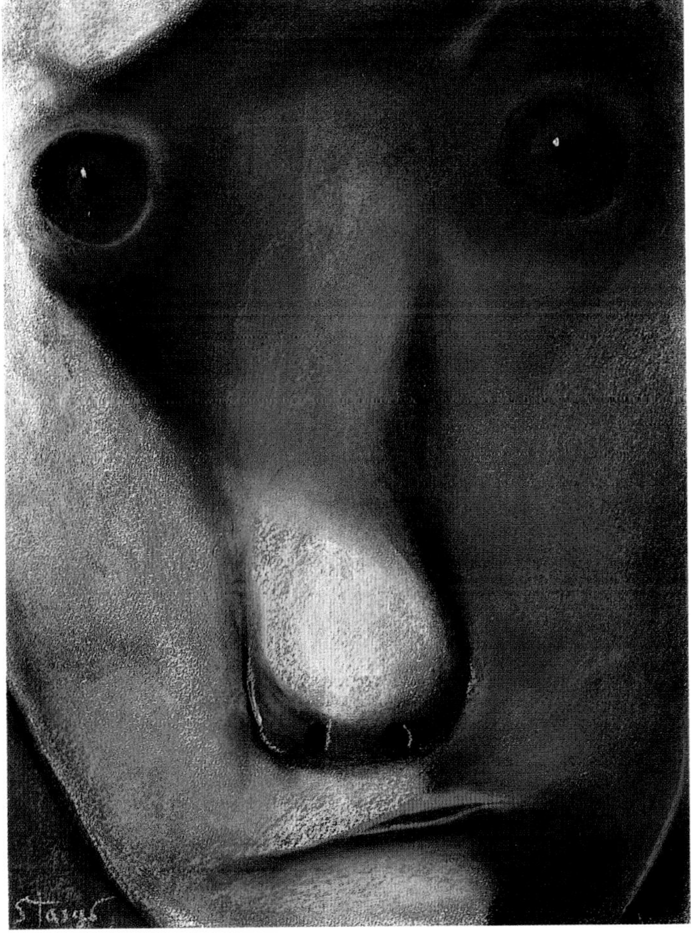

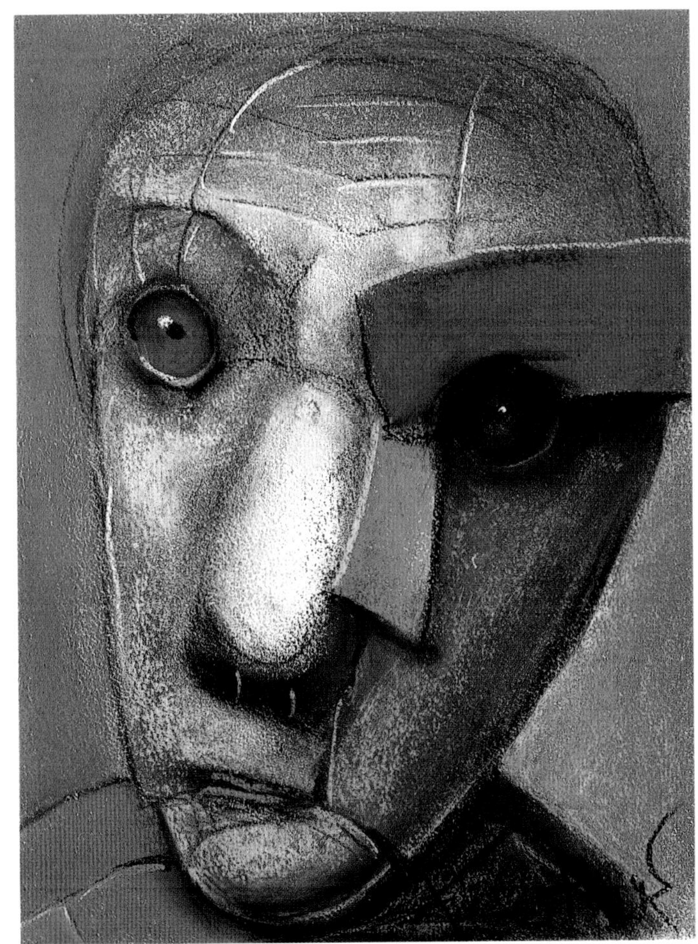

19-22 Faces 顔のイラストレーション 1988

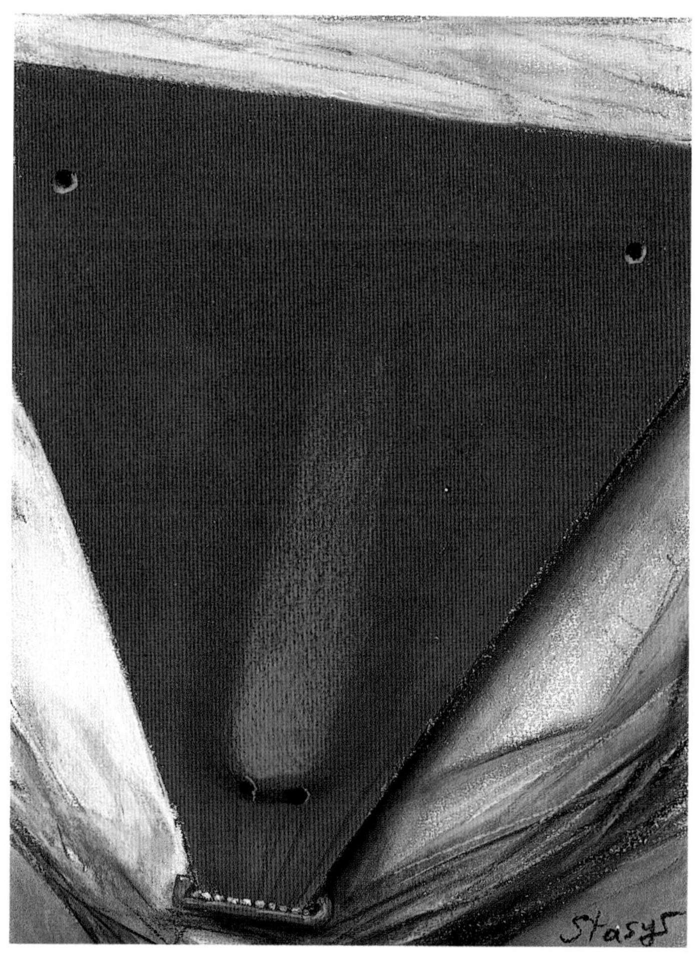

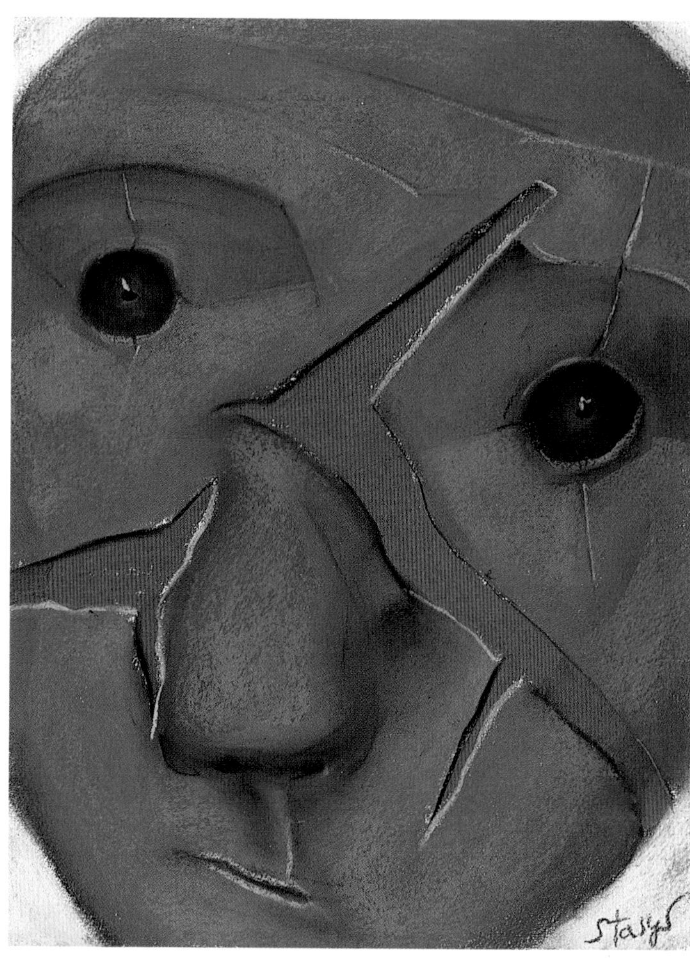

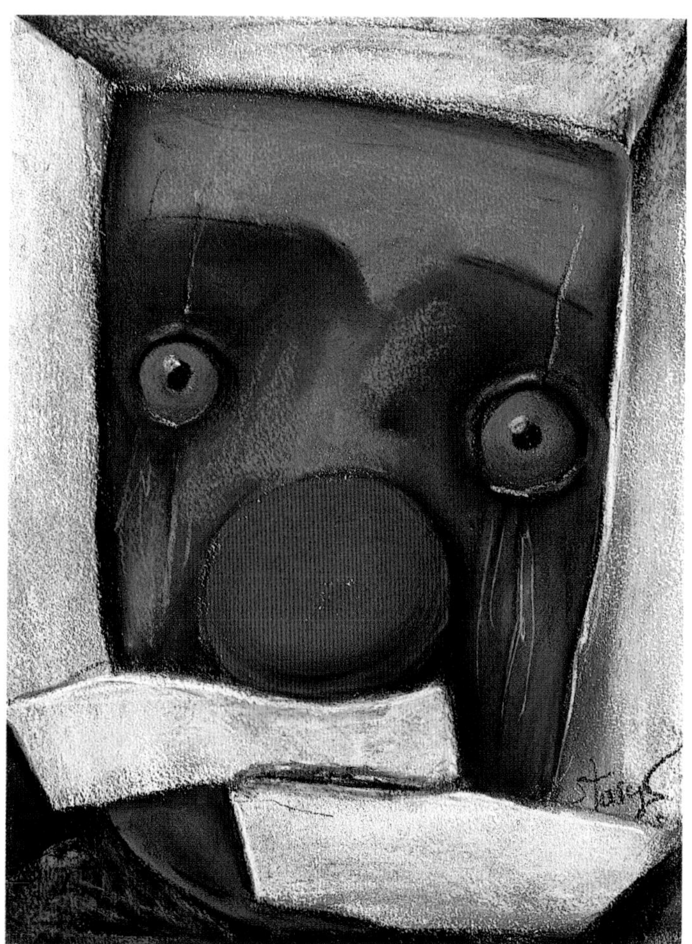

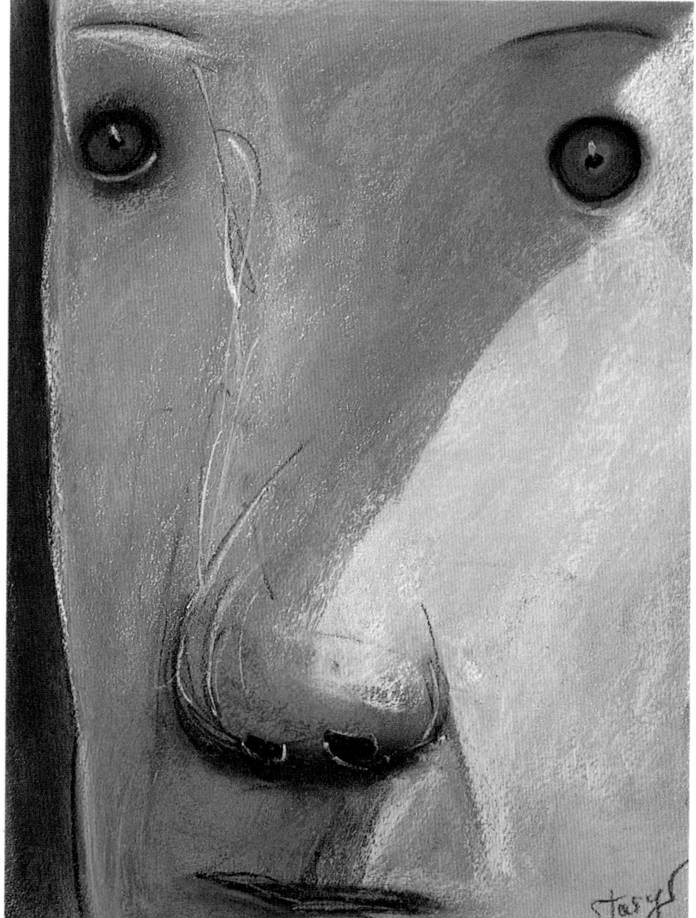

23-26 Faces 顔のイラストレーション 1988

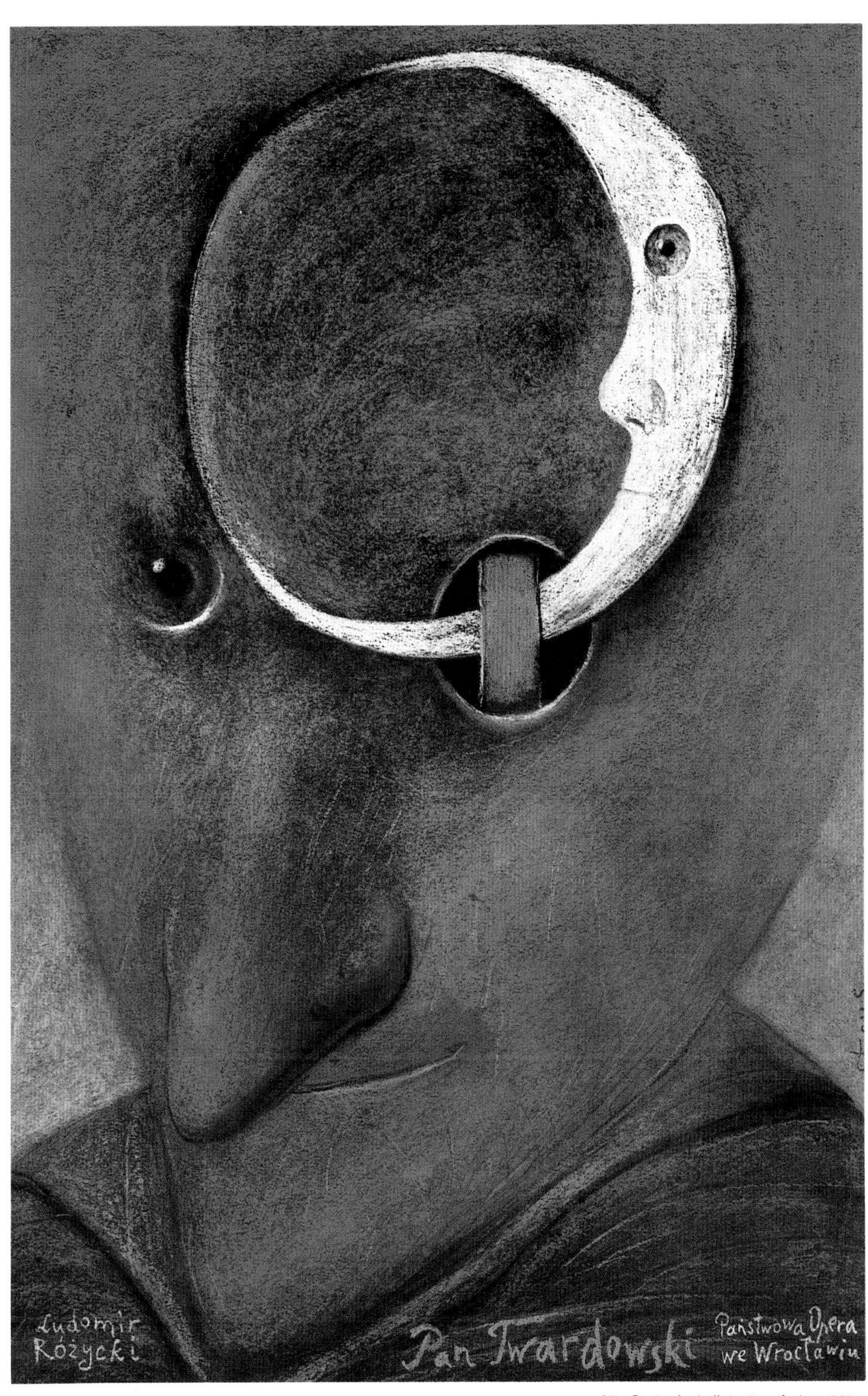

27 Poster for ballet バレエポスター 1987

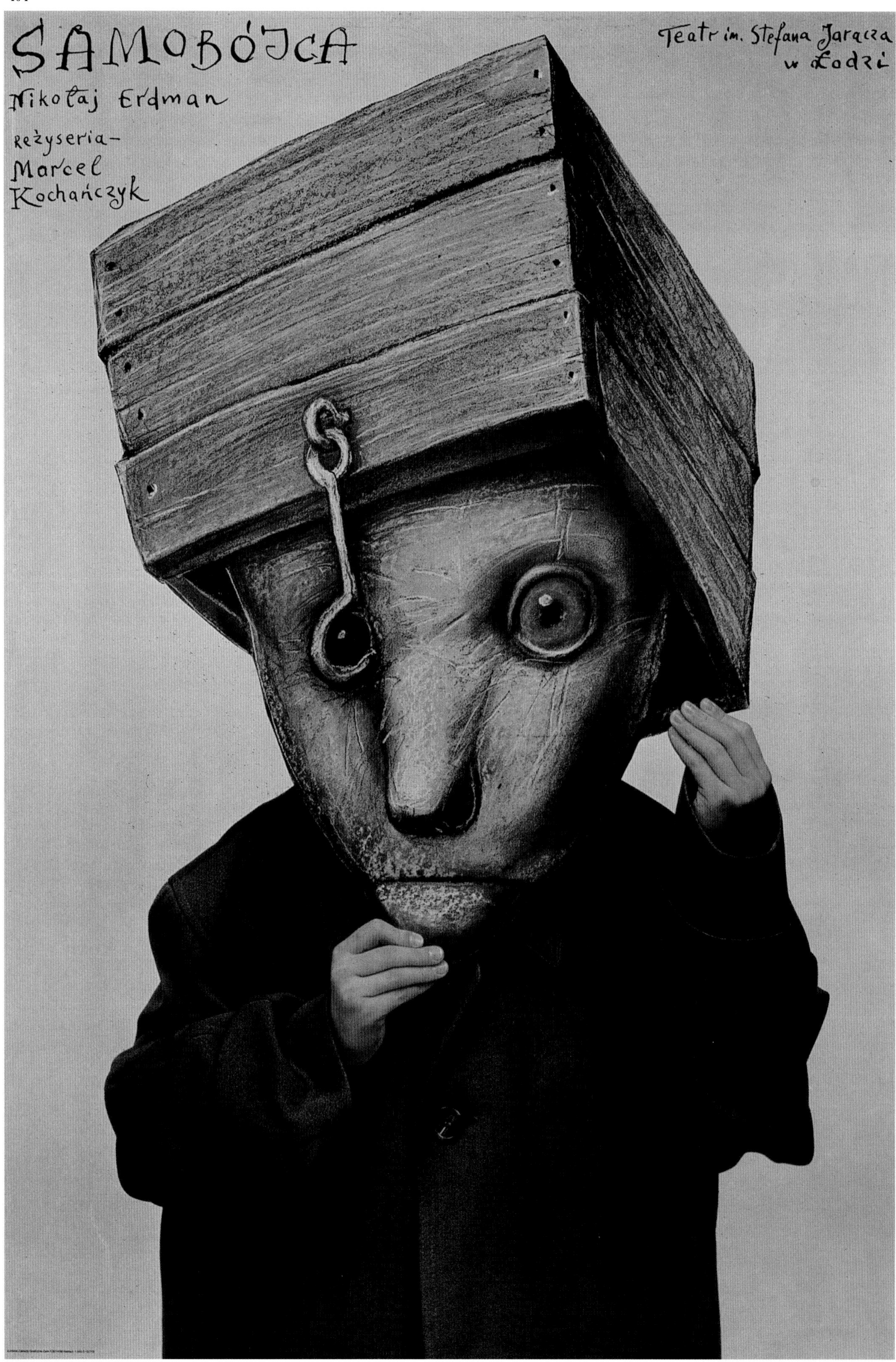

28 Poster for stageplay 演劇ポスター 1988

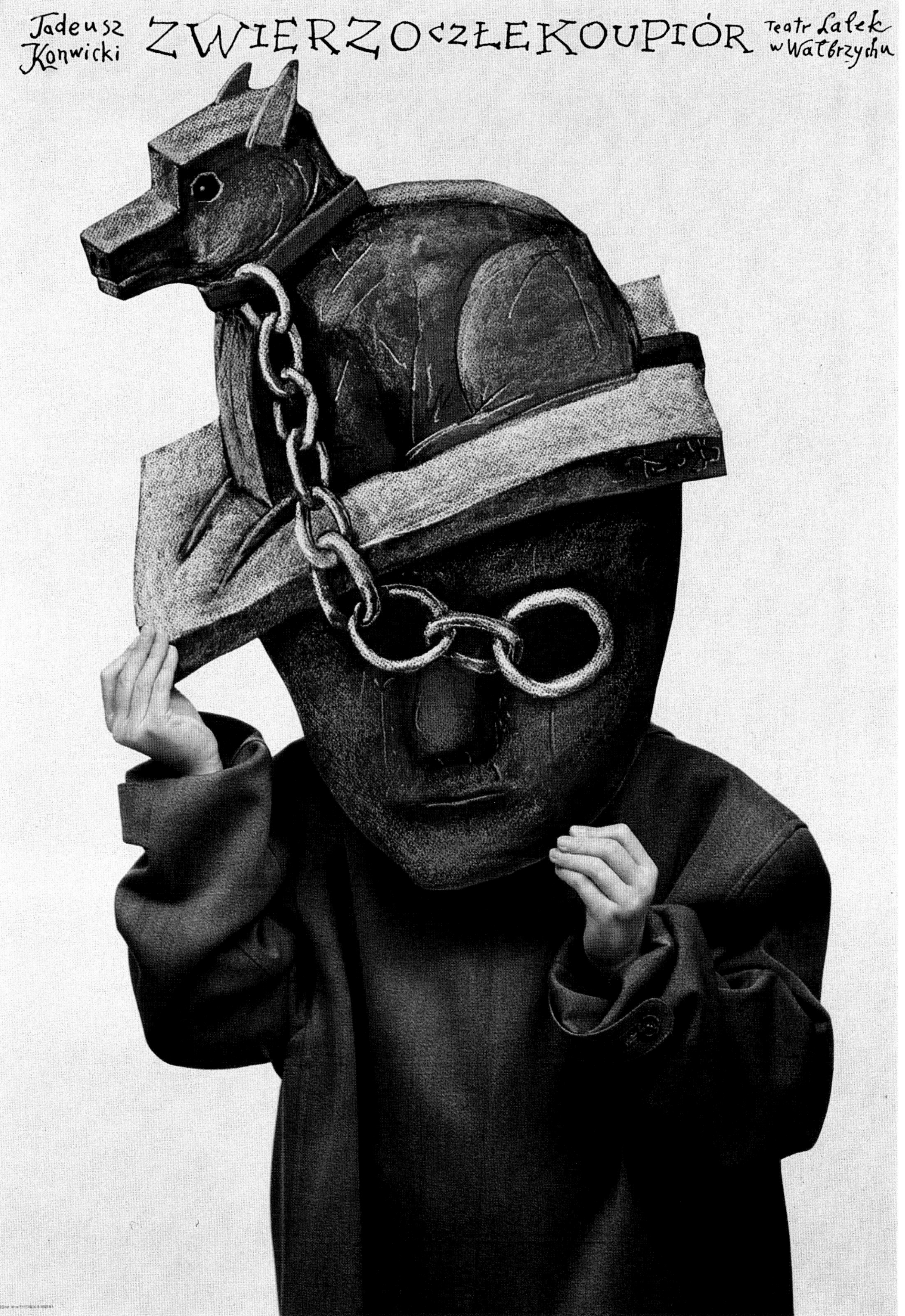

29 Poster for puppet show 人形劇ポスター 1988

YOSHIO HAYAKAWA 早川良雄

Koichi Sato 佐藤晃一

Now in his seventies, Yoshio Hayakawa is producing works of ever more dazzling delight. To visit one of his exhibitions is like setting foot inside a florist shop in spring. So vivid are Hayakawa's colors, they are almost erotic.

This notion is not mere fancy, actually. In Japanese, the word for "color," *iro*, is also used to connote "sex" or "eroticism." In the contemporary Western view, this dual significance may be interpreted as a sign of culture still in a stage of pre-differentiation. But in Japan, *iro*'s double-layered word value embodies a larger intuitive notion: namely, that sex is the manifestation of all life. Hayakawa's recent works reinforce this view.

Hayakawa is by no means alone in his sentient approach to creativity. In fact it is a trait commonly shared by many creative individuals, such as he, born in the greater Osaka region. When these artists come in contact with the intellectual ambience of Tokyo, their sensual world is intruded upon by a wedge of rationality. The result is a style of Japanese graphic design that is both fertile with imagination and tenacious in purpose.

When Hayakawa made his debut shortly after WWII, he was initially hailed as a precocious genius who embodied the fiercely avant-garde penchant of his contemporary Osaka. Then, after a fateful meeting with Yusaku Kamekura—the so-called "ruler-and-compass philosopher"—Hayakawa left Osaka and moved to Tokyo. From that time he transformed from the skilled freehand artist he had been to a full-fledged art director.

In his first series of one-man shows in Tokyo in those early days, Hayakawa explored the theme of "Shape." Employing spartan configurations of flat surfaces in unified geometric motifs, he sublimated his innate artistic sensibilities to the metaphysical level in a brilliant marriage of "color" as he had known in Osaka and "shape" as he had learned in Tokyo. At the time, it was believed that Hayakawa was finally emerging from his brushwork period and entering a larger world of mechanically inspired design.

These expectations aside, in his fourth "Shape" exhibition Hayakawa nonetheless abandoned the medium of the silk screen and reverted to expressing himself through freehand drawings. Moreover, from about the seventh show in the series he reduced the size of his studio and returned to working in solitude.

Wherein lies the significance of this turn of events? Hayakawa's turnabout might perhaps be viewed as a natural course for a man his age. And yet, I believe there is a greater reason for his creative about-face: his innate nature as an "artist."

To be a "designer" demands making decisions. By "decision" I refer here to the need to discard something personal—not to the romantic notion of abbreviating something for the sake of a specific design. For Hayakawa, making a leap to a mechanically ruled "designer" must have been quite painful. Hayakawa, I believe, is an "artist" rather than a "designer" not because he draws pictures but because he is a man who could not endure the agony of having to discard his artistic sensibilities for the sake of his profession.

Hayakawa's works are filled with a profound "gentleness," a sense of the "whole" with nothing lost. They have a universal appeal that touches every human heart deeply. For this reason, he is highly respected by the younger generation and eminently admired overseas.

70才を過ぎて早川良雄の仕事はますますその明るさを増している。個展の会場に足を踏み入れると、そこは春さきの花屋のようだ。色の中に色気が立ち上っている。

日本語の「いろ」という言葉には英語の"color"という意味と"sex"という2つの意味がある。これを西洋近代から見れば「未分化な文化」ということになるが「色は宇宙の命の現われだ」という総合的な直感がそこにはある。早川の近作はそのことを僕に思い起こさせるのである。どこまでも有機的で未文化だからこそ、僕たちはそこに花の香りを覚え、網膜は幸福のカシミヤに包まれたようになるのにちがいない。

ところで、このような情緒的傾向はひとり早川だけのものではない。関西出身のクリエーターに共通した資質であり、彼等が東京の知的な文化風土に出合うことによって、情緒的世界に合理のクサビが打ち込まれ、強靱で豊かな日本のグラフィックデザインが育ってきた事情はよく知られている。第2次大戦後間もない頃の大阪の、強烈な前衛性とモダニズムの風を一身に具現化したような、早熟の天才としてデビューした早川の場合は、定規とコンパスの哲人・亀倉雄策と運命的に出会い、上京する。そしてそれまでの手描きの達人とは異質なアートディレクターの仕事も多く手がけ、その事務所からは沢山のすぐれた後進を輩出させている。当時の東京での個展シリーズ『形状』では、単一な幾可形態をモチーフにしたベタ面の禁欲的な構成を示し、天分の感性を形而上学的なレベルにまで昇華させている。「東のカタチ」と「西のイロ」の見事な結婚の実例である。いよいよ早川は肉筆の甘い沼を出て、さらに大きなデザインのメカニズムの世界へと進んでゆくように思われた。

ところが『形状』の4回目からはシルクスクリーンをやめ、手描きの表現にもどってしまった。また7回目の頃にはスタジオも縮小し、ひとりの作家として元の自分自身に帰ってしまったのである。

これらのストーリーは何を意味しているのだろう。印刷による展覧会も、高齢での事務所管理も容易なことではない。だからこれは当然のなりゆきとも言える。だが早川の場合、それ以外の重大な理由が潜んでいるように僕は思う。それは早川が本質的に「芸術家」だったということである。

デザインには決断が要る。決断とは、何かを切り捨てることだ。それは作画上の省略といったロマンチックなものではない。そして早川にとってはその飛躍はおそらく痛みであったと察せられるのだ。僕が「芸術家」と呼ぶのは「絵かき」という意味ではなく、その痛みに耐えきれない人、という意味である。

そのかわり早川の仕事には深々とした「やさしさ」があり、「全体」が具わっている。若い世代からも敬愛され、海外からの評価も高いということは、とりもなおさず人間の心に染みる普遍性を宿しているということに他なるまい。

それゆえであろう、早川の女性にはどこか母のイメージがある。造形の奥底にあたたかい母親のような匂いが立ちこめているからだ。時代のトレンドから少し身を引いたところで、この母親はいつまでも若く美しい。そして僕たちデザインの子供から見れば、早川の大きく豊かな存在こそが、自分たちのデザインの母親のような気がするのである。

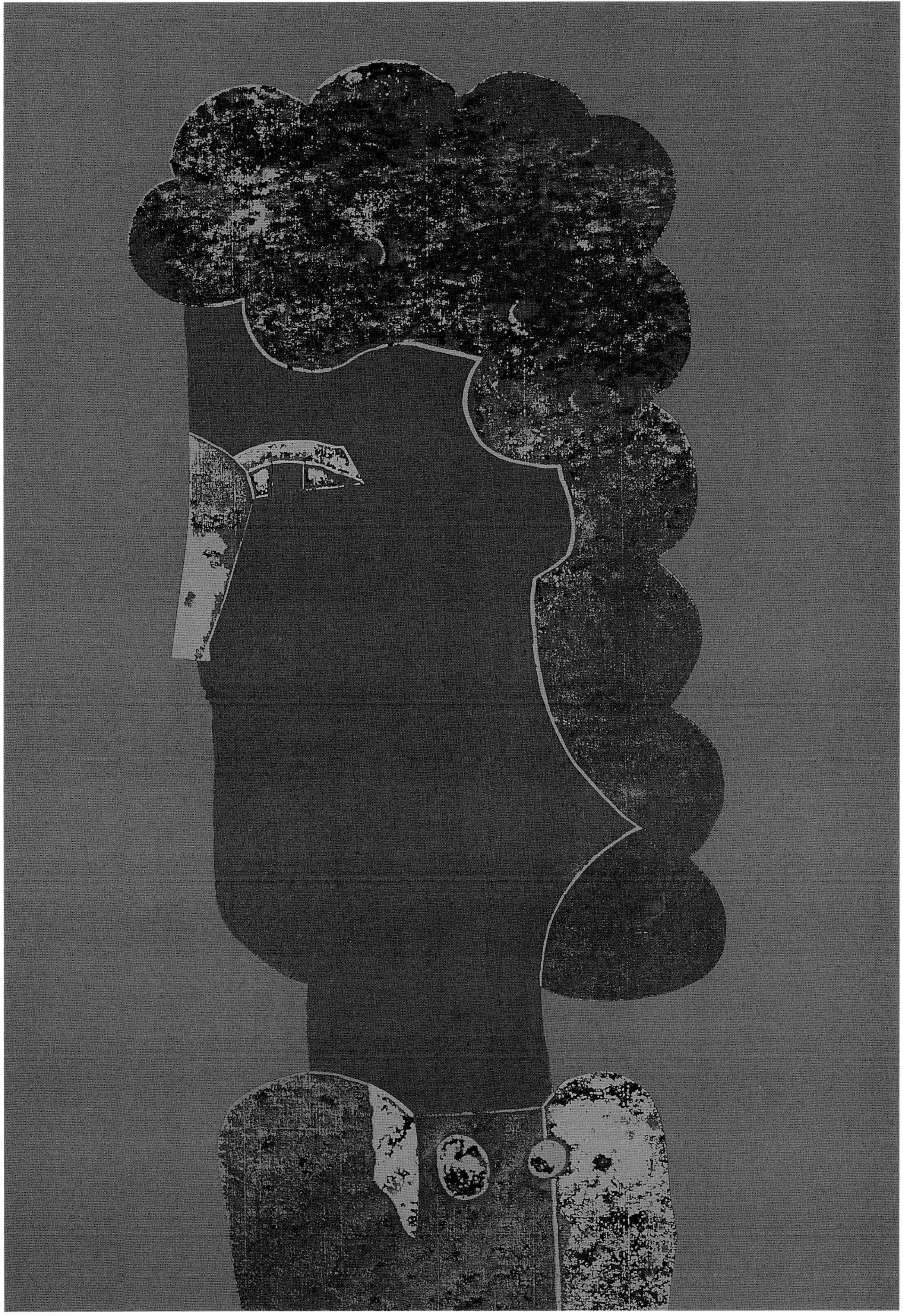

1968

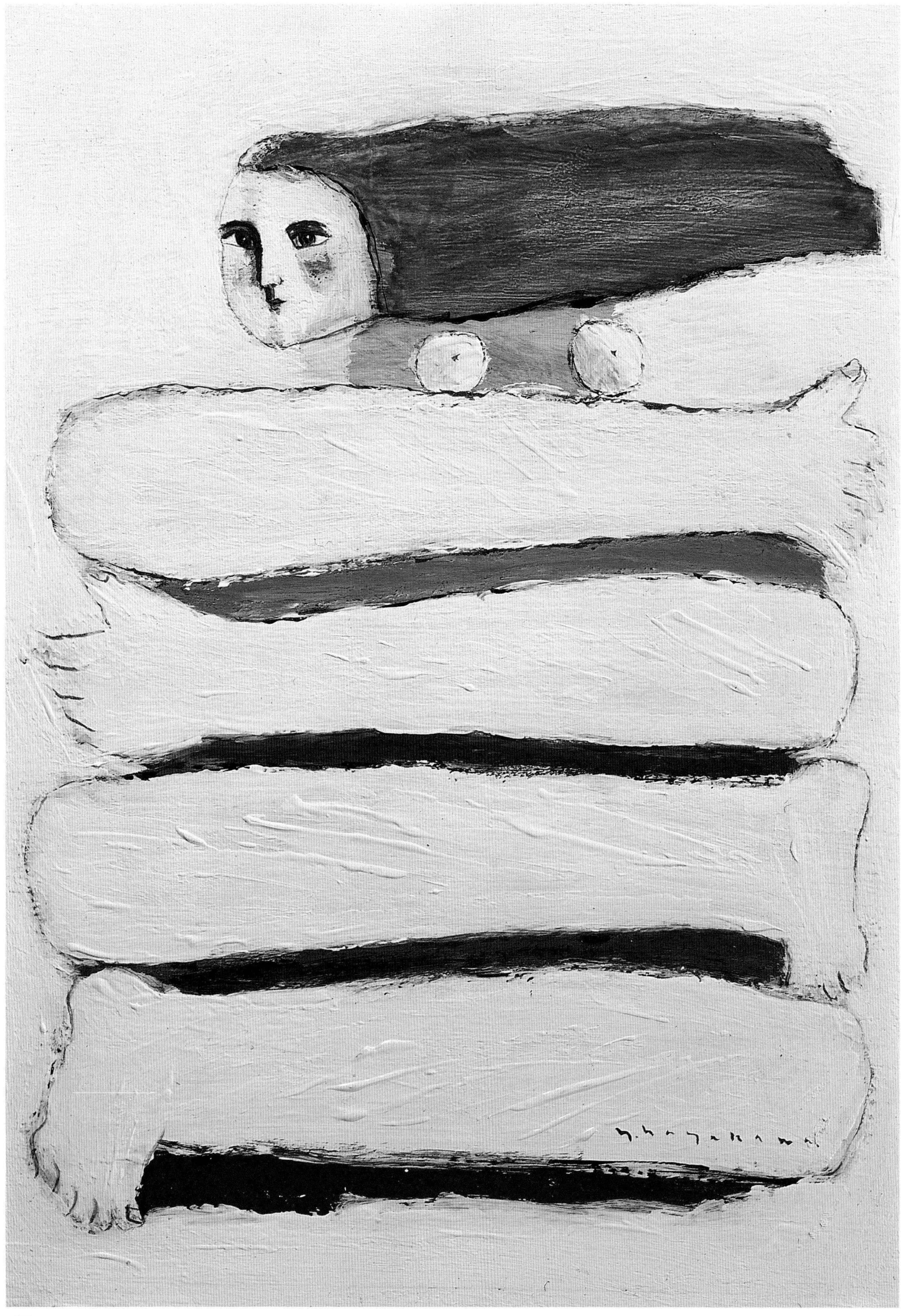

1973

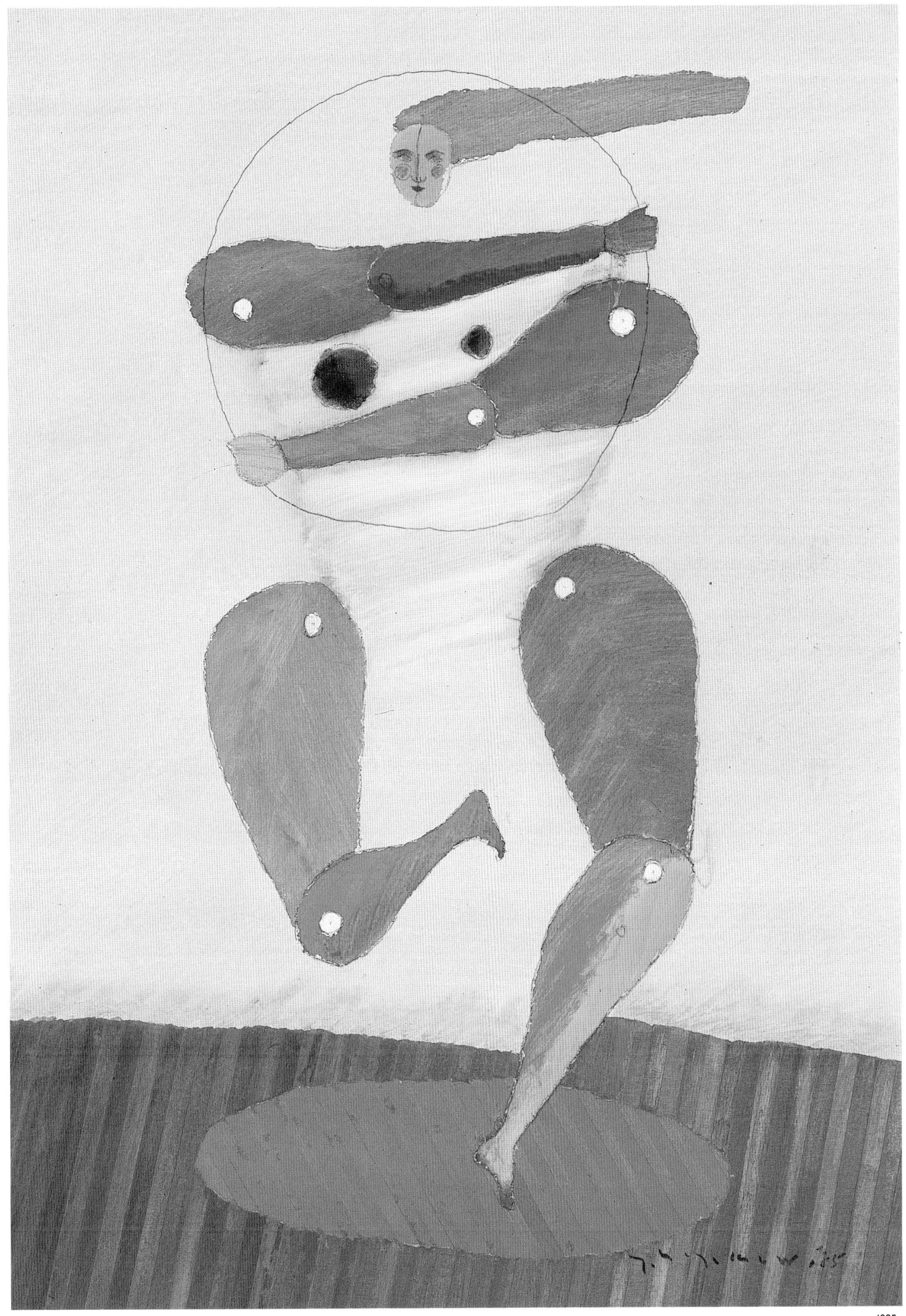

1985

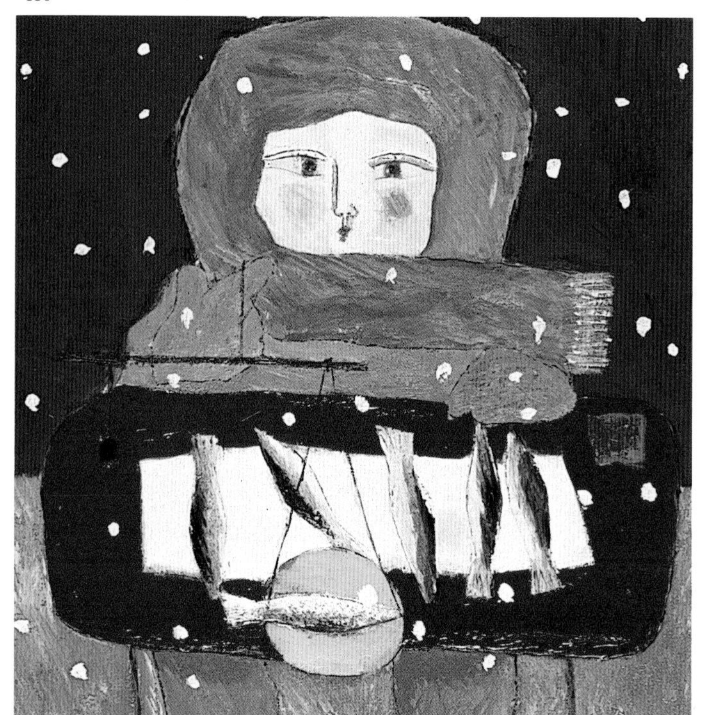

1971

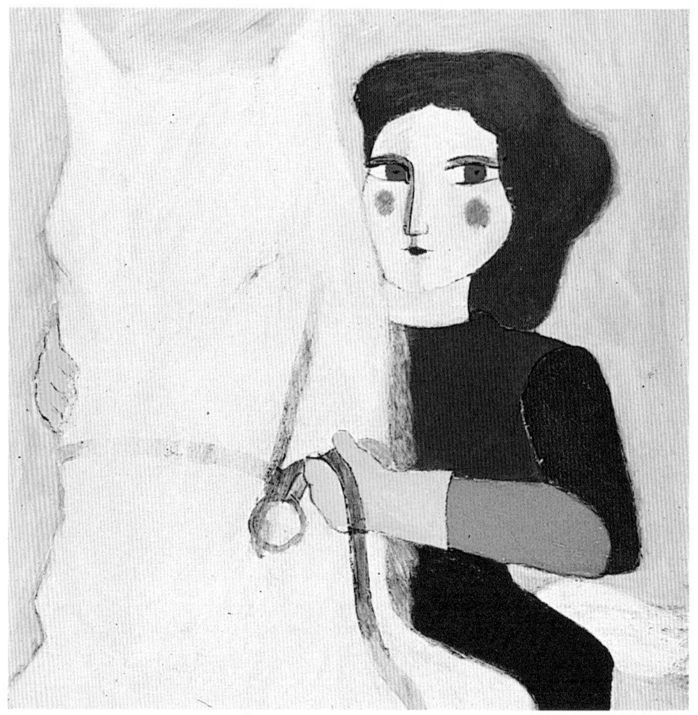

1972

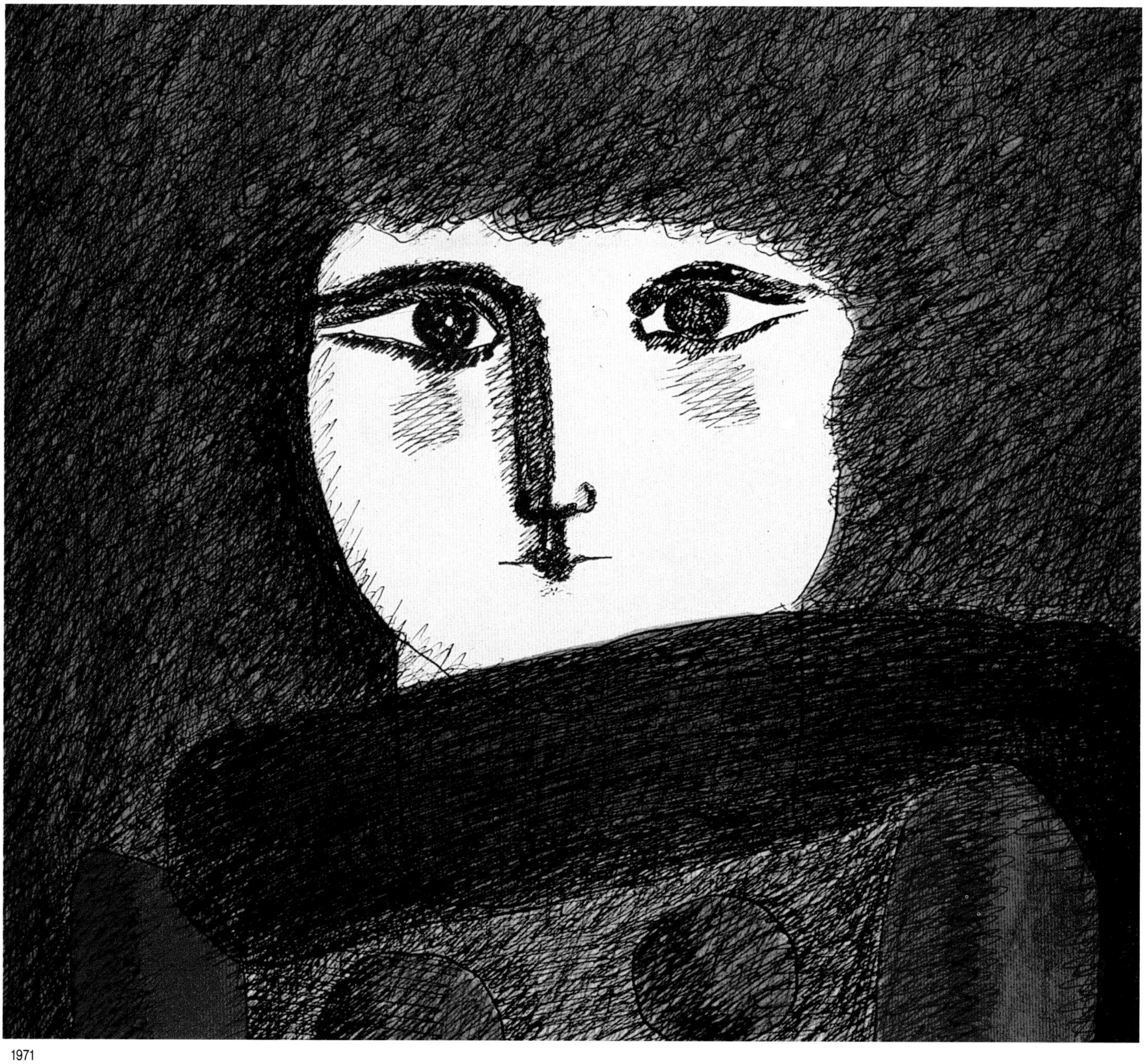

1971

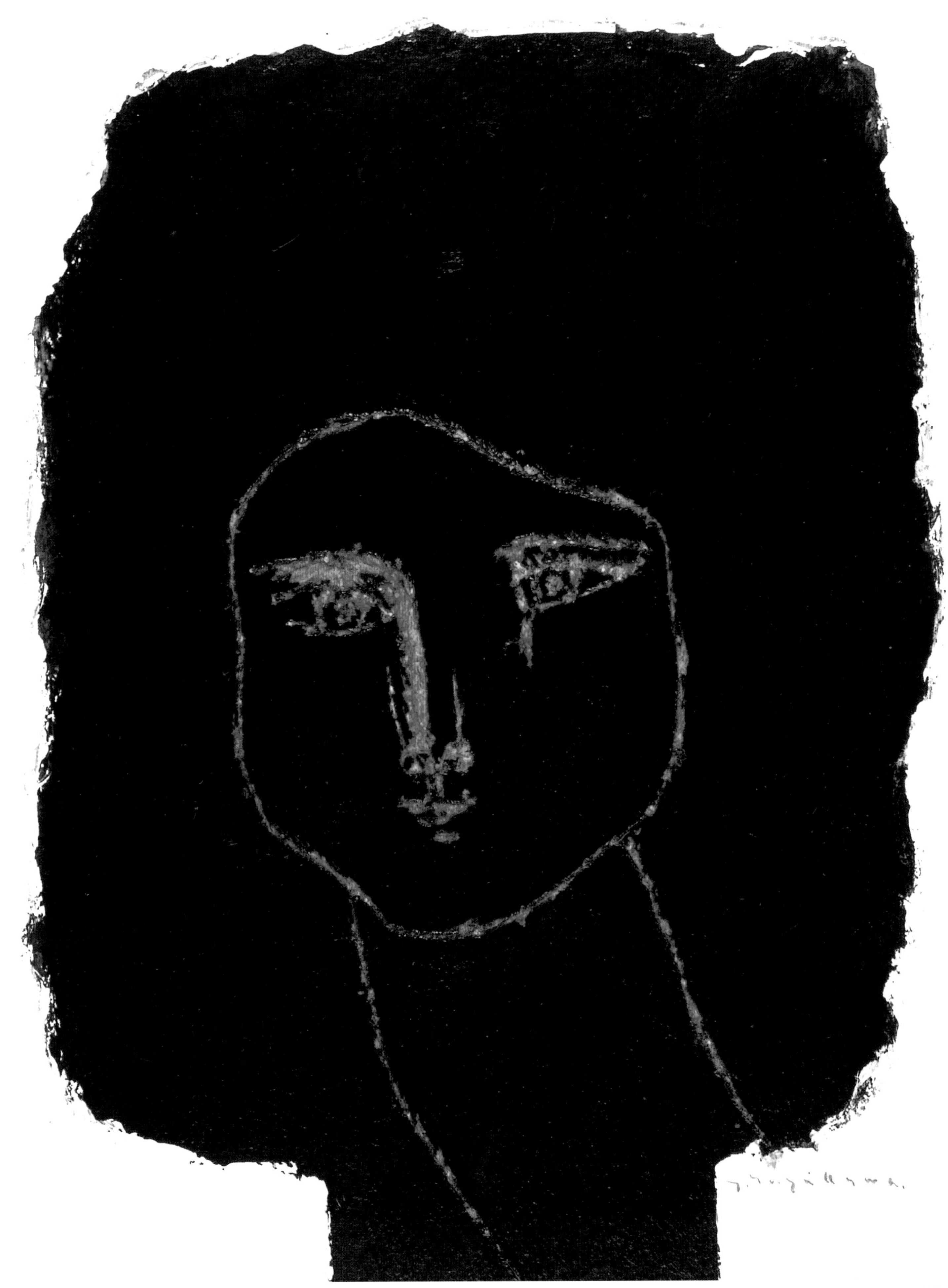

1975

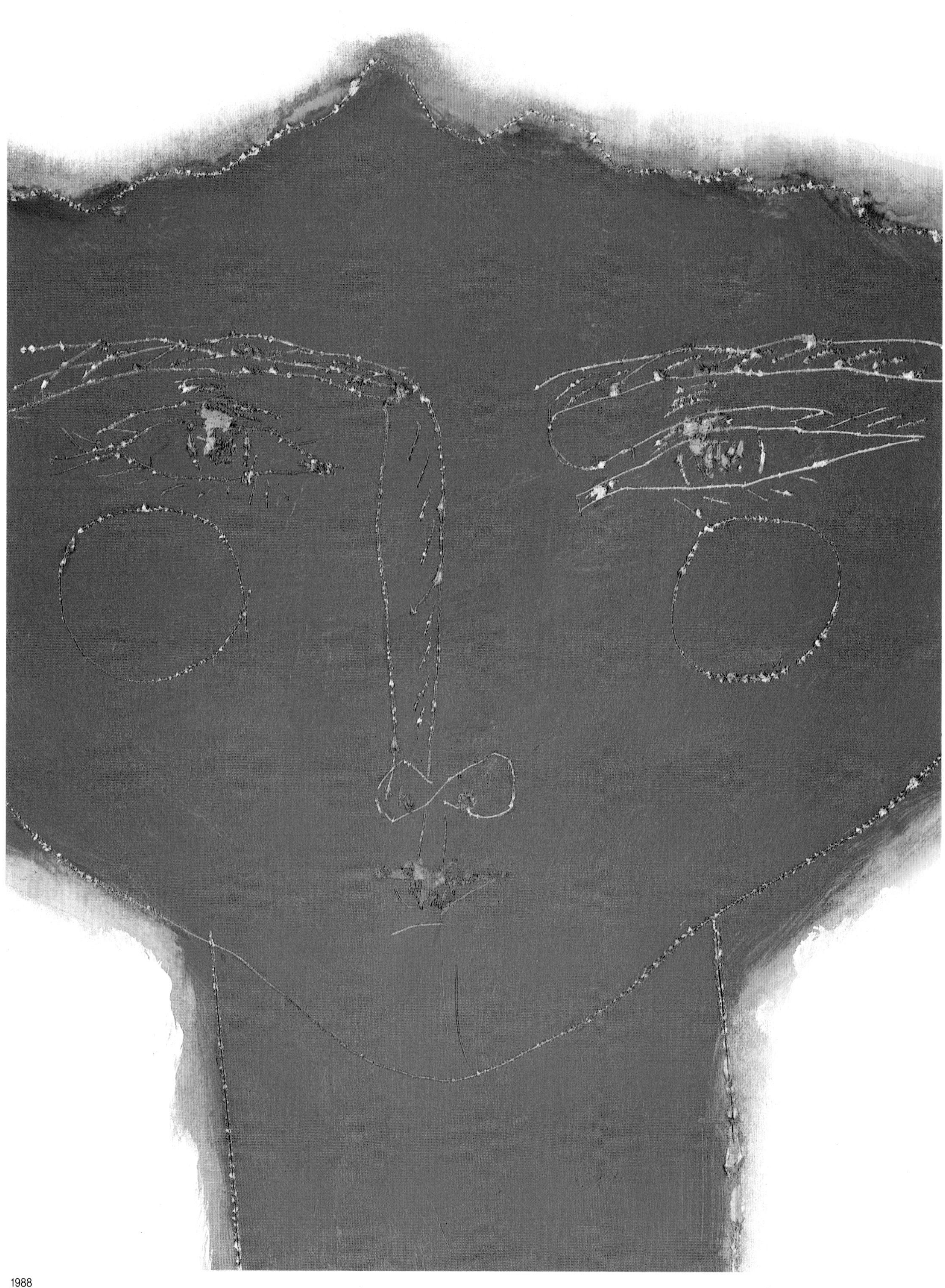

1988

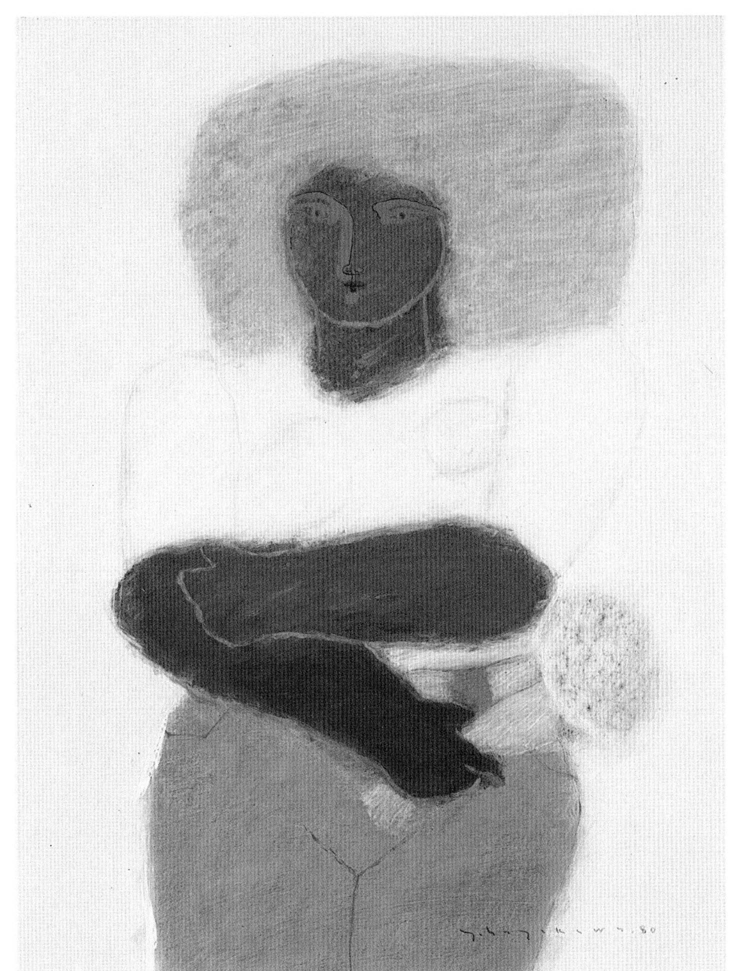

1980

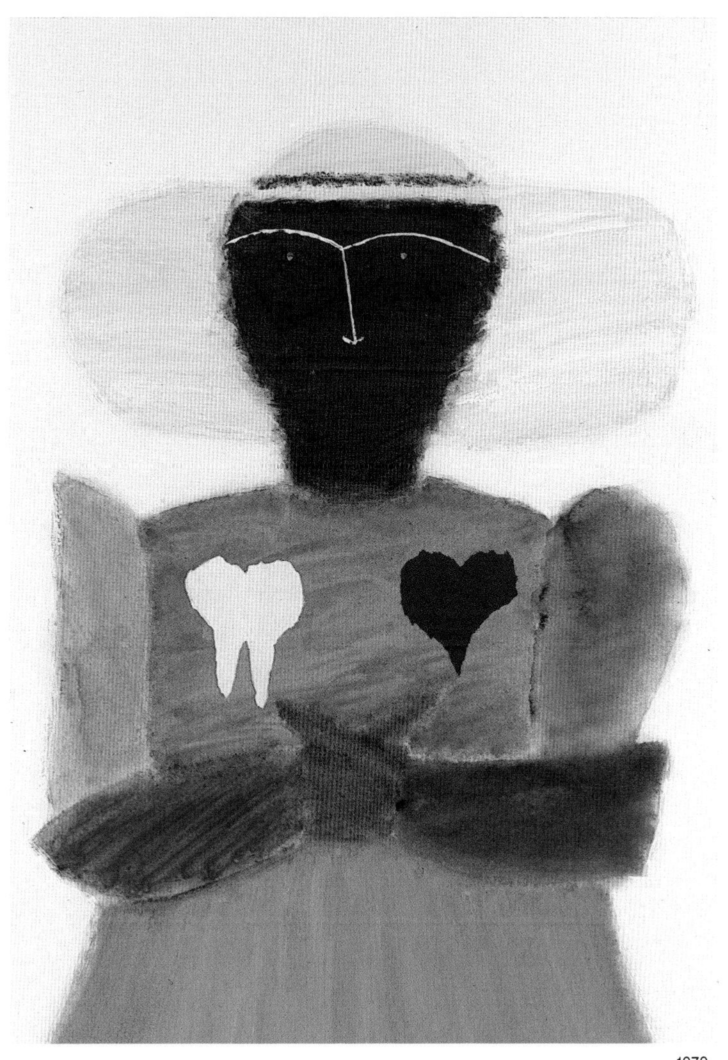

1979

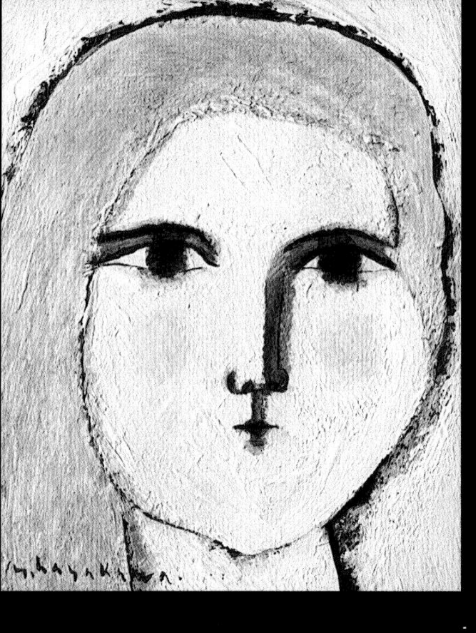
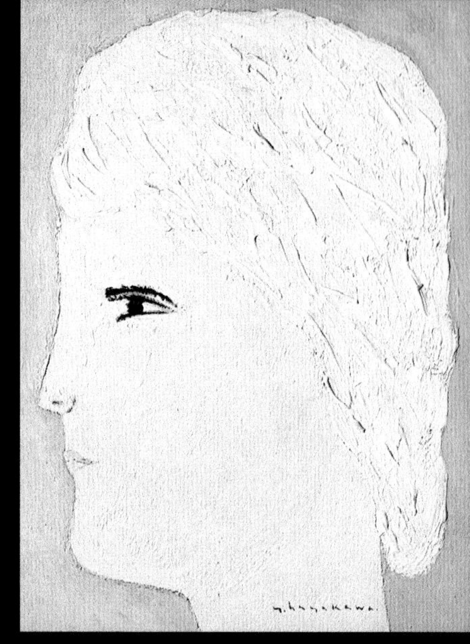
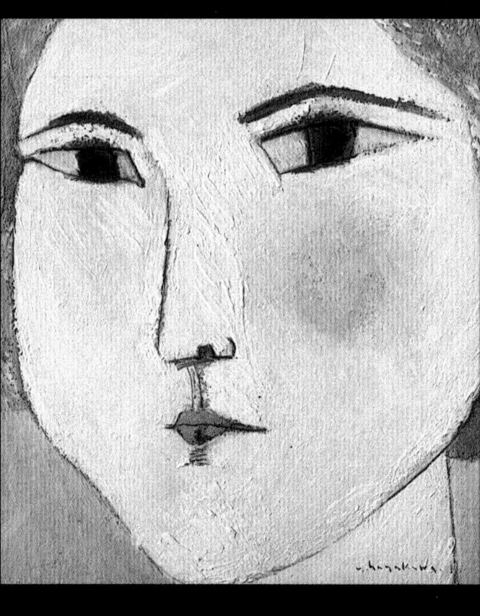
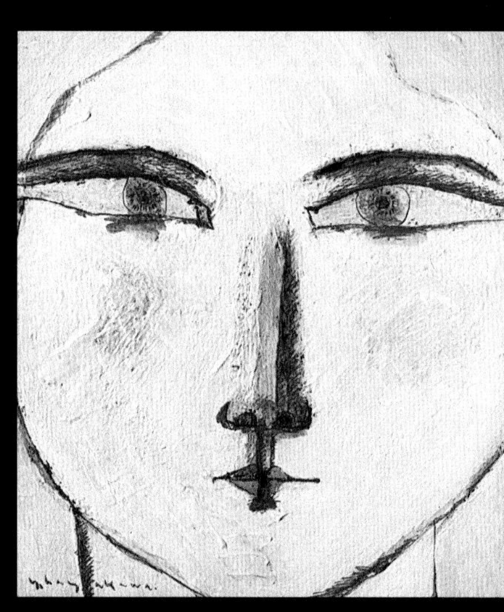
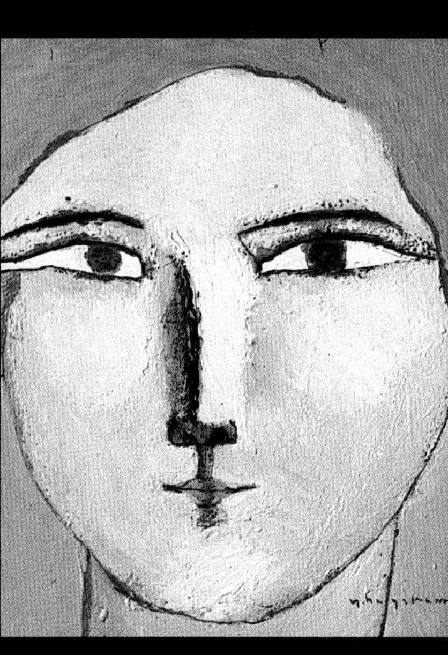
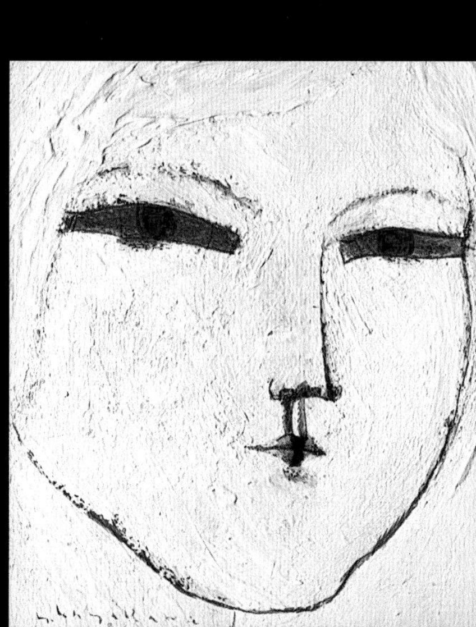

1970

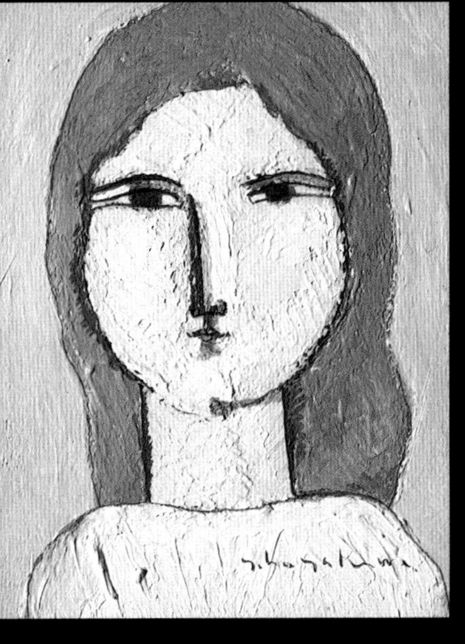
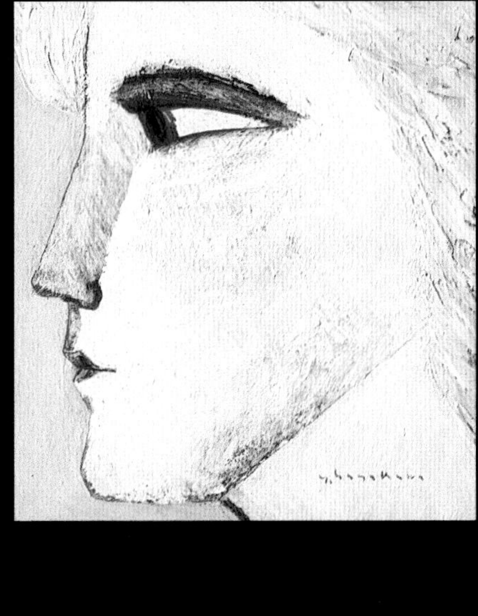
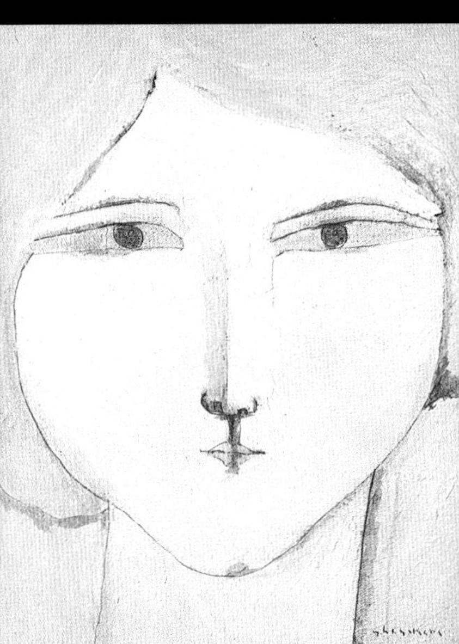
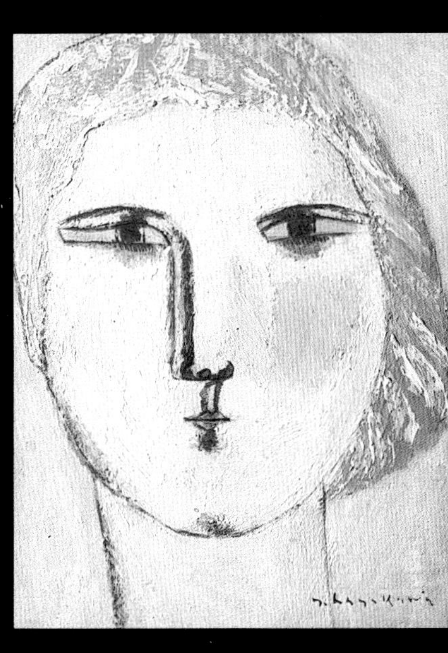
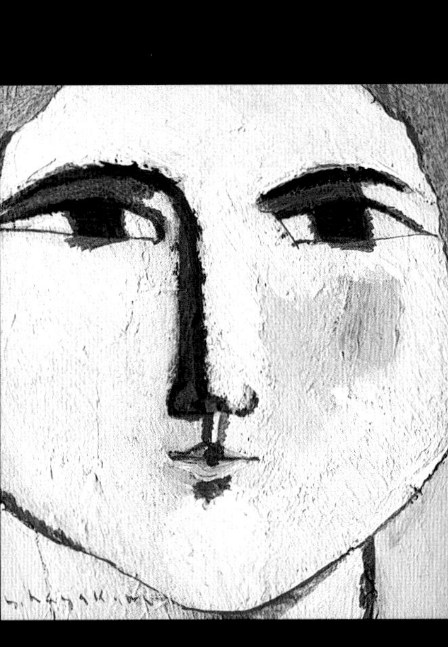
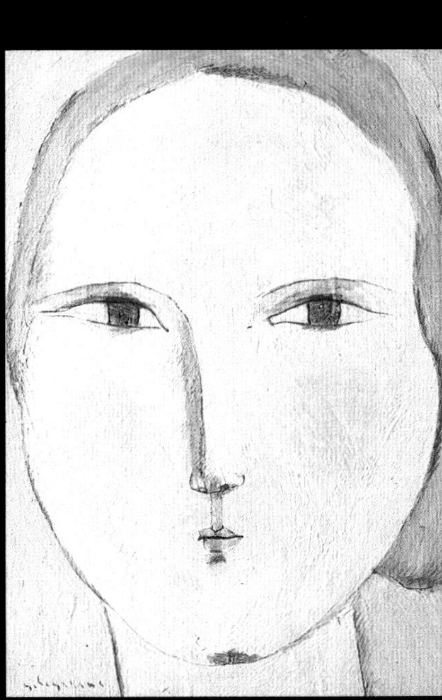

1970

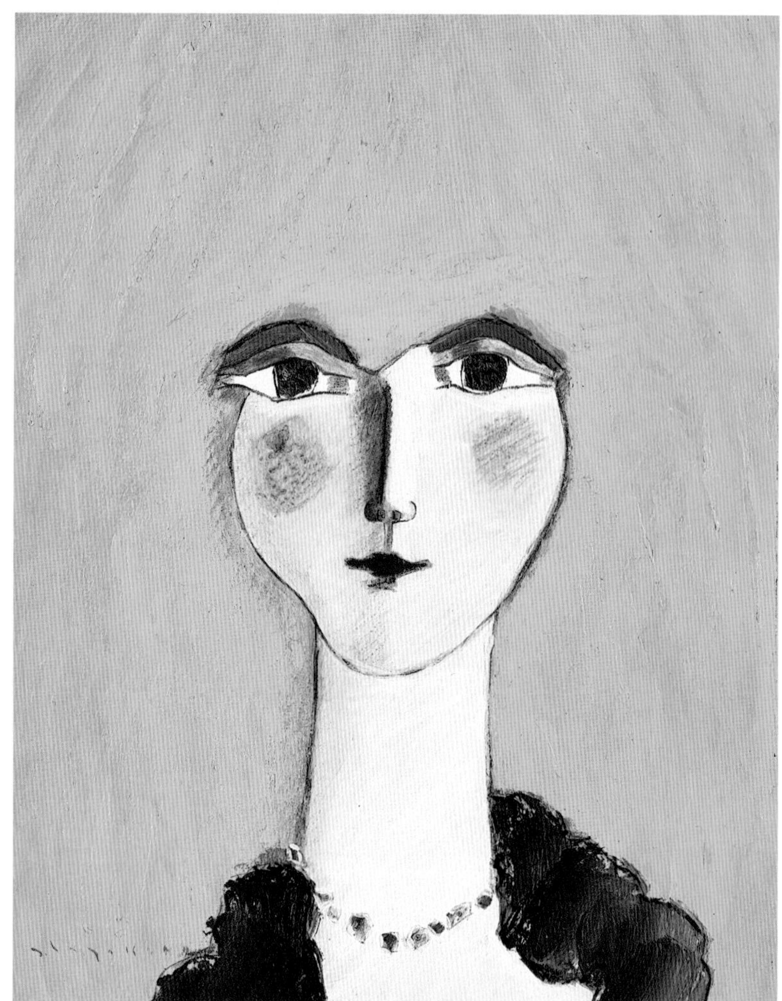

1976

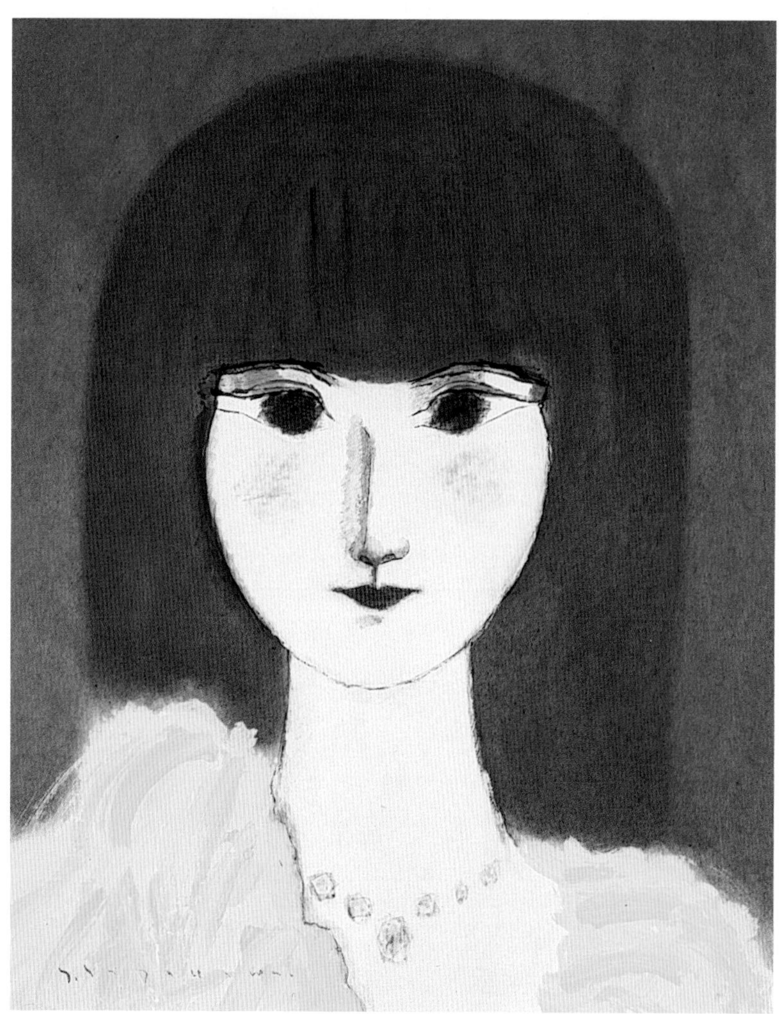

1976

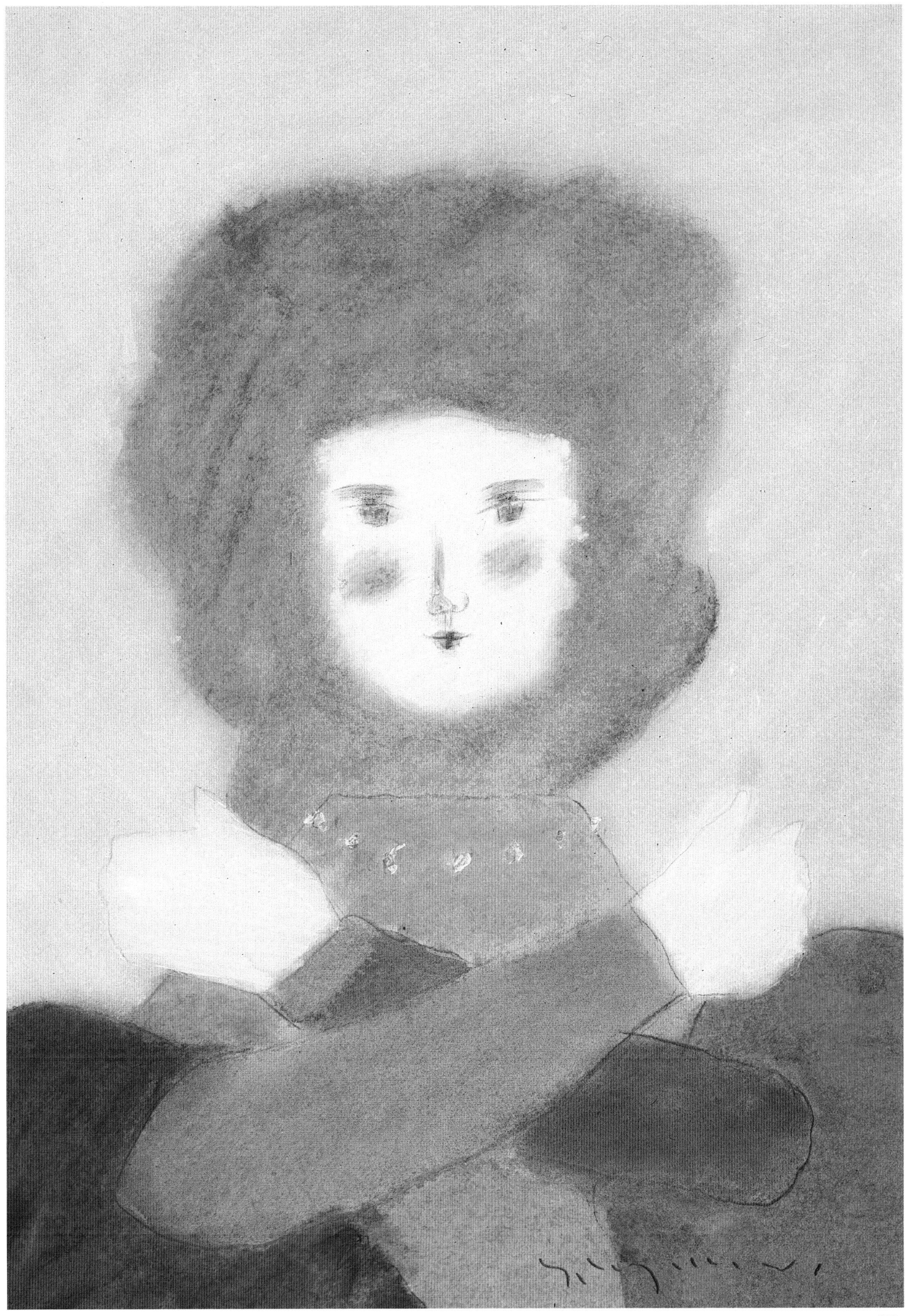

1985

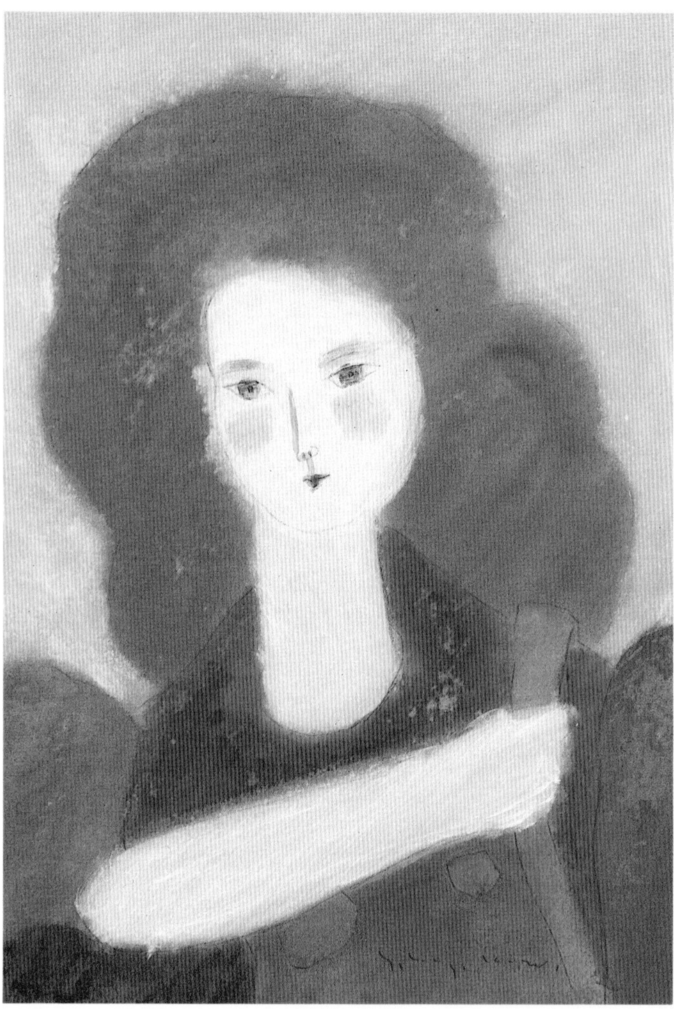

1985

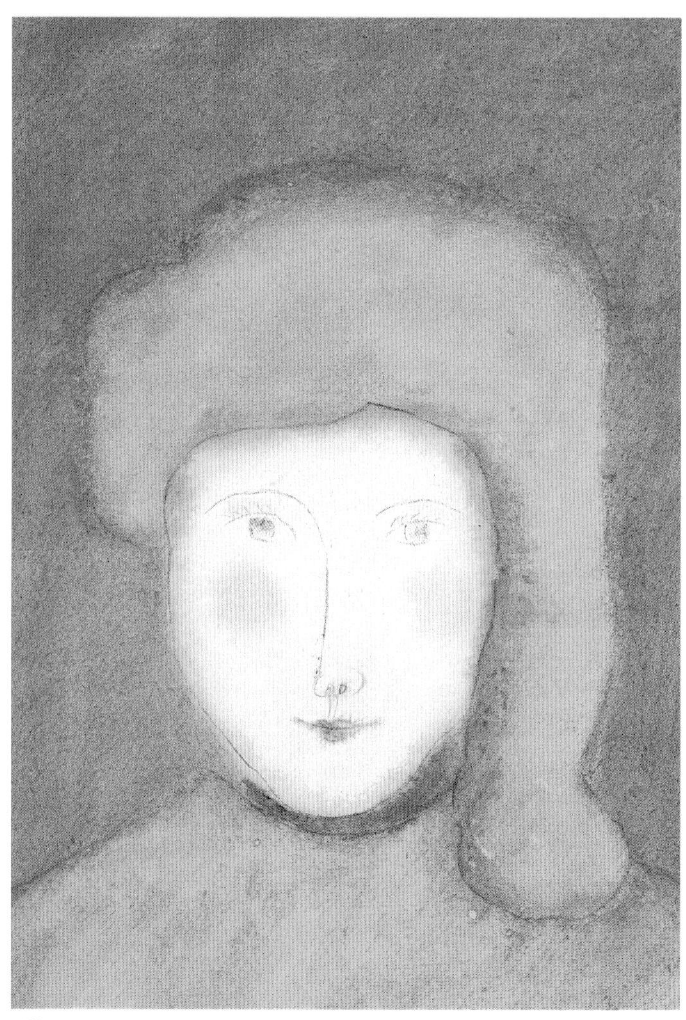

1986

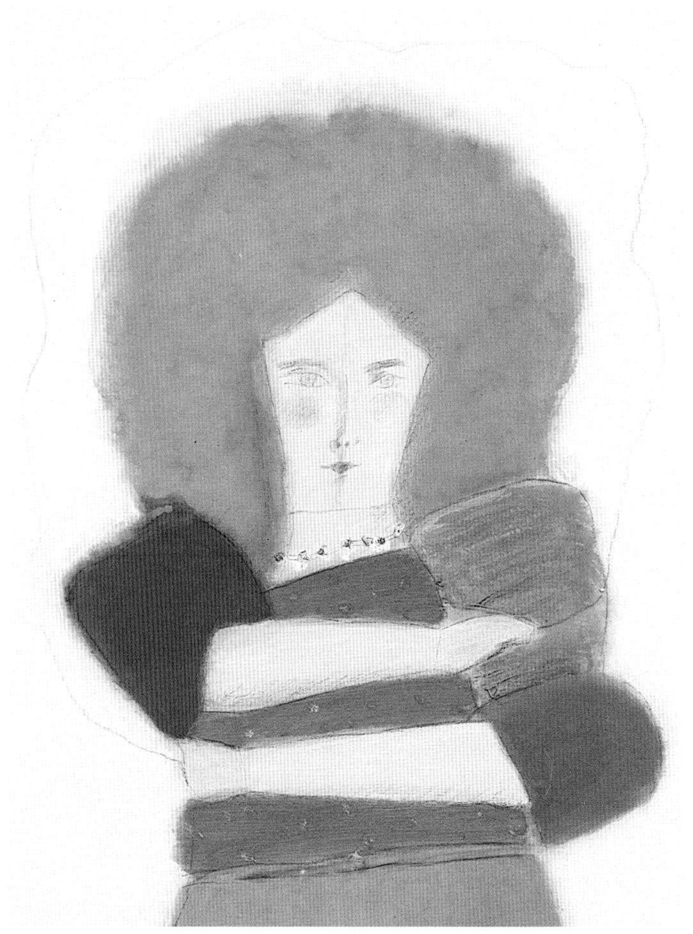

1986

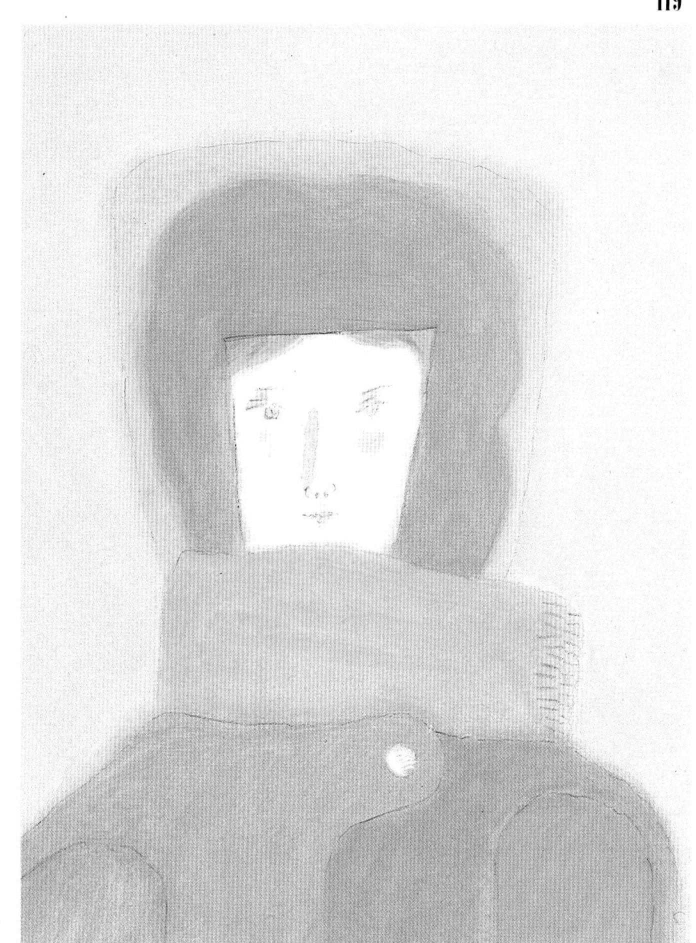

1987

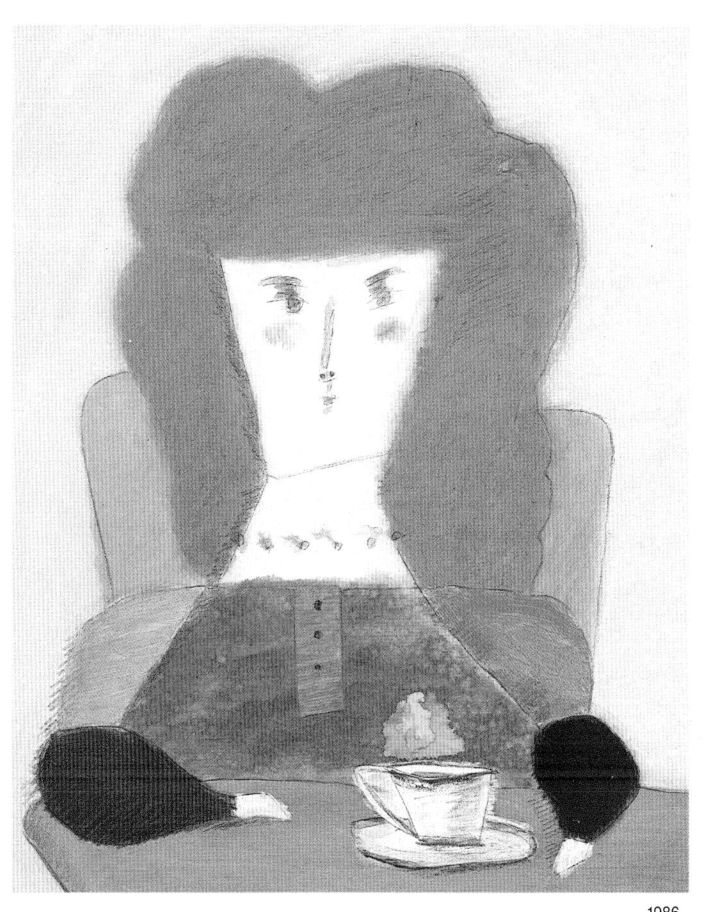

1986

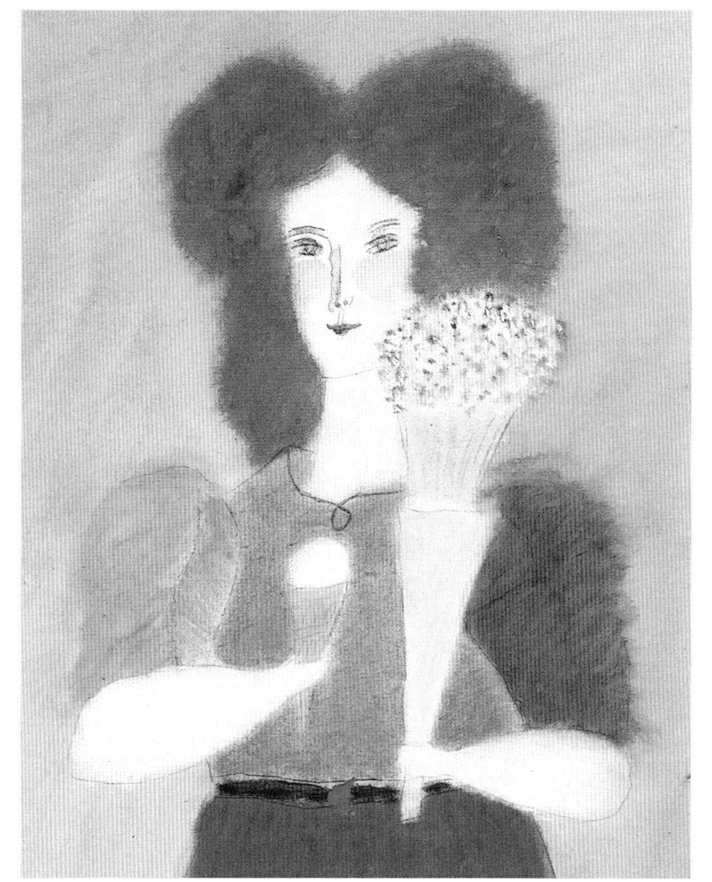

1986

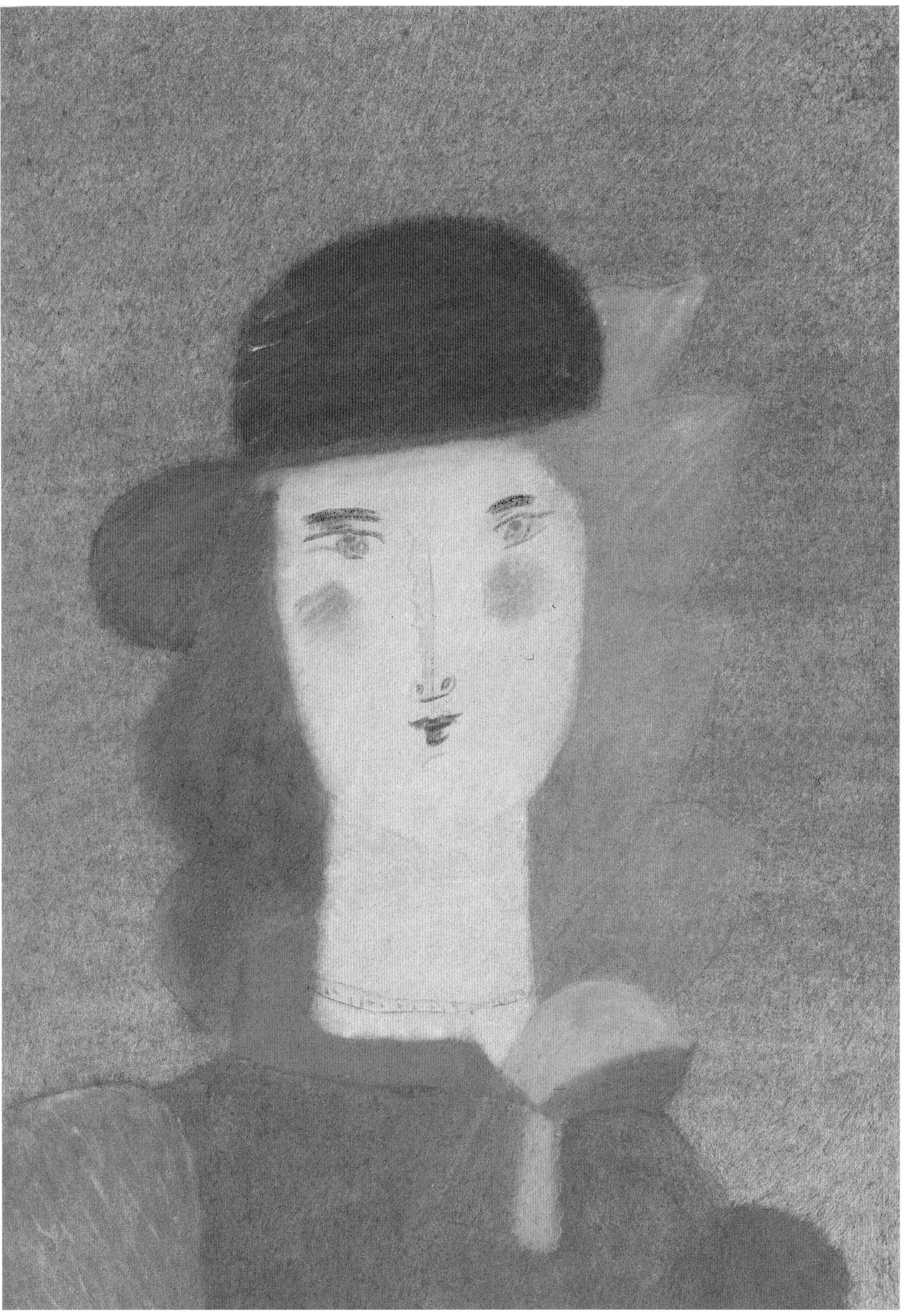

1988

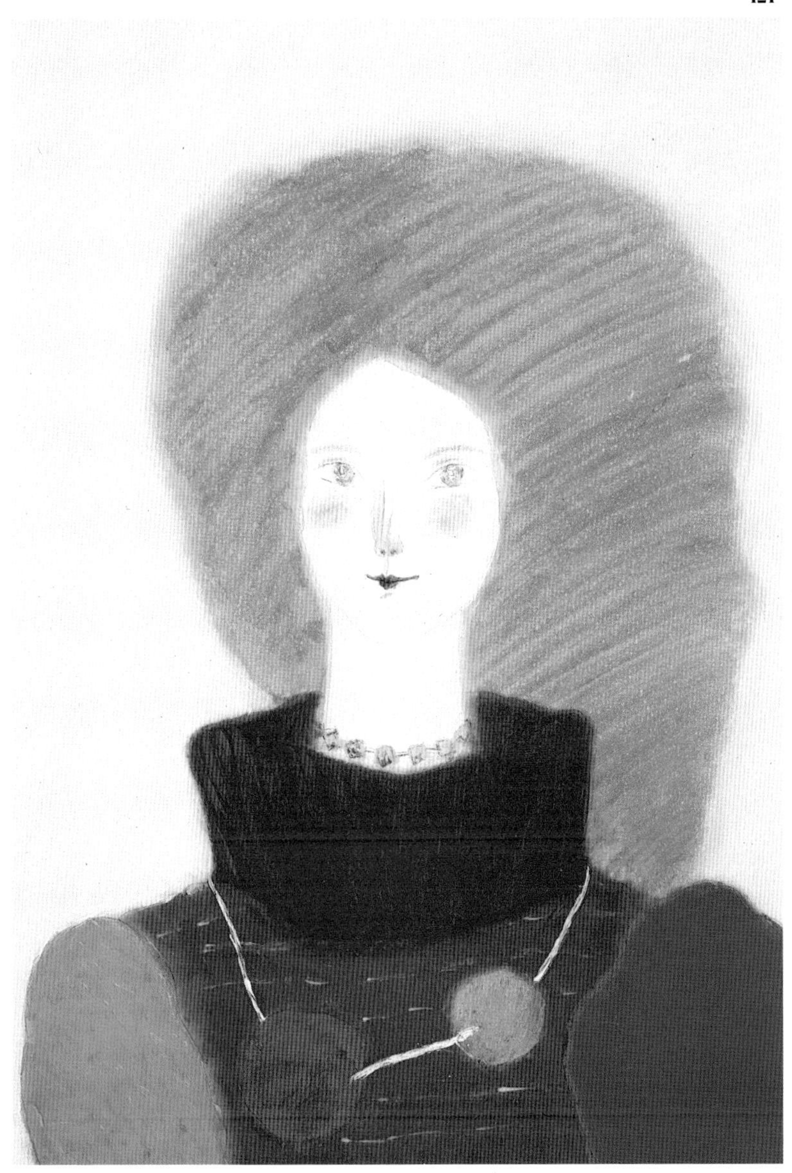

1983

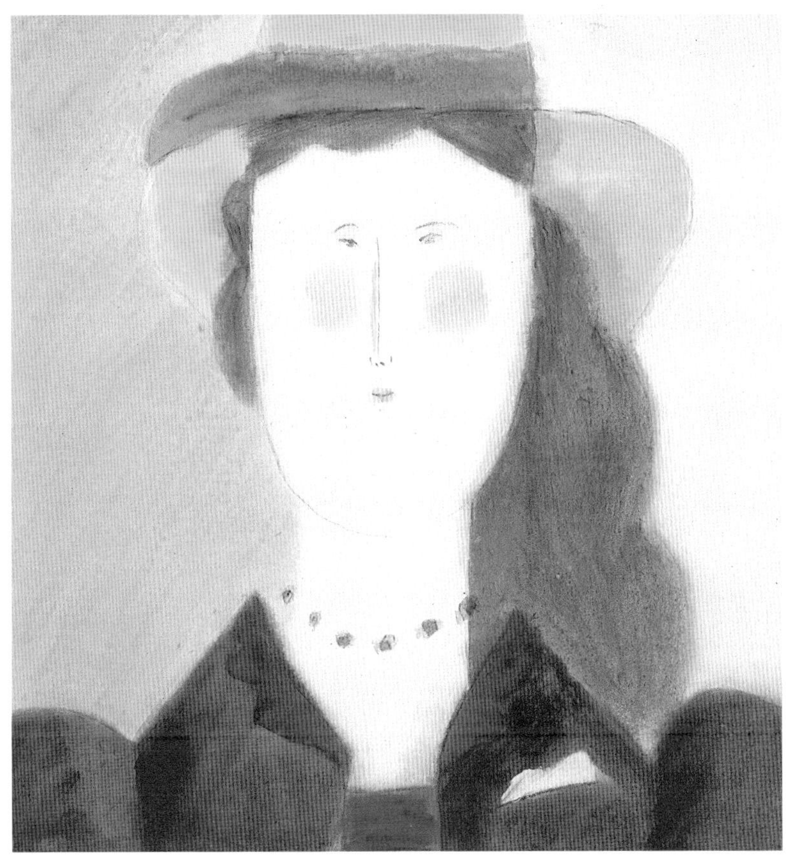

1986

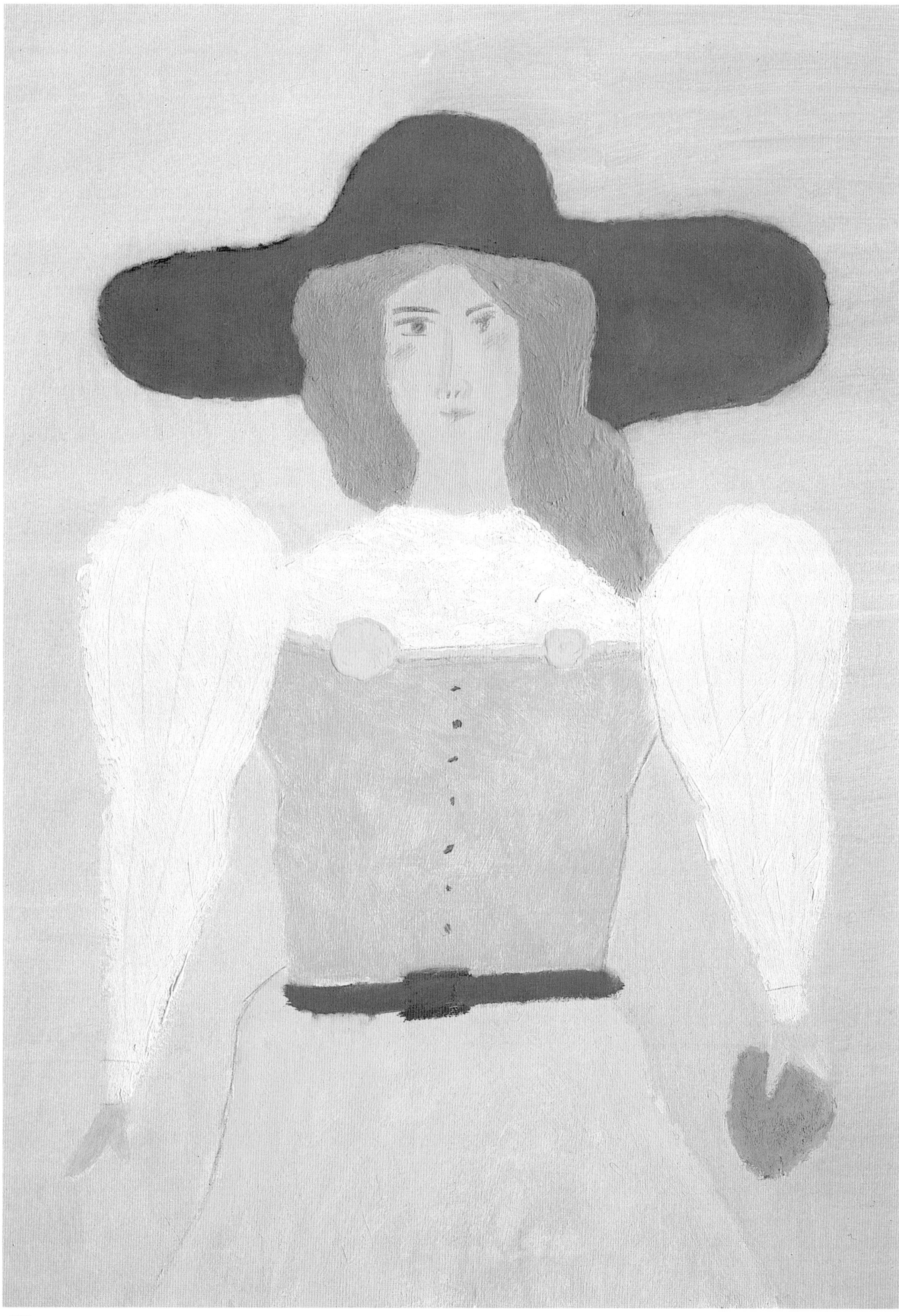

1988

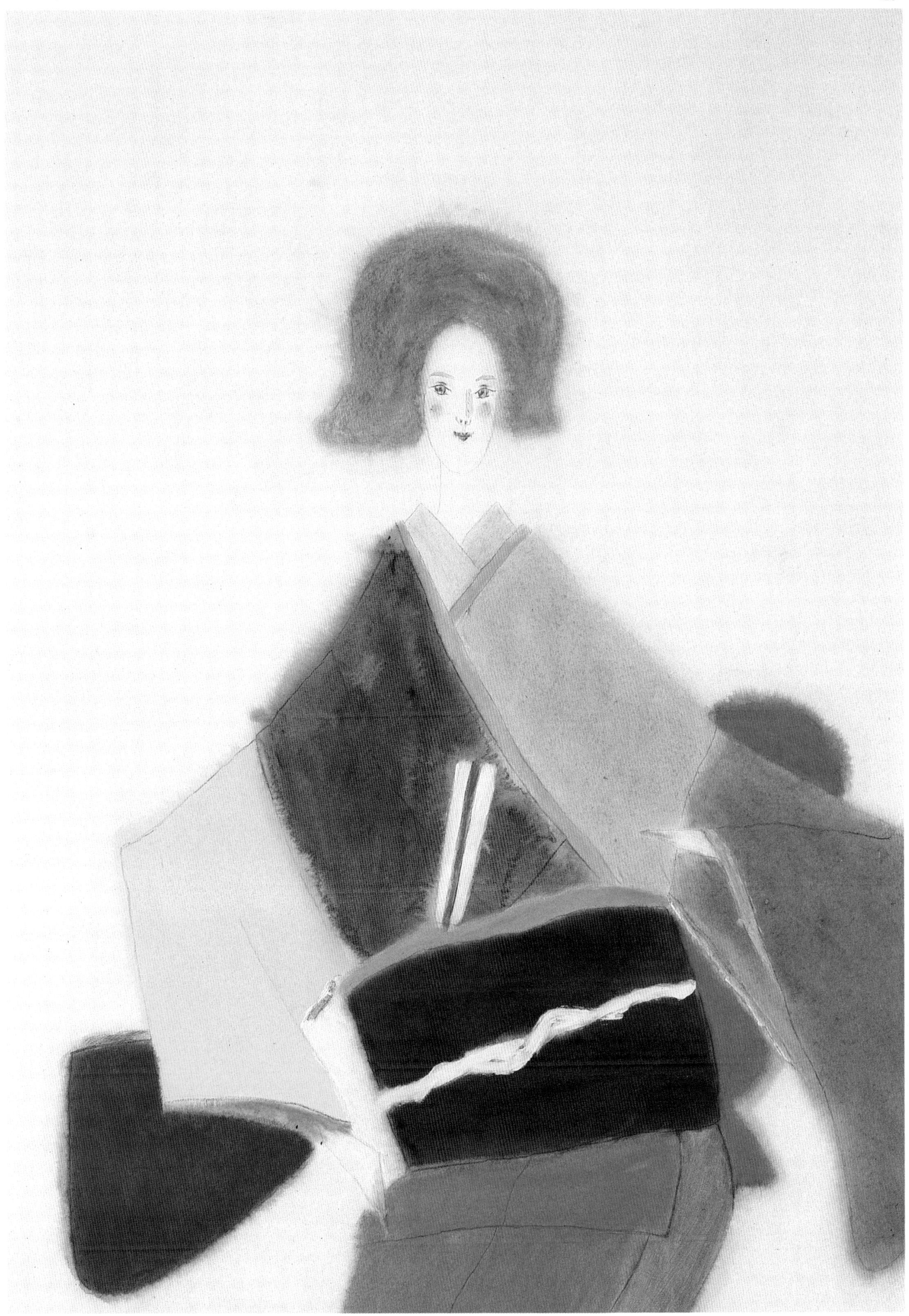

1986

1984

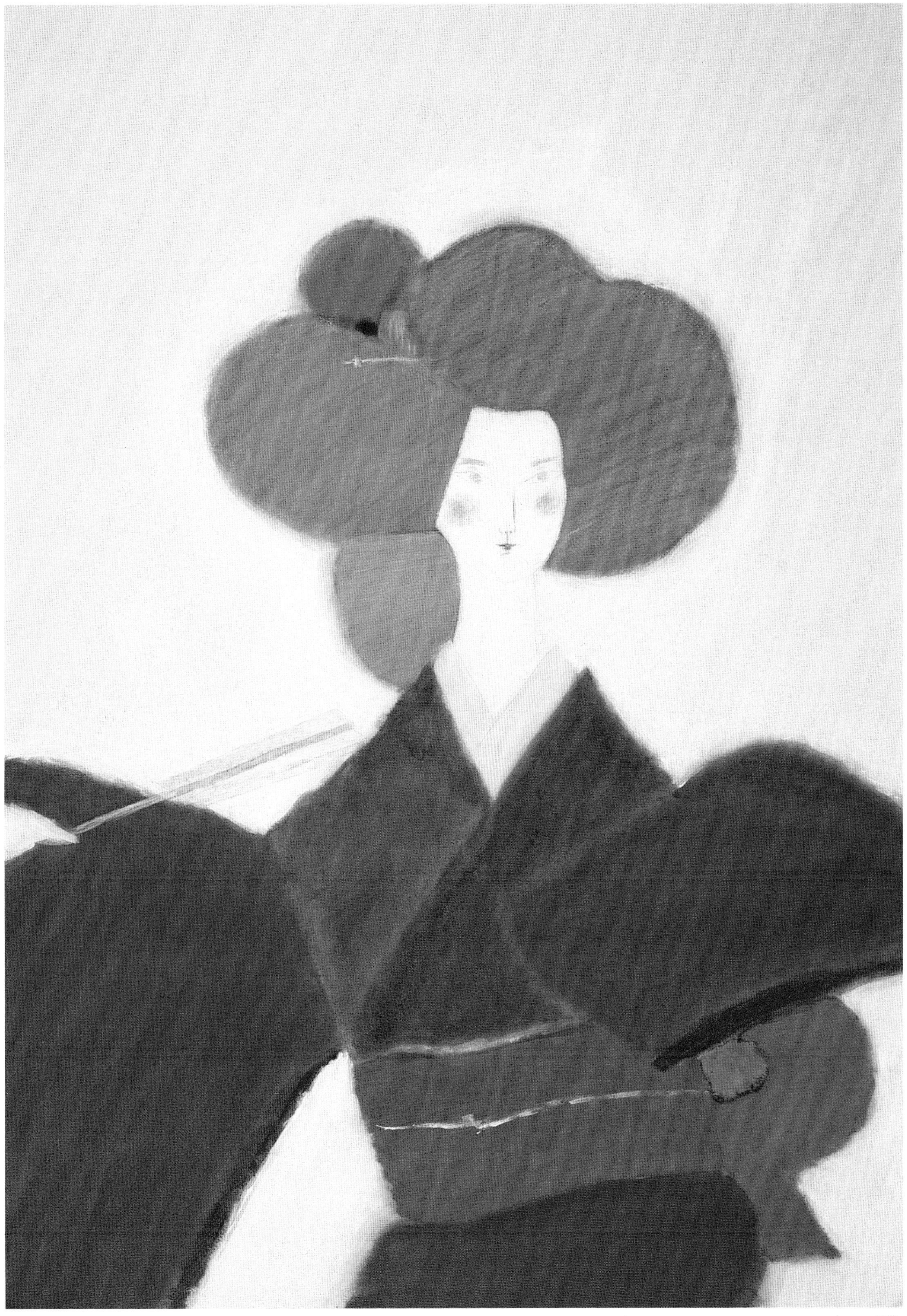

1984

MAKOTO SAITO サイトウ・マコト

Kazumasa Nagai 永井一正

Yesterday I saw Makoto Saito's "Blue Bone" for the first time in some while. It captured my attention with tremendous impact: a single blue bone rising starkly at the center of an all-white periphery. It was part of an exhibition entitled "Contemporary Expression in Background, Interspace and Margin." This unusual show aimed to demonstrate how Japan's unique sense of "background, interspace and margin" is manifested in contemporary works.

Saito was one of the youngest designers selected to participate. His depiction of a solitary blue bone deeply impressed me as a compression of Japanese sensibilities—a work in which a plain perimeter is transformed into a space embued with high tension. Although on first impression Saito may perhaps seem at odds with traditional Japanese sensibilities, on closer scrutiny one recognizes that he identifies closely with the Japanese art tradition in his use of marginal space in his poster as a whole.

Saito's distinctive design qualities are most strongly manifested in his posters, especially outsize horizontal posters. Before Saito appeared on the design scene, designers generally seemed unable to deal meaningfully with an area of this size. Then Saito came along and, with a stroke of brilliance, raised this size poster's aesthetic to a pinnacle.

In Saito's posters the subject is positioned at the center and the large areas to either side are left blank. These margin areas are not simply empty space, however, but a realm that is marked by a high level of tension. The tension is created not only by the exquisite balance with the central form but also by the density, or extreme compression, of the photo or collage at the center. So intense is the compression that it seems to send out vibrations in rippling effect into the white space around it. The overall effect has a powerful impact on the viewer, like the numbing punch packed by a champion boxer.

It is the tremendous speed with which this phenomenon occurs and stimulates our visual sense that constitutes the inherent appeal of Saito's designs. Moreover, this invigorating sense of speed in Saito's works is what differentiates his designs from Japanese art traditions—traditions which he carries on simultaneously, nonetheless. Indeed, it is because he is able to fuse tradition and innovation in this way that Saito has garnered worldwide acclaim and numerous awards.

If Saito is to continue to attract attention, though, he must continuously set the pace for his contemporaries. To do so he is forever making bold statements, as a means of forcing himself to the precipice of his art in order to stir himself on to greater achievements. The reason he gives weight to winning prizes, also, is because he uses such awards as incentives for self-improvement.

As the 1980s draw to a close, we find ourselves in a period characterized by a pervasive mood of vacuousness. Today's youth are dominated by sensations of inertia, loss, hollowness. Nostalgia for past times rings poignantly. Though Makoto Saito is quite apart from these "trends," I believe he too shares today's loneliness and sense of loss. In his case, however, he does not allow himself to be swayed by these sentiments. Instead, he continuously abandons what has become too comfortable. He continuously seeks to upset the balance. He continuously strives to take up the new challenges of the times in which he lives.

それは周囲に白の余白を充分に残しながら、中央に屹立し強いインパクトで私の眼を捕えた。昨日私は久々にサイトウマコトのブルーの骨と対面した。埼玉県立近代美術館の「地・間・余白—今日の表現から」の展覧会の会場でのことである。土田麦僊、福田平八郎から吉原治良、岡田謙三、そして荒川修作、高松次郎等々「地・間・余白」という日本独特の感性が今日の表現の中にどのようにあらわれてきているか、という問いに答えようとするユニークな展覧会である。出品作家のなかでも最も若手の1人として選ばれたサイトウの1本のブルーの骨が中央に立っている作品が、明確に日本的感性を凝縮し、余白を緊迫した空間に変えながら現代を鋭く切りさいているのが印象に残った。

サイトウと伝統的な日本的感性とは一見あい容れないように思えるが、この骨の作品はもともと仏壇の会社のポスターとしてデザインされたものであるから当然としても、ポスター全体を通じて余白を生かすという感性において日本美術の伝統をアイデンティティとして内包していることに気付く。

サイトウのデザインの特質を最も強く表わしているのはポスターである。しかもB倍版横位置のポスターだと思う。サイトウの出現までデザイナー達はこの大きさをもてあましている観があったが、サイトウはB倍版ポスターの美学を見事に完成させた。それ等は造形が中央に位置し、横位置の左右に大きくほとんど白に見える薄いアミ点の入った余白が広がっている。そしてその余白が単なる空きではなく、はりつめた空気感を感じさせるのは、造形としての絶妙のバランス感覚もさることながら、中央の写真、又そのコラージュの造形密度、つまりぎりぎりに凝縮することによってその反撥作用としてそれを見る者の眼に、優れたボクサーのストレートパンチのように飛び込んでくる強さによって、余白にまでその震動が波紋のように広がっているためである。サイトウのデザインの魅力は私達の眼を刺激するスピード感であると思う。

サイトウが日本の伝統を継承しながら、それ等との違いはこの爽快なスピード感であり、それが現代のグラフィックデザイナーとして数々の受賞とともに世界からも注目される存在たらしめている理由であろう。だからサイトウが注目され続けるためには闇を切り裂き、光を捕えながら時代の最先端を疾走し続けなければならない。サイトウが常に強気で発言するのも、自分を自分で追いつめて断崖に立たせることによってふるい立たせようということに他ならない。又サイトウが賞にこだわり続けるのも、スピードランナーがストップウォッチでそのスピードを確認していくように、そして更に記録をのばしていくように、自分への挑戦なのである。

昭和も終り平成の時代になりながらも、世紀末のためか、現代は空白感の漂う時代であり、無力感、喪失感、空虚といった風潮が若者達を支配する。そして過去を懐かしむノスタルジアにひたろうとする。サイトウはそれ等の風潮とは無縁である。しかしサイトウとて孤独に苦しみ現代の喪失感を共有していると思う。ただそれ等に流される自分自身が許せない。居心地の良い場を捨て続け、バランスをくずし続け、常に時代への挑戦者であり続けようとする。

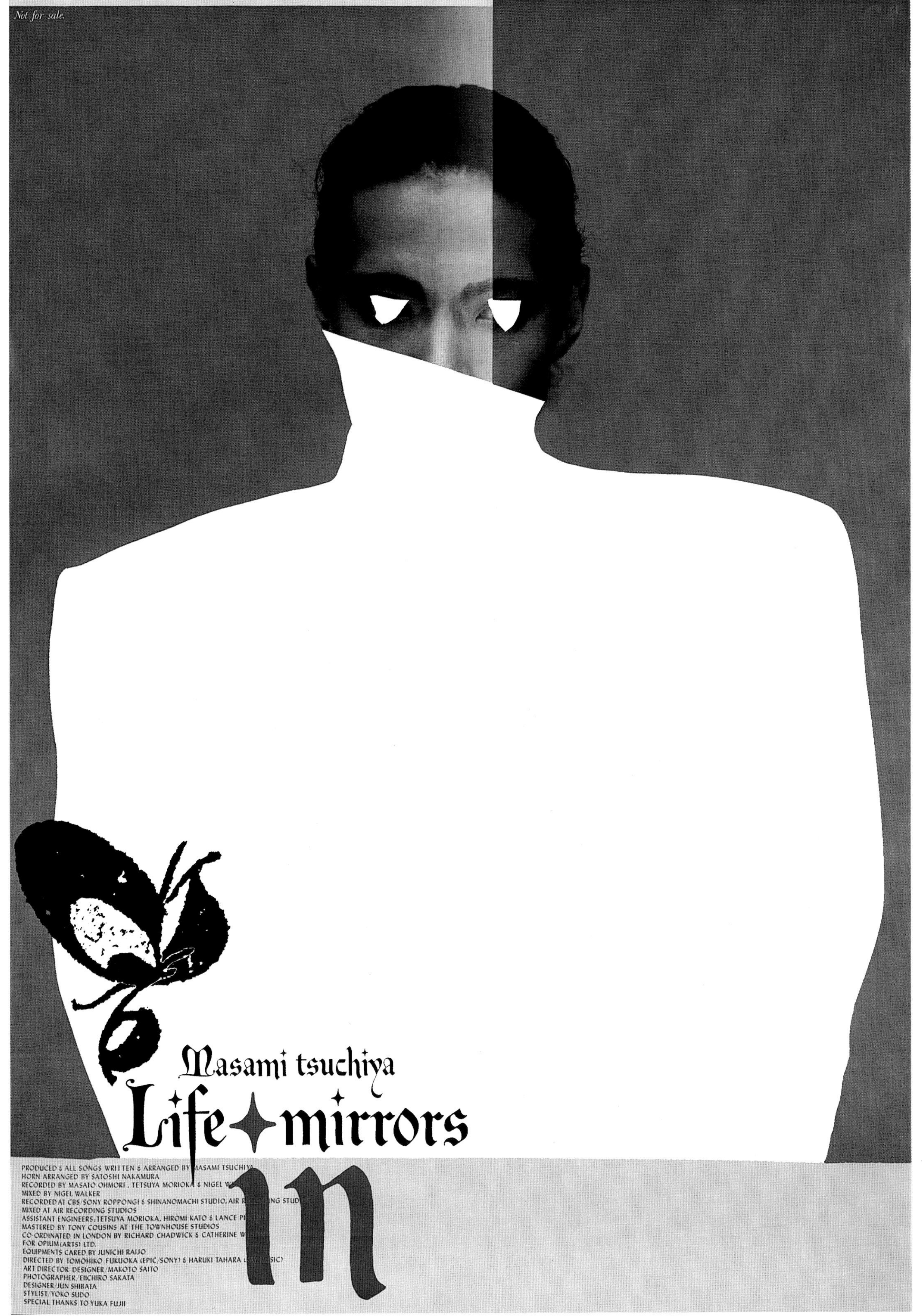

1 Record album poster アルバムのポスター 1987

Onward.
Fashion-Being

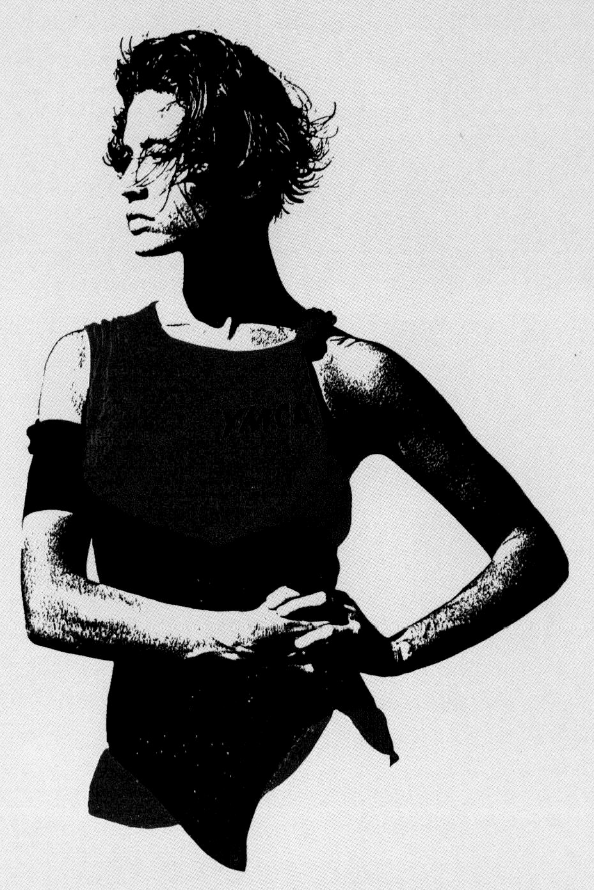

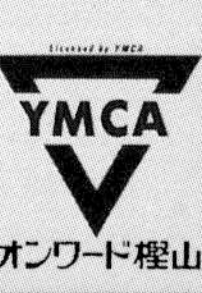

2 Sportswear poster スポーツウエアのポスター 1984

Onward.
Fashion-Being

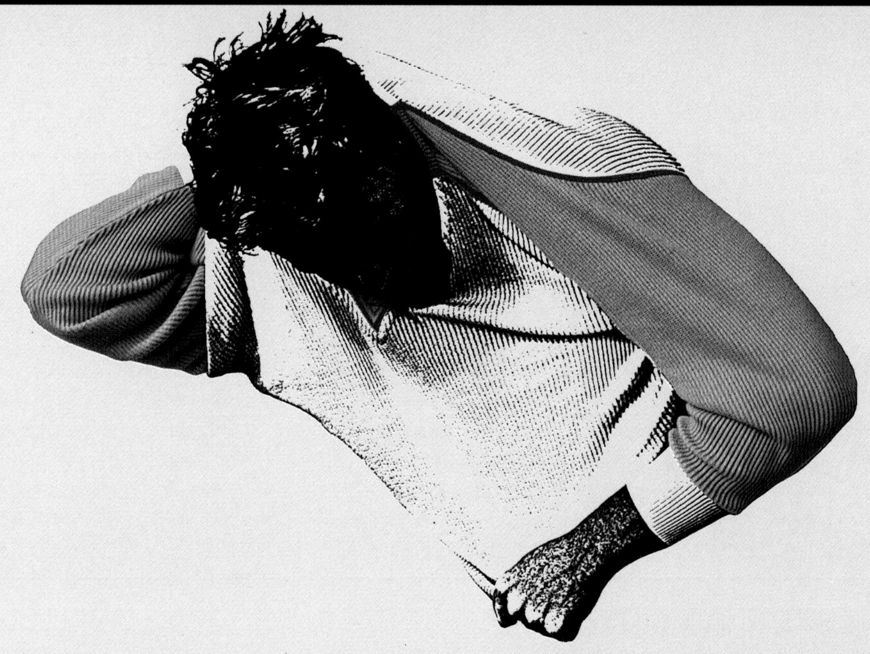

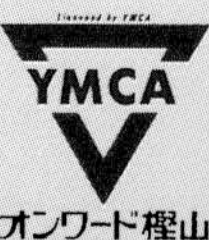

3 Sportswear poster スポーツウエアのポスター 1984

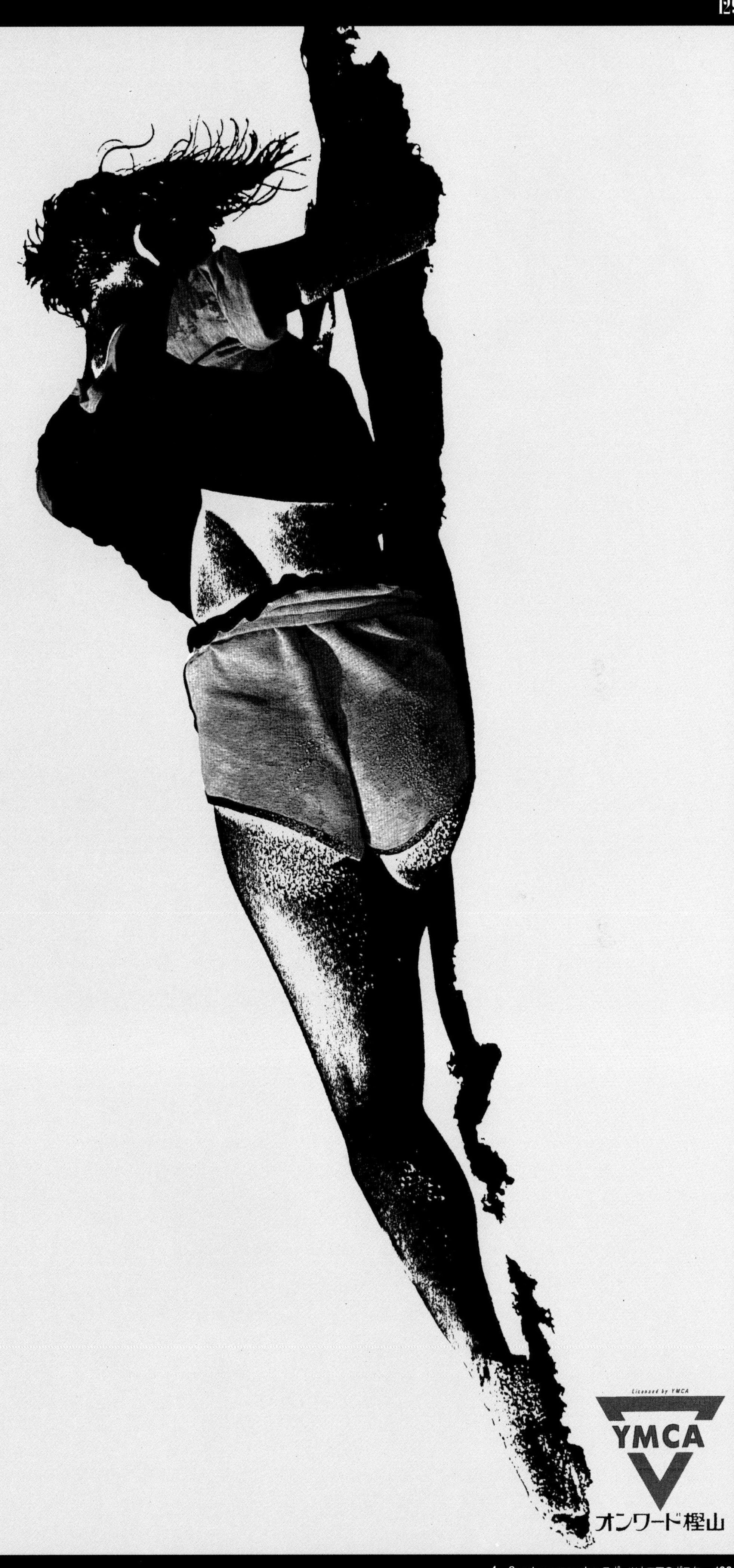

4 Sportswear poster スポーツウエアのポスター 1984

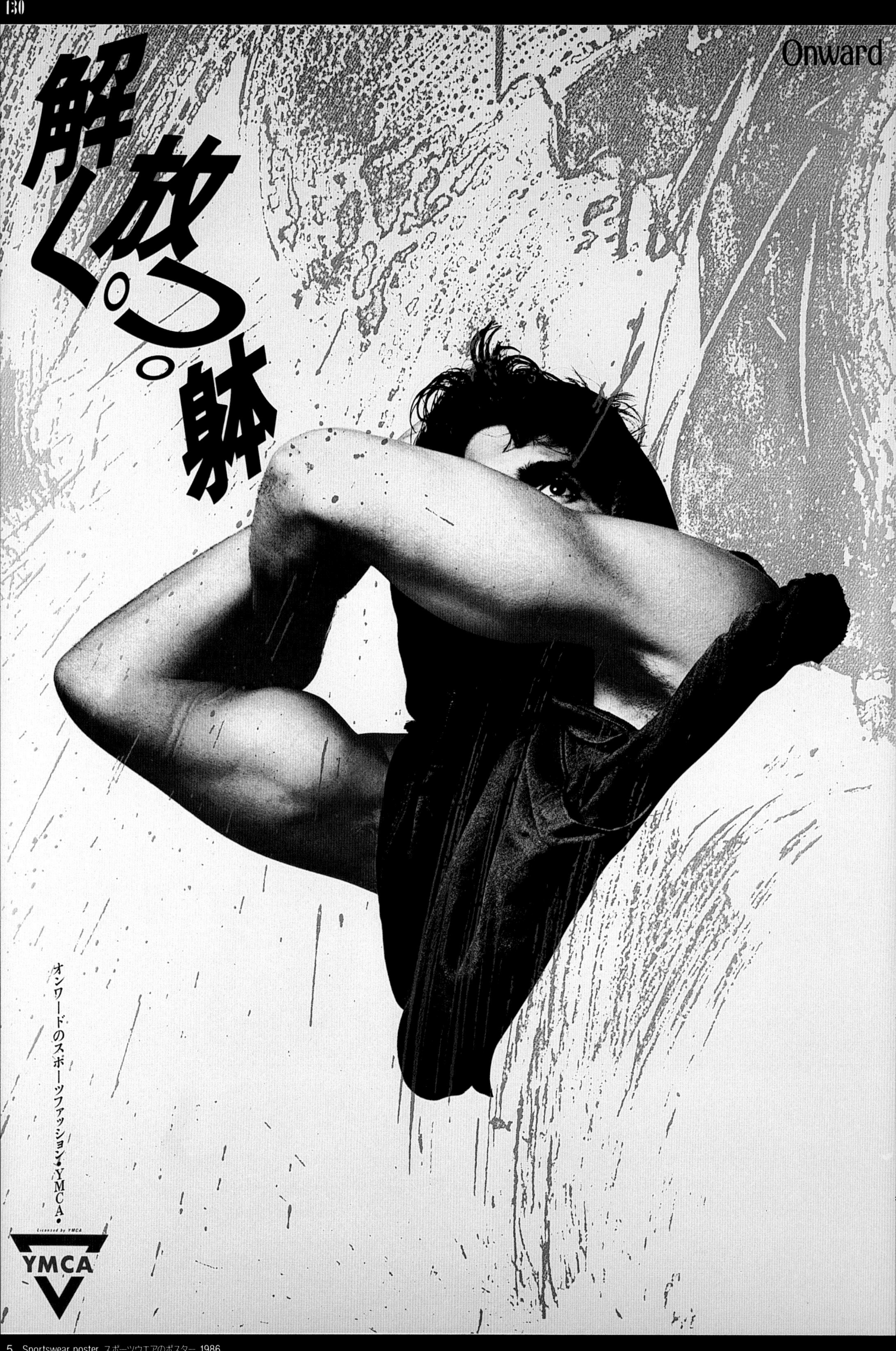

5 Sportswear poster スポーツウエアのポスター 1986

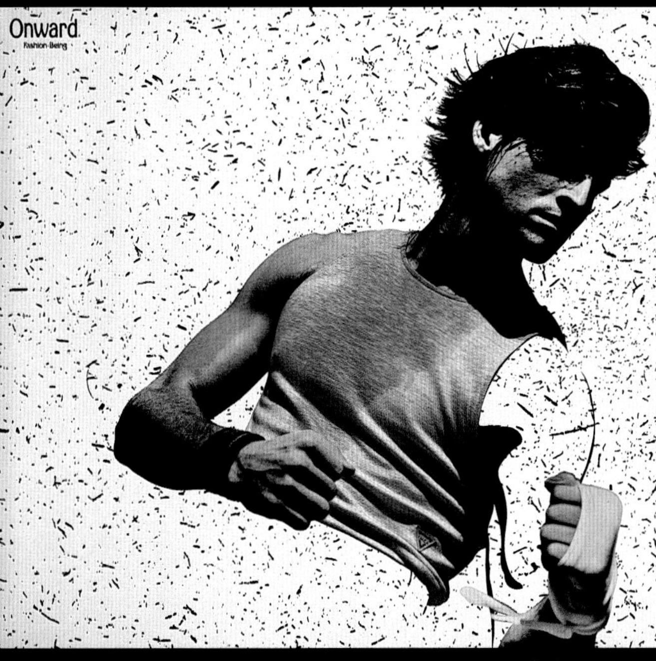

6 Sportswear poster スポーツウエアのポスター 1985

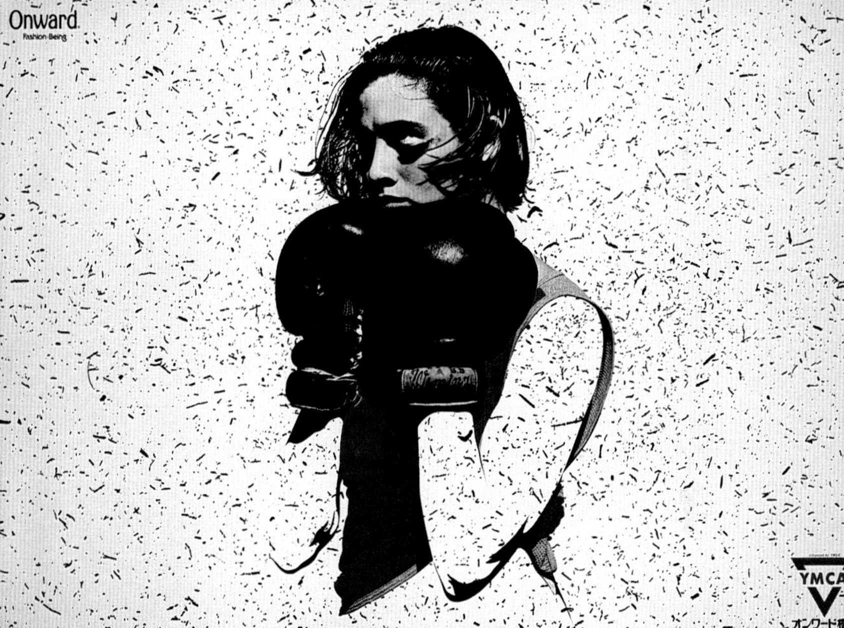

7 Sportswear poster スポーツウエアのポスター 1985

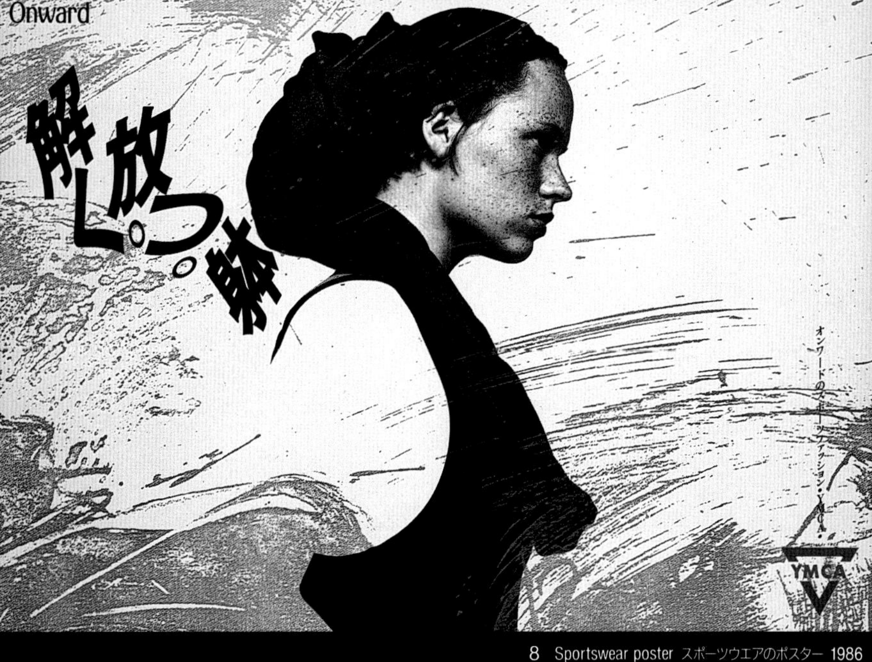

8 Sportswear poster スポーツウエアのポスター 1986

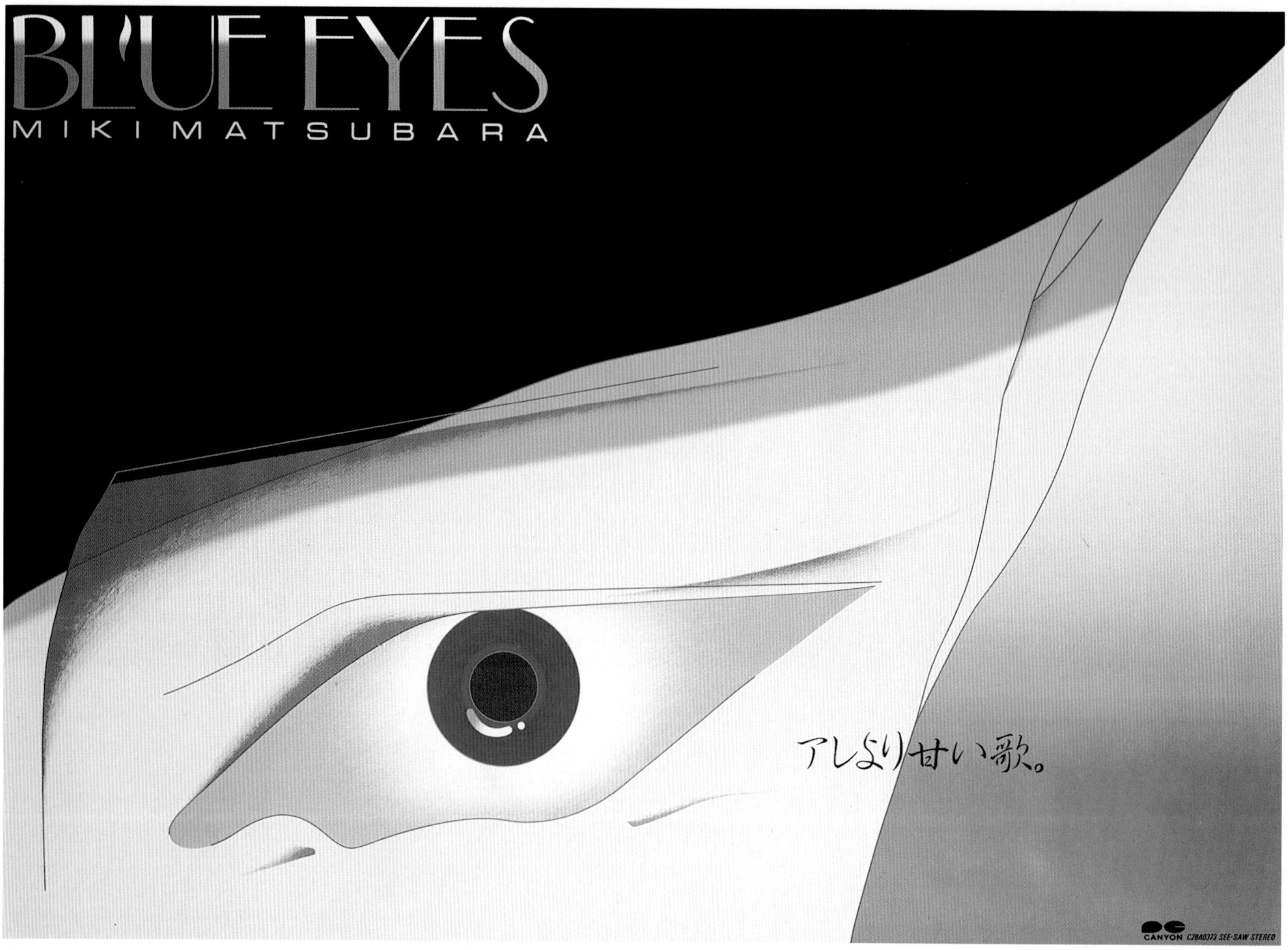

9 Record album poster アルバムのポスター 1985

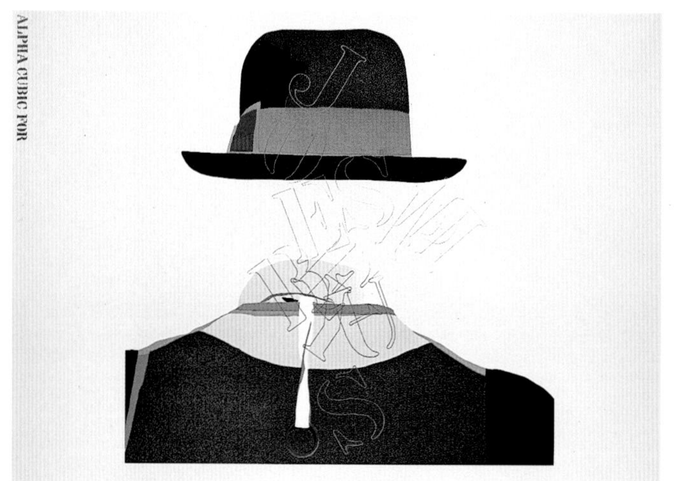

10 Fashion poster ファッションブランドのポスター 1984

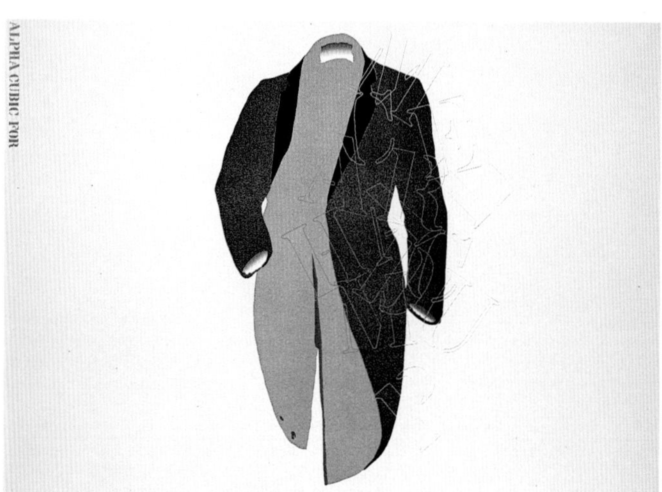

11 Fashion poster ファッションブランドのポスター 1984

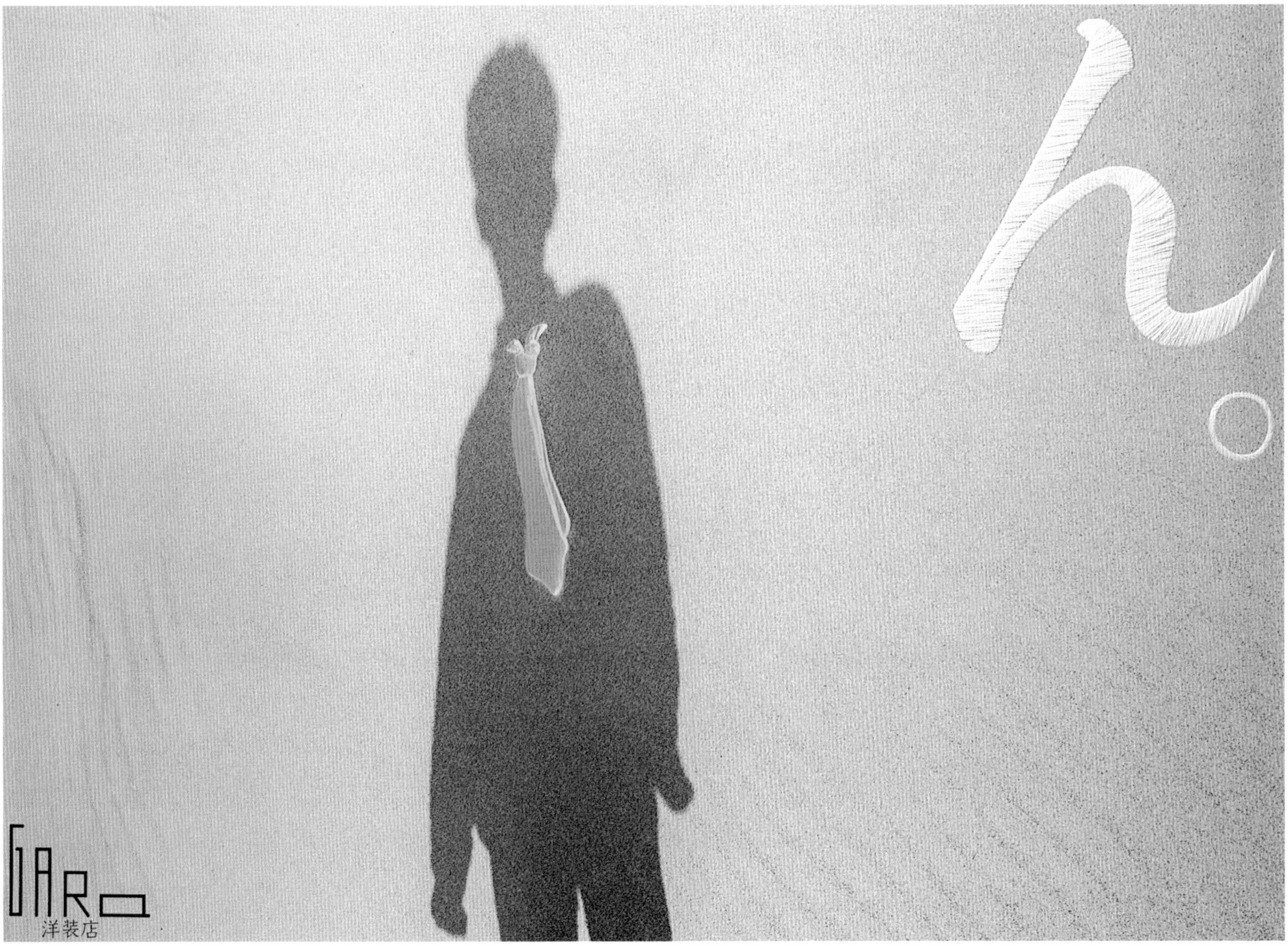

12 Fashion poster ファッションブランドのポスター 1984

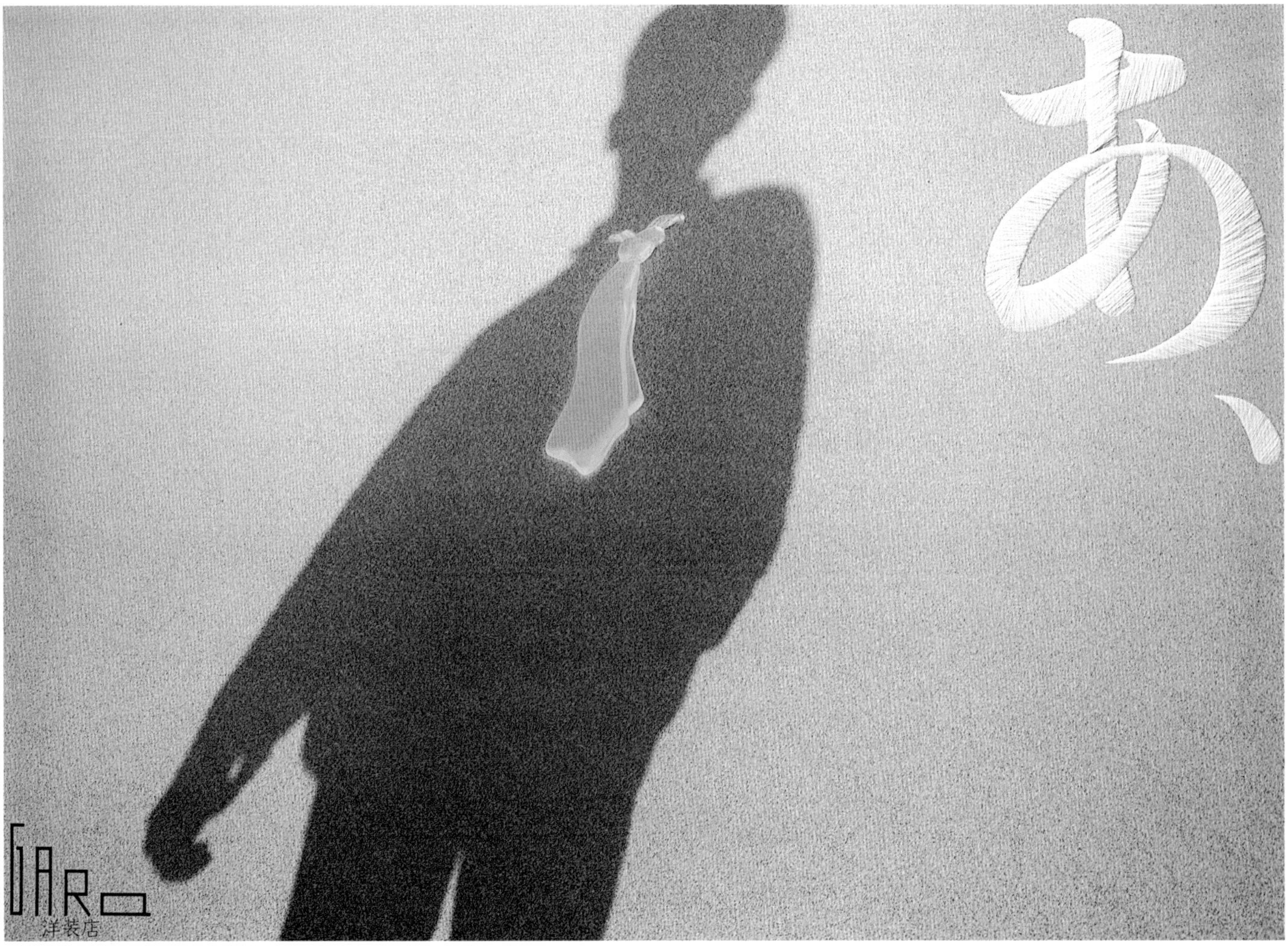

13 Fashion poster ファッションブランドのポスター 1984

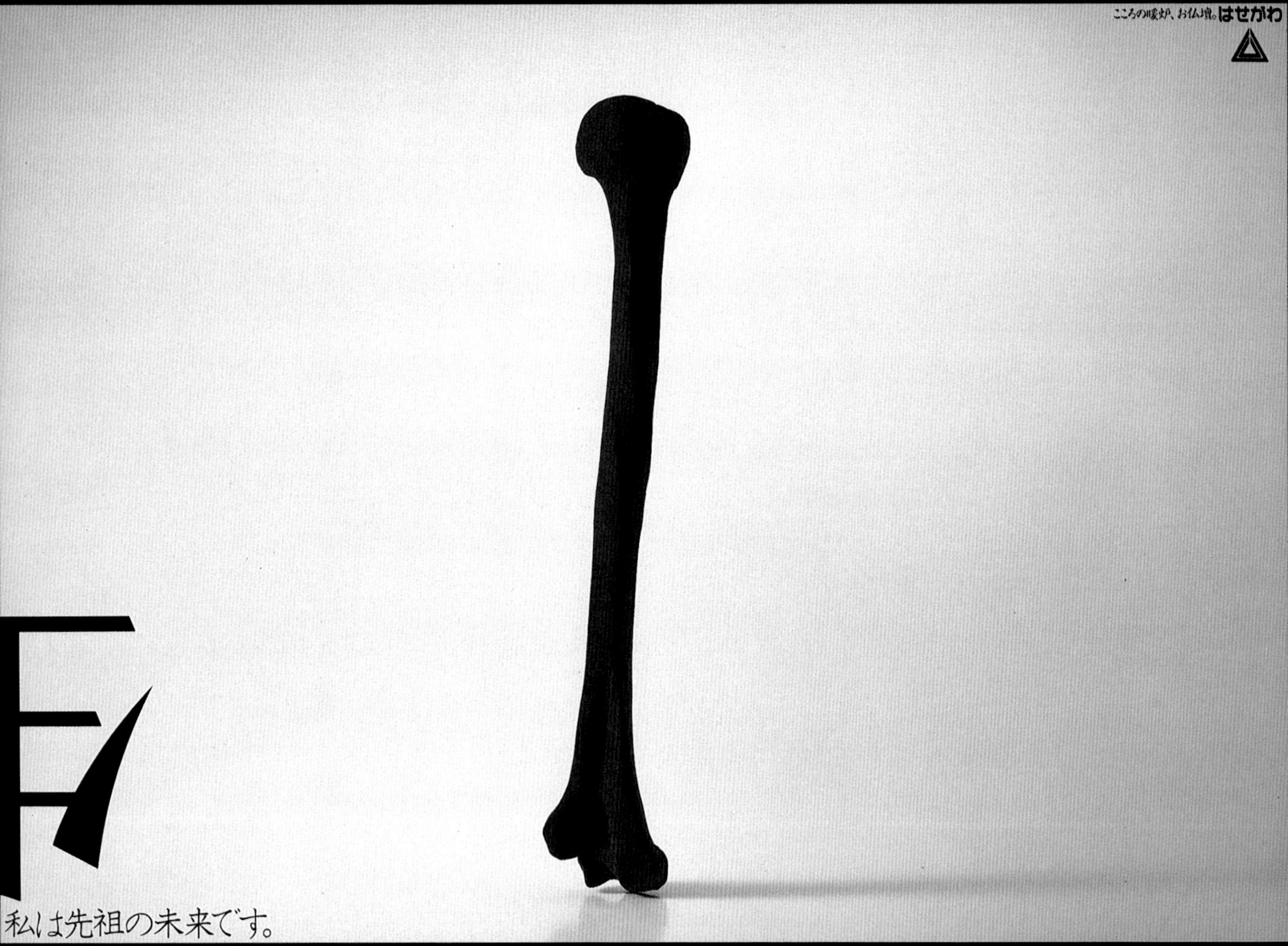

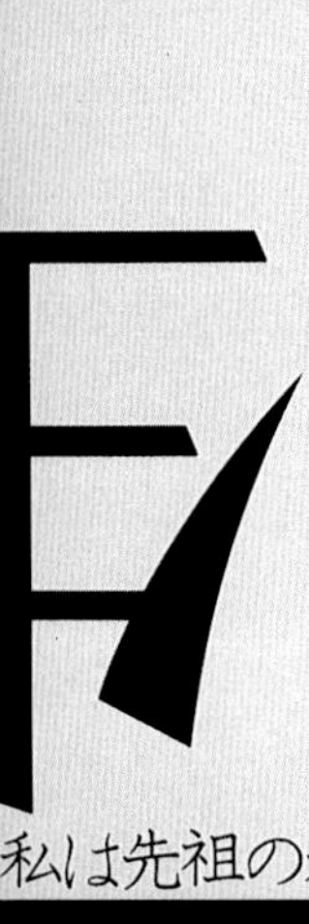

14 Poster for shop selling Buddhist altars and accessories 仏具店のポスター 1985

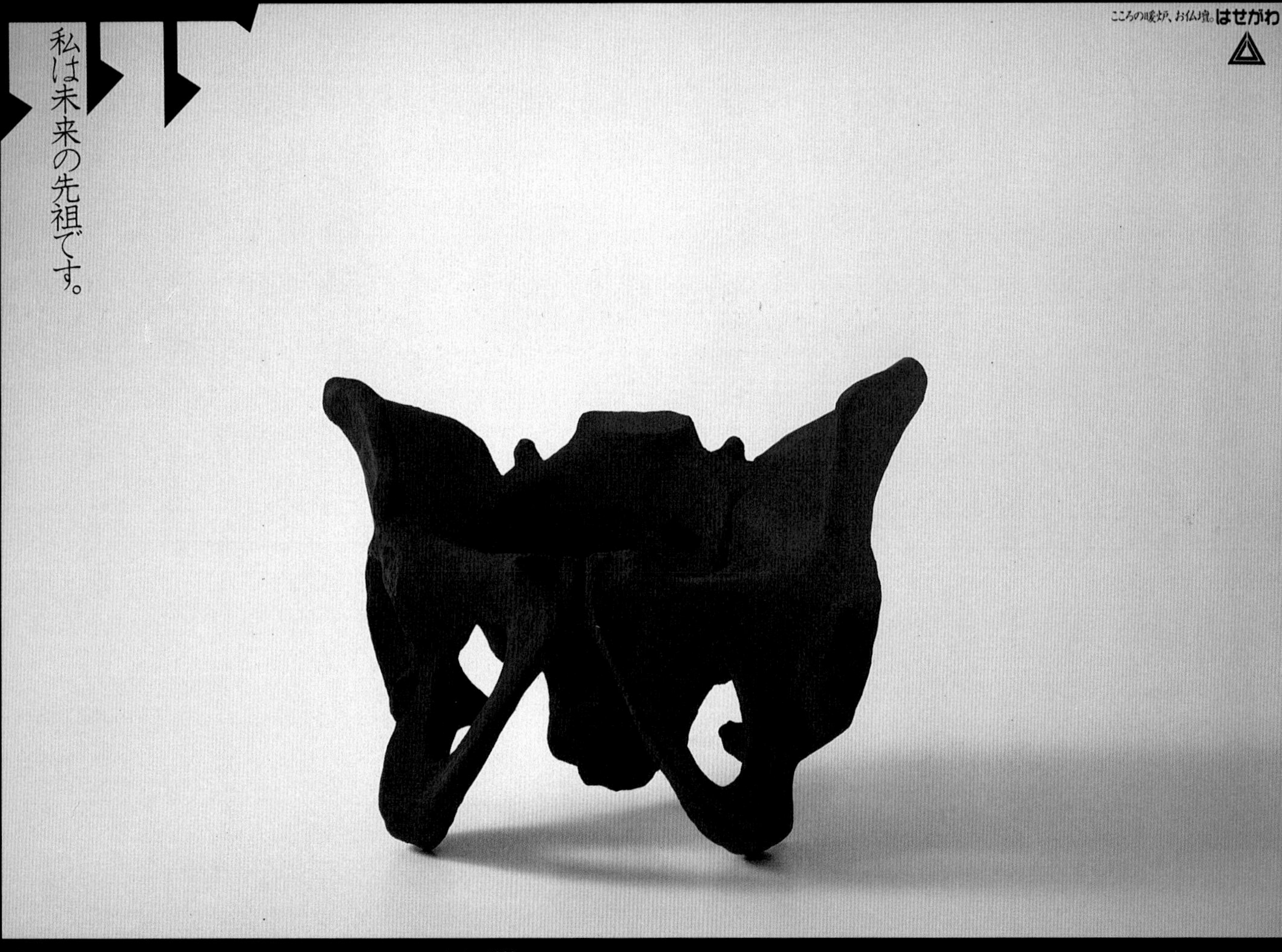

15 Poster for shop selling Buddhist altars and accessories 仏具店のポスター 1985

日本をどうする? 身近なモノ選びから、そんな大きな設問にとりくんでみる。
ムカシの人が「見立て」と呼んでいた方法にならって。
ジャパン・クリエイティブ。西武が1986年以降の生活提案に挑戦。渋谷店でまず展開します。
衣・食・住の局面で、モノづくり、モノ選びにクリエイティブな力を注ぎこみ
現在感覚の見立てを切りひらきます。「変わるモノ、変わらないモノ、日本のデザイン展」その他各階に
クリエイターの参加を得て、10月3日(木)→29日(火)日本のデザインの10月はシブヤで。

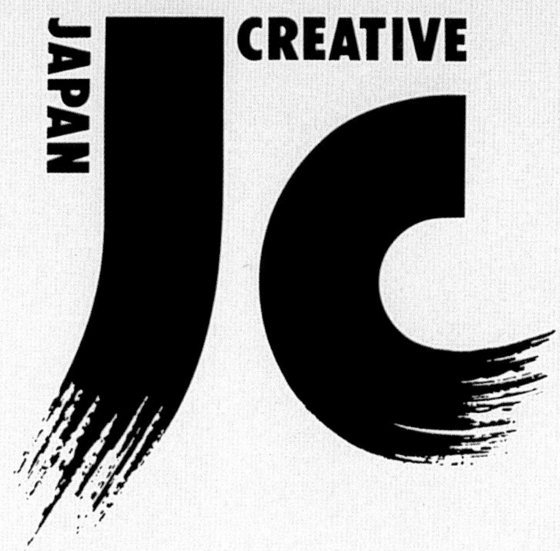

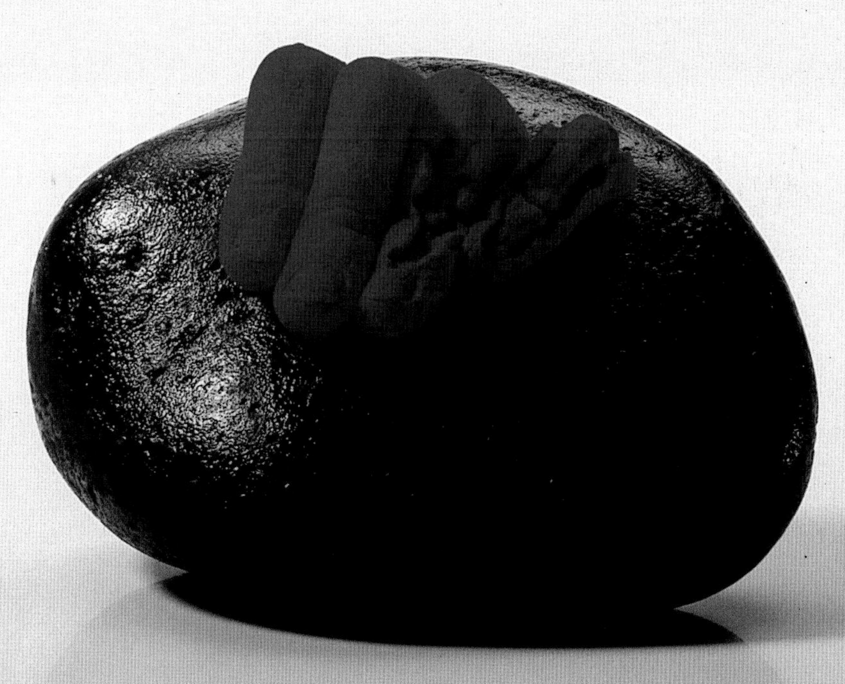

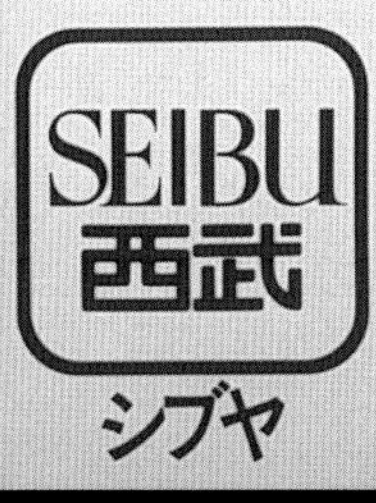

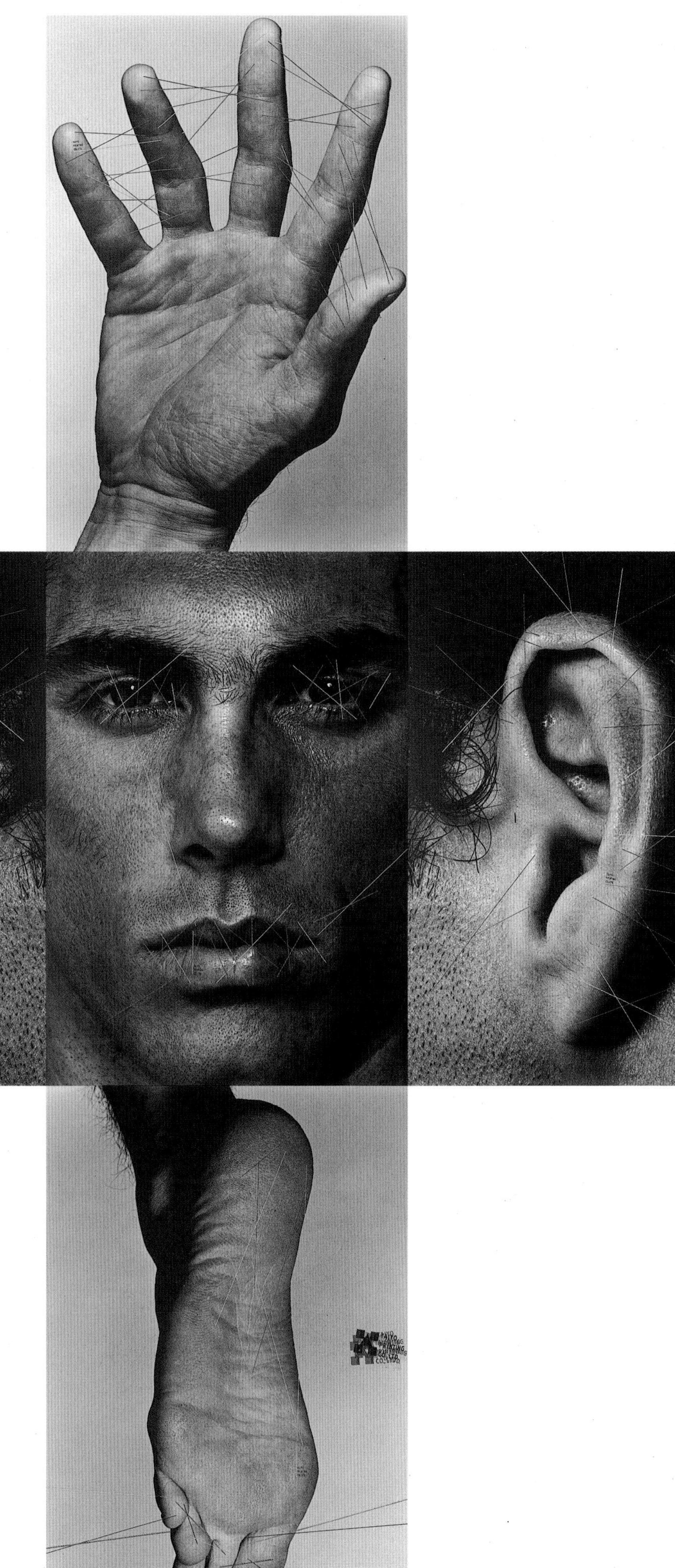

17 Printing company poster 印刷会社のポスター 1988

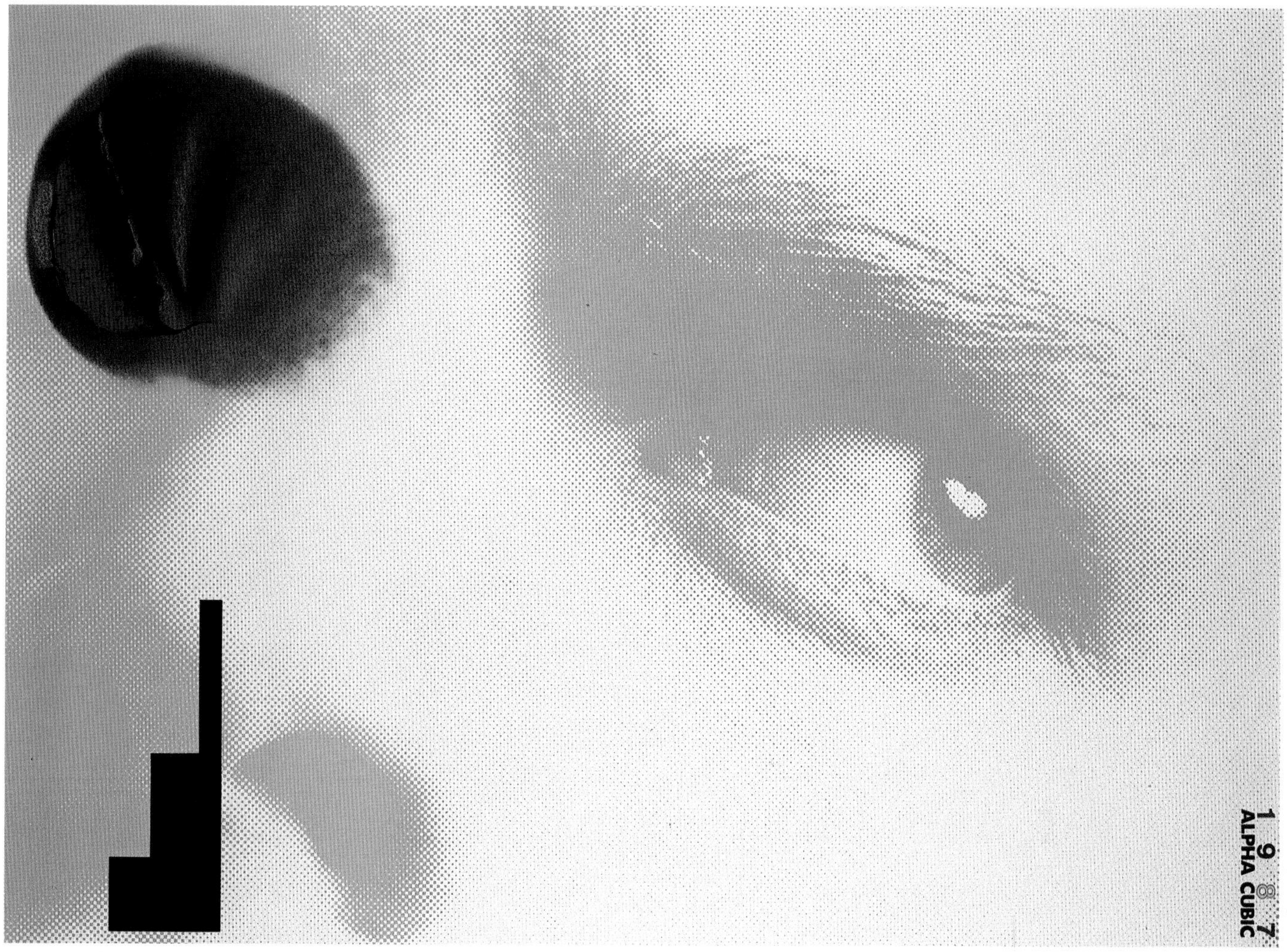

18 Fashion poster ファッションブランドのポスター 1987

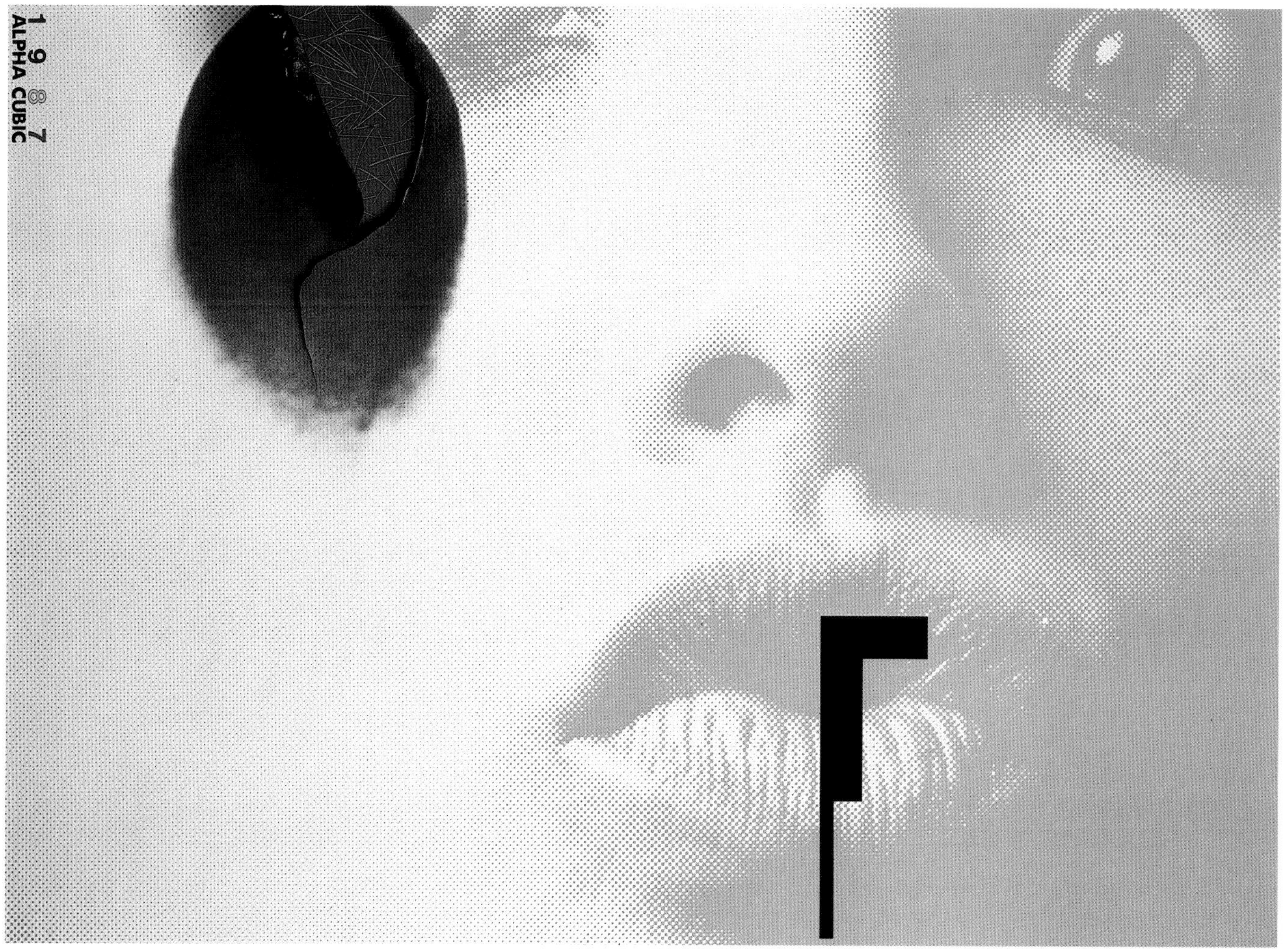

19 Fashion poster ファッションブランドのポスター 1987

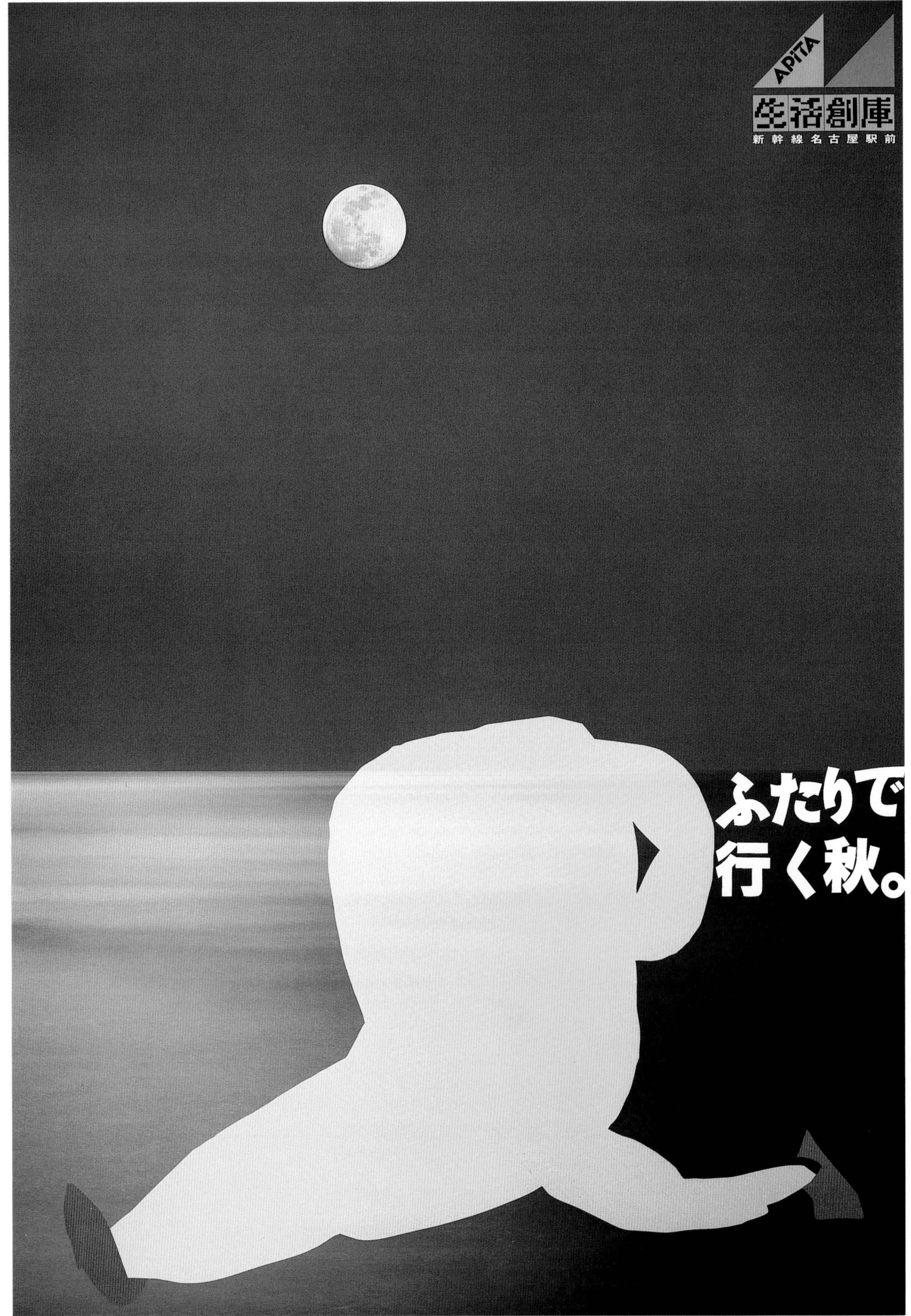

20 Poster for shopping mall ショッピングセンターのポスター 1987

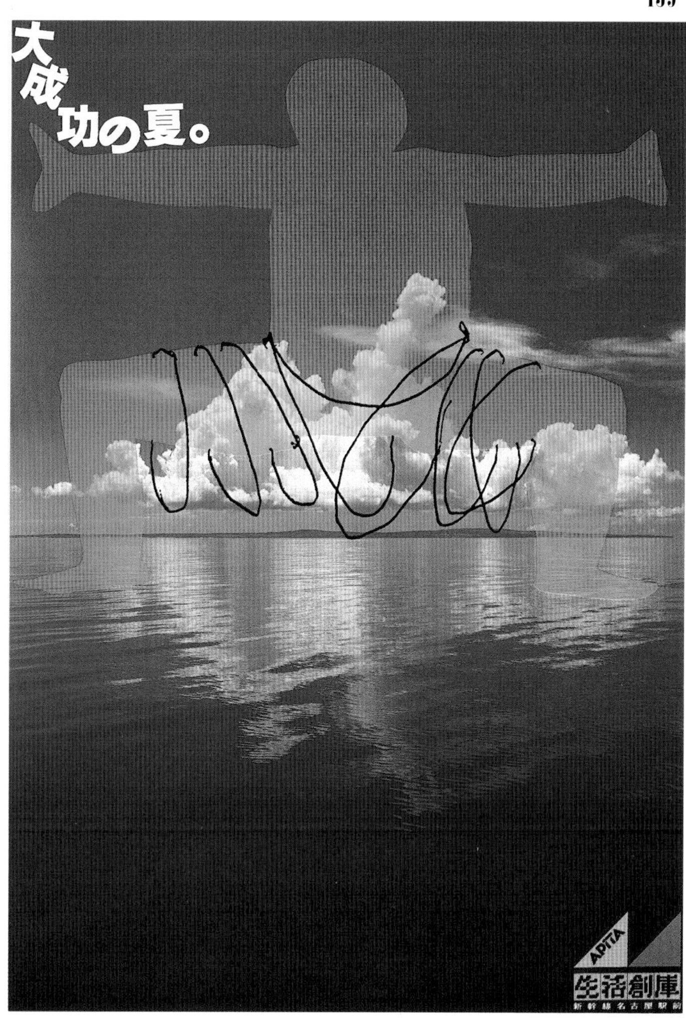

22 Poster for shopping mall ショッピングセンターのポスター 1987

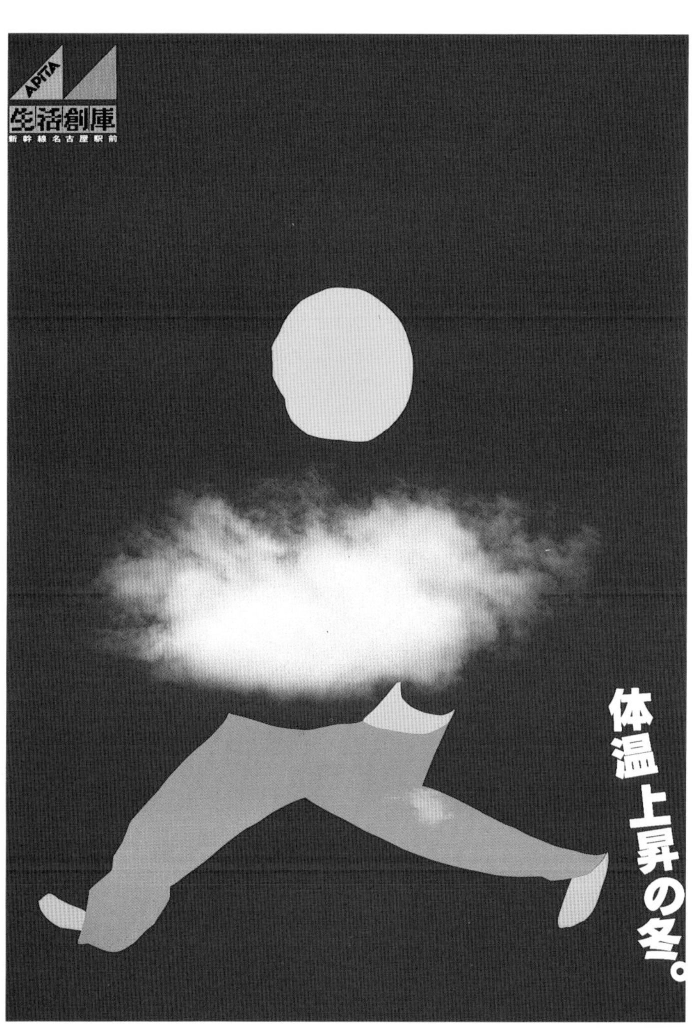

21 Poster for shopping mall ショッピングセンターのポスター 1987

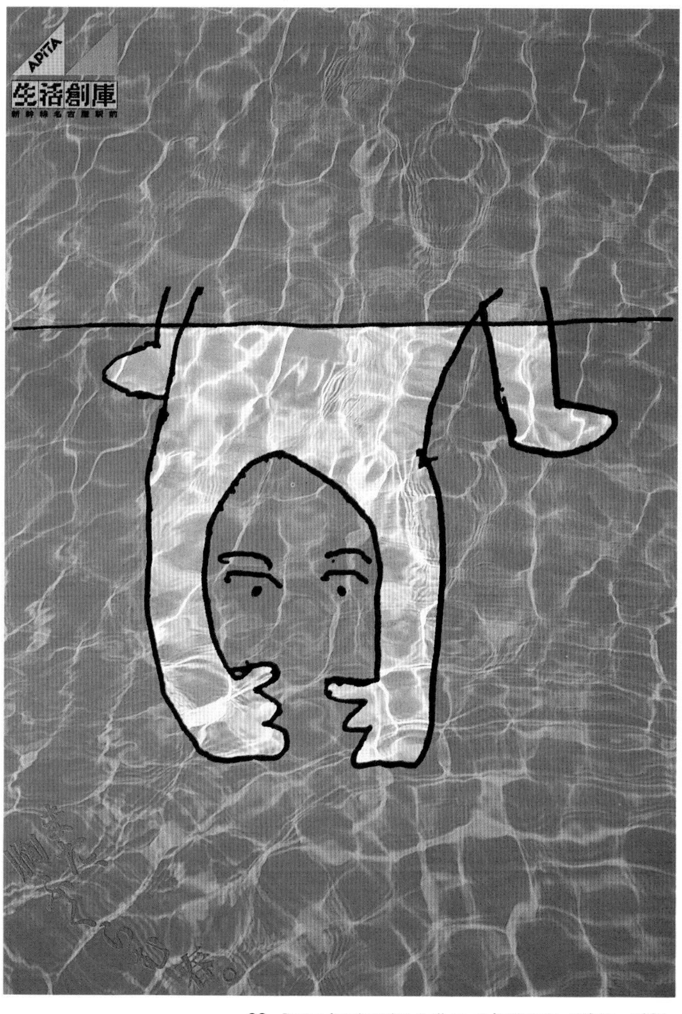

23 Poster for shopping mall ショッピングセンターのポスター 1987

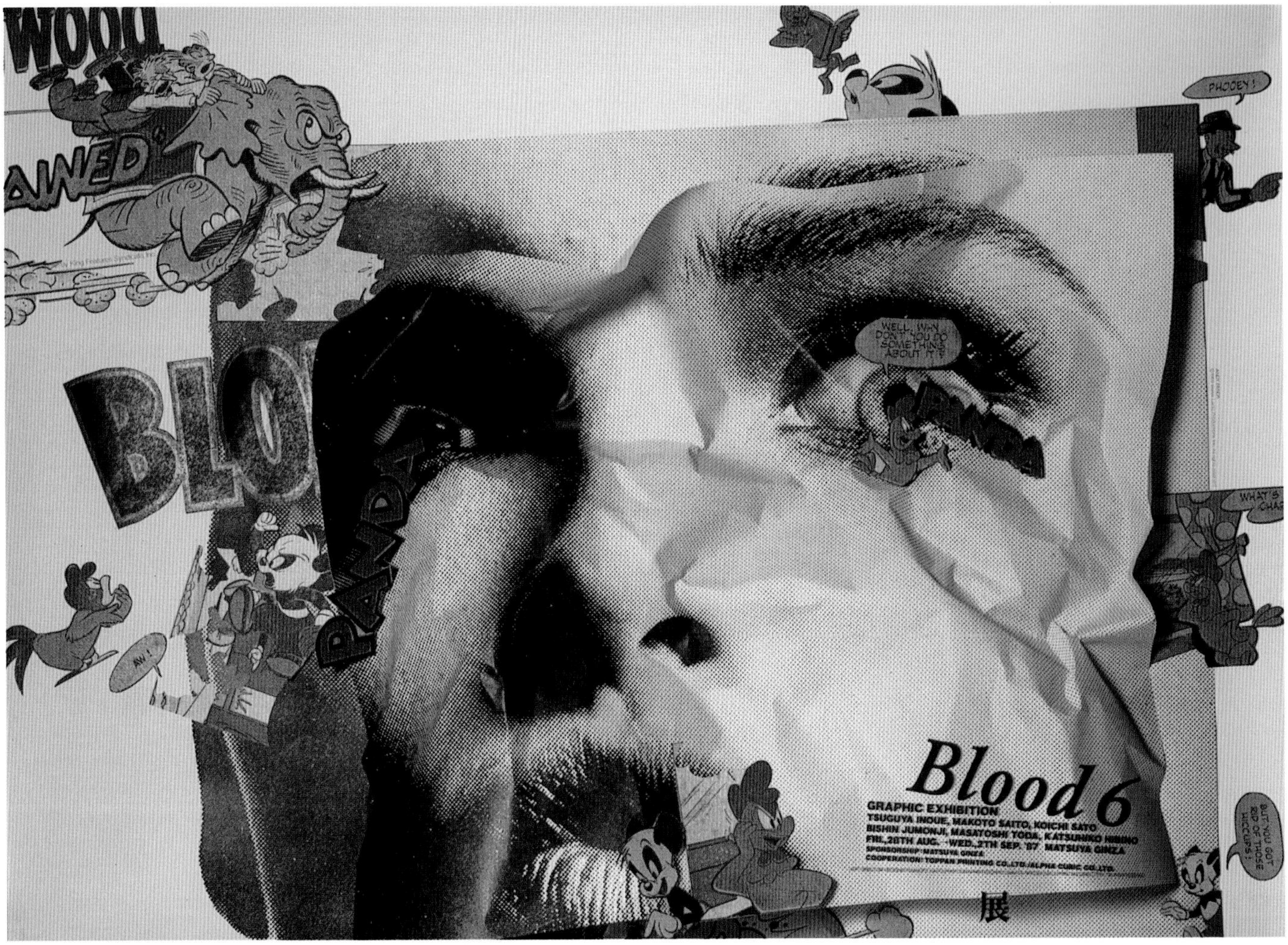

24 Exhibition poster 展覧会ポスター 1987

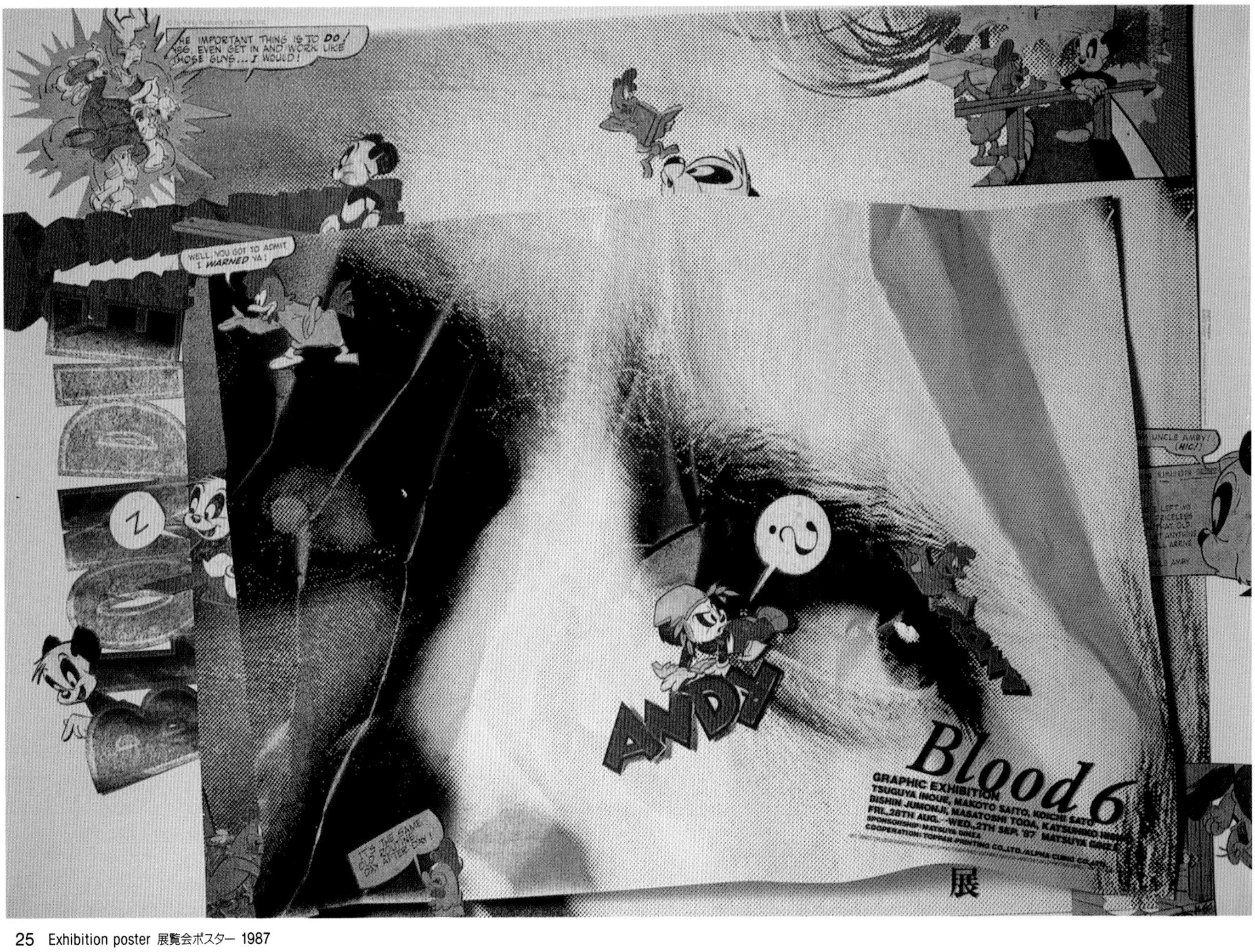

25 Exhibition poster 展覧会ポスター 1987

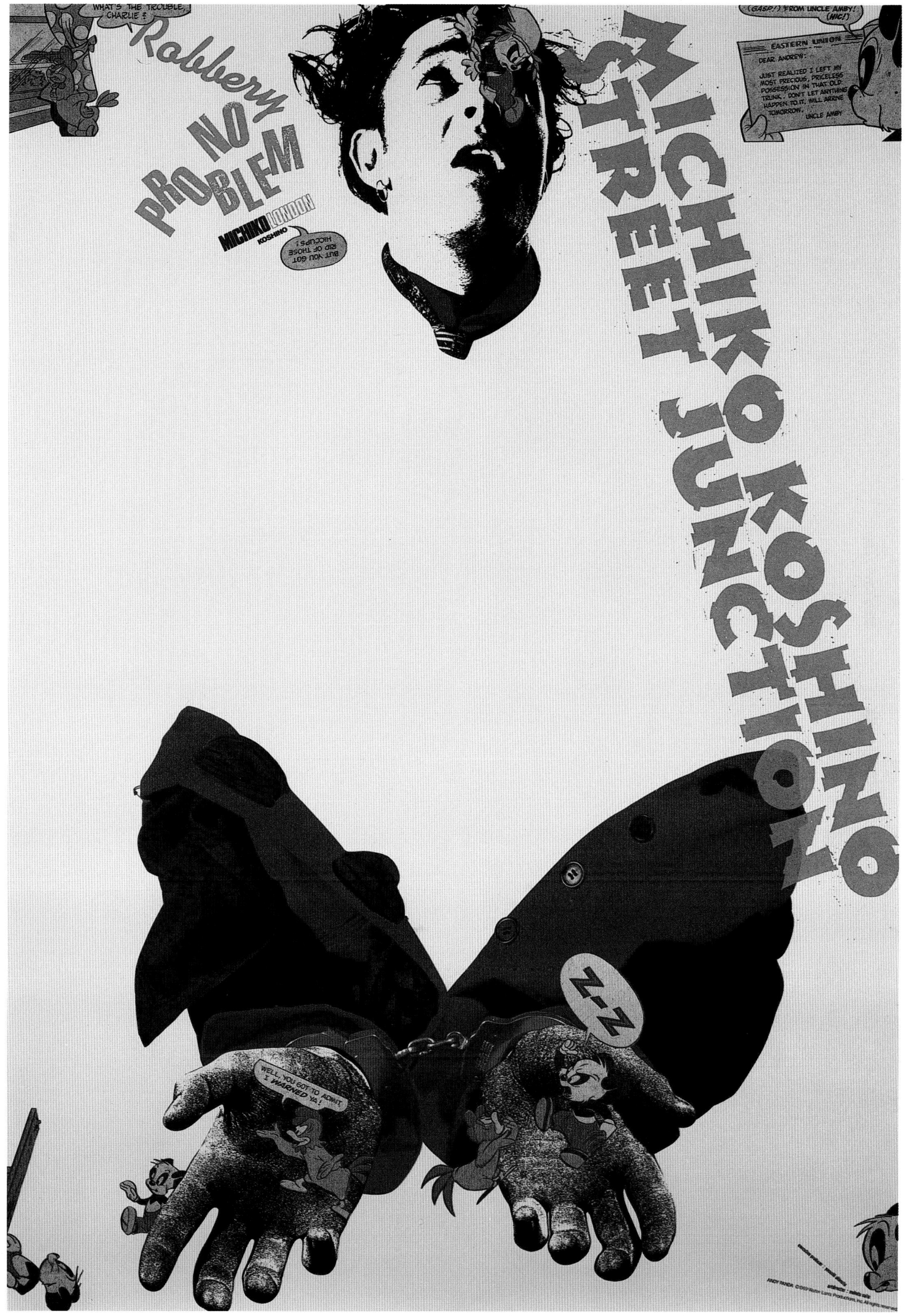

26 Fashion show poster ファッションショーポスター 1987

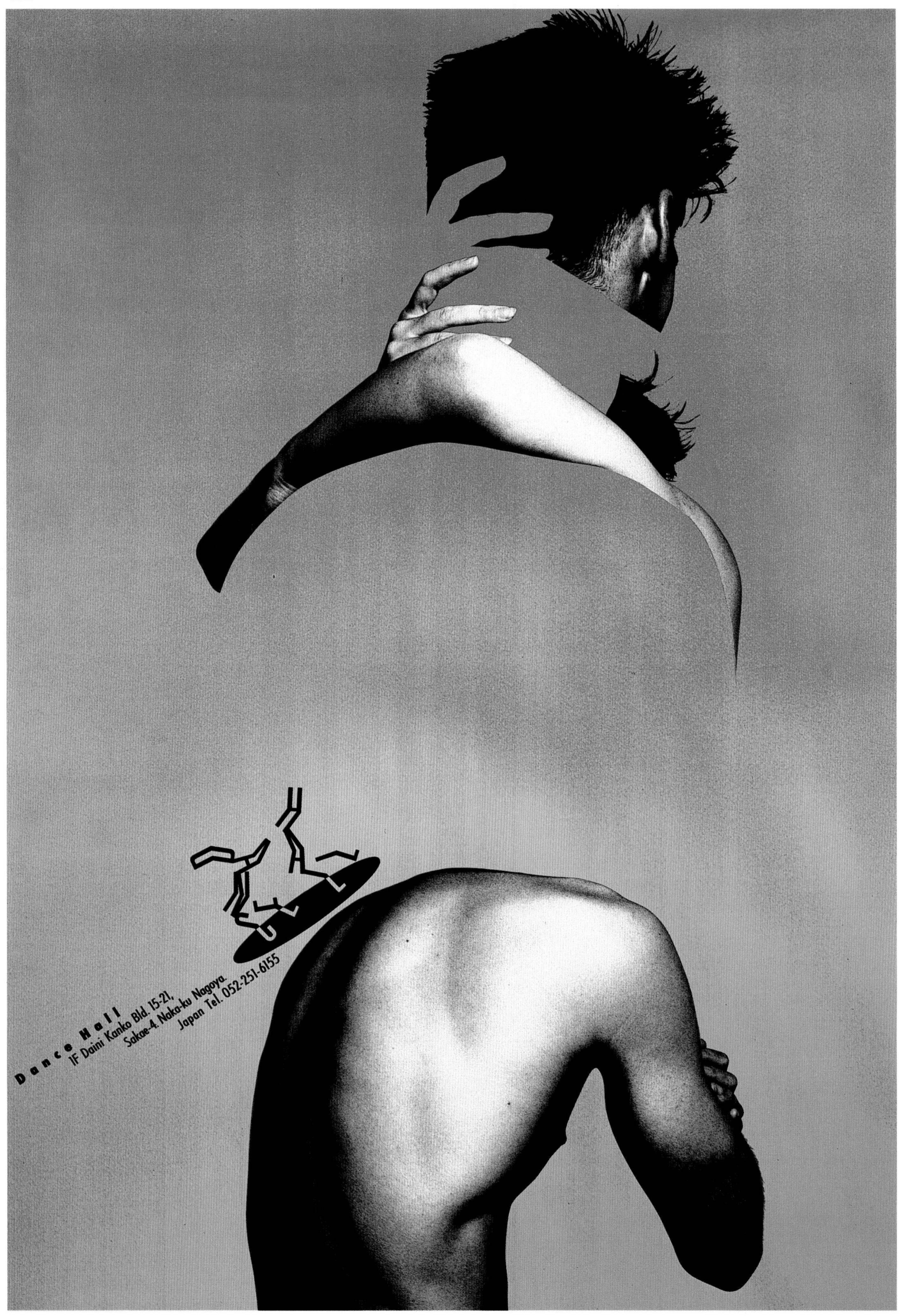

27 Discotheque poster ディスコのポスター 1986

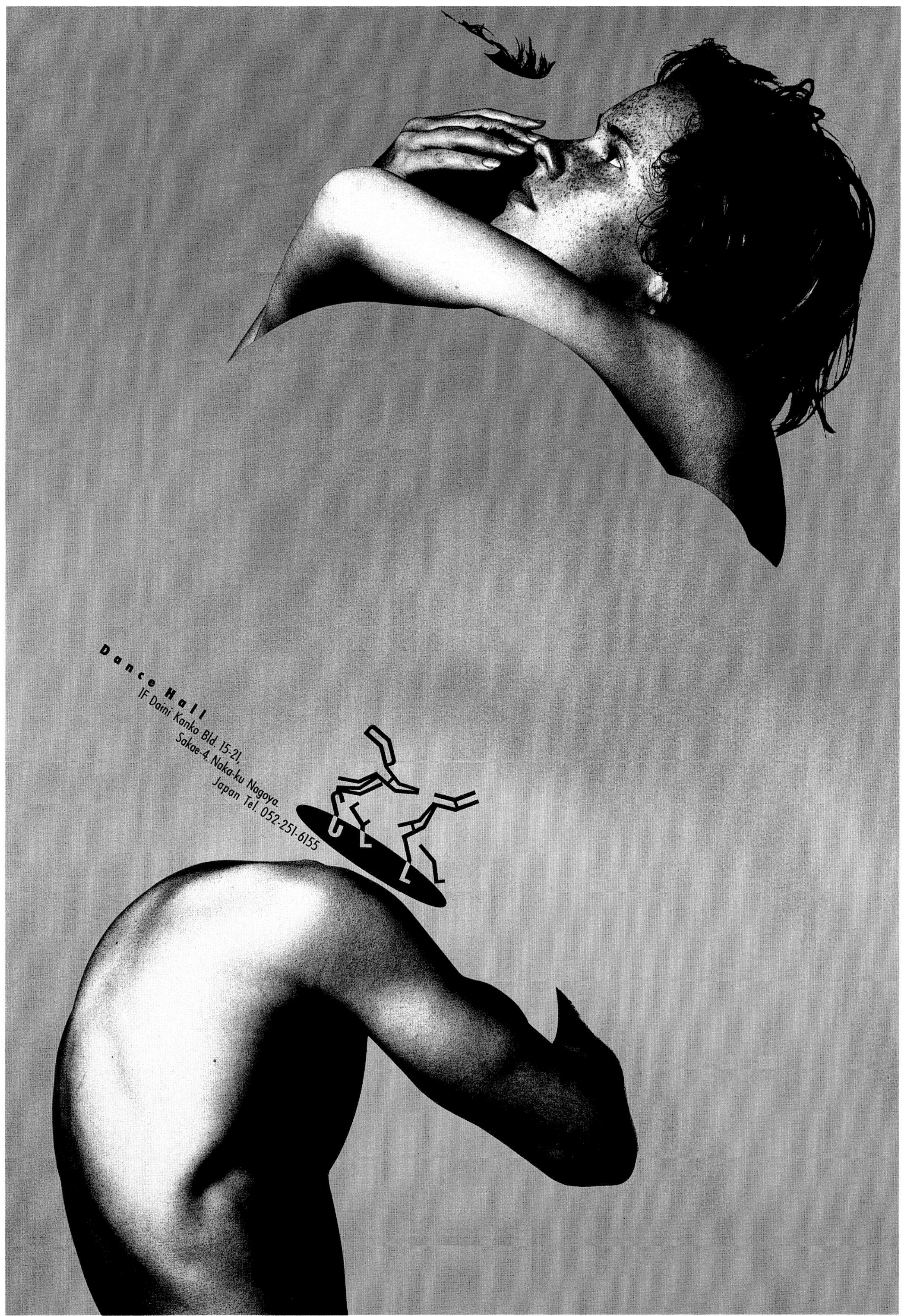

28 Discotheque poster ディスコのポスター 1986

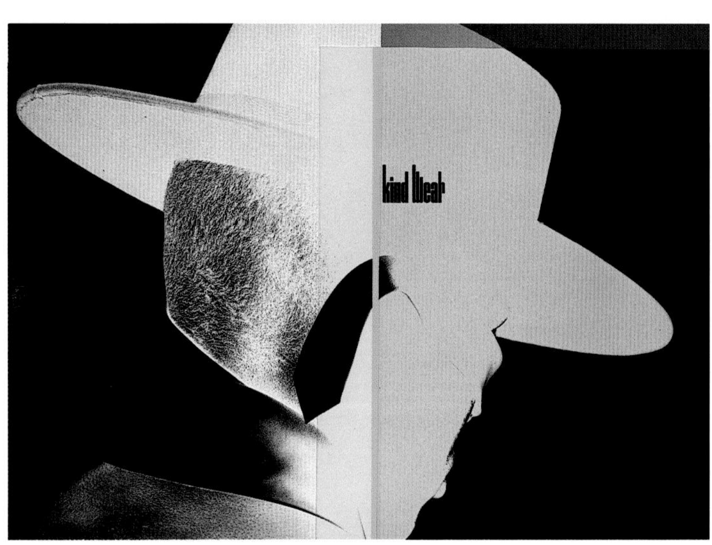

29 Fashion poster ファッションブランドのポスター 1988

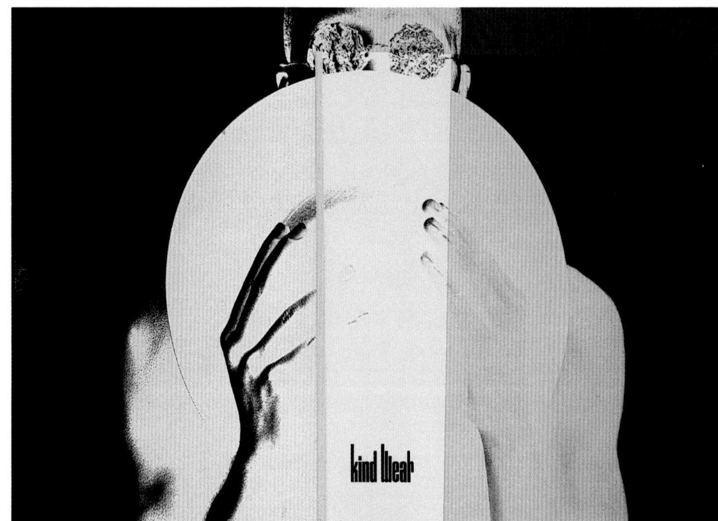

30 Fashion poster ファッションブランドのポスター 1988

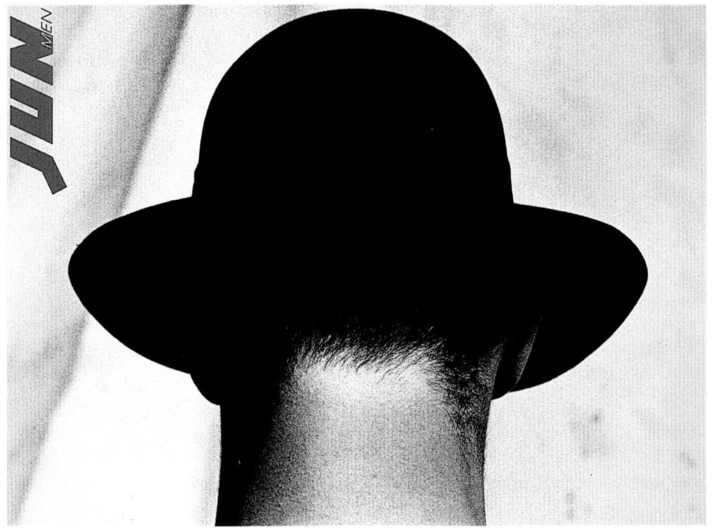

31 Fashion poster ファッションブランドのポスター 1986

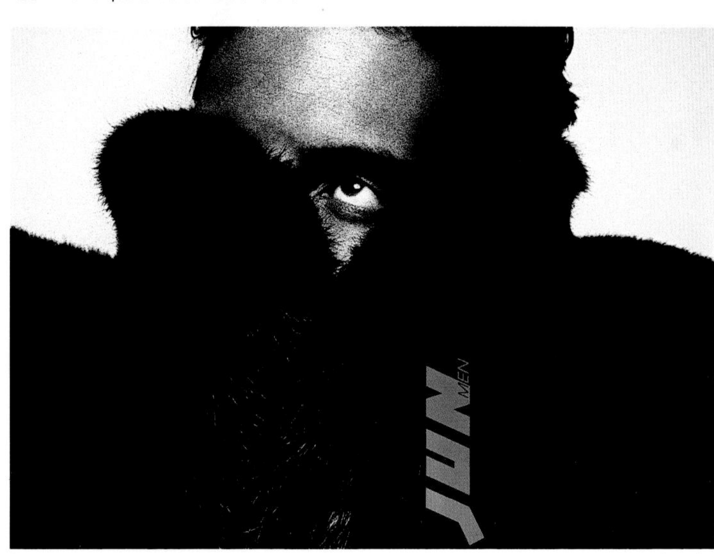

32 Fashion poster ファッションブランドのポスター 1986

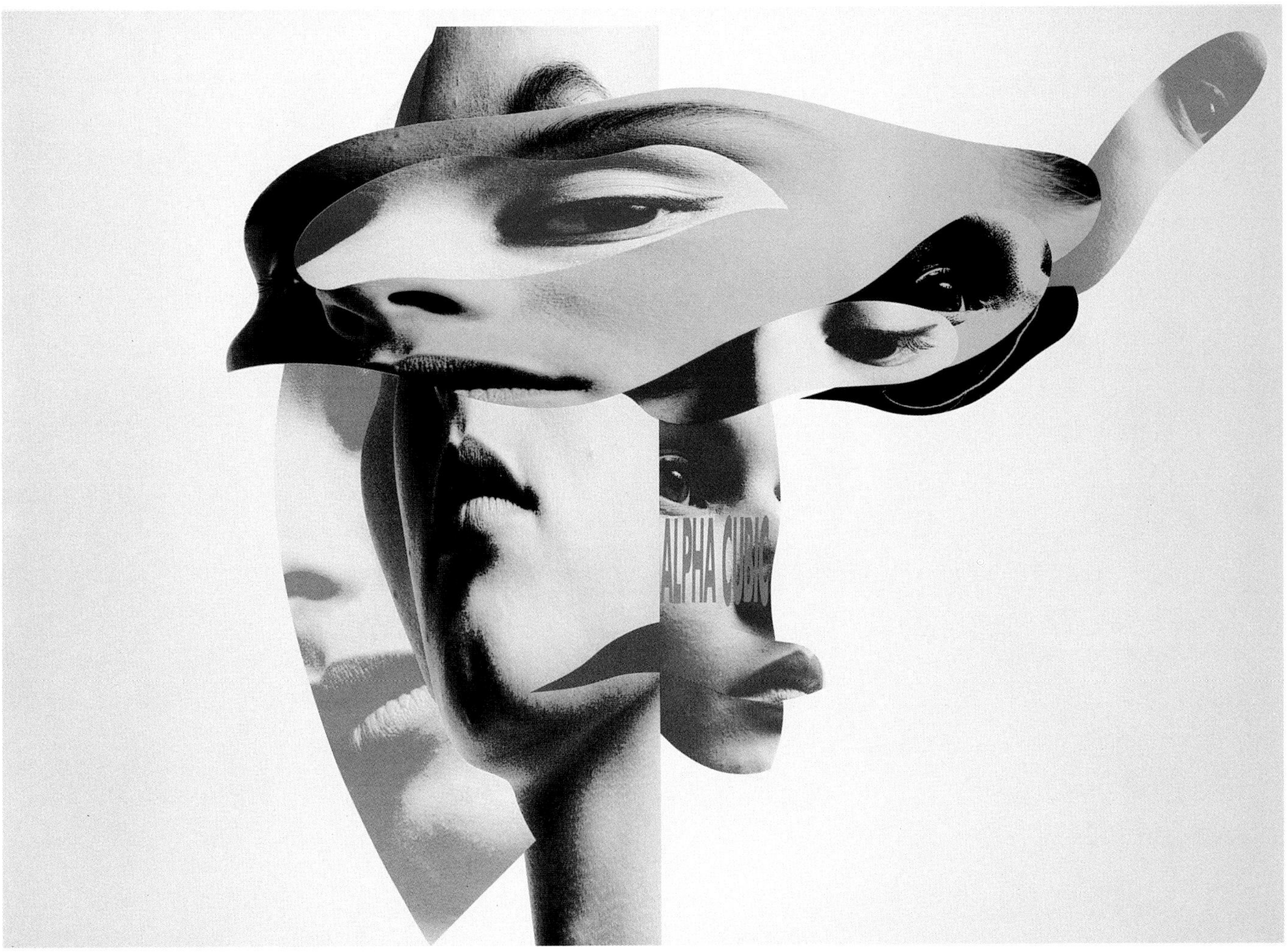

33 Fashion poster ファッションブランドのポスター 1988

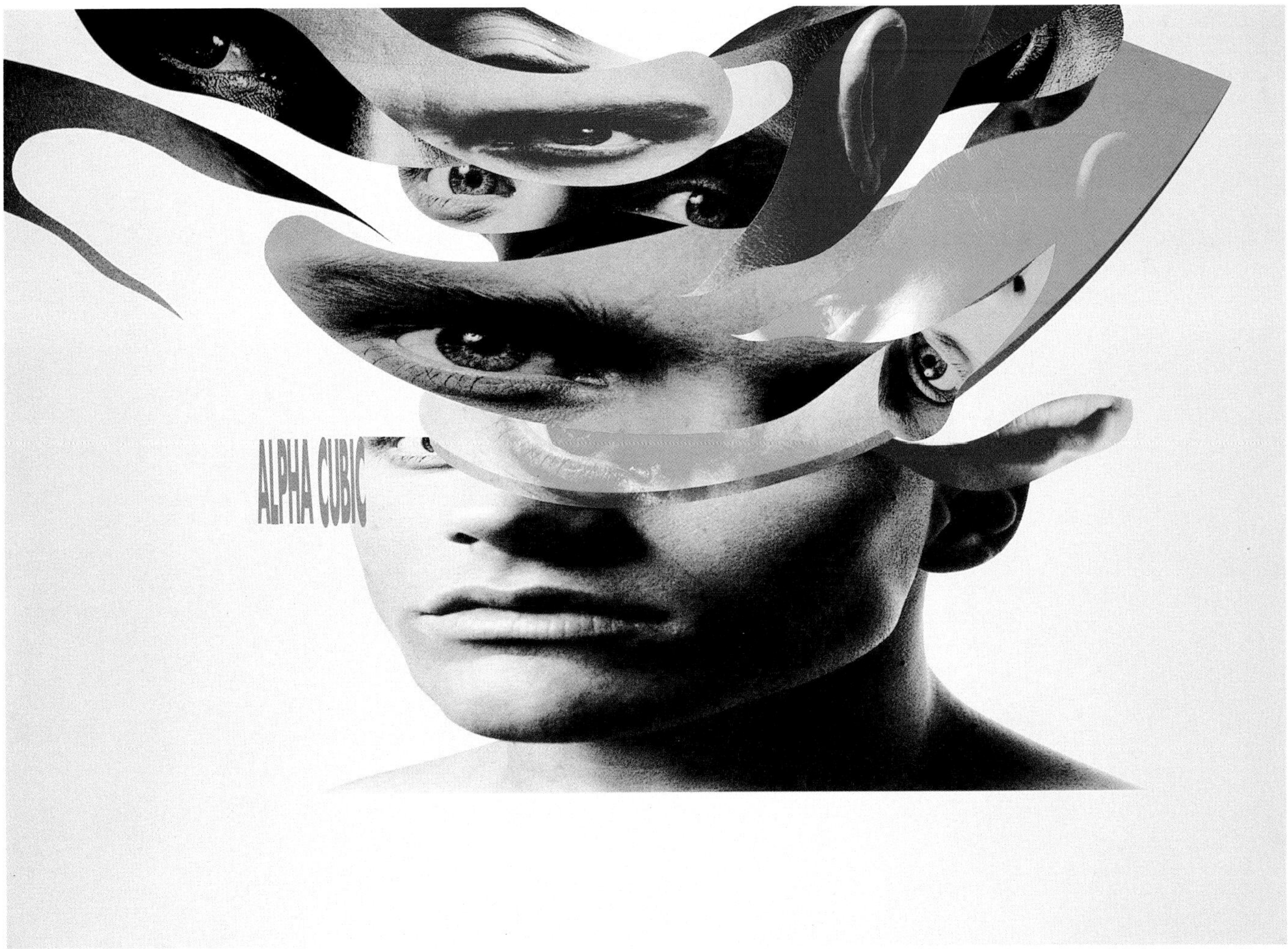

34 Fashion poster ファッションブランドのポスター 1988

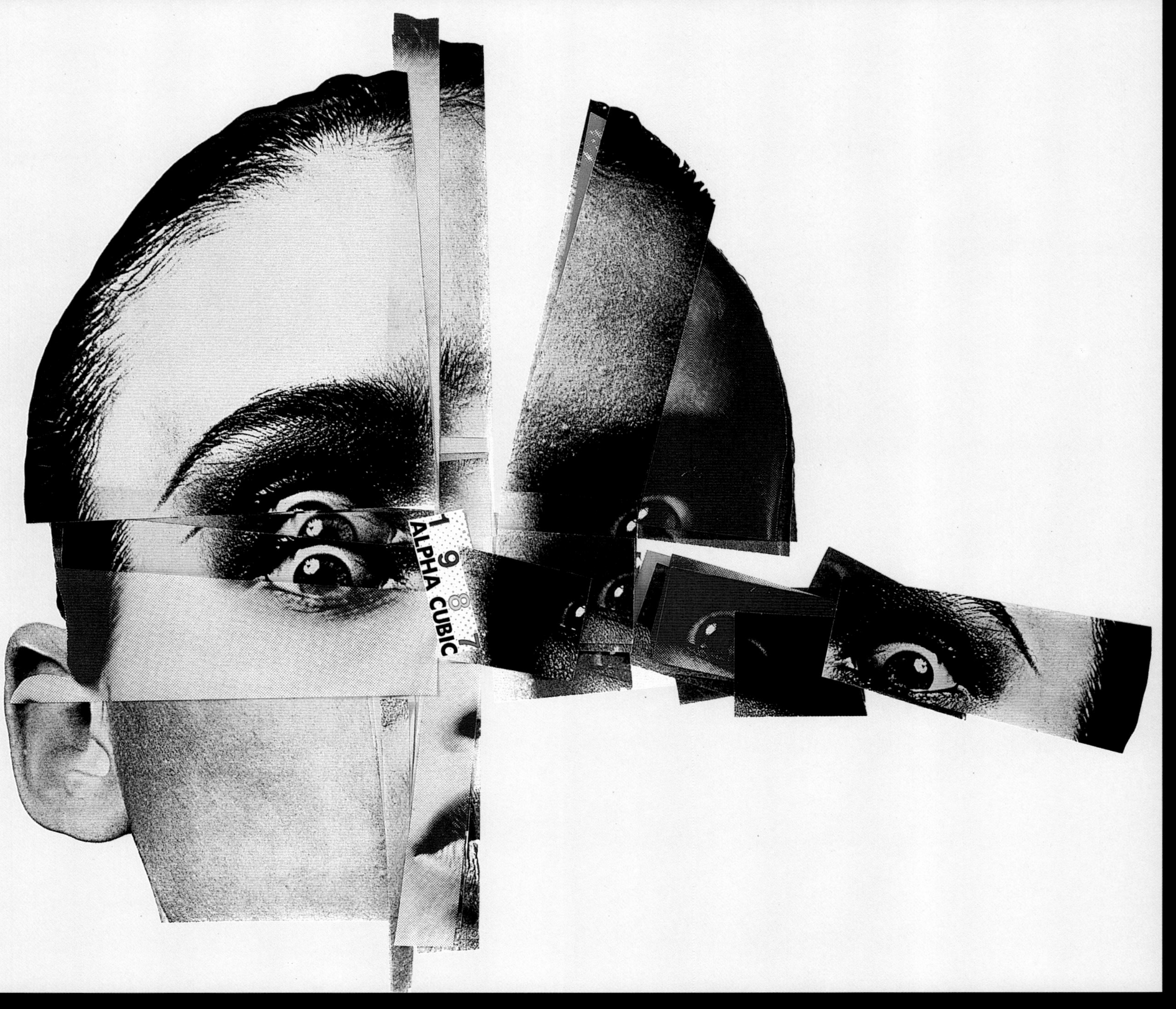

35 Fashion poster ファッションブランドのポスター 1987

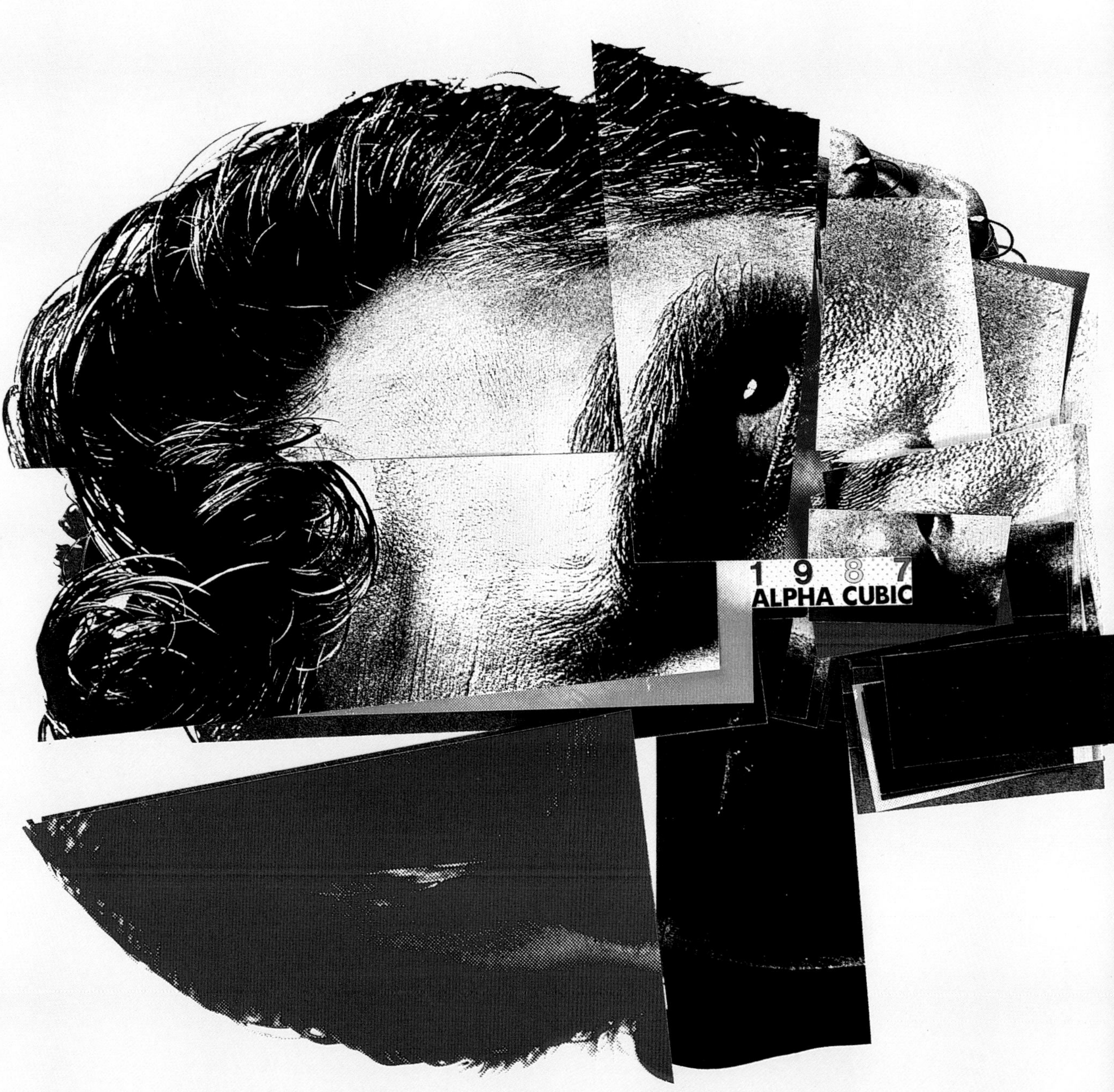

36 Fashion poster ファッションブランドのポスター 1987

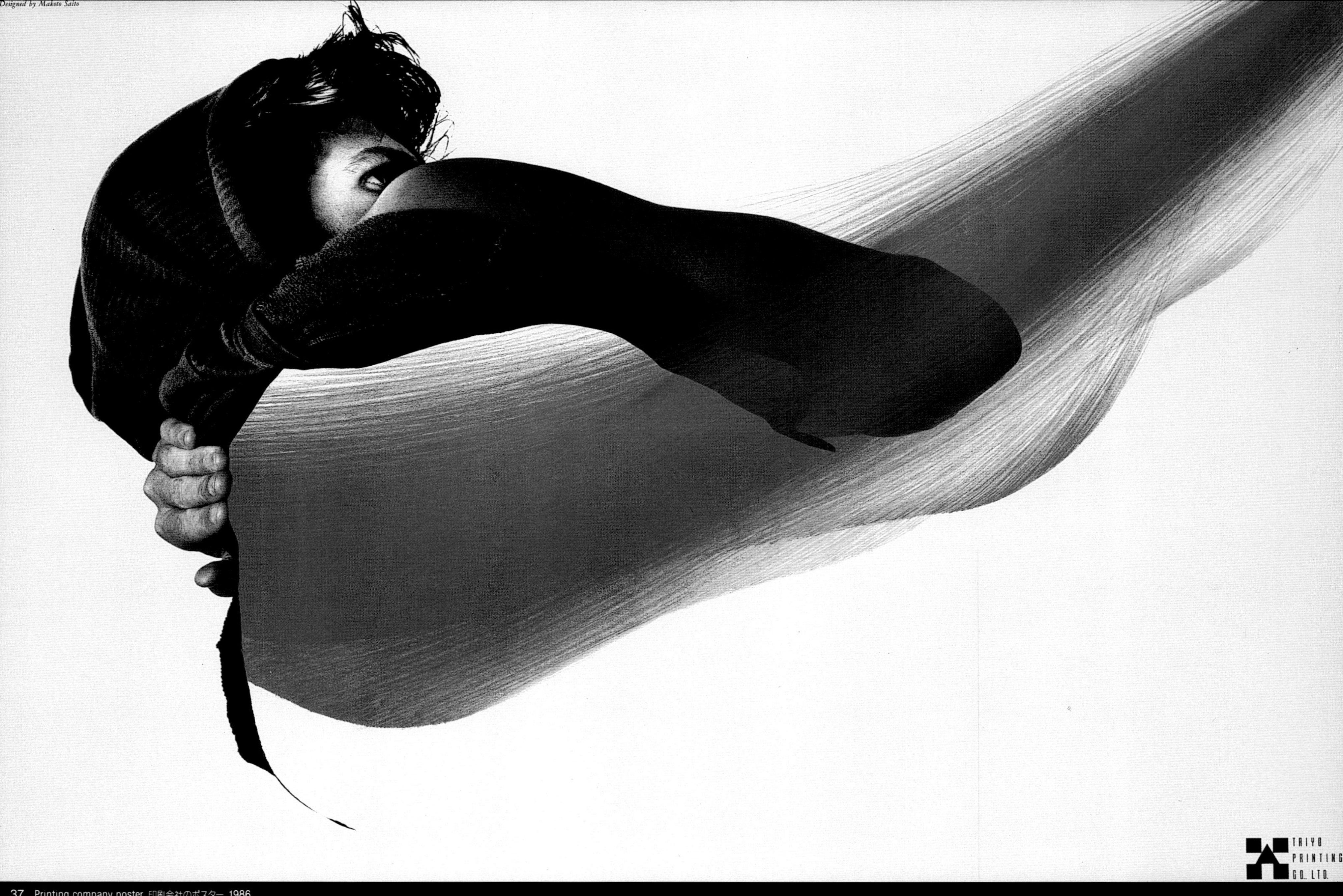

37 Printing company poster 印刷会社のポスター 1986

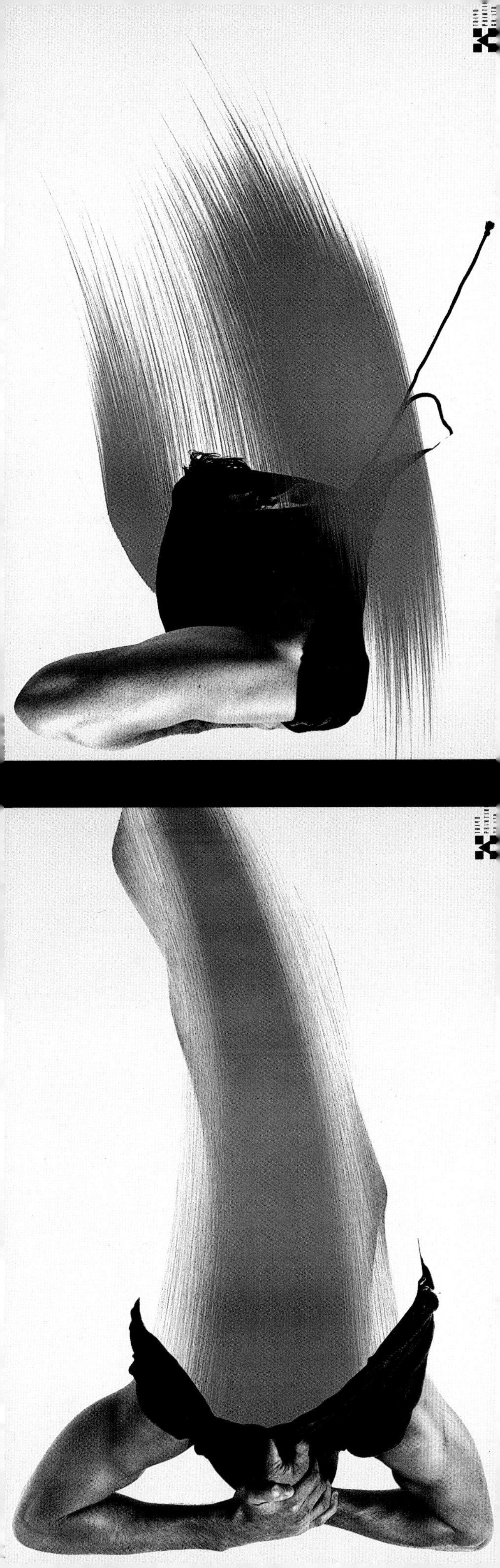

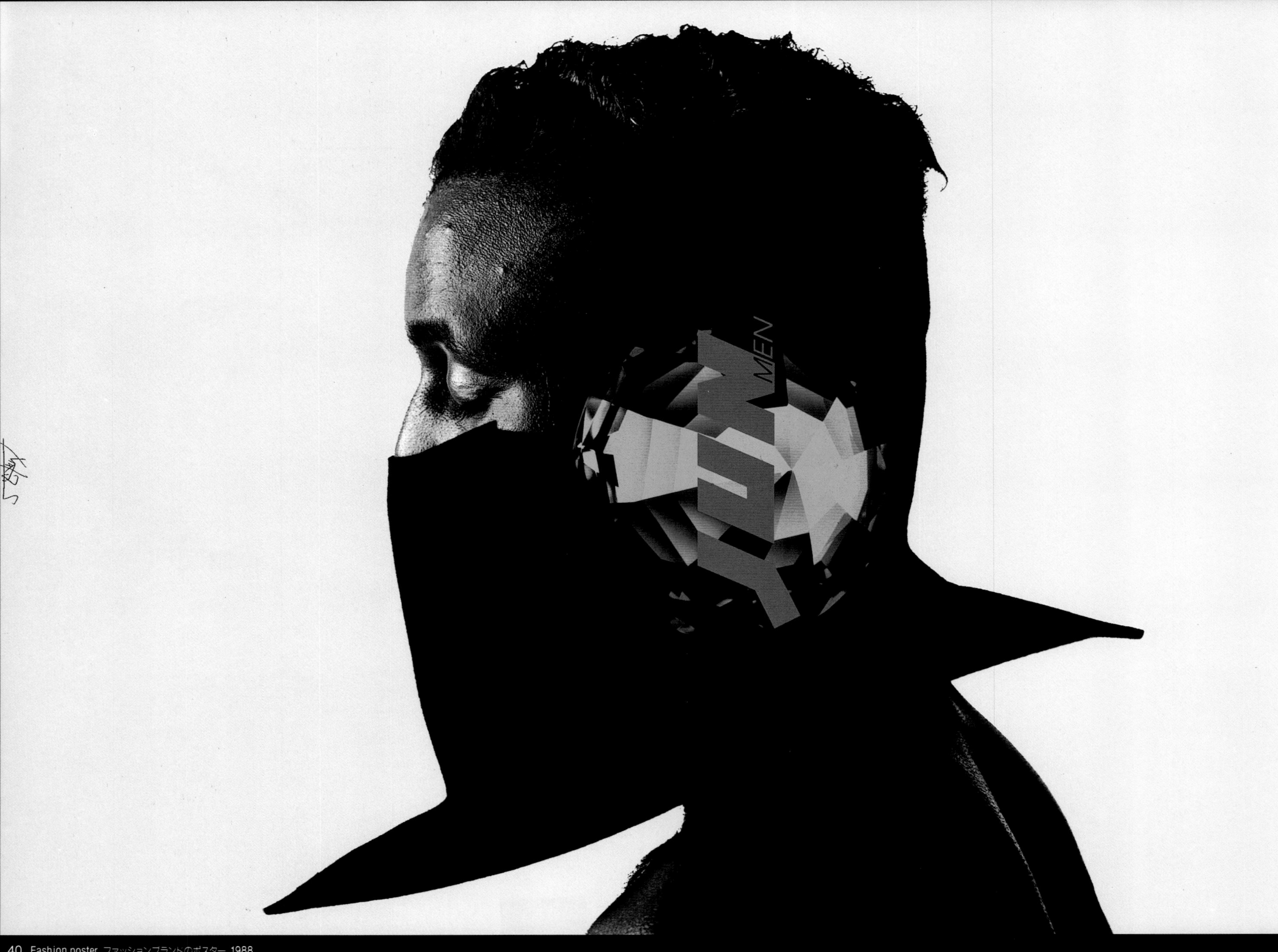

40 Fashion poster ファッションブランドのポスター 1988

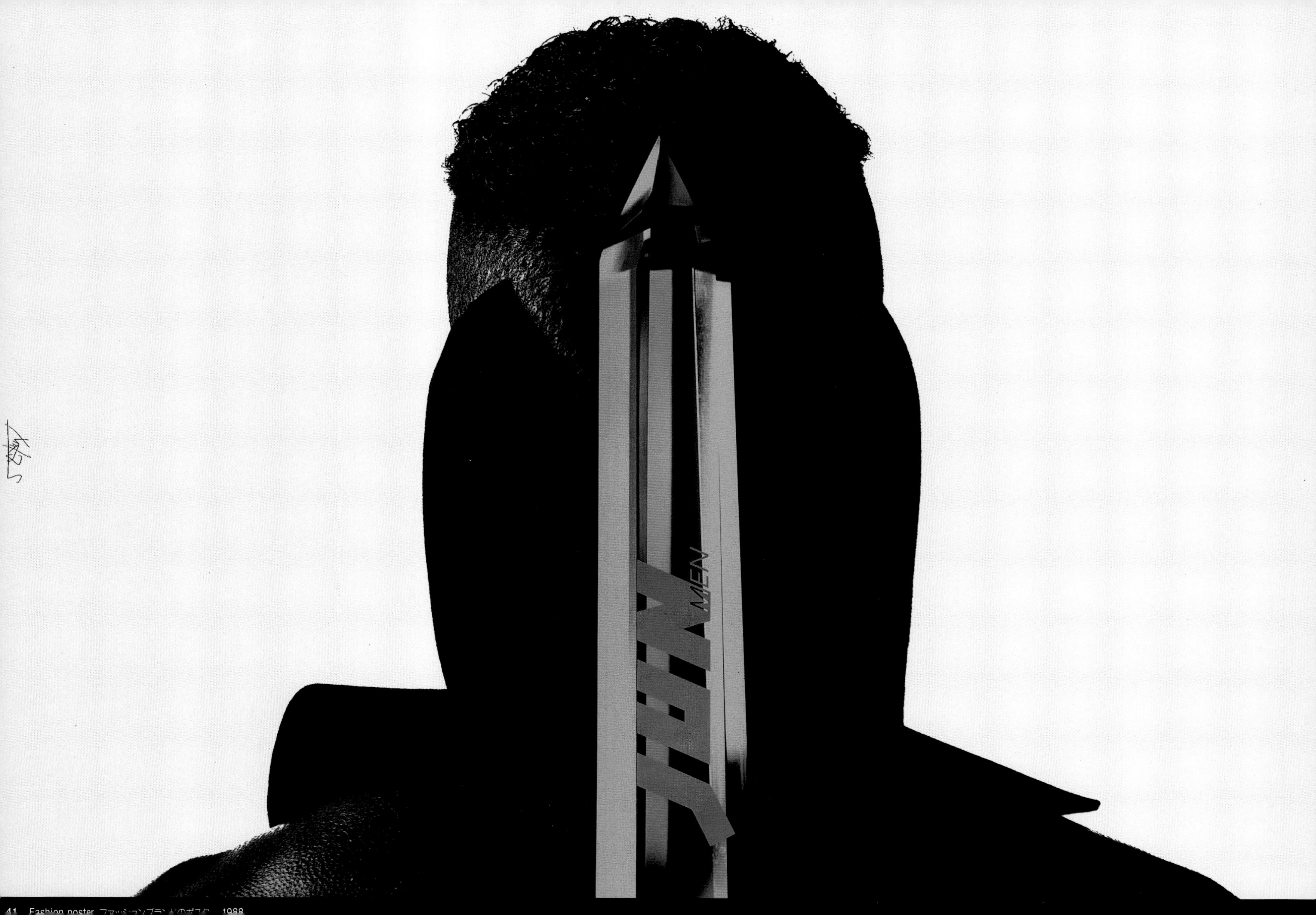

41 Fashion poster ファッションブランドのポスター 1988

Editor's Viewpoint 編集者の視点

JAPANESE FAMILY CRESTS 日本の紋章

Yusaku Kamekura 亀倉雄策

In Japan, every family has its own crest passed down from generation to generation. This contrasts with family insignia in the West which are possessed only by royalty or territorial lords.

The use of family emblems in Japan is said to have originated during the Heian Period (794-1185). This was an age when the aristocracy held political rein, and family crests served as their lofty symbols.

During the ensuing Kamakura Period (1185-1333), political control passed into the hands of samurai warriors. Through this course of events the warrior class came to embrace family crests.

In the Sengoku Period (1482-1558), a period of persistent internecine warfare, heraldic insignia adorned flags and banners taken into battle to intimidate the enemy. By hoisting their crested pennants high on the battlefield, warrior generals transformed grisly, life-threatening combat into glorious encounters with death. Coats-of-arms thus became symbols of the aesthetics of war.

With the arrival of the Edo Period (1600-1868), the Japanese archipelago was unified under a central administration that maintained peace for nearly 300 years. This was an age of self-imposed isolation from the outside world. As might be expected, however, enduring peace gradually weakened the warrior class, and economic power shifted to urban merchants. This eventuality spread possession of crests to tradesmen and farmers as well.

Tradesmen, wishing to ensure their financial fortune, frequently incorporated coins, balance weights and similarly auspicious items into their crest designs. On the other hand, farmers, seeking to invite good harvests, chose motifs such as rice plants and sickles, or, in fear of drought or other natural calamity, designs based on the sun, moon, stars, lightning, clouds and such.

Kabuki actors too came to possess their own insignia during this period, normally adopting a design that artfully restyled the first character of their stage name. With this crest they would flamboyantly adorn their stage costumes, dressing room curtains, bathrobes, folding fans, handtowels and other paraphernalia in order to create a recognizable image for themselves and win publicity. Their avid admirers are said to have flocked to purchase these goods.

In my view, the Japanese crest constitutes one of the starting points of modern graphic design. The origins of Japanese art forms are many and varied—from the Rimpa School with its simplified ornamentation and rich sensuality, to Ukiyo-e with its stylized characters and scenery. Japanese crests, with a history longer than either the Rimpa School or Ukiyo-e, achieved a level of design that is truly brilliant: the epitome of concise abbreviation and simplified symbolism.

Through the course of history, the art of creastmaking was passed down by the hand of the craftsman. During this process, superfluous lines and shapes were gradually eliminated, eventually yielding forms of perfect simplicity. The ultimate product has thereby come to be imbued with powerful expressive assertiveness. Moreover, the Japanese crest is a marvel of sophisticated taste, uncannily modern even by today's standards.

Although the precise number of crests extant in Japan is unknown, it is estimated to range anywhere up to 10,000 to 20,000. The crests illustrated in this volume have been selected from among 4,940 designs in the standard catalogs.

日本では、どの家庭も紋章を持っている。西洋の紋章の様に王様とか領主だけが持っているのではなく、どの家でも必ず先祖伝来の家紋を持っている。紋章の起源は平安時代だと言われている。この頃は貴族が政治を握っていて、文芸、特に詩歌が盛んで、しかも恋愛は爛熟期だったという。だから紋章は貴族のしるしだったのだ。鎌倉時代になって貴族の手から政治は武士の手に移ってしまった。従って武士も家紋を持つ様になり、やがて戦国時代になった。各地に蜂起した武将達の間で天下を統一する戦いが続いた。そこで家紋は戦場での目印として旗に大きく描かれ、敵に対する威嚇の役目を果たす様になった。この時代の戦争は極めて美術的と言ってもよい程、武士達は華麗な鎧や、工芸的な飾りのある刀を持って戦場に臨んだ。そして自分の家紋の旗を背負って戦ったのだから、それこそ死と対面するという凄惨さを逆に華やかで芸術的な死闘としたのである。だから紋章は戦争の美学の象徴でもあったのだ。

やがて国は統一され、江戸時代に入ると世界に前例のない300年という長い平和と鎖国の時代が続く。戦争がないので自然武士は軟弱になり、従って経済は町人の手に移ってしまった。紋章は商人や農民の家でも持つ様になった。面白いのは、商人は金儲けを願う為に銭や秤の分銅や升などを家紋のテーマにした。また農民は豊作を祈るために稲や鎌、或は干魃など自然への恐怖心からか太陽、星、月、稲妻、雲といったモチーフにしたものが多い。自分の芸名の頭文字を巧みに紋章化したのは歌舞伎役者達だった。彼等はその紋章を舞台衣装に派手にちりばめたり、楽屋ののれん、浴衣、扇子や手拭などにつけてイメージ作りと宣伝に大きな効果をあげた。ファンは競って、それらのグッズを買い求めたという。

日本の紋章は、現代グラフィックデザインの原点のひとつだと思う。日本的な造形の原点は色々あるが、例えば琳派の様に装飾性をシンプルに凝縮し、しかも豊かな情感を持つものから、浮世絵の様に人物や風景を様式化して、それが版画という技法でさらに単純化したものまである。日本の紋章は前述の琳派や浮世絵よりも歴史が古いだけに、簡潔な省略法や単純化された象徴性が見事と言っていい程明快なデザインになっている。

紋章は、長い時代の流れの中で、次々と職人の手の中で伝承されてきた。伝承されたと言っても人間の知恵は、無駄な線や、無理な形を時代の流れの中で削りとって、シンプルな形態に完成させた。しかも、その表現や説得力は力強い自己主張を持っている。さらに紋章の素晴らしいところは、大変都会的な感覚で洗練されていることである。

紋章は、普通着物の背とか両袖につける。だから直径3センチ程の小さなものだ。その小さな形から、見る人に訴えかける強い力を感ずる。しかも、その小さな形を商店の正面ののれんに直径2メートルに拡大すると、さらに強い造形力を発揮するのに驚かされる。

紋章の全部の数は、どの位あるのか知らないが1万とも2万とも言う。しかし、この本に載せた紋章は4940個の中から選んだものである。

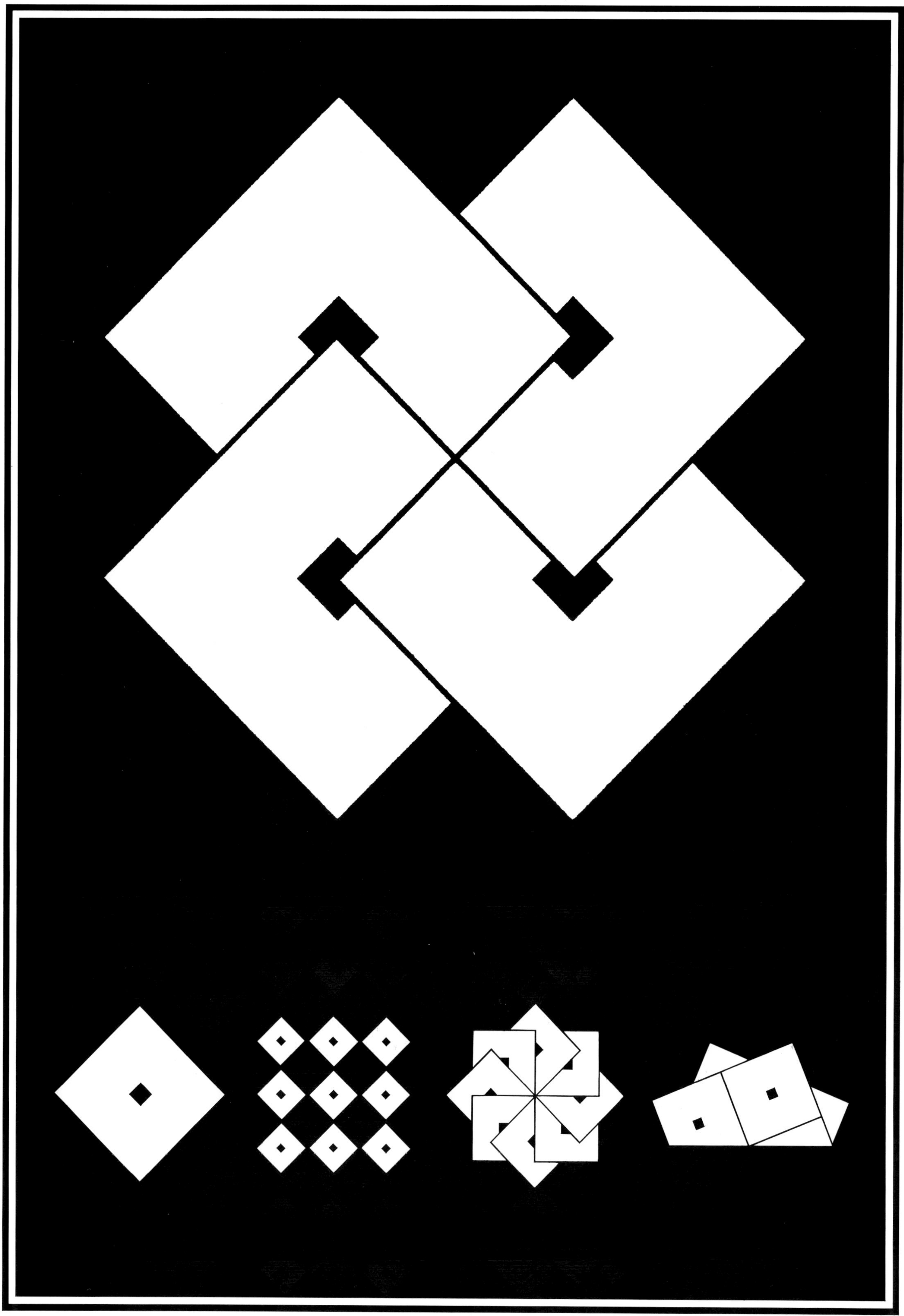

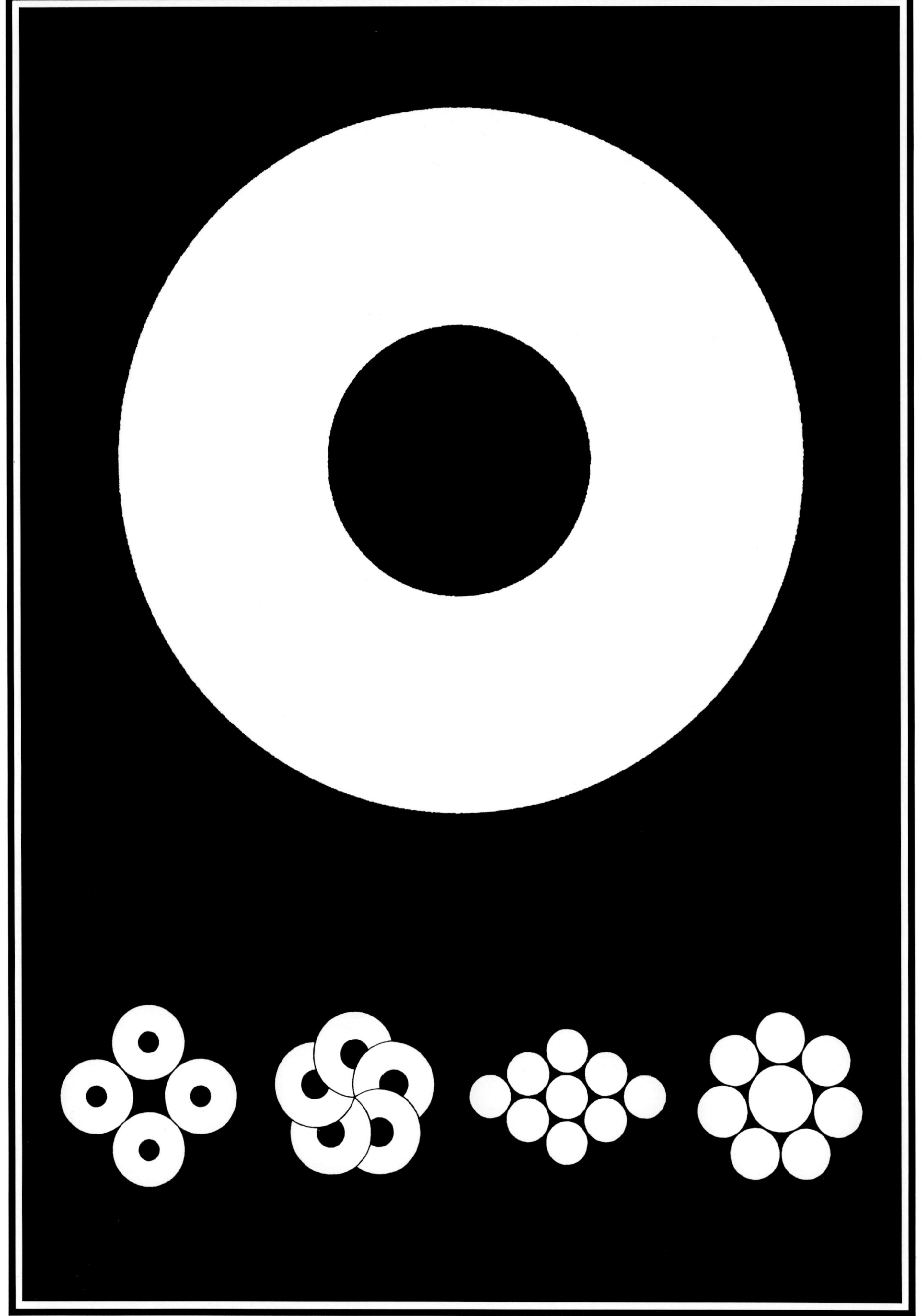

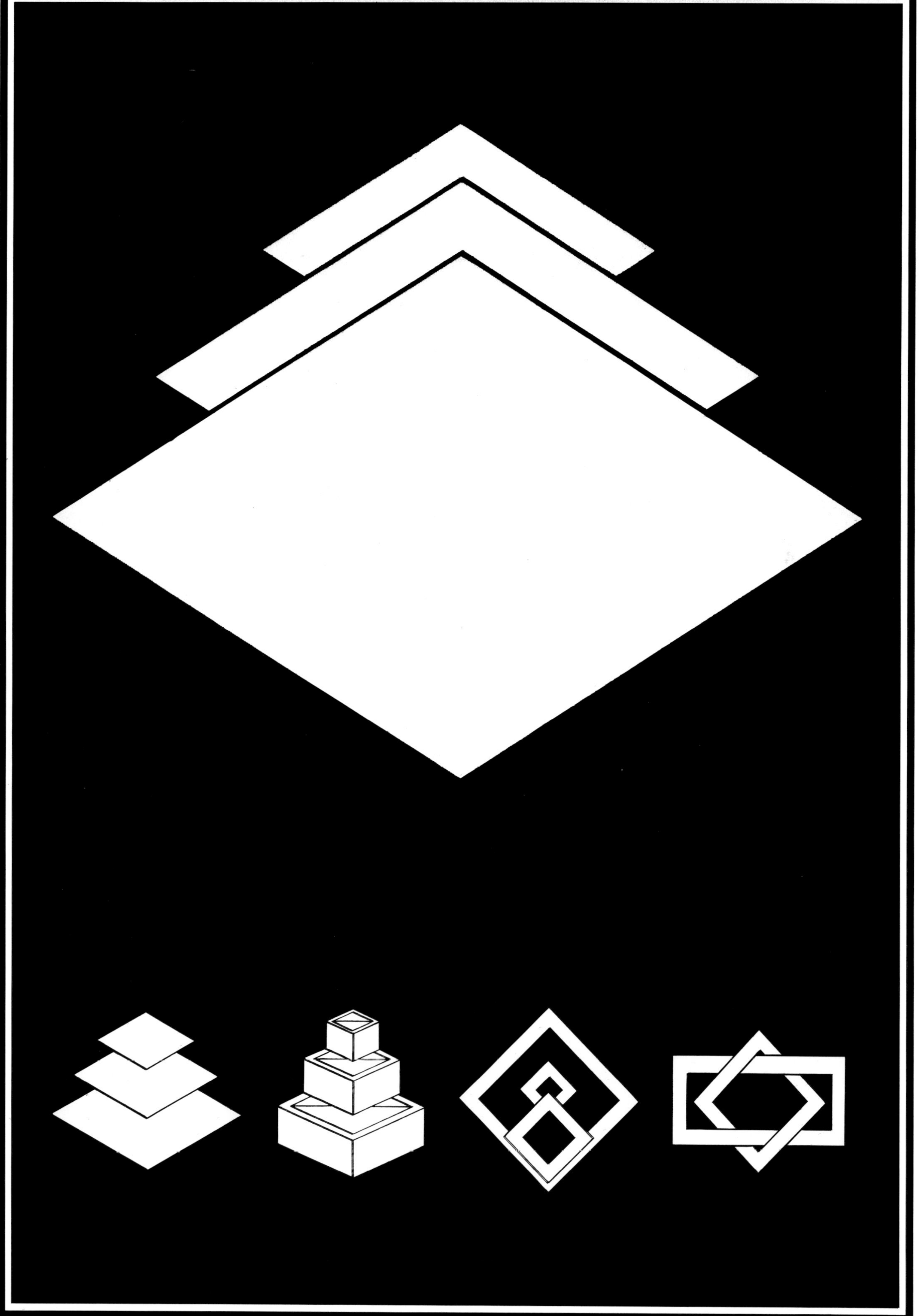

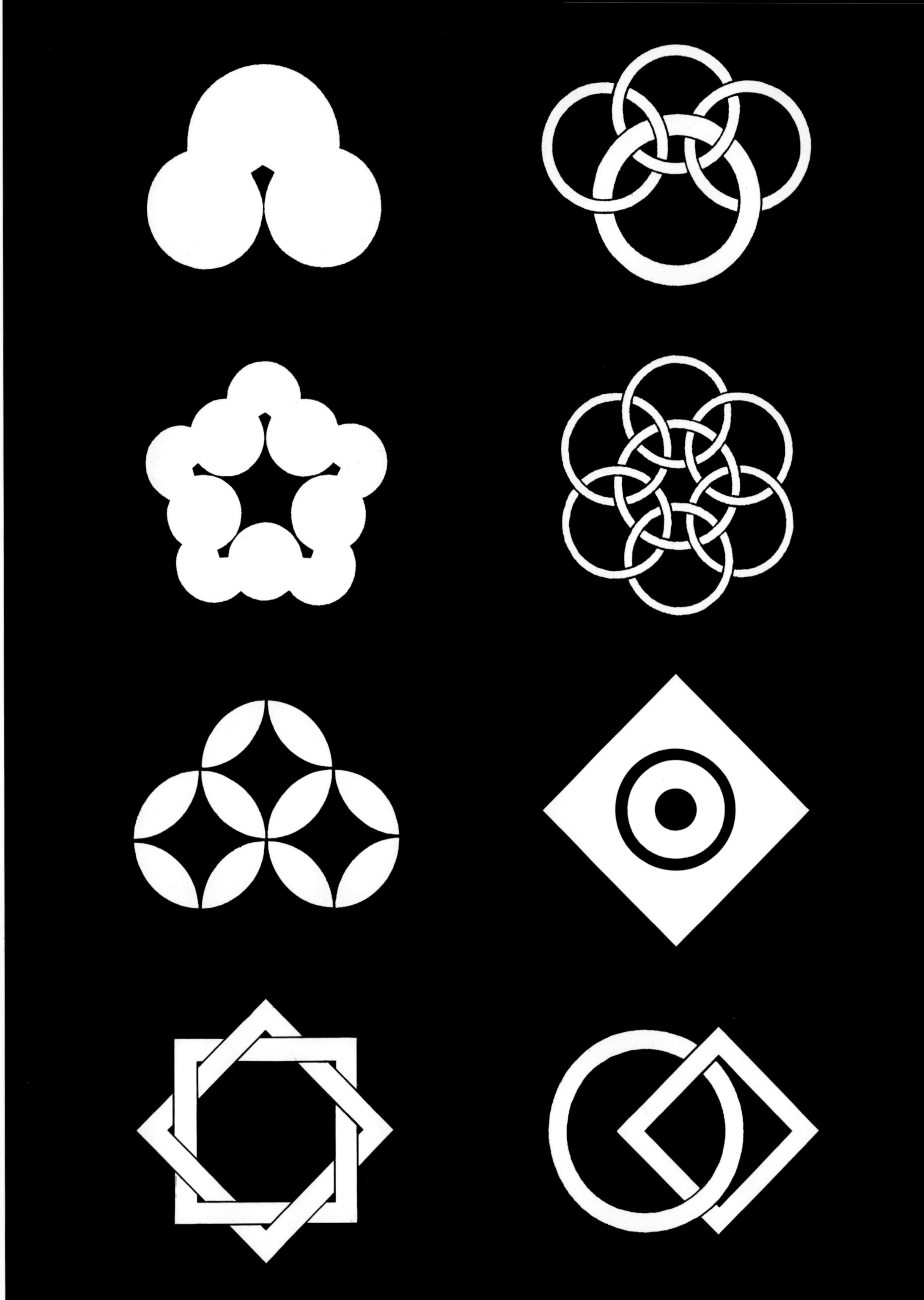

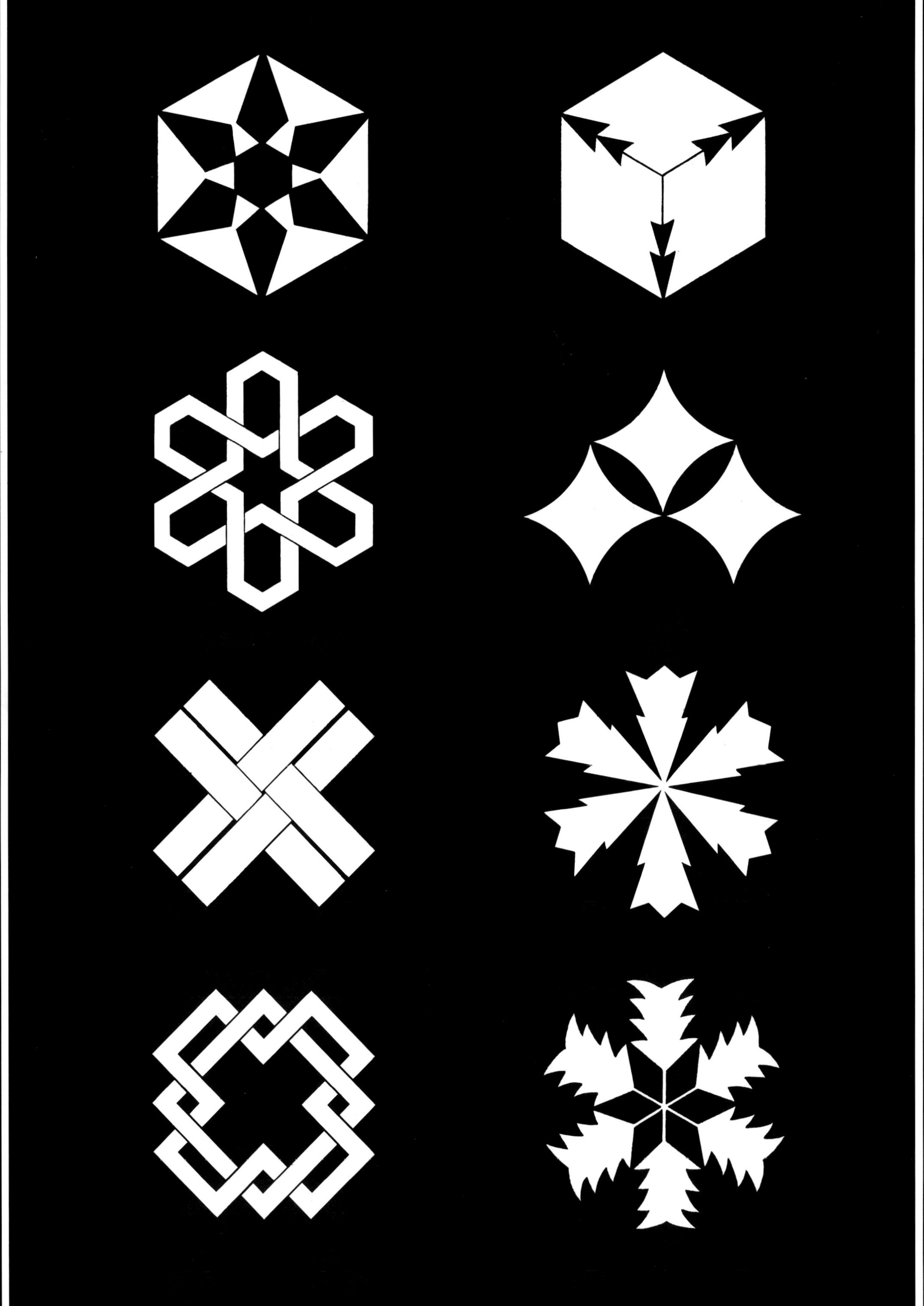

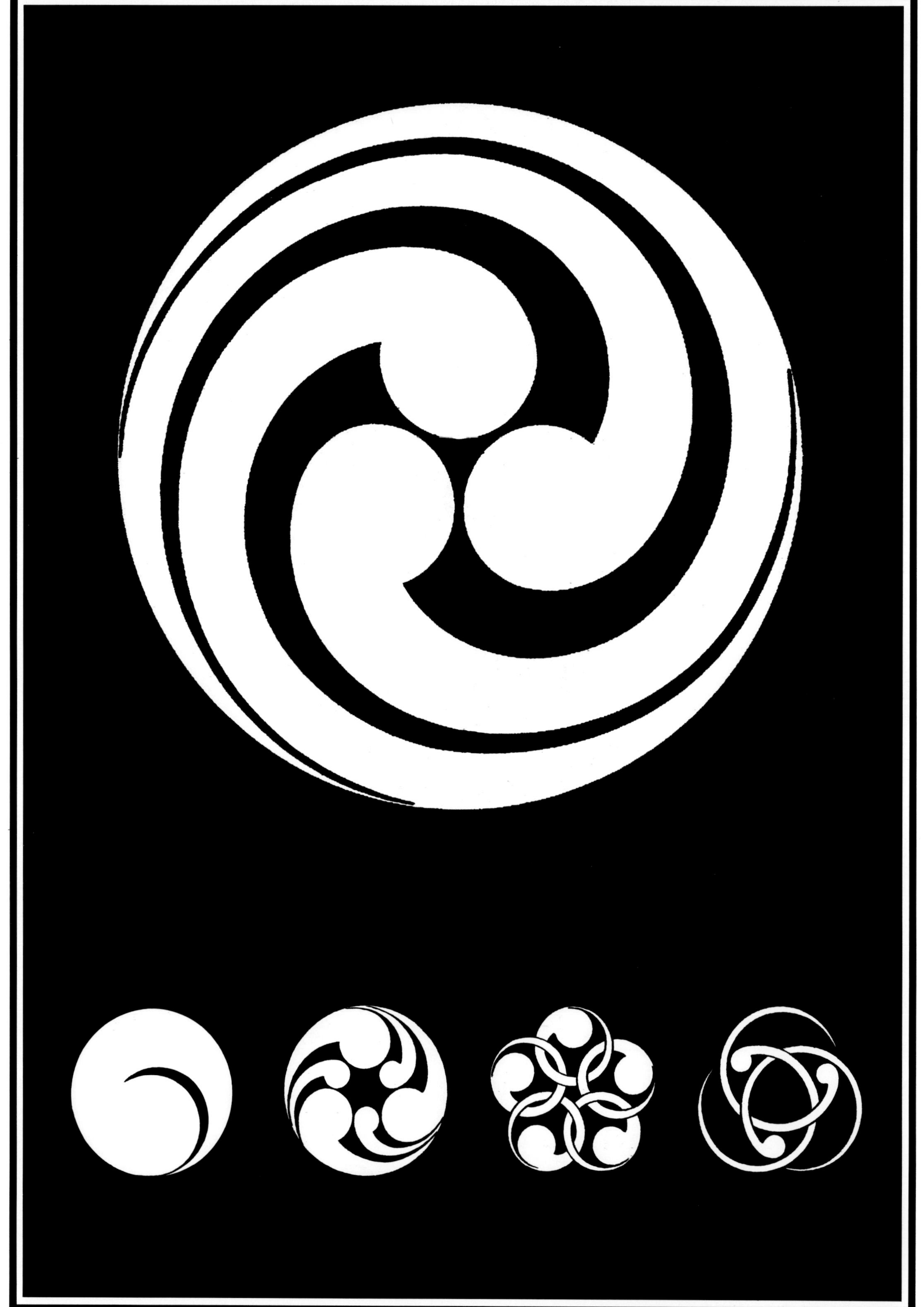

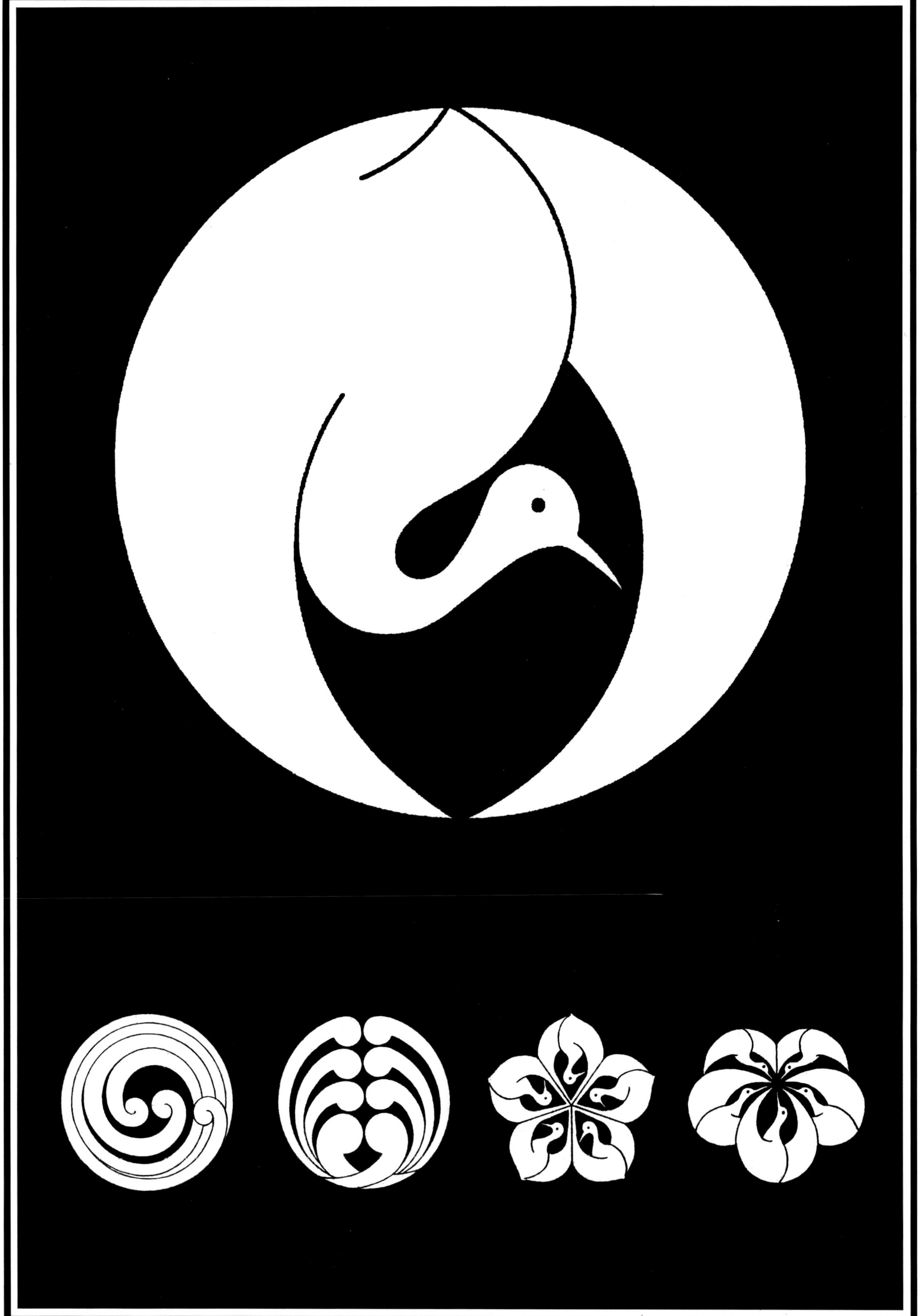

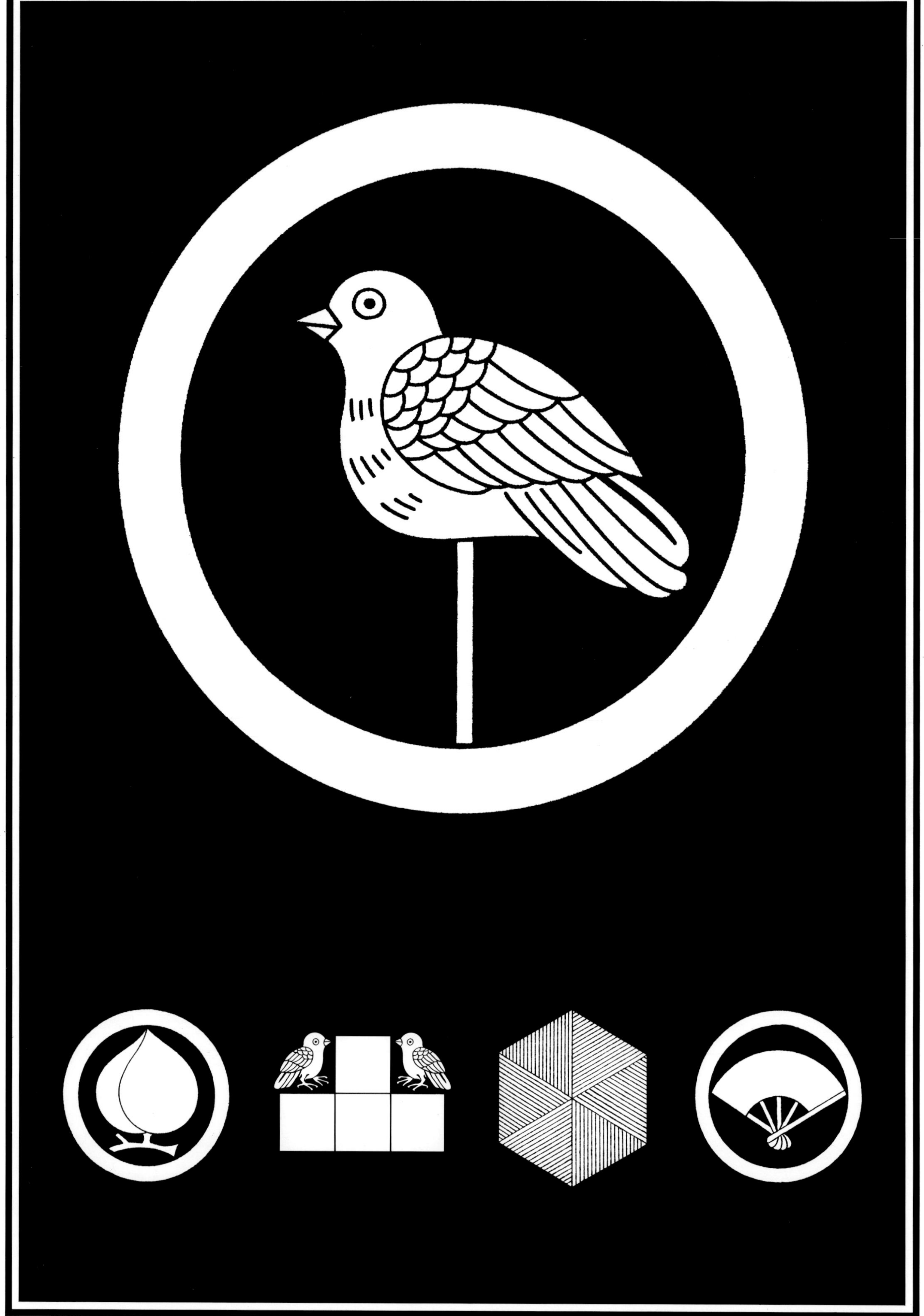

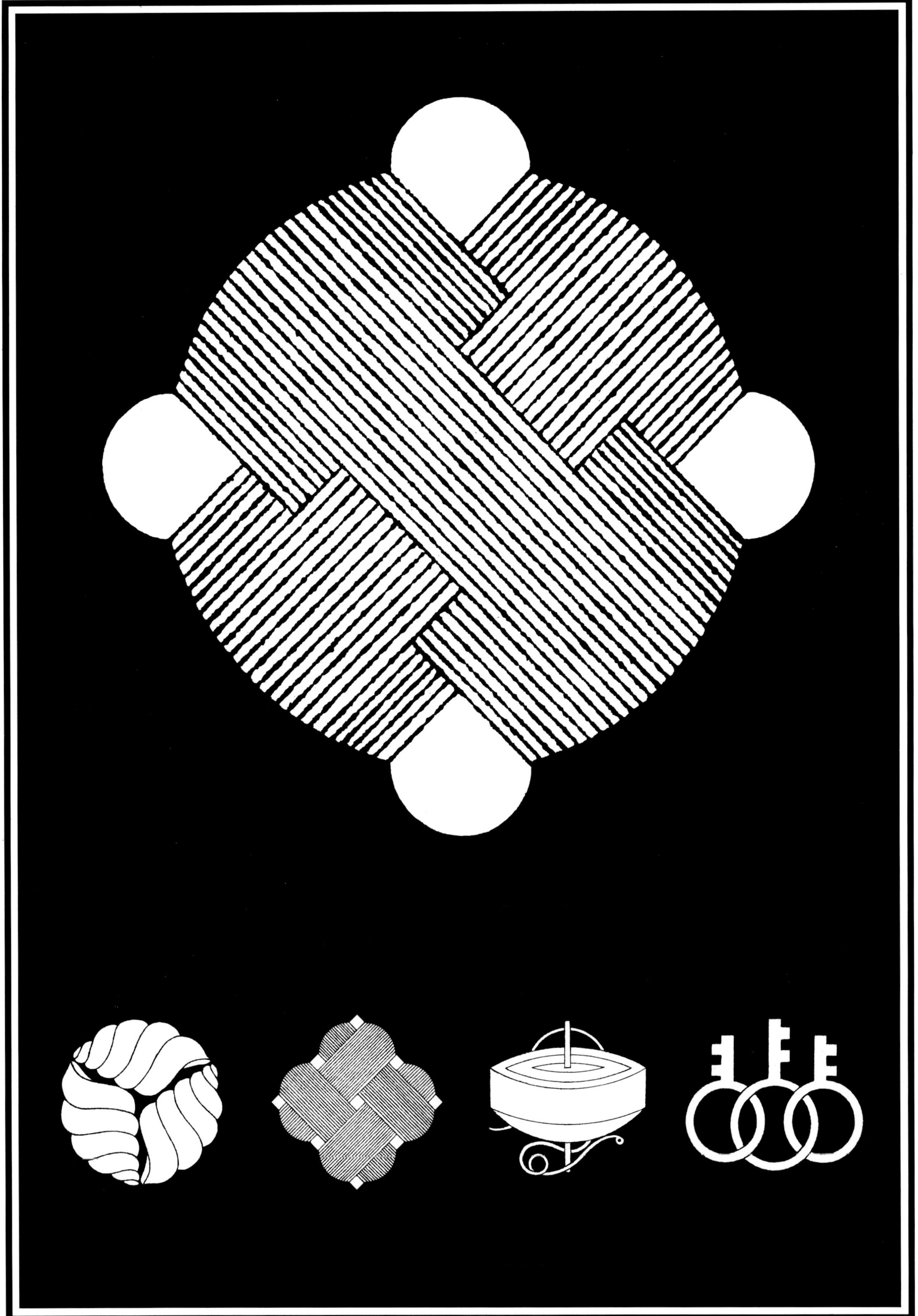

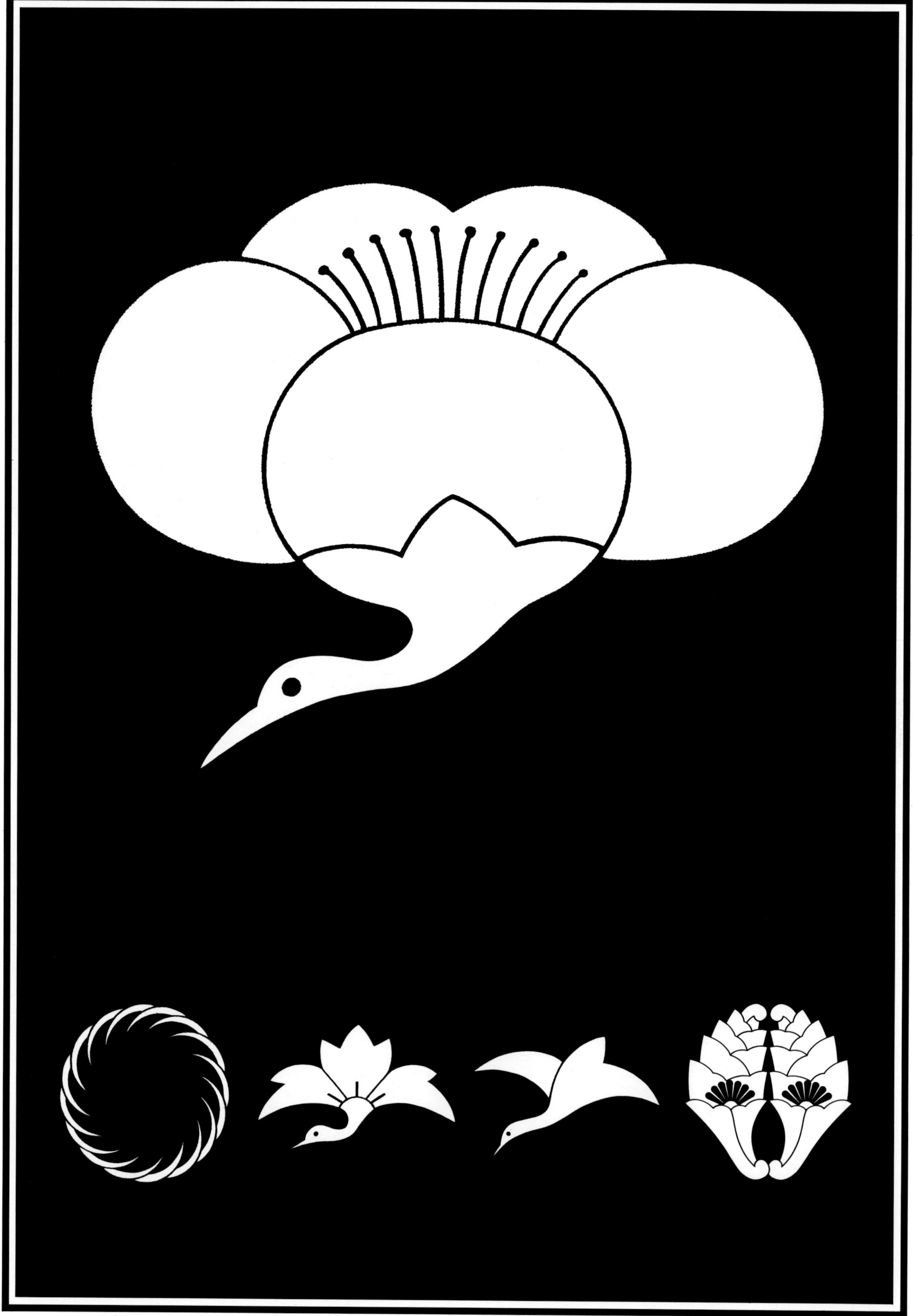

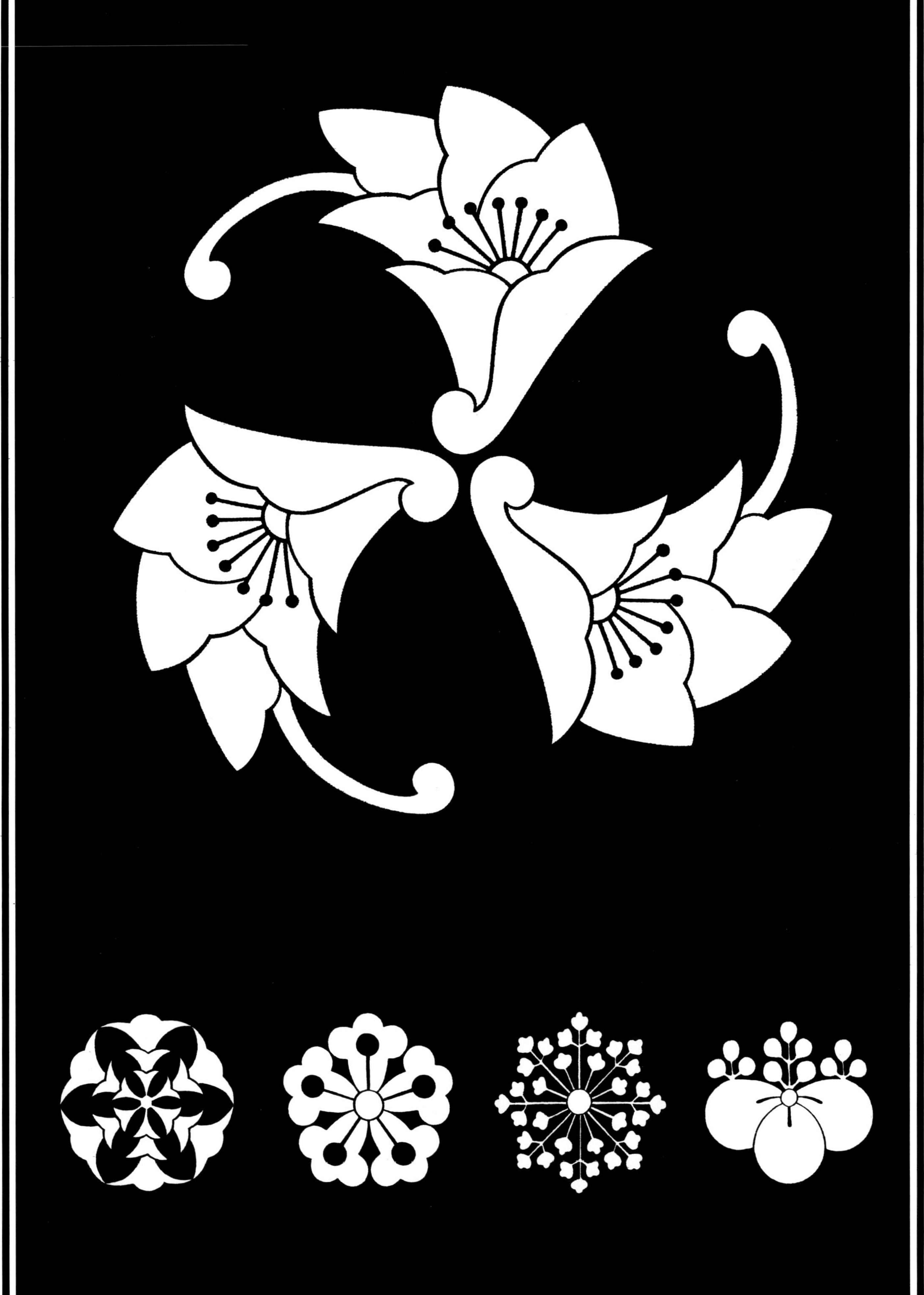

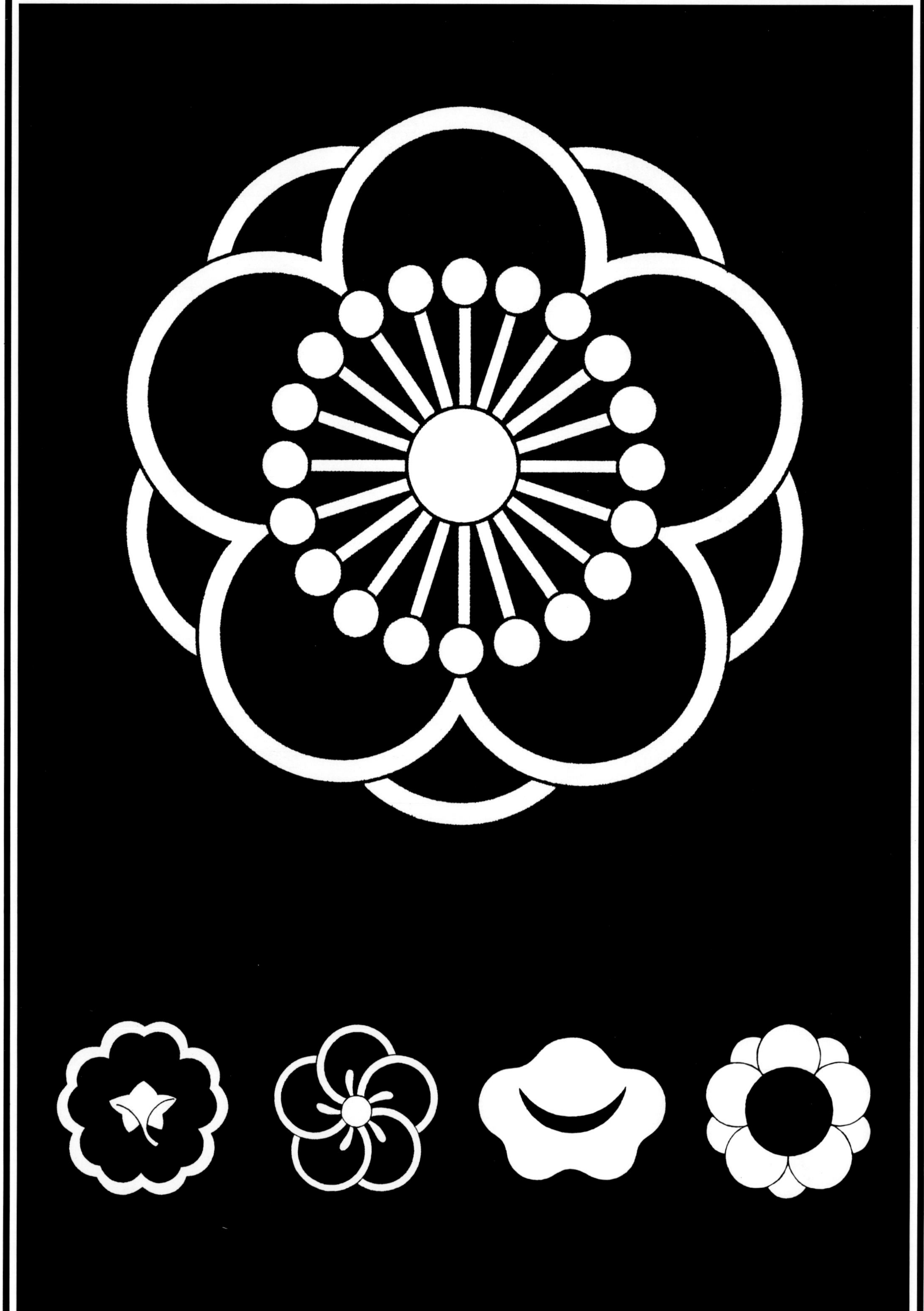

ARTISTS' PROFILES
作家略歴

IKKO TANAKA
田中一光

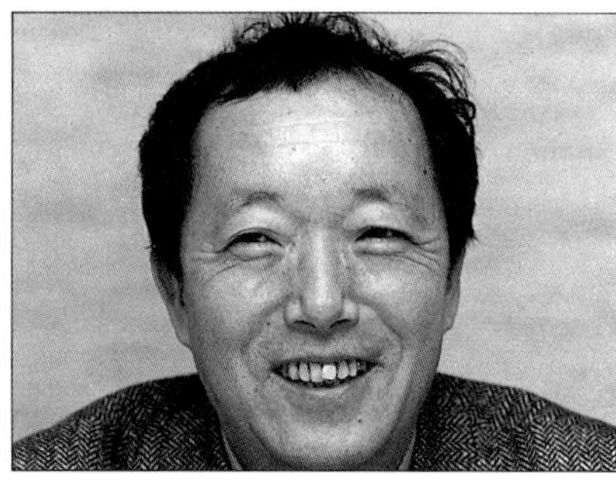

JAPAN
1930 Born in Nara, Japan.
1950 Graduated from Kyoto City College of Fine Arts.
1960 Received the "Gold Medal" from Tokyo ADC.
1968 Received the "Silver Prize" at the International Poster Biennial, Warsaw.
1973 Received the "Membership Award" from Tokyo ADC.
Received the "Mainichi Industrial Design Award."
1980 Produced and designed the "Japan Style" exhibition at the Victoria and Albert Museum, London.
Received the "Recommended Artist's Award" from the Ministry of Education, Japan.
1984 Received the "Bronze Prize" at the International Poster Biennial, Warsaw.
Produced and designed at the "Japanese Design—Tradition and Modernity" exhibition in Moscow.
1985 Received the "2nd Prize" in the Cultural Category at the International Poster Biennial, Lahti, Finland.
1986 Received the "Award of Excellence" from Tokyo ADC.
Received the "Gold Award" from the New York ADC.
1987 One-man shows: "Ikko Tanaka: Crossroad of Design" at Seibu Museum of Art, Tokyo; "Ikko Tanaka at Cooper Union" at Cooper Union, New York; "Ikko Tanaka L.A.—Graphic Designs of Japan" at Japanese American Cultural and Community Center, Los Angeles.
Received the "International Jury's Award" at ZGRAF 5 international exhibition of graphic design in Yugoslavia.
1988 One-man shows: "Design of Ikko Tanaka" at Nara Prefectural Museum of Art, Nara; "Ikko Tanaka Affichiste" at Musée de la Publicité, Paris.
Received the 29th "Mainichi Artist's Award."

1930 奈良市生まれ
1950 京都市立美術専門学校(現京都芸大)卒業
1959 第9回 日本宣伝美術会会員賞受賞
1960 東京アートディレクターズクラブ金賞受賞
1968 ワルシャワ国際ポスタービエンナーレ銀賞受賞
1973 講談社出版文化賞受賞
東京アートディレクターズクラブ会員賞受賞
第19回 毎日デザイン賞受賞
1980 「ジャパンスタイル展」企画・展示設計 ビクトリア&アルバート美術館
昭和54年度芸術選奨文部大臣新人賞受賞
1983 日本宣伝賞 第4回山名賞受賞
1984 モスクワ「日本のデザイン 伝統と現代展」企画・展示
ワルシャワ国際ポスタービエンナーレ文化部門銅賞受賞
1985 フィンランド第6回ラハチ国際ポスター・ビエンナーレ 文化部門第2位受賞
東京アートディレクターズクラブ会員賞受賞
1986 ニューヨークアートディレクターズクラブ金賞受賞
東京アートディレクターズクラブ会員最高賞受賞
1987 個展「田中一光デザインのクロスロード展」西武美術館
個展「Ikko Tanaka at Cooper Union」ニューヨーク
個展「Ikko Tanaka L.A. Graphic Designs of Japan」ロスアンジェルス
ツグラフ5国際グラフィックデザイン展 国際審査賞受賞
1988 個展「田中一光デザイン展」奈良県立美術館
第29回毎日芸術賞受賞
個展「Ikko Tanaka Affichiste」パリ・広告美術館

BRUNO BRUNI
ブルーノ・ブルーニ

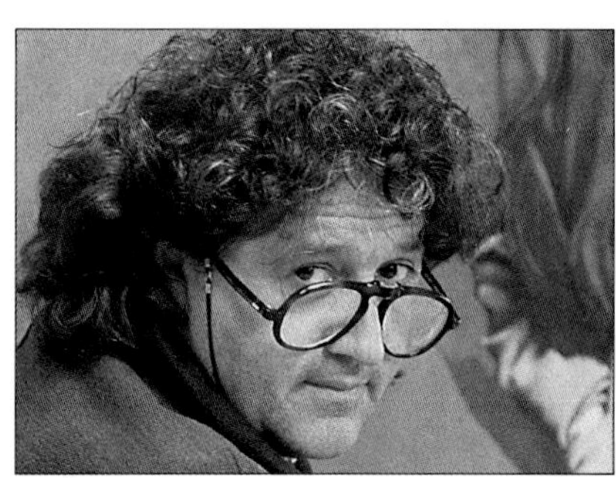

ITALY
1935 Born in Gradara (Pesaro).
1953-59 Studied at the Instituto d'Arte di Pesaro.
1959-60 London
1960-65 Studied at the Staatliche Hochschule fur Bildende Kunste in Hamburg, with Gresko and Wunderlich.
1967 Received the Lichtwark prize stipend of the Freie und Hansestadt, Hamburg.
Since 1959 individual exhibitions in;
Pesaro, Florence, London, Rome, Hamburg, Berlin, Milan, Frankfurt, Amsterdam, Tokyo, New York, Melbourne, Leningrad...
1977 International Senefelderprize

Major exhibitions:
1970 Gallery Torcoliere, Rome
1977 Gallery Brockstadt, Hamburg
1978 Hermitage Museum, Leningrad
1981 Plazzo Ducale, Urbino
1982 Touring exhibition, U.S.A.
1984 Gallerie Steltman, Amsterdam
1984 International Art Fair, Basel
1987 Castello Gradara, City of Gradara, Italy

イタリア
1935 グラダラ(ペザロ)に生まれる
1935-59 ペザロ美術学院で学ぶ
1959-60 ロンドン滞在
1960-65 ハンブルグ造形大学で学び、グレスコ、ウンダーリッヒに師事
1976 ハンブルグ市からリッチワーク奨学金をうける
1959年より個展開催
ペザロ、フィレンツェ、ロンドン、ローマ、ハンブルグ、ベルリン、ミラノ、フランクフルト、アムステルダム、東京、ニューヨーク、メルボルン、レニングラード、他(―1976)
1977 国際セネフェルダー賞を受ける。

主な個展歴
1970 トルコリエーリ画廊/ローマ
1977 ブロックスタット画廊/ハンブルグ
1978 エルミタージュ美術館/レニングラード
1981 ドゥカーレ宮/ウルビーノ
1982 アメリカ巡回展
1984 ステルトマン画廊/アムステルダム
1984 国際アート・フェア/バーゼル
1987 回顧展・グラダラ宮/グラダラ市主催/イタリア

PAUL RAND
ポール・ランド

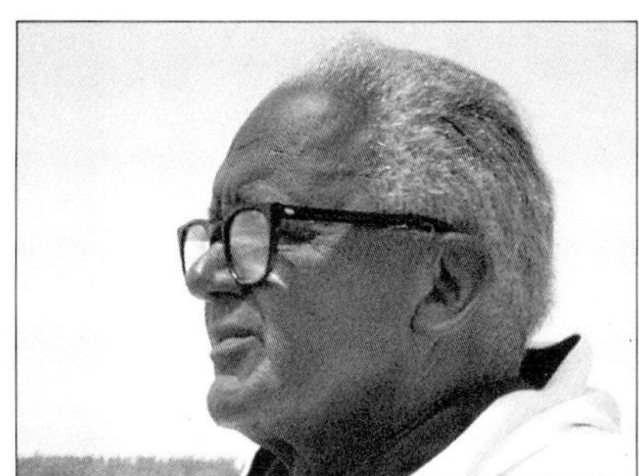

U.S.A.
Paul Rand studied at Pratt Institute, Parsons School of Design and the Art Student League, under George Grosz.
At 23 he became the art director of "Esquire" and "Apparel Arts" and subsequently spent 13 years as creative director of a New York advertising agency. Since 1956 he has been a consultant to IBM, Cummins Engine Company and, for many years, Westinghouse Electric Corporation.
Since 1956 he has also taught at Yale University School of Art, where he is now Professor Emeritus of Graphic Design. Since 1977 he has taught in the Brissaga, Switzerland Yale summer school program.

Among his awards are: Doctor of Fine Arts (Hon) from Philadelphia College of Art, Parsons School of Design, the University of Hartford, School of Visual Arts; Doctor of Letters (Hon) from Kutztown University; Master of Arts from Yale University; Royal Designer for Industry, the Royal Society of Arts, London; Hall of Fame of the New York Art Directors Club; gold medal of the American Institute of Graphic Arts, and medal of the Type Directors Club. He is also a President's Fellow of the Rhode Island School of Design and an honorary professor of Tama University, Tokyo. In 1987 he was awarded the first $25,000 Florence Prize for Visual Communication.

アメリカ
プラット・インスティテュート、パーソンズ・スクール・オブ・デザイン、アート・スチューデント・リーグ、ジョージ・グロスの門下等で学ぶ。23歳で雑誌「エスクワィア」「アパレル・アーツ」のアートディレクターに抜擢され、その後13年間ニューヨークの広告代理店でクリエイティブディレクターとして活躍する。1956年からは長年、IBM、カミンズ・エンジン社、ウエスティングハウス電機会社などのコンサルタントを務め、一方、イェール大学美術学部で教鞭をとり、現在はグラフィックデザインの名誉教授となっている。1977年からは、スイスのブリサーガで行なわれる、イェール大学サマープログラムでも教えている。

受賞と栄誉
フィラデルフィア美術大学、パーソンズ・スクール・オブ・デザイン、ハートフォード大学、ビジュアル・アート・スクール名誉芸術博士号、クッツタウン大学名誉文学博士号、イェール大学名誉文学修士号。ロンドン英国芸術学士院、王室工業デザイナーの称号。ニューヨーク・アートディレクターズクラブ・ホールオブフェーム。アメリカ・グラフィックアート研究所より金メダル。タイプディレクターズクラブよりメダル。ロードアイランド・デザインスクールの名誉校友、多摩美術大学名誉教授。1987年第1回フローレンス賞。

STASYS EIDRIGEVIČIUS
スタシス・エイドリゲヴィチウス

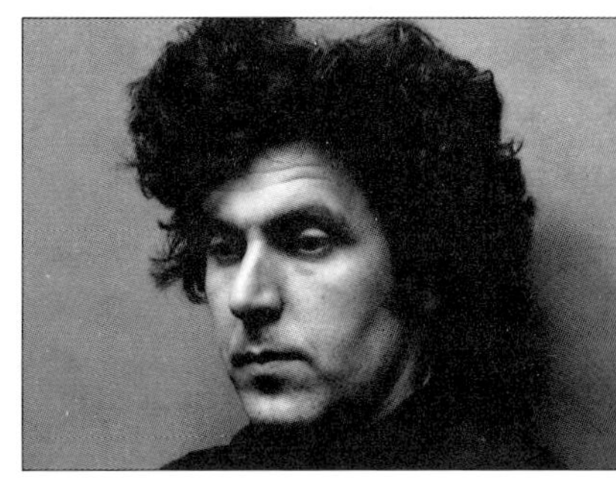

POLAND
1949 Born in Mediniskiai, Lithuania.
1968 Graduated from School of Applied Arts in Kaunas.
1973 Graduated from Art Institute of Vilna and became freelance artist and illustrator.
1989 Currently residing and working in Warsaw, Poland.

Awards:
Honorary Medals at 6th, 7th and 8th International Biennale of Contemporary Ex Libris in Malbork, Poland.
"Third Prize" at 16th International Ex Libris Congress in Lisbon, Portugal.
Gold Plaques at two international exhibitions of illustrations for children's books in Bratislava, Czechoslovakia.
"Grand Prize" at Children's Book Contest in Barcelona, Spain.
"Grand Prize" at World Poster Salon in Paris.

ポーランド
1949 リトアニア共和国メディニスキアイに生まれる
1968 カウナス応用芸術学校卒業
1973 ヴァルナ芸術大学卒業
フリーランスとなり、絵画、彫刻、本のイラストなどを行なう
1989 現在ポーランドのワルシャワに在住

受賞歴
第6、7、8回マルボルク現代国際蔵書票ビエンナーレ(ポーランド)にて名誉勲章、第16回リスボン国際蔵書票コンクール(ポルトガル)第3位、ブラティスラバ国際児童書イラスト展(チェコ)金賞2回、バルセロナ児童書コンテスト(スペイン)グランプリ、パリ世界ポスターサロン(フランス)グランプリ など多数

YOSHIO HAYAKAWA
早川良雄

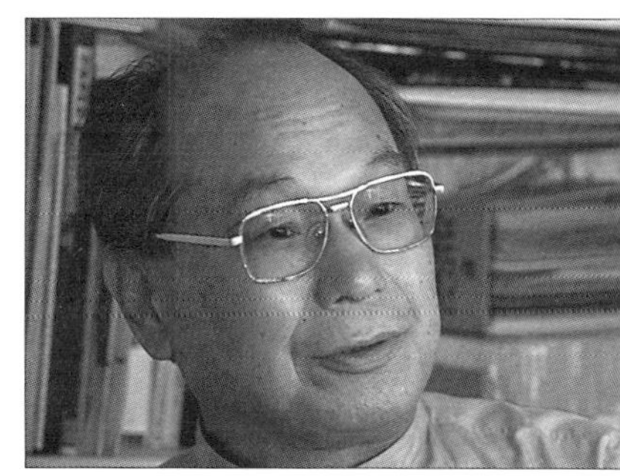

JAPAN
1917 Born in Osaka, Japan.
1936 Graduated from Osaka High School of Industrial Arts.
1954 Received "Osaka Prefectural Art Award."
1955 Received "1st Mainichi Industrial Design Award."
Participated in "Graphic '55" exhibition.
Became member of Alliance Graphique Internationale (AGI).
1960 Served as panelist at World Design Conference, Tokyo.
1970 Participated in "Fundamental Color Plan" of EXPO '70, Osaka.
1973 Served as panelist at ICSID, Kyoto.
1978 Received "Minister of International Trade and Industry Award" at 13th Book Cover Contest.
1981 Received "12th Kodansha Culture Award" for book design.
1982 Awarded Medal with Purple Ribbon from the Japanese Government.
1984 Awarded the 4th Class Order of the Sacred Treasure from the Japanese Government.
1988 Received the "5th Yamana Prize" at the Japan Advertising Awards.

1917 大阪生まれ
1936 大阪市立工芸学校図案科卒業
1954 大阪府芸術賞受賞
1955 第1回毎日産業デザイン賞受賞
国際グラフィックデザイナー連盟(AGI)会員となる
「グラフィック '55展」参加
1960 「世界デザイン会議」(東京)パネリスト
1970 「日本万国博覧会」(大阪)色彩基本計画に参加
1973 「世界インダストリアル会議」(京都)パネリスト
1978 第13回造本装幀コンクール通産大臣賞受賞
1981 第12回講談社出版文化賞受賞
1982 昭和57年度紫綬褒章授章
1984 日本宣伝賞第5回山名賞受賞
1988 勲四等旭日小授章

MAKOTO SAITO
サイトウ・マコト

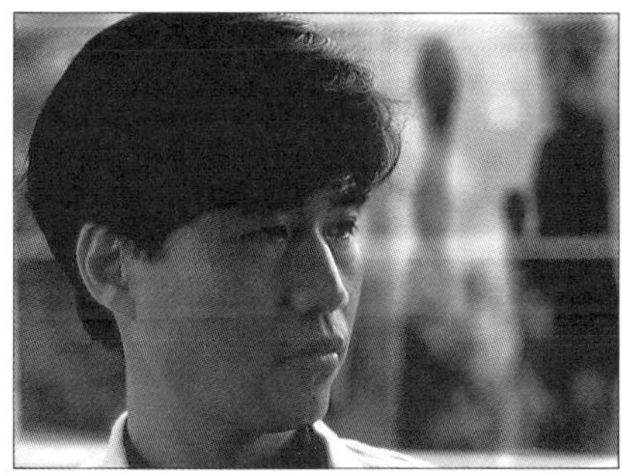

JAPAN
1952 Born in Fukuoka, Japan.
1978 Received "Peter Anderson Special Encouragement Award" at International Art Exhibition, Philadelphia.
Received "Special Prize" at 6th Warsaw International Poster Biennale.
1982 Received "Tokyo ADC Award."
1983 Received "Tokyo ADC Highest Award."
1984 Received "Tokyo ADC Award."
Received "Gold Prize" and two "Bronze Prizes" at Japan-U.S. Graphic Design Exhibition.
Received "Special Prize" at Lahti International Poster Biennale in Finland.
Received "Gold Prize" and "Project Prize" at 9th and 10th Warsaw International Poster Biennale.
1985 Received "Tokyo ADC Members Award."
Received "Second Prize" at International Print Exhibition in Germany.
Received "Gold Prize" and "Bronze Prize" at

1st International Poster Biennale, Toyama.
Received "Award for Excellence" at 1st International Poster Exhibition of France.
1986 Received "Award for Excellence" at 11th Warsaw International Poster Biennale.
Held one-man exhibition at Warsaw National Museum of Modern Art.
Participated in Three Art Directors Exhibition (with Masatoshi Toda and Tsuguya Inoue) at Palais Royal in Paris.
Received "Award for Excellence" at 2nd International Poster Exhibition of France.
1987 Received "Third Prize" at 7th Lahti International Poster Biennale.
Received "Mainichi Design Award."
Received "Gold Award" at 1st New York ADC International Exhibition.
Received "Award for Excellence" at 3rd International Poster Exhibition of France.
1988 Received "Gold Prize" and "Bronze Prize" at 2nd International Poster Biennale, Toyama.
Received "Gold Award" at 2nd New York ADC International Exhibition.
1989 Received "Gold Award" and "Silver Award" at 3rd New York ADC International Exhibition.

1952 福岡県生まれ
1978 フィラデルフィア国際美術展ピーターアンダーソン特別奨励賞
第6回ワルシャワ国際ポスタービエンナーレ特別賞
1982 東京アートディレクターズクラブ賞
1983 東京アートディレクターズクラブ最高賞
1984 東京アートディレクターズクラブ賞
日米グラフィックデザイン展金賞、銅賞2個
ラハティポスタービエンナーレ(フィンランド)特別賞
第9、10回ワルシャワ国際ポスタービエンナーレ金賞、プロジェクト賞
1985 東京アートディレクターズクラブ会員賞
ドイツ国際版画展2席
第1回世界ポスタートリエンナーレトヤマ金賞、銅賞
第1回フランスポスター国際展優秀賞
1986 第11回ワルシャワ国際ポスタービエンナーレ特別賞
ワルシャワ国立近代美術館個展
パレロワイヤルにてアートディレクター3人展
(パリ市主催、戸田正寿、井上嗣也と共に)
第2回フランスポスター国際展優秀賞
1987 第7回ラハティ国際ポスタービエンナーレ第3位
毎日デザイン賞
第1回ニューヨークアートディレクターズクラブ国際展金賞
第3回フランスポスター国際展優秀賞
1988 第2回ニューヨークアートディレクターズクラブ国際展金賞
第2回世界ポスタートリエンナーレトヤマ金賞、銅賞
1989 第3回ニューヨークアートディレクターズクラブ国際展金賞、銀賞

CONTRIBUTORS' PROFILES

評論執筆者紹介

MAMORU YONEKURA
Art critic. Feature editor of Asahi Shimbun (Newspaper).

SHUNSUKE KIJIMA
Art critic. Professor of Kyoritsu Women's University.

SHIGEO FUKUDA
Graphic designer. Member of AGI and JAGDA. Inductee in New York ADC Hall of Fame.

HIROSHI KOJITANI
Graphic designer. Vice-president of ICOGRADA. Director of JAGDA and Tokyo Designers Space.

KOICHI SATO
Graphic designer. Member of AGI, JAGDA, Tokyo ADC and Tokyo Designers Space.

KAZUMASA NAGAI
Graphic designer. Member of AGI. Vice-president of JAGDA.

YUSAKU KAMEKURA
Graphic designer. Member of AGI. President of JAGDA and Japan Design Committee. Editor of CREATION.

米倉 守
美術評論家
朝日新聞学芸部編集委員

木島俊介
美術評論家
共立女子大学教授

福田繁雄
グラフィック・デザイナー
AGI会員、JAGDA会員、ニューヨークADCホールオブフェイム

麹谷 宏
グラフィック・デザイナー
ICOGRADA副会長、JAGDA理事、東京デザイナーズスペース理事

佐藤晃一
グラフィック・デザイナー
AGI会員、JAGDA会員、東京ADC会員、東京デザイナーズスペース会員

永井一正
グラフィック・デザイナー
AGI会員、JAGDA副会長

亀倉雄策
グラフィック・デザイナー
AGI会員、JAGDA会長、日本デザインコミッティ理事長、本誌編集長

掲載資料のご提供を感謝致します

イタリアフォルニ画廊東京店
ギンザ・グラフィック・ギャラリー